IET COMPUTING SERIES 37

Handbook of Big Data Analytics

IET Book Series on Big Data – Call for Authors

Editor-in-Chief: Professor Albert Y. Zomaya, University of Sydney, Australia

The topic of Big Data has emerged as a revolutionary theme that cuts across many technologies and application domains. This new book series brings together topics within the myriad research activities in many areas that analyse, compute, store, manage and transport massive amounts of data, such as algorithm design, data mining and search, processor architectures, databases, infrastructure development, service and data discovery, networking and mobile computing, cloud computing, high-performance computing, privacy and security, storage and visualization.

Topics considered include (but not restricted to) IoT and Internet computing; cloud computing; peer-to-peer computing; autonomic computing; data centre computing; multi-core and many core computing; parallel, distributed and high-performance computing; scalable databases; mobile computing and sensor networking; Green computing; service computing; networking infrastructures; cyberinfrastructures; e-Science; smart cities; analytics and data mining; Big Data applications and more.

Proposals for coherently integrated International co-edited or co-authored handbooks and research monographs will be considered for this book series. Each proposal will be reviewed by the Editor-in-Chief and some board members, with additional external reviews from independent reviewers. Please email your book proposal for the IET Book Series on Big Data to Professor Albert Y. Zomaya at albert.zomaya@sydney.edu.au or to the IET at author_support@theiet.org.

Handbook of Big Data Analytics

Volume 2: Applications in ICT, security and business analytics

Edited by
Vadlamani Ravi and Aswani Kumar Cherukuri

The Institution of Engineering and Technology

Published by The Institution of Engineering and Technology, London, United Kingdom

The Institution of Engineering and Technology is registered as a Charity in England & Wales (no. 211014) and Scotland (no. SC038698).

The Institution of Engineering and Technology
Michael Faraday House
Six Hills Way, Stevenage
Herts, SG1 2AY, United Kingdom

www.theiet.org

British Library Cataloguing in Publication Data
A catalogue record for this product is available from the British Library

ISBN 978-1-83953-059-3 (hardback Volume 2)
ISBN 978-1-83953-060-9 (PDF Volume 2)
ISBN 978-1-83953-064-7 (hardback Volume 1)
ISBN 978-1-83953-058-6 (PDF Volume 1)
ISBN 978-1-83953-061-6 (2 volume set)

Typeset in India by MPS Limited
Printed in the UK by CPI Group (UK) Ltd, Croydon

Contents

About the editors

Vadlamani Ravi is a professor in the Institute for Development and Research in Banking Technology (IDRBT), Hyderabad where he spearheads the Center of Excellence in Analytics, the first-of-its-kind in India. He holds a Ph.D. in Soft Computing from Osmania University, Hyderabad and RWTH Aachen, Germany (2001). Earlier, he worked as a Faculty at National University of Singapore from 2002 to 2005. He worked in RWTH Aachen under DAAD Long Term Fellowship from 1997 to 1999. He has more than 32 years of experience in research and teaching. He has been working in soft computing, evolutionary/neuro/fuzzy computing, data/text mining, global/multi-criteria optimization, big data analytics, social media analytics, time-series data mining, deep learning, bankruptcy prediction, and analytical CRM. He published more than 230 papers in refereed international/national journals/conferences and invited chapters. He has 7,356 citations and an *h*-index of 40. He also edited a book published by IGI Global, USA, 2007. He is a referee for 40 international journals and an Associate Editor for *Swarm and Evolutionary Computation*, Managing Editor for *Journal of Banking and Financial Technology*, and Editorial Board Member for few International Journals of repute. He is a referee for international project proposals submitted to European Science Foundation, Irish Science Foundation, and book proposals submitted to Elsevier and Springer. Further, he is listed in the top 2% scientists in the field of artificial intelligence and image processing, as per an independent study done by Stanford University scientists (https://journals.plos.org/plosbiology/article?id=10.1371/journal.pbio.3000918). He consults for and advises various India banks on their Analytical CRM, Fraud Detection, Data Science, AI/ML projects.

Aswani Kumar Cherukuri is a professor of the School of Information Technology and Engineering at Vellore Institute of Technology (VIT), Vellore, India. His research interests are machine learning, information security. He published more than 150 research papers in various journals and conferences. He received Young Scientist fellowship from Tamil Nadu State Council for Science & Technology, Govt. of State of Tamil Nadu, India. He received an inspiring teacher award from The New Indian Express (leading English daily). He is listed in the top 2% scientists in the field of artificial intelligence and image processing, as per an independent study done by Stanford University scientists (https://journals.plos.org/plosbiology/article?id=10.1371/journal.pbio.3000918). He executed few major research projects funded by several funding agencies in Govt. of India. He is a senior member of ACM and is associated with other professional bodies, including CSI, ISTE. He is the Vice Chair of IEEE taskforce on educational data mining. He is an editorial board member for several international journals.

About the contributors

P.J.A. Alphonse received an M.Tech. degree in Computer Science from Indian Institute of Technology, Delhi and a Ph.D. degree in Mathematics & Computer Science from National Institute of Technology, Tiruchirappalli. He is currently working as a professor in National Institute of Technology, Tiruchirappalli. His research interests include graph theory and its algorithms, wireless and ad hoc networks and cryptography and network security. He is a life member of the ISTE and ISC.

Sarath Babu received a Bachelor's degree in Computer Science and Engineering from Kerala University, India, in 2015 and a Master's degree in Network Engineering from APJ Abdul Kalam Technological University (KTU), Kerala, India, in 2018. He is currently pursuing a Ph.D. degree with the National Institute of Calicut (NITC), India. His research interests include vehicular communications, designing routing protocols and communication in ad hoc wireless devices.

Imanol Bilbao-Quintana, a Ph.D. student from the University of the Basque Country, Spain, is a visitor at KEDRI from 25 October 2017 to 25 April 2018.

Wolfgang Breymann is the head of the group Finance, Risk Management and Econometrics at Zurich University of Applied Sciences. He is among the originators of project ACTUS for standardizing financial contract modelling and a member of the Board of Directors of the ACTUS Financial Research Foundation. He is also a founding member of Ariadne Business Analytics AG. His current work focuses on the automation of risk assessment to improve the transparency and resilience of the financial system.

Nils Bundi is a Ph.D. candidate in Financial Engineering at Stevens Institute of Technology. His research focuses on modelling financial contracts in a formal, rigorous way and the application thereof in financial network theory. Nils is a founding member of the Algorithmic Contract Types Unified Standards, an initiative funded by the Sloan Foundation to create a machine-executable description of the standard contracts in finance. His expertise includes financial data, mathematics and technology.

K. Chaitanya is a technology lead from Infosys Limited, India. He is currently pursuing a Ph.D. from National Institute of Technology, Warangal. He holds an M. Tech. degree from University College of Engineering, JNTU Kakinada. He was awarded with "Most valuable player for the year" and "Award of excellence" awards in Infosys. His research areas include evolutionary algorithms, social networks, Big Data and cloud computing.

A. Chandrasekar is currently the Professor and Head of the Department of Computer Science and Engineering at St. Joseph's College of Engineering, Chennai. He has authored refereed journals and conference papers and patents in various fields such as computer security, image processing and wireless communications. His research interests revolve around network security, signal and image processing, computer vision antenna design, etc. He has received several performance awards and best paper awards.

Aswani Kumar Cherukuri is a professor at the School of Information Technology and Engineering, Vellore Institute of Technology, Vellore, India. His research interests are information security and machine learning. He has executed few research projects funded by the Department of Science and Technology, Govt. of India; Department of Atomic Energy, Govt. of India; and Ministry of Human Resources Development (MHRD) Govt. of India. His *h*-index is 26 and has 2,200 citations as per Google scholar.

Akhilesh Kumar Gangwar received his B.Tech. degree in Computer Science and Engineering from Cochin University of Science and Technology (CUSAT) and his M.Tech. in artificial intelligence from University of Hyderabad. His Master's dissertation research focused on fraud detection and sentiment analysis using deep learning. Currently he is working as a deep learning engineer.

Rohit Gavval was an M.Tech. (AI) student at University of Hyderabad, Institute for Development and Research in Banking Technology, Hyderabad. He is the Director for Cognitive Data Science at Lotusdew Wealth and Investment Advisors, Hyderabad. His research areas of interest are NLP, social media analytics, evolutionary computing and CUDA programming.

Akshay Raj Gollahalli received a B.Tech. degree from the Jawaharlal Nehru Technological University, Hyderabad, India, in 2011. He received his Ph.D. degree from the Knowledge Engineering and Discovery Research Institute, Auckland University of Technology, Auckland, New Zealand.

Currently, he is an engineer in AUT Ventures. He is involved in the development of NeuCube framework for data modelling in spiking neural network architectures.

Kalavala Revanth Harsha holds a dual degree from Indian Institute of Technology (ISM) Dhanbad. He is a data science and ML enthusiast. His areas of interest include NLP with a focus on financial applications. Currently, he is working as a software developer at Samsung Research Institute, Noida.

Chittaranjan Hota currently working as a full Professor of Computer Science at BITS, Pilani Hyderabad Campus, has completed his Ph.D, M.E and B.E all in Computer Science and Engineering. He has been involved in teaching, research and academic administration over the past three decades at BITS, Pilani and other

Indian and universities abroad. His research work on Traffic engineering in IP networks, Big data, Code tamper-proofing, and Cyber security has been funded generously by various funding agencies like Intel, TCS, DeitY, Progress software, MeitY, UGC, and NWO (NL) over the past two decades. Over these years, he has active foreign research collaborations in universities like, Aalto University, Finland; Vrije University, Netherlands; UNSW, Sydney; City university, London; and University of Cagliari, Italy. He has more than 130 research publications at various conferences and journals and has guided more than 10 PhD students over these years. He is currently working on building secure Bio-CPS devices under the National Mission on Interdisciplinary Cyber Physical Systems with funding support from DST (Govt of India).

Sumaiya Thaseen Ikram is an associate professor with 14 years of teaching and research experience in the School of Information Technology and Engineering, Vellore Institute of Technology, Vellore, Tamil Nadu, India. Few of her publications in the domain of intrusion detection are indexed in Springer, Elsevier and SCI. Sumaiya has 430 citations in Google Scholar and her h-index is 9. Her areas of research are cybersecurity, machine learning and cyber-physical systems.

Sk Kamaruddin is a Ph.D. scholar at Institute for Development and Research in Banking Technology, Hyderabad and University of Hyderabad. He did his M.C.A. from Utkal University, Bhubaneswar in 2000. He has 14 years of teaching experience. He published 6 conference papers that have a total citation count of 47. His research interests are machine learning, data mining natural language processing, Big Data analytics and distributed parallel computation.

Nikola K. Kasabov (M'93–SM'98–F'10) received the M.S. degree in Computing and Electrical Engineering and the Ph.D. degree in Mathematical Sciences from the Technical University of Sofia, Sofia, Bulgaria, in 1971 and 1975, respectively. He is currently the Director and the Founder of the Knowledge Engineering and Discovery Research Institute and a professor of Knowledge Engineering with the School of Computing and Mathematical Sciences, Auckland University of Technology, Auckland, New Zealand.

His major research interests include information science, computational intelligence, neural networks, bioinformatics, neuro-informatics, speech and image processing in which areas he has published more than 650 works.

Arya Ketan has been part of Flipkart since its early days and is currently a senior software architect. He is passionate about developing features and debugging problems in large-scale distributed systems. Nowadays, he is working in the big data platform of Flipkart which powers near real time and batch computation on eCommerce datasets. He completed his bachelors in engineering from NIT, Trichy, India in 2008.

Rasmi Ranjan Khansama received his M.Tech. degree from the University of Hyderabad, Hyderabad, India in 2017. He is currently working as an assistant professor in Computer Science and Engineering, C.V. Raman Global University,

Bhubaneswar, India. His research interests include time-series data analysis, deep learning and big-data analysis.

Gang Li, an IEEE senior member, is an associate professor in the school of IT, Deakin University (Australia). He serves on the IEEE Data Mining and Big Data Analytics Technical Committee (2017 Vice Chair), IEEE Enterprise Information Systems Technical Committee, IEEE Enterprise Architecture and Engineering Technical Committee and as the vice chair for IEEE Task Force on Educational Data Mining. He served on the Program Committee for over 200 international conferences in artificial intelligence, data mining and machine learning, tourism and hospitality management.

Xiao Liu received his Ph.D. degree in Computer Science and Software Engineering from the Faculty of Information and Communication Technologies at Swinburne University of Technology, Melbourne, Australia in 2011. He is currently a senior lecturer at School of Information Technology, Deakin University, Melbourne, Australia. Before that, he was teaching at Software Engineering Institute, East China Normal University, Shanghai, China. His research areas include software engineering, distributed computing and data mining, with special interests in workflow systems, cloud/fog computing and social networks.

Sanket Mishra is a PhD scholar at BITS Pilani Hyderabad Campus, Hyderabad, India, where his research work in the area of Machine learning is supported through TCS PhD fellowship. Prior to his PhD, he holds a Masters in Computer Sc. from Utkal University, Odisha. He has pursued joint research in the area of Smart city with Prof Abhaya Nayak's group at Macquarie University, Sydney, Australia. He has been an invited guest speaker to deliver a hands-on session on "IoT and Serverless computing" at IIIT, Guwahati, Assam. He has also served as guest reviewer in IEEE Access and Springer journals. His research interests include Stream processing, Event processing, Internet of Things, Machine learning, etc.

J.V.R. Murthy is a professor, Director of Incubation Centre and IPR at Jawaharlal Nehru Technological University (JNTU) Kakinada, India. Prior to joining JNTU, he served for reputed companies such as William M. Mercer, Key Span Energy and AXA Client solutions in the USA. He submitted a project titled "Establishing a Blockchain-based Financial Information Sharing Ecosystem with Intelligent Automation" in collaboration with University of Missouri. He is a Recipient of Obama-Singh Initiative grant, in collaboration with Chicago State University USA. He received A.P. State Government's, Best Teacher award. He published more than 65 research papers in international journals/conferences, including IEEE and Elsevier Sciences. Thirteen scholars were awarded Ph.D. under his guidance. He was appointed as Independent Director, Kakinada Smart City Corporation Ltd. and chairmen, Nominations and Remunerations Committee by Ministry of Urban Development Government of India. His research interests are data mining, Big Data, machine learning and artificial intelligence.

Remya Krishnan Pacheeri is a research scholar in the Department of Computer Science and Engineering at National Institute of Technology (NIT), Calicut. She received a B.Tech. degree with distinction and Honours in Computer Science Engineering from Calicut University, Kerala and an M.Tech. degree with distinction in Computer Science and Engineering from Rajagiri School of Engineering and Technology, Kerala. Her research interests include security in vehicular ad hoc network.

Lakshmikanth Paleti is a research scholar at Jawaharlal Nehru Technological University, Kakinada. He is currently working as an associate professor in Department of Computer Science and Engineering at Kallam Haranadhareddy Institute of Technology, Chowdawaram, Guntur. He received his M.Tech. degree from JNTUK, Kakinada in Computer Science and Engineering. His research interests are social network mining, Big Data and data mining.

Arun Raj Kumar Parthiban is working as a faculty in the Department of Computer Science and Engineering (CSE) at National Institute of Technology (NIT) Calicut, Kozhikode. He has 15 years of teaching and research experience. His research interests include designing protocols in networks and intrusion detection systems. He has published papers in SCI/SCIE indexed journals and conferences. He is an IEEE senior member and an ACM member.

Syam Kumar Pasupuleti received an M.Tech. degree in Computer Science and Technology from Andhra University and a Ph.D. degree in Computer Science from Pondicherry University. He is an assistant professor in the Institute for Development and Research in Banking Technology (IDRBT), Hyderabad. His research interests are in the area of cloud computing, security and privacy, cryptography and IoT. He is a member of the IEEE.

Radha Krishna Pisipati is a professor at National Institute of Technology (NIT) Warangal, India. Prior to joining NIT, Krishna served as the Principal Research Scientist at Infosys Labs, faculty at IDRBT (a research arm of Reserve Bank of India), and a scientist at National Informatics Centre, Govt. of India. He holds double Ph.Ds. from Osmania University and IIIT—Hyderabad. His research interests are data mining, Big Data, social networks, e-contracts and workflows.

Jayashree Pougajendy is currently a research scholar in the Department of CSE at Indian Institute of Technology Hyderabad. She received her Master's degree with a gold medal from National Institute of Technology, Puducherry and a Bachelor's degree with distinction from Pondicherry Engineering College. Her research interests broadly span the areas of deep learning, Bayesian deep learning and network security. She has published papers in conferences and SCI/SCIE indexed journals.

Praveen Kumar Premkamal received an M.Tech. degree in Computer and Information Technology from Manonmaniam Sundaranar University. He is currently doing Ph.D. at National Institute of Technology, Tiruchirappalli. His research interests include cloud computing, Big Data and cryptography. He is a life member of the ISTE.

S. Radhika is currently an associate professor from the School of Electrical and Electronics Engineering at Sathyabama Institute of Science and Technology. She completed her Ph.D. with research title "Design of Adaptive Filtering Algorithms for Acoustic Echo Cancellation Application." Her areas of research include adaptive signal processing, sparse signal processing, machine learning biomedical signal processing and graph signal processing. She has published several articles in international and national journals and conferences.

Kumar Ravi is working as a data architect with HCL Technologies, Noida. He worked on several projects related to predictive analytics, anomaly detection, NLP, time series mining and decision analysis. He did his Ph.D. in Computer Science from University of Hyderabad and IDRBT. He authored 20 papers. He has 956 citations as per Google scholar indexing. His research area includes NLP, image processing, time series mining and recommender systems.

Vadlamani Ravi has been the professor at the Institute for Development and Research in Banking Technology, Hyderabad since June 2014. He obtained his Ph.D. in the area of Soft Computing from Osmania University, Hyderabad and RWTH Aachen, Germany (2001). He authored more than 230 papers that were cited in 7,880 publications and has an h-index 42. He has 32 years of research and 20 years of teaching experience.

Gillala Rekha obtained her M.C.A. from Osmania University and M.Tech. from JNTUH. She completed her Ph.D. from SRU and is currently working as an associate professor in CSE Department at KL University, India. Her research interests are machine learning, pattern recognition, deep learning and data mining and specifically working on imbalance problems pertaining to real-world applications.

Neelava Sengupta received the B.Tech. degree from the Maulana Abul Kalam Azad University of Technology, Kolkata, India, in 2009. He received his Ph.D. degree from the Knowledge Engineering and Discovery Research Institute, Auckland University of Technology, Auckland, New Zealand.

He was an Engineer with the Centre for Development of Advanced Computing, Pune, India, and a Research Assistant with the University of Hildesheim, Hildesheim, Germany. He is involved in the development of novel algorithms for integrated data modelling in spiking neural network architectures.

Karthick Seshadri is working as an assistant professor in the Department of Computer Science and Engineering at NIT Andhra Pradesh. His areas of research interest include Big Data analytics, machine learning, probabilistic graphical modelling, Bayesian learning, approximation and randomized algorithms and distributed and parallel algorithms. He has about 9 years of teaching experience and 4 years of experience in IT industry in firms, including Morgan Stanley. He enjoys teaching algorithms.

Durvasula Venkata Lakshmi Narasimha Somayajulu is a professor at National Institute of Technology (NIT) Warangal, India. Prior to joining NIT, he completed M.Tech. from Indian Institute of Technology (IIT), Kharagpur and Ph.D. from

IIT Delhi. Currently, he is a director (on deputation) of Indian Institute of Information Technology, Design and Manufacturing, Kurnool. His research interests are databases, information extraction, query processing, Big Data and privacy.

Keesara Sravanthi is pursuing her Ph.D. degree from GITAM University, India. She is currently working as an assistant professor in Malla Reddy Engineering College, Hyderabad, Telangana, India. Her areas of interest are machine learning, deep learning, etc.

Kurt Stockinger is a professor of Computer Science, Director of Studies in Data Science at Zurich University of Applied Sciences (ZHAW) and Deputy Head of the ZHAW Datalab. His research focuses on Data Science (Big Data, Natural Language Query Processing, Query Optimization and Quantum Computing). Previously he worked at Credit Suisse, Berkeley Lab, Caltech and CERN. He holds a Ph.D. in Computer Science from CERN/University of Vienna.

Vaidyanathan Subramanian is a full-stack engineer working in the Flipkart Cloud Platform (FCP). He has been with Flipkart for the past 6 years and has worked on a broad range of technologies spanning distributed systems, big data, search engines, core backend, front-end and mobile. He completed his bachelors in engineering from VIT, Vellore (India) in 2008.

Amit Kumar Tyagi is an assistant professor (senior grade) and a senior researcher at Vellore Institute of Technology (VIT), Chennai Campus, India. His current research focuses on machine learning with Big Data, blockchain technology, data science, cyber-physical systems and smart and secure computing and privacy. He has contributed to several projects such as "AARIN" and "P3-Block" to address some of the open issues related to the privacy breaches in vehicular applications (like Parking) and medical cyber-physical systems. He received his Ph.D. Degree from Pondicherry Central University, India. He is a member of the IEEE.

Foreword

The *Handbook of Big Data Analytics* (edited by Professor Vadlamani Ravi and Professor Aswani Kumar Cherukuri) is a two-volume compendium that provides educators, researchers and developers with the background needed to understand the intricacies of this rich and fast-moving field.

The two volumes (Vol. 1: Methodologies; Vol. 2: Applications in ICT, Security and Business Analytics) collectively composed of 26 chapters cover a wide range of subjects pertinent to database management, processing frameworks and architectures, data lakes and query optimization strategies, toward real-time data processing, data stream analytics, fog and edge computing, artificial intelligence and Big Data and several application domains. Overall, the two volumes explore the challenges imposed by Big Data analytics and how they will impact the development of next generation applications.

The Handbook of Big Data Analytics is a timely and valuable offering and an important contribution to the Big Data processing and analytics field. I would like to commend the editors for assembling an excellent team of international contributors who managed to provide a rich coverage on the topic. I am sure that the readers will find the handbook useful and hopefully a source of inspiration for future work in this area. This handbook should be well received by both researchers and developers and will provide a valuable resource for senior undergraduate and graduate classes focusing on Big Data analytics.

Professor Albert Y. Zomaya
Editor-in-Chief of the *IET Book Series on Big Data*

Foreword

It gives me an immense pleasure in writing the foreword for this excellent book on *Handbook of Big Data Analytics—Applications*. This handbook is the second in the two-volume series on Big Data analytics. Throughout history it is clear that the applications of theories and technologies have brought not only the attention of the community closer but also their usefulness to society at large. Big Data analytics theories and frameworks are no exception. Due to the big data–driven era created by the 4th paradigm of science and fuelled by the 4th industrial revolution (industry 4.0), Internet of Things (IoT), there is a massive demand for performing analytics on Big Data in order to derive value from it. Big Data analytics found spectacular applications in almost all sectors such as health, finance, manufacturing, marketing, supply chain, transport, government, science and technology and fraud detection. Further, applying Big Data analytics is helping the organizations, businesses and enterprises to explore new strategies, products and services.

Contributions to this volume deal with Big Data analytics (BDA) in a variety of cutting-edge applications, including Big Data streams, BDA for security intelligence, e-commerce business workflows, automated analytics, algorithmic contracts and distributed ledger technologies for contract-driven financial reporting, leveraging neural network models such as self-organizing map, wavelet neural network, radial basis function neural network and spiking neural network for financial applications with Big Data in GPU environments, IoT Big Data streams in smart city applications, and Big Data–driven behaviour analytics. The editors of this volume have done a remarkable job of carefully selecting these application areas and compiling contributions from prominent experts. I like to congratulate the editors for bringing out this exciting volume and the authors of the individual chapters for their noteworthy contributions.

This two-volume series covers the Big Data architecture, frameworks and applications in specified fields and some of the individual contributions are a result of extensive research. I am sure that this volume on applications of BDA would further ignite more innovations, applications and solutions in Big Data–driven problem areas. Hence, I strongly recommend this volume as a text book or a reference book to the undergraduate and graduate students, researchers and practitioners who are currently working or planning to work in this important area.

Rajkumar Buyya, Ph.D.
Redmond Barry Distinguished Professor
Director, Cloud Computing and Distributed Systems (CLOUDS) Lab
School of Computing and Information Systems
The University of Melbourne, Australia

Preface

Big Data analytics (BDA) has evolved from the performing analytics on small, structured and static data in the mid-1990s to the current unstructured, dynamic and streaming data. Techniques from statistics, data mining, machine learning, natural language processing and data visualization help derive actionable insights and knowledge from Big Data. These insights help the organizations and enterprises in improving their productivity, business value, innovation, supply chain management, etc. The global BDA market value is expected to touch around $17.85 billion by 2027 at an annual growth rate of 20.4%. This edited volume of the *Handbook of Big Data Analytics—Applications* contains a delectable collection of 16 contributions illustrating to the reader the applications of BDA in domains such as finance, security and customer relationship management.

Chapter 1 highlights how BDA can be leveraged in addressing security-related problems, including anomaly detection and security monitoring, while preprocessing Big Data in various applications, sparsity is a major concern. Chapter 2 proposes a sparsity-aware data selection scheme for adaptive filtering algorithms. Software defined networking (SDN) provides a dynamic and programmed approach to efficient network monitoring and management. Chapter 3 discusses the SDN in IoT Big Data environment and security aspects of SDN and IoT routing. Chapter 4 focuses on the issue of security of Big Data storage in cloud. Authors proposed a novel cipher text policy attribute-based signcryption method. The proposed method is aimed at achieving efficiency and flexible access control. Managing and processing Big Data streams is an important task in BDA . Privacy preservation is a major concern due to the presence of attack vectors across different levels of Big Data processing. Chapter 5 provides a detailed discussion on various privacy-preserving techniques for different steps in Big Data life cycle. Behaviour data is fundamentally raw data arising out of the customers' behaviour and actions. It is distinct from demographic, geographic and transactional data of customers. Performing analytics on such data provides hitherto unknown actionable insights and derives value to business applications. Chapter 6 provides a deep insight into the Big Data and behaviour analytics and its future trends. IoT data streams provide huge volumes of data and predicting both simple and complex events from these streams is a challenging task. Chapter 7 addresses this issue with an adaptive clustering approach based on agglomerative clustering. Further, a novel 2-fold approach is proposed in finding the thresholds that determine triggering points. E-Commerce applications heavily use BDA. Authors of Chapter 8 focus on the gender-based recommendations to provide more customization. The proposed approach along with feature extraction for gender-based classification was demonstrated on Big Data platforms. Chapter 9 presents recommender systems with a detailed taxonomy. Further, it illustrates how their performance can be enhanced with BDA support. Chapter 10 provides an interesting case study of BDA in India's popular e-commerce company Flipkart. Authors describe the challenges involved in architecting distributed and analytical systems at scale. Performing regression on Big Data is a challenging task due to the presence of voluminous data.

Authors of Chapter 11 propose a semi-supervised learning architecture called Parallelized Radial Basis Function Neural Network (PRBFNN) and implemented it in Apache Spark MLlibrary. Chapter 12 introduces a novel framework for performing visual sentiment analysis over bank customer complaints. The framework employs self-organizing feature maps and implements it using CUDA in the Apache Spark environment. Chapter 13 discusses parallel wavelet neural networks for BDA in banking applications. The proposed model is demonstrated in GPU environment and tested its performance against the conventional CPU implementation. Chapter 14 proposed three variants of the parallel evolving spiking neural networks for predicting Indian stock market movement and implemented in GP-GPU environment.

Chapter 15 dwells on the design of parallel clustering algorithms to handle the compute and storage demands of the applications that handle massive datasets. Further, this chapter presents a detailed taxonomy of clustering techniques that would be a rich source of information for readers. Chapter 16 discusses the technological elements required to implement financial reporting with a focus on automated analytics pipeline. Further, parallel programming technologies based on Hadoop and Spark are explored for large-scale financial system simulation and analysis.

We as editors hope that contributions of this volume will spur curiosity among researchers, students and practitioners to pitch in a wide range of new applications and optimizations to the current applications. Many other domains such as cybersecurity, bioinformatics, healthcare, several science and engineering disciplines, agriculture and management will stand benefitted by these case studies as these are generic in nature and can be customized to suit any application.

Vadlamani Ravi
Aswani Kumar Cherukuri

Acknowledgements

At the outset, we express our sincere gratitude to the Almighty for having bestowed us with this opportunity, intellect, thoughtfulness, energy and patience while executing this exciting project.

We are grateful to all the learned contributors for reposing trust and confidence in us and submitting their scholarly, novel work to this volume and their excellent cooperation in meeting the deadlines in the whole journey. It is this professionalism that played a great role in the whole process enabling us to successfully bring out this volume. We sincerely thank Valerie Moliere, Senior Commissioning Book editor, IET and Olivia Wilkins, Assistant Editor, IET for their continuous support right from the inception through the final production. It has been an exhilarating experience to work with them. They provided us total freedom with little or no controls, which is necessary to bring out a volume of this quality and magnitude.

We are grateful to the world renowned expert in Big Data analytics and cloud computing, Dr. Rajkumar Buyya, Redmond Barry Distinguished Professor and Director of the Cloud Computing and Distributed Systems (CLOUDS) Laboratory at the University of Melbourne, Australia for being extremely generous in writing the foreword for these two volumes, in spite of his busy academic and research schedule.

Former Director IDRBT, Dr. A.S. Ramasastri deserves thanks for his support to the whole project.

Last but not least, Vadlamani Ravi expresses high regard and gratitude to his wife Mrs. Padmavathi Devi for being so accommodative and helpful throughout the journey as always. Without her active help, encouragement and cooperation, projects of scale cannot be taken up and completed on schedule. He owes a million thanks to her. He acknowledges the support and understanding rendered by his sons Srikrishna and Madhav in the whole project.

Aswani Kumar Cherukuri sincerely thanks the management of Vellore Institute of Technology, Vellore for the continuous support and encouragement toward scholarly works. He would like to acknowledge the affection, care, support, encouragement and understanding extended by his family members. He is grateful to his wife Mrs. Annapurna, kids, Chinmayee and Abhiram, for always standing by his side.

Vadlamani Ravi, IDRBT, Hyderabad
Aswani Kumar Cherukuri, VIT, Vellore

Introduction

Vadlamani Ravi[1] and Aswani Kumar Cherukuri[2]

While many technical drivers—distributed computing/GP-GPU computing, inges-tion, storage, querying, analytics, in-memory analytics, in-database analytics, etc.—fuelled spectacular, mature advancements in data engineering and analytics of the Big Data analytics (BDA), the business and scientific drivers too fuelled the humungous growth of this exciting field.

On the business side, obtaining 360° view of the customers became essential for the successful and profitable implementation of comprehensive end-to-end customer relationship management in service industries; network and cybersecurity having generated unprecedented amounts of data needed a computational paradigm for successful detection and prevention of cyber fraud attacks. On the scientific side, the "deluge" of data in its various forms, be it in aerospace industry, drug discovery, physics, chemistry, agriculture, climate studies, environmental engi-neering, smart power grids, healthcare, bioinformatics, etc., also propelled the need for having a paraphernalia of a new paradigm coupled with solutions to analyse and offer easier problem-solving ways and means for better decision-making. In other words, all the 5Vs became prominent in all the aforementioned disciplines.

Further, new paradigms such as cloud computing, fog computing, edge com-puting, IoT and 5G communications all are important beneficiaries of BDA. In healthcare, the recent Nobel Prize in medicine was awarded to two researchers working in gene editing—an area that requires a good amount BDA. Similarly, the large hadron collider experiment to simulate the big bang theory underneath the earth's surface in Europe would have been a nonstarter but for the effective use of BDA. Ophthalmology and other medical fields are also immensely benefited by the advent of BDA. Further, BDA together with new AI a.k.a. deep learning algorithms is making irreversible changes in many scientific and business domains. Network and cyber fraud detection is increasingly becoming a complex task owing to the presence of Big Data in the form of volume, velocity and variety. Social media and social network analysis together with the concepts of graph theory are making waves in busting out syndicate fraud. Again, these fields are replete with Big Data.

Majority of the machine learning methods, viz., evolutionary computing algorithms, many neural network training algorithms, clustering algorithms, clas-sifiers, association rule miners and recommendation engines are by design parallel

[1]Center of Excellence in Analytics, Institute for Development and Research in Banking Technology, Hyderabad, India
[2]School of Information Technology & Engineering, Vellore Institute of Technology, Vellore, India

and hence are thoroughly exploited by researchers in order to propound their distributed and parallel counterparts. Third-generation neural networks, viz., spiking neural networks that perform incremental learning for data coming at a fast pace were also benefited by BDA.

As a consequence, BDA became a backbone and fulcrum of all scientific endeavours that have both scientific and business ramifications. One can only ignore this exciting field at his/her peril.

Chapter 1

Big data analytics for security intelligence

Sumaiya Thaseen Ikram[1], Aswani Kumar Cherukuri[1], Gang Li[2] and Xiao Liu[2]

There is a tremendous increase in the frequency of cyberattacks due to the rapid growth of the Internet. These attacks can be prevented by many well-known cybersecurity solutions. However, many traditional solutions are becoming obsolete because of the impact of big data over networks. Hence, corporate research has shifted its focus on security analytics. The role of security analytics is to detect malicious and normal events in real time by assisting network managers in the investigation of real-time network streams. This technique is intended to enhance all traditional security approaches. The various challenges have to be addressed to investigate the potential of big data for information security.

This chapter will focus on the major information security problems that can be solved by big data applications and outlines research directions for security intelligence by applying security analytics. This chapter presents a system called seabed, which facilitates efficient analytics on huge encrypted datasets. Besides, we will discuss a lightweight anomaly detection system (ADS) that is scalable in nature. The identified anomalies will aid us to provide better cybersecurity by examining the network behavior, identifying the attacks and protecting the critical infrastructures.

1.1 Introduction to big data analytics

In the past, cyberattacks were executed in a simple and random way. Nowadays, attacks are systematic and exist for long term. Also, it is challenging to analyze data and identify the anomalous behavior because of the volume and random changes in the dissemination of network data. Thus, solutions using big data techniques are essential.

Big data analytics (BDA) provides comprehensions that are implicit, beneficial and previously unknown. The underlying fact is that there are behavioral or usage patterns that exist in big data. Mathematical models are applied by BDA to fit on these patterns by deploying various data mining approaches such as association rule

[1]School of Information Technology and Engineering, Vellore Institute of Technology, Vellore, India
[2]School of Information Technology and Engineering, Deakin University, Melbourne, Australia

mining, cluster analysis, predictive analytics and prescriptive analytics [1]. The perceptions of these methods are characterized on interactive dashboards thereby assisting the corporations to improve their profits, maintain the competitive verge and augment their CRM.

In the recent years, cybersecurity has emphasized on identification of improper behavior pattern by monitoring network traffic. In traditional techniques, hackers can easily render the intrusion detection system (IDS), antivirus software and firewalls to be ineffective. This is because these approaches scan incoming data against existing malware signatures. This state is very critical due to the petabytes and exabytes of data being transferred daily within computer networks, thereby hiding their presence effectively and instigating austere damage.

The unique features of BDA are given as follows:

- an agile decision-making technique with monitoring and investigation of real-time network data for network managers;
- dynamic identification of access pattern for both known and previously unknown malicious behavior, network traffic flow, which is relevant to all cyber threat categories;
- improved detection ability for suspicious behavior in real time (least possible false-positive rate (FPR));
- full visibility (360° vision) in real time of network movement and malfunctions by providing suitable dashboard-based visualization methods;
- the previously mentioned necessities are managed and applicable to big data software and hardware.

1.2 Big data: huge potentials for information security

Many enterprises proposing security solutions [2–4] emphasize the prospects and benefits of big data for security and have published white papers. Possible research directions are accentuated in the working group's report of citizen science association (CSA) [5]. Rivest Shamir and Adleman also recommends a steady move to the intelligence-driven security model [6]. The benefit of the model in comparison to the conventional security information and event management (SIEM) systems is the ability to investigate the most diverse and unused data to a larger extent than before.

The infrequent pattern of network users are analyzed by network-based intrusion detection and the rapid interface speed requires BDA for the development.

Network analysis is accomplished on relatively high-volume data by deploying conventional approaches such as supervised techniques, which is summarized in Table 1.1. However, big data solutions handle huge stream data and also minimize false-negative and false-positive rates.

The network traffic information, for example, users, routing traffic, and network applications are analyzed using NetFlow [16] that is a network protocol. Analysis on the data captured by NetFlow is widely utilized for studies on network anomaly detection as it can identify the malicious traffic information. Network anomaly detection models are constructed by soft computing, machine learning,

Table 1.1 Comparison of big data analytics for intrusion detection

Approach	Abnormalities	Dataset	Technique	Experimental analysis
A big data model to minimize modification of network traffic, thereby improving the accuracy and decreasing the false-negative rate [7]	U2R, R2L, Probe and DoS	KDD CUP99	Decision tree KNN, K-means and random forest	Accuracy rate: 98.6% on DoS, 56.1% on U2R, 77.2% on R2L and 95.4% on normal data
Apache Spark Cluster deployed for DDoS detection method [8]	DDoS	Capturing normal traffic data and 2000 DARPA LLDOS 1.0	Spark with ANN	Accuracy value of 94%
Big data techniques for analyzing network traffic [1]	SYN/FIN attack, NULL and XMAS scan	NCCDC	Hive and HDFS	Visual representation of investigational results
Hadoop for real-time IDS in a high-speed big data setting [9]	DoS, U2R, R2L, Probing	NSL-KDD, KDD 99 and DARPA	Naïve Bayes, SVM, REPTree, J48, random forest, conjunctive rule and Hadoop	The best classifiers in terms of true-positives are REPTree and J48 which is 99.9%
Multivariate dimensionality reduction analysis [10] for real-time DDoS attack identification	Distributed denial of service	KDD Cup 1999 dataset	Techniques such as principal component analysis, multivariate and correlation analysis Technologies such as MATLAB®	Results are presented visually
Hadoop with machine learning for cloud computing to build an anomaly detection model [11]	Poor networks	KDD Cup 99	Approaches such as SVM, naïve Bayes, decision tree and technologies such as Weka, HDFS and MapReduce	Above 90% of accuracy
Apache Storm to develop hybrid intrusion detection system in real time [3]	DDoS	ISCX2012	Neural networks Storm, CC4 and multilayer perceptron neural networks	The average accuracy obtained is 89%

(Continues)

Table 1.1 (Continued)

Approach	Abnormalities	Dataset	Technique	Experimental analysis
Anomaly-based intrusion identification implemented at various TCP/IP layers [4]	Systematic downloading, DDoS attacks and abusive Internet access	Campus LAN logs of a proxy server and edge router traces	Time series analysis, pattern analysis and machine learning	Results are presented visually
Traffic anomaly identification using a novelty entropy mode [12]	DoS, DDoS, DRDoS port scan	Collection of IPFIX data from a university's router edge	Shannon entropy, MapReduce and APSE	Better performance in APSE than Shannon entropy in terms of identification of malicious traffic
Graph and streaming analytics using big data architectures [13]	Contextual anomalies and advanced persistent threats	SIEM data	MapReduce, Kafka, Tableau, GemfireXD, D3.js and Apama	The anomaly clusters contain the average accuracy and recall which are given as follows: extremely high [0.7,0.9], high [0.75,0.7], medium [0.9,0.9], low [0.8,0.95] and extremely low [1.0,0.4]
Traffic split with hash function to identify network anomalies using a MapReduce framework [14]	Sasser, SMB, NetBIOS, Ping, RPC and additional attacks	MAWI traffic archive	MapReduce, hash algorithm	The average F-score is 0.88
Random forests in quasi-real-time utilized for end-to-end botnet detection [15]	Bot attacks (Zeus Storm, Conficker, Kelihos/Hlux)	Campus network traffic and CAIDA	Hive, Tshark, Mahout, random forest	The average accuracy is 99.7%

density and distance-based approaches. One such technique used by the authors [17] is the clustering technique that does not need predefined class labels. This technique is a widely utilized approach for detecting anomalies [17].

1.3 Big data challenges for cybersecurity

Momentous potential has been recognized for BDA to cybersecurity. However, the true potential can be comprehended only if we address the several challenges given as follows:

1. Privacy: There is a need to develop privacy preserving big data applications because building privacy violations is easier.
2. BDA for advanced persistent threats (APT) detection: New detection algorithms are in complete demand which can process substantial data from dissimilar data sources. Few proof-of-concept deployments for the identification of security events exist that utilize BDA and demonstrate superior results [4,12,18].
3. High-performance cryptography: Various symmetric and asymmetric algorithms such as attribute-based encryption are developed for preventing attacks on the availability, consistency and reliability of big data [19] and encrypted data search techniques.
4. Security investigation on big data datasets: It is impossible to understand the ground truth from the data that is progressively gathered. Tremendous amount of events are comprised in the datasets but identifying what is benign and/or where attack has initiated remain as challenges [18].
5. Data origin problem: The provision for the expansion of data sources for processing creates an uncertainty in each data source in big data. Hence, the legitimacy and integrity of data deployed in our tools have to be reconsidered. The effects of maliciously inserted data can be identified and minimized by combative machine learning and robust statistics [13,14].
6. Security visualization: There is an ample increase in the amount of research and development in the emerging area of visualization technology [15,20]. Commercial and open-source data visualization tools are available for security [21]. However, it is elementary with graphs, pie charts and pivot tables in spreadsheet excel.
7. Skilled personnel: There is a huge shortage of skilled personnel for successful implementation of big data for information security. One of the critical elements is appropriately skilled personnel for deployment.

1.4 Related work on decision engine techniques

Decision engine (DE) approaches have been categorized into five types: classification, clustering, knowledge, combination and statistical approaches as illustrated in Table 1.2.

Table 1.2   Intrusion detection using decision management techniques

Decision management approaches	Benefits	Weaknesses
Classification [22–24]	Correct labeling of network data increases precision and minimizes false-positives	• More consumption of resources • Underlying statement is that each classifier has to be constructed separately
Clustering [25–27]	Processing time is shortened and class label is not essential for grouping data	• Construction of normal profile for improving the effectiveness of the technique • Upgradation of profile requires higher time
Knowledge [27,28]	Increased accurateness to distinguish existing attacks	• Malicious statements are described using static rules • Substantial processing time
Combination [29–31]	Few parameters are adjusted for augmenting accuracy	• Enormous effort and time for the integration of approaches
Statistics [32–34]	• Minimal consumption of resources • Correct baseline adaptation results in better accurateness	• Baseline selection requires precise analysis • New attack categories are defined by new functions

A network-based ADS using support vector machine (SVM) and hierarchical clustering was developed by Horng *et al.* [22] to enhance the accuracy by reducing the time for training the model. Similarly, another network-based ADS utilizing naïve Bayes, *K*-means and artificial neural network (ANN) was built by Dubey *et al.* [24] to boost the accuracy of malicious events. Nevertheless, the underlying assumption in classification-based IDS is that individually every classifier has to be attuned and they require more resources than statistical approaches.

Clustering, which is an unsupervised machine learning approach, groups a set of data elements on the basis of the identical features of the samples; for instance, measure of distance or probability. Different clustering techniques, namely, hierarchical, *K*-means and fuzzy *C*-means, were analyzed by Nadiammai and Hemalatha [26] to develop a network-based ADS. The authors [26] stated that fuzzy *C*-means was superior in comparison to other techniques in terms of accuracy and complexity.

Data points are classified according to class labels by creating a pattern set from input data in knowledge-based approaches. Temporal logic conditions are utilized to build a logical structure called EAGLE, which is suggested by Naldurg *et al.* [27] for developing an intrusion detection framework. Hung *et al.* [28]

presented a network-based ADS using an ontology approach. The advantages of knowledge-based algorithms are flexible and robust in nature to identify attacks for small-scale systems. They also result in high detection rate only if there is substantial information regarding normal and abnormal patterns. However, because of the challenge in dynamically updating the rules, false-positives are high and there is no data pertaining to audit for normal and intrusion data.

Ensemble and fusion-based ADS classifies data samples using combination-based techniques. A payload network-based ADS with high speed was built by Perdisci *et al.* [31] to improve detection precision using an one-class SVM ensemble. Another network-based ADS [29] deployed sampling and weighted majority technique to build an integration of accurate classifiers using PSO-generated weights. In comparison to single approaches, combination-based approaches yield enhanced correctness rate. Conversely, they depend on a hybridization degree to integrate the result of number of classifiers which, in turn, results in high cost of computation for heavy network traffic.

Statistical built techniques measure the anomaly event using means and standard deviation that are of first order, second order such as correlation measure and hypothesis testing and mixture models that are of third order. An unsupervised statistical approach developed by Fan *et al.* [32] was analyzed using Bayesian inference based on finite generalized Dirichlet mixture models (DMMs) to classify the anomalous and legitimate events. A network-based ADS [3] utilized a Gaussian mixture model to select the parameter for each component and quantity of mixture components in real-time environment.

1.5   Big network anomaly detection

Conventional supervised techniques are deployed on enormous volume of network data to distinguish anomalies from normal event. Large and stream data can be handled by big data solutions to lessen false-positive and false-negative rates. Various big data techniques developed for IDS with regard to year wise-distribution, type of anomaly identified is detailed in Table 1.3.

1.6   Big data for large-scale security monitoring

Centralized IDS, namely, Snort [40], Bro [41] and Suricata [42], can analyze network packets and can identify intrusions. These systems analyze and correlate data obtained from several network components and diverse network points.

A service model is developed [6] for network security application. The architecture developed includes honeypots, gathered cybersecurity intelligence. Payloads, flow data and signature alert data about attackers are gathered and recorded by honeypots. The correlation between honeypot and client is analyzed and determined by Google page ranking. However, DNS data and HTTP traffic are not included.

Table 1.3 Big data approaches for intrusion detection

Year	Approaches	Anomalies	Data	Experimental analysis
2018	IDS for big data implemented using PCA and mini batch *K*-means (PMBKM) with Calski Harabasz indicator for clustering efficiently [35]	Network anomalies	KDDCup99 dataset	PMBKM is efficient in comparison with *K*-means, *K*-means with PCA and mini batch *K*-means
2018	Spark-chi-SVM model for intrusion detection [36]	Network anomalies	KDD99	High performance, efficient for big data and lowers the training time
2018	IDS using decision tree which can be deployed in fog computing setting [37]	All 22 network attacks	KDDCUP 99	Effective and accurate
2017	Big data analytics using DMM for anomaly detection [38]	Network datasets	NSL-KDD and UNSW-NB15	Identified the attacks efficiently
2016	Big data model to avoid the influence due to network traffic distribution using KNN, decision tree, *K*-means and random forest. The model enhanced the precision and decreased the false-negatives [7]	DoS, Probe, R2L and U2R	KDD Cup99	Accuracy: 93.9% on probe, 98.6% on DoS, 56.1% on U2R, 77.2% on R2L and 95.4% on normal data
2016	DDoS detection technique implemented in Apache Spark Cluster using ANN [39]	DDoS	Normal generated traffic data and 2000 DARPA LLDOS 1.0	94% accuracy obtained
2016	Big data techniques for analyzing network traffic using HDFS and Hive [1]	SYN/FIN attack, NULL scan, XMAS scan	NCCDC	Visual representation of results
2016	A real-time IDS for extremely high speed big data setting using SVM, naïve Bayes J48, REPTree, random forest, conjunctive rule implemented in Hadoop [1]	DoS, U2R, R2L and Probing	DARPA, KDD 99, NSL-KDD	True-positive rate of 99.9% is obtained for REPTree and J48 that are the best classifiers
2016	PCA and multivariate dimensionality reduction technique for a real-time DDoS attack detection [9]	DDoS	1999 KDD Cup data	Visual representation of results
2016	Hadoop with machine learning and cloud computing to build an anomaly detection model. The model deployed Weka, HDFS, MapReduce and techniques like naïve Bayes, SVM and decision tree [10]	Poor connections	KDD Cup 99	Accuracy above 90%

Year	Method	Anomaly/Attack type	Dataset	Results
2016	Identification of malicious traffic using adaptive stream projected outlier detector [11]	DoS, R2L, U2R and Probing	KDD Cup 99 and generated data	Visual representation of results
2015	Machine learning, time series and pattern analysis for developing an anomaly-based intrusion detection to be deployed at different layers of TCP/IP (network/application) [3]	DDoS attacks, invasive Internet access and organized downloading	Campus LAN and edge router traces used to capture proxy server logs	Visual representation of results
2015	Traffic anomaly detection using MapReduce with APSE and Shannon entropy [4]	DoS, DDoS, DRDoS port scan	IPFIX data captured at a university's edge router	APSE shows better performance in comparison to Shannon entropy
	Graph and streaming analytics using big data architectures for a live operation. Technologies deployed are GemFireXD, MapReduce, Kafka, Apama, D3.js and Tableau [12]	Relative anomalies advanced persistent threats	Large global 500 company SIEM data	Anomaly groups with average recall and precision given below: very low [1.0,0.4], low [0.8,0.95], medium [0.9,0.9], very high [0.7,0.9] and high [0.75,0.7]
2015	A real-time hybrid intrusion detection model using CC4, multilayer perceptron neural networks and apache storm [2]	DDoS	2012 ISCX dataset	Average accuracy is 89%
2015	MapReduce framework to identify network anomalies using Hashdoop that analyzes traffic with hash calculation and cyclic redundancy check [13]	NetBIOS, SMB, Ping, Sasser, RPC and other attacks	MAWI traffic archive	F-Score: 0.88
2014	Analyzing NetFlow data using Hadoop MapReduce jobs were executed on Amazon servers using Hive to identify watering whole attack, thereby evaluating the competence of various data formats [15]	Watering hole attack	CAIDA	Number of reducers is very important in Hive. Hadoop MapReduce has an effective sequence file format
2014	A framework for anomaly detection and forensics using EWMA, PCA, MEDA, Timelines and oMEDA [20]	Firewall access attempts, IRC background activity, Parsing errors, IRC activity, DNS attacks and FTP attempts to outer nodes	Mini challenge 2 VAST 2012	Visual representation of results

Scalable network intrusion detection is addressed in the following papers [43–46]. Traffic processing and content inspection are parallelized [43,44] thereby processing several gigabits of data per second. This is obtained by multi core CPUs and multiple GPUs. The IDS has no serialized component because every operation is mapped to a suitable device after parallelization [43]. Suricata network intrusion detection system (NIDS) [42] proposed a solution for load balancing. Snort or Suricata is based on stateful IDS that relies on in-depth traffic analysis. Hence, these methods fully exploit computer capacity and require optimization of traffic analysis.

In the following section, we discuss about NIDS. Performance analysis of Shark and Spark appears to be best in comparison to other scenarios such as large-scale security monitoring.

One of the persistent security problems is the detection and prevention of network intrusions which has been studied from the past 30 years [47]. In 1987, IDS [48] was first proposed. The research still remains open owing to the dynamic progress of diverse information to be analyzed. In addition, identification of critical features for intrusion detection processing the heavy volume of dissimilar data and novel firewall policies to cope with attackers is also a challenging issue. Examples of NIDS are Snort [40], Bro [41] and Suricata [42]. The traffic of various protocols like HTTP, SIP, DNS is evaluated to determine anomalies. Rules that rely on signatures are defined to identify the anomalous traffic behavior. When an anomaly is encountered, IDS raises an alarm or the communication is halted (intrusion prevention system).

IP flow data is collected by Internet Service Providers which has the challenge of dealing with heavy traffic. Flow data discards the payload and is an aggregated traffic. Hence, privacy of users is preserved. The characteristics of flow record are IP version, timestamp, total packets and bytes exchanged, source and destination IP addresses and their corresponding ports. A unified approach for analyzing the data coming from diverse sources such as honeypots, DNS monitoring and standalone IDS is also an issue. In this chapter, system architecture for intrusion detection and prevention is proposed. The architecture analyzes various traffic such as HTTP, DNS, honeypot data and IP flow records. Intrusion detection utilized each of the traffic separately and detected efficiently [49–53]. Three various storage systems are integrated in the similar data storage and processing facility.

1.7   Mechanisms to prevent attacks

Asymmetric homomorphic encryption schemes such as Paillier [22] are typically used in present solutions. One scenario where it can be useful is if data is created and analyzed by diverse parties (Figure 1.1). Alice upload the data to the cloud after encryption by public key, and Bob submits the queries and decrypts using private key to obtain the results. Another solution is the protection mechanism for frequency attacks built on supplementary information. This attack has also been proved against deterministic encryption [8]. Defense against such attacks is devised

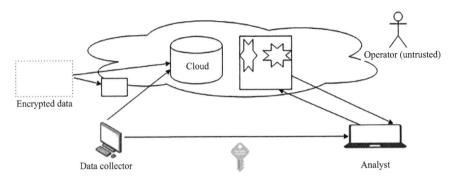

Figure 1.1 Motivating scenario

by an encryption technique called Splayed Additively Symmetric Homomorphic Encryption (SPLASHE) by expanding sensitive columns to numerous columns such that each new column relates to data for each distinctive element in the original column. In this technique, widening and deterministic encryption are padded with counterfeit entries to overthrow frequency attacks thereby limiting the overhead of computation and storage.

ASHE and SPLASHE are used in a system called seabed for proficient analytics over huge encrypted datasets. Seabed comprises a client-side planner and proxy. For each new data set the planner is applied once and transforms the plain text to encrypted text by selecting suitable encryption schemes for individual column according to the type of queries every user wishes to perform. The queries are rewritten for the encrypted schema visibly by the proxy and also decrypt the results obtained from the cloud. These computations cannot be accomplished directly on the cloud. Many optimizations in the seabed preserve the bandwidth, storage and computation costs of ASHE low. Therefore, it is acquiescent to the hardware acceleration that is offered on modern CPUs.

Paillier [22] introduced additive homomorphism wherein two cipher texts can be added to obtain a new cipher text that decrypts to the sum of two encrypted values (i.e., $C(x) + C(y) = C(x + y)$). The cloud can compute aggregation directly on the encrypted data because of the previous feature. Fully homomorphic systems [15] and systems with different homomorphism are used to determine random functions on encrypted data. There are various cipher texts for each value in homomorphic encryption because of the arbitrary nature. These schemes provide standard semantic security, which means that no attacker can obtain data about the plain text, given the cipher text. In certain situations the cloud has to view some property of the encrypted values also known as property preserving encryption. One such example is to compute a join. The randomness would prevent the cloud to match up to the encrypted values. Therefore, deterministic encryption [8] can be used in this situation. Conversely, these schemes are vulnerable to frequency attacks [5] because each item i is mapped to precisely one cipher text $C(i)$. Consider an example where a column contains a small value such as name of country, and the cloud identifies the value as Europe which will be more common in the data, the attacker can search for the most common cipher text and deduce that this cipher text will decrypt to that corresponding plain text. Another example of a property preserving encryption scheme is the selection of rows based on a series of values such as timestamps that are stored in an encrypted column. Order preserving encryption [10] is used to decide whether $x < y$, given only $C(x)$ and $C(y)$. There is a trade-off between confidentiality, functionality and performance as it is obvious if the cloud can perform the comparison, then the attacker can also perform the same.

APT that are previously unknown are developing which bypass existing security approaches. Big data analysis is the new security paradigm that can react to these attacks and can act as a central security management. Big data model is used for mining data from diverse sources to identify earlier unknown threats [54].

1.8   Big data analytics for intrusion detection system

1.8.1   Challenges of ADS

An ADS often faces potential challenges because of its effective design. Construction of normal profile to differentiate it from anomaly [20,25,31,44] could discover the challenges for ADS.

- Creating a profile with all probable normal samples is a complex task due to the inaccurate margin between malicious and normal events. FPR and false-negative rate increase when a normal pattern is characterized as an attack.
- Careful analysis is required to design the architecture of scalable and adaptive ADS. This is because the stealth and spy attacks [12] also have pattern similar to normal events.
- The processing time and FAR can increase if real-time identification is not addressed appropriately. There are two reasons: (i) noisy or irrelevant features of network traffic; (ii) adoption of lightweight detection techniques to handle the issue.
- ADS requires quality datasets for learning, evaluating and validating which is a major concern. Extensive variety of contemporary normal and malicious observations should be properly labeled. However, analyzing the data requires huge effort which establishes a reliable truth table with malware and normal events.
- Building an ADS architecture for a large-scale setting is demanding for SCADA and cloud computing. This is because of the presence of multiple nodes in a centralized or distributed environment. The performance of ADS is also affected due to the large amount of data transfer with heavy speed among the nodes.

1.8.2   Components of ADS

The four major components of ADS are

1. data source,
2. preprocessing,
3. DE approach and
4. a defense response depicted in Figure 1.2.

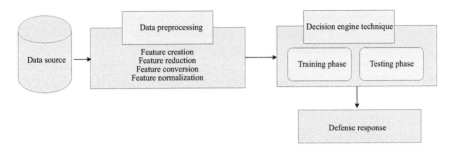

Figure 1.2   Components of ADS

Data source module: The primary part of ADS which sends the network or host audit data to the DE. The input obtained from DE is utilized to classify the samples as normal or attack [55]. Offline datasets containing a range of normal and malicious events, namely, UNSW-NB15, NSLKDD and KDDCUP 99, are used for assessing the performance of DE.

Data preprocessing module: This module plays an important phase in the framework that involves learning, handling and altering the audit input records. A pattern set is created after removing duplicated and noisy features. DE obtains the patterns to identify anomalous events and thereby enhancing the performance. The various functions of DE are (i) feature creation; (ii) feature reduction; (iii) feature conversion and (iv) feature normalization.

Feature creation: Different tools, namely, Netmate, BRO-IDS and NetFlow, are used for creating a set of features from network or host data. Mining of feature subset of UNSW-NB15 and NSL-KDD datasets is necessary else IDS cannot operate on raw data.

Feature reduction: Irrelevant and repeated features are excluded in feature selection and extraction techniques. Principal component analysis (PCA) [8] is used after extraction of original features to transform the records from high to a low dimension space.

Feature conversion: Symbolic feature types are converted into numeric values as data with symbolic values cannot be utilized by statistical DE and analytics.

Feature normalization: The features are scaled to a precise range, for instance [0,1]. The statistical nature of the attributes is retained as the measure eliminated the raw data bias.

DE module: An efficient design for detection of intrusive events is critical for large-scale real-time setting. The effectiveness of IDS is measured by suitable selection of functions for DE, training and testing stages. The complete defense will be compromised if it is not efficient.

Security response module: Attack actions are prevented by taking a decision explained by the administrators or system. Whenever there is a malicious incident, an alert will be sent to the administrator to prevent the activity.

Figure 1.3 depicts effective and lightweight ADS [26]. The major modules are logging, capturing and DMM-based DE. The network data is collected in the first

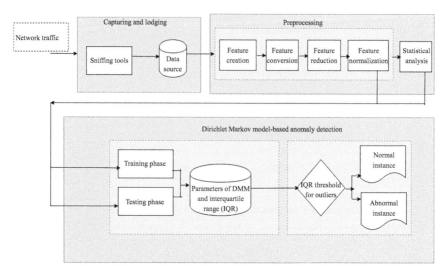

Figure 1.3   ADS framework

module and analyzed in the second to advance the performance. The experimental analysis has been done on UNSW-NB15 and NSL-KDD datasets. Thus, a lower FAR and higher precision is obtained.

An attribute of network traffic in the first phase is created by analyzing network connections for a particular time interval. Sniffing traffic from the router positioned at every node is one of the best options to analyze network data. Thus, only relevant network packets are aggregated [33,34]. Network data is filtered in the preprocessing phase by transforming symbolic attributes to numeric ones. This conversion is performed because only numeric data is handled by DMM-based statistical approach. The performance is improved by selecting the contributing features which reduces the computation time for the DE in real time.

1.8.2.1   Capturing and lodging module

Network data is sniffed and processed by the DE. An IXIA perfect storm tool [5,9] can analyze wide range of network fragments and produces various web application traffic such as Google, YouTube, Skype and Facebook. The tool can impersonate normal and abnormal network records.

1.8.2.2   Preprocessing module

In this module, feature conversion is performed as the first step to modify symbolic into numeric features as DMM-based ADS can operate only on numeric features. PCA is used for feature reduction, which is a widely used dimensionality reduction approach, and the other advantages are reduced usage of memory, data transfer and processing time. The major advantage is improved precision [14,16]. Normalization of feature eliminates the bias of raw data and transforms the feature value so that the attributes can be easily visualized and processed.

1.9 Conclusion

Encryption can be easily bypassed by recent unknown attacks. Hence, big data that is arising as a new promising prototype is in need for classifying such attacks. Big data can analyze heavy volumes of dissimilar data which is transforming the background of information security. Though many solutions are provided by big data, the challenges of big data which are detailed in this chapter have to be analyzed to realize the true scope. The various challenges in this domain are detection of APT and data leaks, visualization of security to analyze forensic, fraud and criminal intelligence are in the initial stages of research community. Revolutionary contributions are awaited from the researchers in this area to create substantial impact to the industry development.

In this chapter, two novel encryption techniques, ASHE and SPLASHE, for encrypted data to prevent from frequency attacks are discussed. A big data model for identification and prevention of unknown cyberattacks is also analyzed. The framework has three modules such as logging and capturing, preprocessing and statistical DE. Network data is sniffed and collected from a large-scale setting. The second module filters and removes the unwanted data to enhance the performance of DE. Finally, the DMM-based ADS identifies the malicious samples using a technique known as lower–upper interquartile range. Thus, the FPR is reduced and this approach can be scaled to SCADA and cloud computing architectures.

Acknowledgment

This study was undertaken with the support of the Scheme for Promotion of Academic and Research Collaboration (SPARC) grant SPARC/2018-2019/P616/SL "Intelligent Anomaly Detection System for Encrypted Network Traffic."

Abbreviations

ADS	anomaly detection system
ANN	artificial neural network
APT	advanced persistent threats
APSE	Adjustable Piecewise Shannon Entropy
DE	decision engine
DMM	Dirichlet mixture model
EWMA	exponentially weighted moving average
FPR	false-positive rate
IDS	intrusion detection system
NIDS	network intrusion detection system
PCA	principal component analysis
SIEM	security information and event management
SVM	support vector machine

References

[1]   Bachupally, Y.R., X. Yuan, and K. Roy. Network security analysis using Big Data technology. In SoutheastCon, 2016. 2016.

[2]   Zhang, J., H. Li, Q. Gao, H. Wang, and Y. Luo. Detecting anomalies from big network traffic data using an adaptive detection approach. Information Sciences, 2015. 318: p. 91–110.

[3]   Mylavarapu, G., J. Thomas, and T.K. Ashwin Kumar. Real-time hybrid intrusion detection system using Apache Storm. In High Performance Computing and Communications (HPCC), 2015 IEEE 7th International Symposium on Cyberspace Safety and Security (CSS), 2015 IEEE 12th International Conference on Embedded Software and Systems (ICESS), 2015 IEEE 17th International Conference on. 2015.

[4]   Sait, S.Y., A. Bhandari, S. Khare, C. James, and H.A. Murthy. Multi-level anomaly detection: Relevance of big data analytics in networks. Sadhana, 2015. 40(6): p. 1737–1767.

[5]   Terzi, D.S., R. Terzi, and S. Sagiroglu. Big data analytics for network anomaly detection from netflow data. In 2017 International Conference on Computer Science and Engineering (UBMK). IEEE, 2017.

[6]   Curry, S., E. Kirda, E. Schwartz, W.H. Stewart, and A. Yoran, "Big Data Fuels Intelligence-Driven Security". White paper, January 2013.

[7]   Yao, H., Y. Liu, and C. Fang. An abnormal network traffic detection algorithm based on big data analysis. International Journal of Computers, Communications & Control, 2016. 11(4).

[8]   Hsieh, C.-J. and T.-Y. Chan. Detection DDoS attacks based on neural network using Apache Spark. In Applied System Innovation (ICASI), 2016 International Conference on. 2016.

[9]   Rathore, M.M., A. Ahmad, and A. Paul. Real time intrusion detection system for ultra-high-speed big data environments. The Journal of Supercomputing, 2016. 72(9): p. 3489–3510.

[10]   Jia, B., Y. Ma, X. Huang, Z. Lin, and Y. Sun. A novel real-time DDoS attack detection mechanism based on MDRA algorithm in big data. Mathematical Problems in Engineering, 2016. 2016.

[11]   Cui, B. and S. He. Anomaly detection model based on Hadoop platform and Weka interface. In 2016 10th International Conference on Innovative Mobile and Internet Services in Ubiquitous Computing (IMIS). 2016.

[12]   Tian, G., Z. Wang, X. Yin, *et al.* Mining network traffic anomaly based on adjustable piecewise entropy. In Quality of Service (IWQoS), 2015 IEEE 23rd International Symposium on. 2015. p. 299–308.

[13]   Puri, C. and C. Dukatz. Analyzing and predicting security event anomalies: Lessons learned from a large enterprise big data streaming analytics deployment. In Database and Expert Systems Applications (DEXA), 2015 26th International Workshop on. 2015.

[14]   Fontugne, R., J. Mazel, and K. Fukuda. Hashdoop: A MapReduce framework for network anomaly detection. In Computer Communications Workshops (INFOCOM WKSHPS), 2014 IEEE Conference on. 2014.

[15]   Singh, K., S.C. Guntuku, A. Thakur, and C. Hota. Big data analytics framework for peer-to-peer botnet detection using random forests. Information Sciences, 2014. 278: p. 488–497.

[16]   He, W., G. Hu, and Y. Zhou Large-scale IP network behavior anomaly detection and identification using substructure-based approach and multivariate time series mining. Telecommunication Systems, 2012. 50(1): p. 1–13.

[17]   Liu, D., C.H. Lung, N. Seddigh, and B. Nandy. Network traffic anomaly detection using adaptive density-based fuzzy clustering. In 2014 IEEE 13th International Conference on Trust, Security and Privacy in Computing and Communications. 2014. p. 823–830.

[18]   Dumitras, T. and D. Shou Toward a standard benchmark for computer security research: The worldwide intelligence network environment (WINE). In Proc. EuroSys BADGERS Workshop, pp. 89–96. ACM, 2011.

[19]   Ganugula, U. and A. Saxena High performance cryptography: Need of the hour. CSI Communications, 2013: p. 16–17.

[20]   Zhou, X., M. Petrovic, T. Eskridge, M. Carvalho, and X. Tao. Exploring Netflow data using Hadoop. In Proceedings of the Second ASE International Conference on Big Data Science and Computing. 2014.

[21]   Alguliyev, R. and Y. Imamverdiyev. Big data: Big promises for information security. In 2014 IEEE 8th International Conference on Application of Information and Communication Technologies (AICT), pp. 1–4. IEEE, 2014.

[22]   Horng, S.J., M.Y. Su, Y.H. Chen, *et al.* A novel intrusion detection system based on hierarchical clustering and support vector machines. Expert Systems with Applications, 2011. 38(1): p. 306–313.

[23]   Ambusaidi, M.A., X. He, P. Nanda, and Z. Tan. Building an intrusion detection system using a filter-based feature selection algorithm. IEEE Transactions on Computers, 2016. 65(10): p. 2986–2998.

[24]   Dubey, S. and J. Dubey. KBB: A hybrid method for intrusion detection. In Computer, Communication and Control (IC4), 2015 International Conference on, pp. 1–6. IEEE, 2015.

[25]   Jadhav, A., A. Jadhav, P. Jadhav, and P. Kulkarni. A novel approach for the design of network intrusion detection system (NIDS). In Sensor Network Security Technology and Privacy Communication System (SNS & PCS), 2013 International Conference on, pp. 22–27. IEEE, 2013.

[26]   Nadiammai, G. and M. Hemalatha. An evaluation of clustering technique over intrusion detection system. In Proceedings of the International Conference on Advances in Computing, Communications and Informatics, pp. 1054–1060. ACM, 2012.

[27]   Naldurg, P., K. Sen, and P. Thati. A temporal logic based framework for intrusion detection. In International Conference on Formal Techniques for Networked and Distributed Systems, pp. 359–376. Springer, 2004.

[28]   Hung, S.S. and D.S.M. Liu. A user-oriented ontology-based approach for network intrusion detection. Computer Standards & Interfaces, 2008. 30(1): p. 78–88.

[29]   Aburomman, A.A. and M.B.I. Reaz. A novel SVM-KNN-PSO ensemble method for intrusion detection system. Applied Soft Computing, 2016. 38: p. 360–372.

[30]   Shiet, J. A technique independent fusion model for network intrusion detection. In Proceedings of the Midstates Conference on Undergraduate Research in Computer Science and Mathematics, vol. 3, pp. 1–3. Citeseer, 2005.

[31]   Perdisci, R., G. Gu, and W. Lee. Using an ensemble of one-class SVM classifiers to harden payload-based anomaly detection systems. In Sixth International Conference on Data Mining (ICDM'06), pp. 488–498. IEEE, 2006.

[32]   Fan, W., N. Bouguila, and D. Ziou. Unsupervised anomaly intrusion detection via localized Bayesian feature selection. In 2011 IEEE 11th International Conference on Data Mining, pp. 1032–1037. IEEE, 2011.

[33]   Fan, W., N. Bouguila, and D. Ziou. Variational learning for finite Dirichlet mixture models and applications. IEEE Transactions on Neural Networks and Learning Systems, 2012. 23(5): p. 762–774.

[34]   Harrou, F., F. Kadri, S. Chaabane, C. Tahon, and Y. Sun. Improved principal component analysis for anomaly detection: Application to an emergency department. Computers & Industrial Engineering, 2015. 88: p. 63–77.

[35]   Peng, K., V.C.M. Leung, and Q. Huang. Clustering approach based on mini batch Kmeans for intrusion detection system over big data. IEEE Access, 2018. 6: p. 11897–11906.

[36]   Othman, S.M., F.M. Ba-Alwi, N.T. Alsohybe, *et al.* Intrusion detection model using machine learning algorithm on Big Data environment. Journal of Big Data, 2018. 5: p. 34. https://doi.org/10.1186/s40537-018-0145-4.

[37]   Peng, K., V. Leung, L. Zheng, S. Wang, C. Huang, and T. Lin. Intrusion detection system based on decision tree over big data in fog environment. Wireless Communications and Mobile Computing, 2018. 2018.

[38]   Moustafa N., G. Creech, and J. Slay. Big data analytics for intrusion detection system: Statistical decision-making using finite Dirichlet mixture models. In: Palomares Carrascosa I., Kalutarage H., and Huang Y. (eds) Data Analytics and Decision Support for Cybersecurity. Data Analytics. Cham: Springer, 2017.

[39]   Hsieh, C.-J. and T.-Y. Chan. Detection DDoS attacks based on neural network using Apache Spark. In Applied System Innovation (ICASI), 2016 International Conference on. 2016.

[40]   Roesch, M. Snort – Lightweight intrusion detection for networks. In Proceedings of the 13th USENIX Conference on System Administration, ser. LISA'99, pp. 229–238. 1999.

[41]   Paxson, V. Bro: A system for detecting network intruders in real-time. In Proceedings of the 7th Conference on USENIX Security Symposium Volume 7, ser. SSYM'98. 1998.

[42]   Open Information Security Foundation (OISF). Suricata Open Source IDS/IPS/NSM engine. 2019. Available at https://suricata-ids.org/.

[43]   Vasiliadis, G., M. Polychronakis, and S. Ioannidis. MIDeA: A multiparallel intrusion detection architecture. In Proceedings of the 18th ACM Conference on Computer and Communications Security, ser. CCS'11, pp. 297–308. New York, NY, USA: ACM, 2011.

[44] Jamshed, M.A., J. Lee, S. Moon, *et al.* Kargus: A highly-scalable software-based intrusion detection system. In Proceedings of the 2012 ACM Conference on Computer and Communications Security, ser. CCS'12, pp. 317–328. New York, NY, USA: ACM, 2012.

[45] Jiang, H., G. Zhang, G. Xie, K. Salamatian, and L. Mathy. Scalable high-performance parallel design for network intrusion detection systems on many-core processors. In Proceedings of the Ninth ACM/IEEE Symposium on Architectures for Networking and Communications Systems, ser. ANCS'13, pp. 137–146. Piscataway, NJ, USA: IEEE Press, 2013.

[46] Gill, H., D. Lin, X. Han, C. Nguyen, T. Gill, and B.T. Loo. Scalanytics: A declarative multi-core platform for scalable composable traffic analytics. In Proceedings of the 22nd International Symposium on High performance Parallel and Distributed Computing, ser. HPDC'13, pp. 61–72. New York, NY, USA: ACM, 2013.

[47] Anderson, J.P., "Computer security threat monitoring and surveillance". Fort Washington, Pennsylvania, Tech. Rep., 1980.

[48] Denning, D.E. An intrusion-detection model. IEEE Transactions in Software Engineering, 1987. 13(2).

[49] Antonakakis, M., R. Perdisci, D. Dagon, W. Lee, and N. Feamster. Building a dynamic reputation system for DNS. In Proceedings of the 19th USENIX Security Symposium. 2010.

[50] Bilge, L., E. Kirda, C. Kruegel, and M. Balduzzi. Exposure: Finding malicious domains using passive DNS analysis. In Proceedings of NDSS. 2011.

[51] Sperotto, A., G. Schaffrath, R. Sadre, C. Morariu, A. Pras, and B. Stiller. An overview of IP flow-based intrusion detection. Communications Surveys Tutorials, IEEE, Third 2010. 12(3): p. 343–356.

[52] François, J., S. Wang, R. State, and T. Engel. BotTrack: Tracking botnets using NetFlow and PageRank. In Proceedings of the 10th International IFIP TC 6 Conference on Networking – Volume Part I, ser. NETWORKING'11, pp. 1–14. Berlin, Heidelberg: Springer-Verlag, 2011.

[53] Kreibich, C. and J. Crowcroft. Honeycomb: Creating intrusion detection signatures using honeypots. SIGCOMM Computer Communication Review, 2004. 34(1): p. 51–56.

[54] Ahn, S.-H., N.-U. Kim, and T.-M. Chung. Big data analysis system concept for detecting unknown attacks. In 16th International Conference on Advanced Communication Technology, pp. 269–272. IEEE, 2014.

[55] Moustafa, N. and J. Slay. UNSW-NB15: A comprehensive data set for network intrusion detection systems (UNSW-NB15 network data set). In Military Communications and Information Systems Conference (MilCIS), 2015, pp. 1–6. IEEE, 2015.

Chapter 2

Zero attraction data selective adaptive filtering algorithm for big data applications

Sivashanmugam Radhika[1] and Arumugam Chandrasekar[2]

Big data sets are characterized by raw data with large dimension, noise accumulation, spurious correlation and heavy-tailed behavior along with measurement outliers. Therefore, a unified approach is inevitable to preprocess the raw data in order to improve the prediction accuracy. In this paper, we present updated data preprocessing framework based on adaptive filtering algorithm with data selection capability together with removal of outliers and noise. The l_1 norm minimization along with a new update rule based on higher order statistics of error enables dimension reduction without any sacrifice in accuracy. Thus, the proposed zero attraction data selective least mean square (ZA-DS-LMS) algorithm can claim for the reduction in the computational cost with the improvement in convergence speed and steady-state mean square error (MSE) without any compromise in the accuracy. Simulations were performed in real and simulated big data to validate the performance improvement of the proposed algorithm in the context of preprocessing for big data analysis.

2.1 Introduction

In the current scenario, the data sets are increasing at a high rate because of the presence of cheap sensors, mobile phones, Internet, etc.; big data is the one characterized by too large data sets which results in problems associated with storage, analysis, sharing, privacy and needs specific processes and algorithms to meet the big data requirement of time and accuracy [1]. Even though the amount of data is very large, the information extracted is very small due to the following reasons: First, the acquired data sets suffer from low quality. The quality of data is mainly impaired by noise and measurement outliers. Noise can be considered as an unrelated factor to the required data that are acquired externally or internally and are capable of altering the information that is gathered from a particular data set [2]. Measurement outliers occur in situations such as during unexpected disruption and circuit saturation [3].

[1]Department of Electrical and Electronics Engineering, School of Electrical and Electronics, Sathyabama Institute of Science and Technology, Chennai, India
[2]Department of CSE, St. Joseph's College of Engineering, Chennai, India

This is unavoidable and expected because sensors are the most widely used primary source of data. These sensors are mostly deployed in open environment together with hard terrain and they work for entire day. So any harsh atmospheric condition may produce noise [4]. Noise may also occur due to technical issues of the devices used or due to the movement of the subjects especially in the case of medical data sets [5]. Second, not all the data in the data set bring new information. This often seen in several big data applications such as medical data sets and econometric data sets. Thus, if these non-innovative data are censored or not selected to take part in the statistical inference, then it is possible to manage the storage and processing problems associated with big data [6]. Third, most of the real data sets are found to have spurious correlation and exhibit heavy-tailed behavior as they are complex in nature as they are obtained from multiple sources [2,7].

Thus, data preprocessing is inevitable to increase the information extracted from various big data sets for big data analysis. Data preprocessing involves the efficient processing of the data before being fed for data analysis. Different literatures speak about the necessity and the work of data preprocessing methods. In [8], an improved filtering method is proposed for data preprocessing. A method based on rigid structure matching is explained in [9] for the noise removal. Experiments done in the context of human motion capture illustrate the effectiveness of the proposed approach. Several adaptive filters that incorporate the data selection feature were proposed for big data application. They include the family of partial update and set membership adaptive algorithms [10–15]. The work of these algorithms is to update the filter coefficients partially or selectively based on certain constraint which is dependent on error. They mainly lack in the number of solution involved as they update the coefficients in blocks. Later, data censoring adaptive algorithms were developed [6,15,16]. The idea behind these algorithms is that non-innovative and noise data are censored to participate in the update recursion which is found to be useful in wireless, ad hoc network, medical data sets and other big data applications. In [3,17,18,20], several data selective adaptive algorithms were developed. The main concept behind this approach is that two thresholds are selected to propose the probability of update. The update rule is based on standard deviation of error which will be more suitable if the error is said to be Gaussian. But the error is found to have heavy and light tail distributions as the big data are generally obtained from various sources and they sometime exhibit heavy tail behavior [2]. Thus, the existing rule [3,17,18] is not suitable in the present context.

In [21], a preprocessing methodology based on combination of principal component analysis method with additive Gaussian noise is proposed. This method is found to reduce the dimension of big data. Statistical evidences indicate that higher order statistics measures the error more accurately than second-order statistics. Literatures such as [19] provide evidence that kurtosis of error performs better than MSE when the error is non-Gaussian. Another aspect often seen in real-time data set is sparsity [7,24]. In order to exploit sparsity to improve the performance of the algorithms, several sparsity aware adaptive algorithms were developed [20,22,23].

Thus, from the different literatures it is evident that the performance of data analysis is better with preprocessing than without preprocessing. Also it is evident that the data preprocessing has a significant role in the data analysis as the quality of data has a direct impact on the accuracy and results obtained from the data analysis. It is also found from the literatures that there is no unified and systematic approach to preprocess the data. All the existing techniques rely only on one or two aspects only. Therefore, it is necessary to develop or construct single efficient smart adaptive data preprocessing approach that can produce quality data along with suitable selectivity so as to reduce the complexity of data model which is particularly important for data analysis process. Hence, this paper focuses on the design and development of adaptive filtering strategies suitable for big data pre-processing application. The main contributions of his paper are as follows.

We propose an updated data preprocessing framework based on adaptive filtering algorithm for big data analysis. An optimized LMS-based data selection adaptive algorithm is proposed. A higher order statistics of error-based update rule is proposed to remove noise and outliers. We propose inclusion of l_1-norm-based term to further enhance the performance of the algorithm.

This chapter is organized as follows: Section 2.2 discusses the system model for data preprocessing using adaptive algorithm. It also discusses the MSE error of the algorithm and the nature of the noise and error sources. The proposed data pre-processing framework is discussed in Section 2.3. A new proposed update rule is also proposed. The proposed updated ZA-DS-LMS algorithm that includes a zero attraction term is also discussed in this section. Simulations are provided in Section 2.4 and the results of the proposed method are discussed and also compared with the original counterpart in this section. Conclusions are presented in Section 2.5 along with the future scope of the proposed work.

2.2   System model

For data preprocessing application, there are lots of surveys already done. As for, as system identification problem is concerned, linear regression is found to provide promising results [4,25–28]. However, it is required to be optimized so as to obtain better performance. For this purpose, an adaptive algorithm is considered. The problem under consideration is for learning an unknown system which is assumed to be linear as shown in Figure 2.1. Here, the work of the adaptive filter is to estimate the signal $y(n)$. For this purpose, an unknown system with input $x(n)$ of length N with zero mean and correlation R given by $x(n) = [x_0(n)x_1(n)x_2(n) \cdots x_N(n)]^T$ is taken. Throughout, n is the time index. Let us assume that the desired signal or reference signal is assumed to be known. The desired response $d(n)$ is modeled as a multiple linear regression model given by

$$d(n) = w_O^T x(n) + v(n) \tag{2.1}$$

where w_O is optimal weight vector and $v(n)$ is the noise source with variance σ_v^2. Here, $y(n) = w^T(n)x(n)$ is estimated output for the filter, $w(n) = [w_0(n)w_1(n)w_2(n) \cdots w_N(n)]^T$ is filter coefficient vector, and $e(n) = d(n) - y(n)$ is error signal. Assuming that the coefficient vector $w(n)$ and the input $x(n)$ are uncorrelated, the MSE at any instant of time n is given by

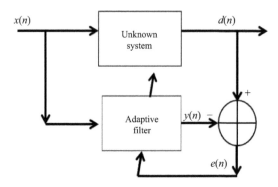

Figure 2.1   Adaptive filter in the context of unknown system identification

$$\varepsilon(n) = E\big[e^2(n)\big] = E\Big[v(n) + (w_O - w(n))^T x(n)\Big]^2 \qquad (2.2)$$

If the weight error vector is given by (2.3) as

$$\tilde{w}(n) = w_O - w(n) \qquad (2.3)$$

the MSE $\varepsilon(n)$ is written as

$$\varepsilon(n) = E\big[v^2(n)\big] - 2E\big[v(n)\tilde{w}^T(n)x(n)\big] + E\big[\tilde{w}^T(n)x(n)x^T(n)\tilde{w}(n)\big] \qquad (2.4)$$

If the error signal and the noise are uncorrelated [10], we obtain (2.5) as

$$\varepsilon(n) = \sigma_v^2 + E\big[\tilde{w}^T(n)x(n)x^T(n)\tilde{w}(n)\big] = \sigma_v^2 + \varepsilon_{excess}(n) \qquad (2.5)$$

where $\varepsilon_{excess}(n)$ the excess MSE and σ_v^2 is the variance of the noise source. Equation (2.5) is very important for adaptive algorithm as it is used for the updation of filter coefficients.

2.3   Proposed data preprocessing framework

In this section, we propose data preprocessing framework based on adaptive filtering approach. Figure 2.2 depicts the process flow. Initially the data sets obtained from different sensors are collected which are called as raw data. These raw data are converted into discrete form as per the required time intervals. These raw data consist of noise term, outliers and also noninformation content in it. The main process of the preprocessing done is shown inside the box in Figure 2.2. Using the initial training data set, adaptive filter parameters are initialized. The coefficients are updated on the basis of update recursion rule for the adaptive filter. For each iteration, the extracted data set is compared with the desired response or the testing data set (which is assumed to be known in advance). The updation is made on the basis of the MSE of the result obtained between the extracted data set and the

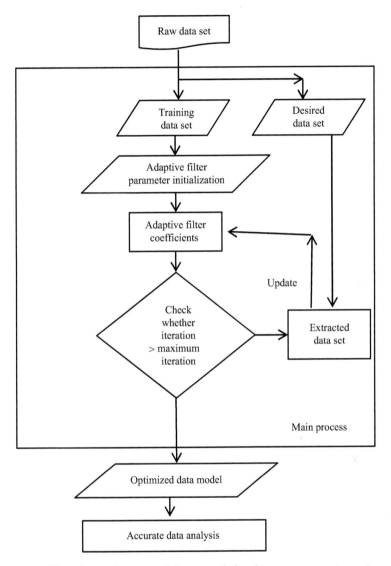

Figure 2.2   Flowchart of proposed framework for data preprocessing using adaptive filter

testing data set. Thus, as per update equation of adaptive filter, the process of updation is repeated for the maximum number of iteration. Finally, the extracted data set obtained is the optimized one. Thus, the work of the adaptive filter is to reduce noise, outlier with data selectivity feature. This optimized data model is further used for big data analysis for efficient prediction. The following section elaborates the concept of main process in detail.

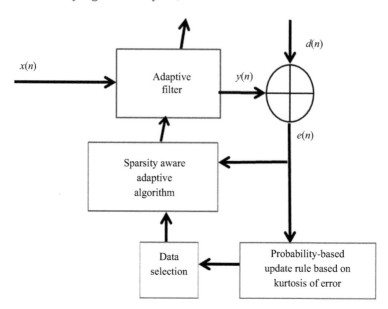

Figure 2.3   Proposed system model

2.3.1   Proposed update rule

The main process of the proposed preprocessing framework is shown in Figure 2.3. The known desired data set is compared with the output from adaptive filter. The error output at each iteration is used for the calculation of MSE and kurtosis of error which are used for data selection as well as for fixing the range for updation of filter coefficients. Conventional update recursion of LMS adaptive filter is given by (2.6) as follows:

$$w(n + 1) = w(n) + \mu e(n)x(n) \tag{2.6}$$

where μ is called the step size. It does not incorporate all these requirements for big data application. Therefore, modified update recursion for adaptive filter is required. Further the improvement of performance is made by the inclusion of sparsity aware term. The modified update recursion is proposed as follows.

Consider a practical application in which the estimated output is obtained. If the error signal is taken and if the standard deviation of error is measured, then it is possible to say that if the standard deviation of error is smaller than some value times of variance of noise, i.e., $|e(n)| < \gamma(n)\sigma_v$, then it implies that there is no new information in the data set due to the signal pair $d(n)$ and $x(n)$. Thus, the updation need not be made. On the other hand, if the mean square value of error is greater than maximum value times of noise $|e(n)| < \gamma_{max}\sigma_v$, it implies that an outlier such as measurement outlier would have occurred, and then also the updation is not made. In both the cases, the data set can be discarded as it directly affects the computational complexity [3]. Based on the previous requirement, the proposed update rule is given by

$$w(n+1) = \left\{ \begin{matrix} w(n) + \mu e(n)x(n) & \text{if } \gamma(n)\sigma_v < \sigma_e(n) < \gamma_{\max}\sigma_v \\ w(n) & \text{otherwise} \end{matrix} \right\} \quad (2.7)$$

Thus, it can be seen that when there is a noise in the input, by use of the condition given in (2.7), the filter coefficients are either updated or not updated. Whenever an outlier has occurred, then as per (2.7), the update is removed and the filter coefficients are made unchanged. Thus, removal of noise and outlier as well as data selectivity is efficiently made.

2.3.2   Selection of thresholds

If the error follows Gaussian distribution, then the update rule based on standard deviation of error provides good performance. It is well known that the noise source is not always Gaussian and the error deviates from Gaussian distribution. If the error distribution deviates much from the shape of Gaussian distribution, mere standard deviation does not provide feasible solution. Therefore, it is required to use higher order statistics of error to obtain a feasible solution. Kurtosis is the measure of fourth power of coefficient which is given by [19] as kurtosis $= E[e^4(n)]/E^2[e^2(n)]$.

The value of $\gamma(n)$ is based on the MSE given in (2.5). The steady state EMSE of LMS is given by [10] as

$$\frac{\mu Tr(R)}{1 - \mu Tr(R)}\sigma_v^2 \quad (2.8)$$

Substituting (2.8) in (2.5), we obtain the value of $\gamma(n)$, the lower threshold as given in (2.9).

$$\gamma(n) = \left(\sqrt{1 + \frac{\mu Tr(R)}{1 - \mu Tr(R)}} \right) \quad (2.9)$$

The value of upper threshold $\gamma_{\max}$ is very important as it decides the elimination of outlier. If $\gamma_{\max}$ depends only on the standard deviation, then it cannot give accurate results for heavy- and light-tailed errors. Therefore, the higher-order statistics of error such as kurtosis as a number or ratio with respect to kurtosis of Gaussian error is used as an upper threshold $\gamma_{\max}$. Therefore,

$$\gamma_{\max} = \sqrt{\frac{k_G}{k_e}} \quad (2.10)$$

where k_e is the kurtosis of error and k_G is the kurtosis of Gaussian distribution. Thus, it can be seen that whenever the error is a heavy-tailed one, then the k_e is a large value. The thresholds are smaller as $k_G = 3$. Hence, the range of the error updation is reduced and hence the heavy-tailed outlier is prevented in the filter coefficients. On the other hand, if there is light-tailed error, the range of updation should be large so as to update the useful information. As expected for light-tailed error, the value of k_e is small and hence the threshold is large. Thus, the previous proposed rule selectively operates on the data and removes all types of outliers.

2.3.3   Sparsity model

Sparsity is one of the common occurrences found in most of the large big data sets such as echo signals, HDTV signals and underwater acoustic signals, [2] and compression sensing algorithms were developed to explore the sparse nature and improve the performance of the algorithm [14]. They work by inclusion of lp norm penalty function to the original cost function of adaptive algorithm. The work of the norm function is to attract the near to zero filter coefficients and thus reduce the computational complexity and increase the convergence. Out of several norm functions, l_1 norm is used as it provides convex minimization, and it is the only norm that considers even smaller coefficients. Thus, the update recursion is given by

$$J(n) = \frac{1}{2}e^2(n) + \rho\|w(n)\|_1 \qquad (2.11)$$

If l_1 norm penalty is also incorporated in the proposed rule, further improvement in convergence and reduction in steady state error for sparse data sets can be obtained. The sparsity-aware-proposed rule is given by (2.12) as

$$w(n+1) = \left\{ \begin{array}{ll} w(n) + \mu e(n)x(n) - \rho \text{sgn}(w(n)) & \text{if } \gamma(n)\sigma_v < \sigma_e(n) < \gamma_{\max}\sigma_v \\ w(n) & \text{otherwise} \end{array} \right\} \qquad (2.12)$$

Generalizing (2.7), we can obtain as

$$w(n+1) = w(n) + \beta(n)\mu e(n)x(n) \qquad (2.13)$$

If l_1 norm penalty term is also included then the update recursion becomes

$$w(n+1) = w(n) + \beta(n)\mu e(n)x(n) - \rho \text{sgn}(w(n)) \qquad (2.14)$$

where ρ is zero attraction controller term that decides the strength of attraction, and $\text{sgn}(w(n))$ is sign function given by

$$\text{sgn}(w(n)) = \left\{ \begin{array}{l} \frac{w(n)}{|w(n)|} \text{ if and } w(n) \neq 0 \\ 0 \text{ if and } w(n) = 0 \end{array} \right\}.$$

$\beta(n)$ is the data selectivity parameter given by

$$\beta(n) = \left\{ \begin{array}{ll} 1 & \text{if } \gamma(n)\sigma_v < \sigma_e(n) < \gamma_{\max}\sigma_v \\ 0 & \text{otherwise} \end{array} \right\} \qquad (2.15)$$

The algorithm is given in form as pseudocode as follows:
Initialization: $x(0) = 0$, $w(0) = 0$, $e(0) = 0$, σ_v^2 is known, select μ, ρ.
Given input $x(n)$,

For time index $n = 1, 2, \ldots$
Compute $\gamma(n)$ and fix $\gamma_{\max}$
Obtain error $e(n)$, standard deviation of error σ_e and $\beta(n)$
If $\beta(n) = 0$, $w(n + 1) = w(n)$
Calculate $\gamma_{\max}$ using (2.10)
Check $\sigma_e(n) > \gamma_{\max}\sigma_v$
If yes $e(n) = 0$, $d(n) = 0$
Else update weights using $w(n + 1) = w(n) + \mu e(n)x(n) - \rho \mathrm{sgn}(w(n))$

2.4   Simulations

In this section, simulation results are presented to validate the performance improvement of the proposed scheme. The results are shown in two different scenarios: one using synthesized data and the other with real data sets all, pertaining to big data application.

Scenario 1: In the first scenario, real data are collected for the prediction of appliances energy use in a low energy building [29]. The work of the adaptive filter is to predict the energy use based on the previous measurements. The measured signal is modeled as AR 1 model. The step size is chosen to be 0.005. In order to calculate the standard deviation of the error, the method used in [12] is adopted. Figure 2.4 illustrates the predicted and original value obtained using the proposed rule given in (2.7). From Figure 2.1, it is evident that the proposed sequence and the original sequence coincide. When the number of data sets used was analyzed, it is found that the data set used is only 32% of the total available data which claims for the reduction in the storage space as expected.

Scenario 2: Consider a speech sequence of length 20,000 samples with a sampling frequency of 8 kHz. The normalized sparsity level is chosen as 0.4 where

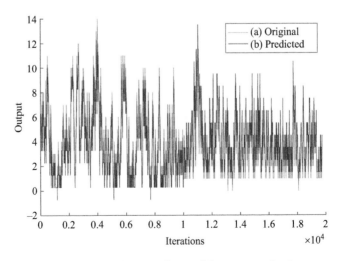

Figure 2.4   Tracking analysis of the proposed scheme

it is obtained as the ratio between total number of sparse terms to the total number of terms. The problem under consideration is the unknown system identification problem. The system and the filter are assumed to be made of the same number of filter coefficients. The input is both white Gaussian and colored. The colored input is obtained by passing white Gaussian noise through first-order AR system with transfer function given by $1/(1-0.8z^{-1})$. The noise is made of both Gaussian and other noise sources. The Gaussian noise has unity variance and the impulsive noise is generated as $k(n)A(n)$ where $k(n)$ is a Bernoulli process with probability of success $[k(n) = 1] = p_r$. MSE in dB scale is used to measure the performance metric of the proposed scheme. The signal-to-noise ratio (SNR) is taken as 30 dB.

The first experiment is done for the sparsity aware data selective LMS algorithm. The parameters of the LMS algorithm are as follows $\mu = 0.001$, $\rho = 0.5 \times 10^{-4}$ for both original and the proposed scheme. In Figure 2.2, the MSE learning curves of the LMS, DS-LMS, ZA-LMS and the proposed schemes are compared for white input. As expected the performance of the proposed one is similar to the ZA-LMS algorithm and it is better than the data selection strategy proposed in [12] and original LMS due to the inclusion of sparsity aware term. Similar conclusions are drawn from Figures 2.3 and 2.4 where the same experiment is repeated for colored inputs for systems of orders 1 and 4, respectively. The number of the times the update is made is found to be almost 35% of the total size of the data set without any compromise in the performance. The second experiment is done with different a outlier, namely, impulsive noise sources with different values of Pr and the performance is measured. As seen from Figures 2.5–2.9, the proposed algorithm provides satisfactory performance for all types of outliers.

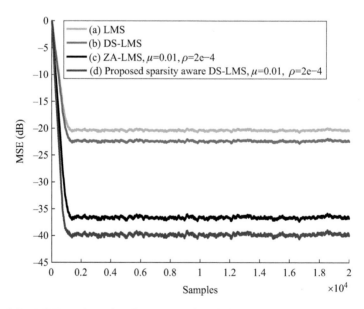

Figure 2.5   MSE analysis for the proposed and the original LMS algorithm for white input

In order to illustrate the data selectivity of the proposed scheme, the simulation is performed for first experiment of scenario 2 where the input is taken as white Gaussian and the SNR is varied as 30, 20, 10 dB, respectively. The step size is chosen as 0.05. For each value, the data sets used are tabulated in Table 2.1. Thus,

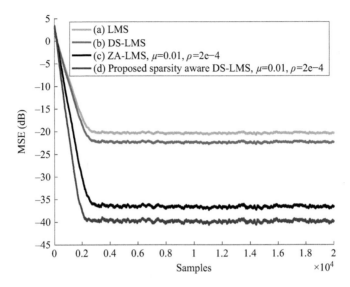

Figure 2.6 MSE analysis for the proposed and the original LMS algorithm for AR 1 input

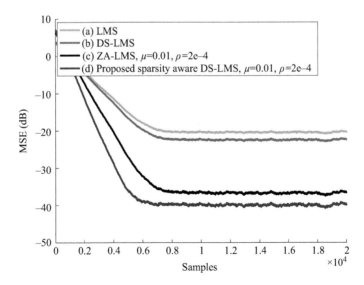

Figure 2.7 MSE analysis for the proposed and the original LMS algorithm for AR 4 input

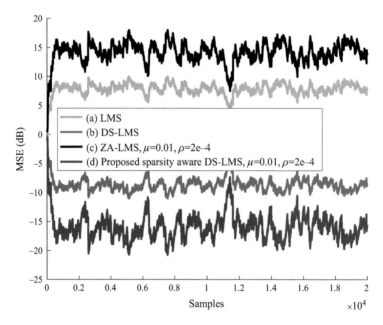

Figure 2.8   MSE analysis for the proposed and the original LMS algorithm for
white input with outlier as impulsive noise with Pr = 0.01

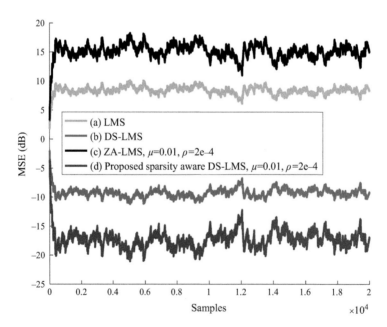

Figure 2.9   MSE analysis for the proposed and the original LMS algorithm for AR
1 input with outlier as impulsive noise with Pr = 0.01

Table 2.1 Data selectivity for varying noise level

Sl. no.	SNR (dB)	Data used (%)
1	30	50
2	20	43
3	10	30

from the table it is evident that as the SNR value is increased, the data usage is also increased which is an evident to prove that the noise and outliers are effectively removed when the SNR is low.

2.5 Conclusions

In this work, sparsity aware data selection scheme for adaptive filtering algorithms pertaining to big data preprocessing were developed. The proposed ZA-DS-LMS algorithm results in lesser computational complexity by the use of the proposed update rule. Further, the non-Gaussian outliers are also removed by preventing the updation of coefficients during the occurrence of noise. Additionally, by the inclusion of l_1 norm sparsity aware term, enhanced performance improvement is obtained. Thus, the proposed scheme is a suitable candidate for big data application where reduction in space, time together with increase in efficiency is obtained. Further research will deal with the application of data selection scheme to information theory criteria based on adaptive algorithms and also on the issues relating to the optimal selection of parameters for adaptive filters.

References

[1]   Härdle, W., Lu, H. H. S., and Shen, X. (Eds.). Handbook of Big Data Analytics. Springer International Publishing, Springer Nature Switzerland; 2018.

[2]   García-Gil, D., Luengo, J., García, S., and Herrera, F. Enabling smart data: Noise filtering in big data classification. Information Sciences, 2019;479:135–152.

[3]   Diniz, P. S. R. On data-selective adaptive filtering. IEEE Transactions on Signal Processing, 2018;66(16):4239–4252.

[4]   Shi, W., Zhu, Y., Huang, T., *et al.* An integrated data preprocessing framework based on apache spark for fault diagnosis of power grid equipment. Journal of Signal Processing Systems, 2017;86(2–3):221–236.

[5]   Fan, J., Han, F., and Liu, H. Challenges of big data analysis. National Science Review, 2014;1(2):293–314.

[6]   Berberidis, D., Kekatos, V., and Giannakis, G. B. Online censoring for large-scale regressions with application to streaming big data. IEEE Transactions on Signal Processing, 2016;64(15):3854–3867.

[7]   Narayanan, A., and Shmatikov, V. Robust de-anonymization of large sparse datasets. In 2008 IEEE Symposium on Security and Privacy, 2008; pp. 111–125.

[8]   Ma, H., King, I., and Lyu, M. R. Effective missing data prediction for collaborative filtering. In Proceedings of the 30th Annual International ACM SIGIR Conference on Research and Development in Information Retrieval, 2007; pp. 39–46.

[9]   Wei, X., Xiao, B., Zhang, Q., and Liu, R. A rigid structure matching-based noise data processing approach for human motion capture. In 2011 Workshop on Digital Media and Digital Content Management, 2011; pp. 91–96.

[10]   Syed, A. H. Adaptive Filter Theory. John Wily and Sons, Inc., Hoboken, NJ, 2003.

[11]   Abadi, M. S. E., and Husøy, J. H. Selective partial update and set-membership sub-band adaptive filters. Signal Processing, 2008;88(10):2463–2471.

[12]   Dogancay, K. Selective-partial-update proportionate normalized least-mean-square adaptive filtering for network echo cancellation. U.S. Patent 2008;7:433,908.

[13]   De Lamare, R. C., and Diniz, P. S. R. Set-membership adaptive algorithms based on time-varying error bounds for CDMA interference suppression. IEEE Transactions on Vehicular Technology, 2008;58(2):644–654.

[14]   Zhang, S., and Zhang, J. Set-membership NLMS algorithm with robust error bound. IEEE Transactions on Circuits and Systems II: Express Briefs, 2014;61(7):536–540.

[15]   Diniz, P. S. R., and Yazdanpanah, H. Data censoring with set-membership algorithms. In IEEE Global Conference on Signal and Information Processing, 2017.

[16]   Wang, Z., Yu, Z., Ling, Q., *et al.* Distributed recursive least-squares with data-adaptive censoring. In IEEE International Conference on Acoustics, Speech and Signal Processing (ICASSP) (pp. 5860–5864), 2017.

[17]   Mendonça, M. O. K., Ferreira, J. O., Tsinos, C. G., *et al.* On fast converging data-selective adaptive filtering. Algorithms, 2019;12(1):4.

[18]   Tsinos, C. G., and Diniz, P. S. R.. Data-selective LMS-Newton and LMS-Quasi-Newton algorithms. In IEEE International Conference on Acoustics, Speech and Signal Processing (ICASSP), 2019.

[19]   Tanrikulu, O., and Constantinides, A. G.. Least-mean kurtosis: a novel higher-order statistics based adaptive filtering algorithm. Electronics Letters, 1994;30(3):189–190.

[20]   Lima, M. V., Ferreira, T. N., Martins, W. A., *et al.* Sparsity-aware data-selective adaptive filters. IEEE Transactions on Signal Processing, 2014;62 (17):4557–4572.

[21]   Da Silva, I. B. V., and Adeodato, P. J. PCA and Gaussian noise in MLP neural network training improve generalization in problems with small and unbalanced data sets. In The 2011 International Joint Conference on Neural Networks, 2011; pp. 2664–2669.

[22] Radhika, S., and Sivabalan, A. ZA-APA with zero attractor controller selection criterion for sparse system identification. Signal Image and Video Processing, 2018;12(2):371–377.

[23] Radhika, S., and Sivabalan, A. Steady-state analysis of sparsity-aware affine projection sign algorithm for impulsive environment. *Circuits, Systems, and Signal Processing* 2017;36(5):1934–1947.

[24] Wang, Y., Chen, Q., Kang, C., Xia, Q., and Luo, M. Sparse and redundant representation-based smart meter data compression and pattern extraction. IEEE Transactions on Power Systems, 2016;32(3):2142–2151.

[25] Karthikeyan, P., Amudhavel, J., Abraham, A., Sathian, D., Raghav, R. S., and Dhavachelvan, P. A comprehensive survey on variants and its extensions of big data in cloud environment. In Proceedings of the 2015 International Conference on Advanced Research in Computer Science Engineering & Technology, 2015; pp. 1–5.

[26] Strohmer, T., and Vershynin, R. A randomized Kaczmarz algorithm with exponential convergence. Journal of Fourier Analysis and Applications, 2009;15(2):262–278.

[27] Needell, D., Srebro, N., and Ward, R. Stochastic gradient descent and the randomized Kaczmarz algorithm. ArXiv e-prints. 2014.

[28] Agaskar, A., Wang, C., and Lu, Y. M. Randomized Kaczmarz algorithms: Exact MSE analysis and optimal sampling probabilities. In Proc. of Global Conf. on Signal and Info. Proc.; Atlanta, 2014; pp. 389–393.

[29] Irvine, U. C. Appliances Energy Prediction Data Set, UCI Machine Learning Repository [http://archive.ics.uci.edu/ml]. Irvine, CA: University of California, School of Information and Computer Science. 2017.

Chapter 3

Secure routing in software defined networking and Internet of Things for big data

Jayashree Pougajendy[1], Arun Raj Kumar Parthiban[2] and Sarath Babu[2]

The Internet of Things (IoT) witnesses a rapid increase in the number of devices getting networked together, along with a surge in big data. IoT causes various challenges, such as quality of service (QoS) for differentiated IoT tasks, power-constrained devices, time-critical applications, and a heterogeneous wireless environment. The big data generated from the billions of IoT devices needs different levels of services, providing big data service based on user requirements which is one of the complex tasks in the network. Software-defined networking (SDN) facilitates interoperability among IoT devices and QoS to the differentiated IoT tasks. SDN introduces programmability in the network by the decoupling of the control plane and data plane. The decoupling of the control logic to a centralized SDN controller drastically reduces power spent on network control on the IoT devices. Also, SDN considerably reduces hardware investments. In this chapter, we focus on discussing the feasibility of using SDN in big data generated by IoT devices. We discuss the architecture of IoT, the relationship between IoT and big data, the arrival of SDN in IoT and big data, routing mechanism, and security aspects of SDN and IoT routing and the application of SDN to IoT.

3.1 Introduction

The availability of small supercomputers with reduced cost increases the feasibility of attaching the small computing device with the physical devices. The growing Internet technology that connects every device to the Internet is known as the IoT. Connecting the gadgets, sensors, and applicants in home, office, industries, hospitals, and public places into the Internet enables data storing, transferring, and sharing of data without human interventions. Billions of IoT devices around the world are now connected to the Internet.

[1]Computer Science and Engineering, Indian Institute of Technology Hyderabad, Hyderabad, India
[2]Computer Science and Engineering, National Institute of Technology Calicut, Kozhikode, India

The connected device collects and shares a massive volume of data in each and every moment, the collected data stored in the cloud and data center available on the Internet. The IoT is a significant contributor of data to big data.

IoT broadens the scope of networking where physical objects or things embedded with micro-electro-mechanical systems are networked together. Not only the cost of data transmission but also its latency for analysis and action increase. Fields such as deep learning have witnessed tremendous success in the tasks of image processing and NLP because of the availability of huge data and data centers. Big data facilitates the identification of deeper patterns and trends in data, which helps organizations in decision- and policymaking. IoT facilitates connecting devices that generate big data in structured (data stored in conventional database systems in the form of tables), unstructured (such as videos/images/audios), or semi-structured form (such as HTML, XML, and JSON formats). That is, with an increasing number of devices connected to IoT, come an increasing amount of data in terms of volume, velocity, variety, veracity, and value (popularly known as the 5Vs of big data). The challenges associated with IoT big data are listed as follows:

1. accessing huge amounts of heterogeneous data from various sources that are in diverse forms such as structured, unstructured, and semi-structured;
2. massively increasing the number of IoT devices in the order of billions;
3. how to store big data as existing data storage platforms are not efficient in storing big data? Storage platforms should be designed in such a manner to facilitate quicker access and faster processing catering to real-time applications;
4. how to quickly process the data to extract meaningful information? This involves challenges such as missing and noisy data;
5. how to ensure security in sharing the data across wide IoT applications and platforms?

IoT also widens its scope to various sectors such as transportation, agriculture, healthcare, surveillance, environmental monitoring. For example, data from sensors in blowout preventers to help oil well operators and in retail environments to monitor customer's browsing behavior are massive in volume and are sent from remote locations to central servers over satellites. This surge in IoT big data demands the need for better handling of workloads and storage in organizations. Also, several devices are to be managed to range from network switches to legacy SCADA (supervisory control and data acquisition) devices. With this high complexity, scalability, and the need for rapid real-time response, manual network management is not feasible.

SDN is a new paradigm shift in current computer networking. SDN is aimed at separating the control and the data planes to facilitate programmability in the network. In a non-SDN environment, there are three planes: the management plane, the control plane, and the data plane. The management plane in the application layer monitors the network and coordinates the functions between the control and the data plane. Protocols under the management plane are SNMP, HTTPS, and SSH.

The SDN devices can efficiently monitor and allocate the network resources on the basis of the user requirement in real time. The global view of the SDN controller supports storing, processing, and effectively sharing of the network resources and big data generated by the IoT devices. There are many data centers deployed in the different regions of the world that are connected through the Internet, as shown in Figure 3.1. Data centers and cloud can be categorized in private-, public-, and hybrid-based services they provide. Many of the data center owners earn money by giving public services. The huge data centers enable SDN inside the data centers, which increases the efficiency in handling resources.

SDN provides a viable solution to manage IoT by bringing in the following capabilities:

1. Centralization of control through software with the knowledge of the complete network.
2. The abstraction of the devices and the protocols used in the network, enabling IoT devices to access huge data, perform analytics, add new sensors, without the knowledge of the underlying infrastructure.
3. Flexibility in SDN to dynamically change network behavior based on the network traffic patterns. SDN is applied to the IoT to dynamically achieve differentiated quality levels to different IoT tasks in heterogeneous wireless networking environments. Differentiated QoS is needed because some IoT tasks fit into hard real time and some into soft real time. For example, IoT tasks such as early earthquake detection, smart city waste management are to be given higher priority than smart parking.

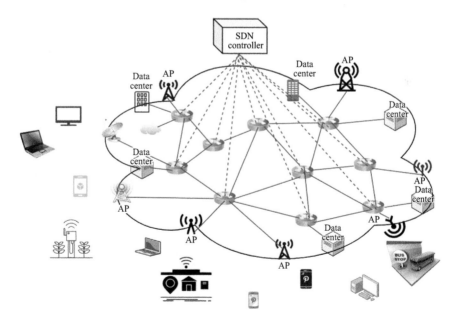

Figure 3.1   Intersection SDN, big data, and IoT

The control and data planes are located in the same layer-3 switching device. The control plane is responsible for making routing decisions based on the routing protocols OSPF, BGP, etc. The routing decisions taken by the control plane are transferred to the data plane where the routes get updated in the forwarding information base (FIB). Based on the forwarding table entries in the data plane, the packets get forwarded in the network. In SDN, decoupling the control plane from the data plane, the control plane of the switches moved to a centralized controller. This decoupling abstracted from the applications that run on top of the controller. Therefore, each switch does not handle the traffic and routing decisions on its own. The controller is used to handle the traffic at the switches. It takes control decisions and is responsible for the installation of the configuration rules in the switches connected to it.

The motivation behind SDN comes from various directions. SDN facilitates the ease of network management compared to the non-SDN environments where the network administrators have to configure all the network devices. It provides software control of the switches in the network through a centralized controller. When there is a change in the network operating systems or the protocols for the network, all the networking devices require modifications, whereas SDN requires only the controller to be modified as the control plane is decoupled from the data plane. It enables centralized control over a virtualized resource in virtualization scenarios like a multi-tenant cloud environment. SDN architecture helps in traffic analysis and anomaly detection scenarios by using the applications that run on top of the controller.

3.2   Architecture of IoT

The generic architecture for the IoT includes five layers [1], such as the perception layer, transport layer, processing layer, application layer, and business layer. Figure 3.2 shows the 5-layer IoT architecture.

1. Perception layer
    The perception layer is analogous to the five senses of a human. This layer gives a physical meaning to everything that is a part of IoT. Sensors such as

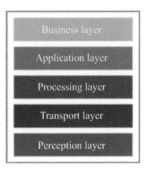

Figure 3.2   Layer IoT architecture

RFID, infra-red sensors, 2D barcode which senses location, temperature, speed, etc. constitute this layer. The technologies used in the perception layer include RFID, 2D barcode, GPS, etc. This layer collects the sensing information from various sensors and converts them into signals to be transmitted to the next higher layer, the transport layer.

2. Transport layer

    The transport layer is also called network layer in the IoT architecture. The main function of this layer is to transfer the data received from the perception layer to the processing layer and vice versa. The key technologies used in this layer include FTTx, 3G, Wi-Fi, Zigbee, and UMB. IoT requires IPv6 as the number of objects getting networked is of a tremendous increase [2]. There will be nearly 25 billion devices under the umbrella of the IoT by the year 2020 [3]. IPv6 constitutes the transport layer of IoT architecture. The IoT has to encompass not only billions of objects, but also various networks. The convergence of various networks in IoT is itself a big challenge and a promising research area.

3. Processing layer

    The main functionality of the processing layer lies in storing, updating, analyzing, and processing of the data received from the transport layer. The key technologies used in this layer include cloud computing and ubiquitous computing. Other technologies include intelligent processing of information stored in the database and handling big data.

4. Application layer

    The application layer consists of the various IoT applications that use the data received from the processing layer. IoT applications include and are not limited to logistics management, smart city traffic control systems, early earthquake detection systems, smart home control, automation systems, etc.

5. Business layer

    This layer deals with the management of all the applications and services related to IoT. It is responsible for the research in IoT related to the business models and profit models for effective business strategies.

The raw data generated by the IoT devices are processed on the basis of the requirements. The raw data are transformed into meaningful information by performing operations such as preparation, calculation, correlation, and analysis. Nowadays, organizations use PaaS services to store and process data instead of using their infrastructure. The cloud service providers provide different services and dynamic resource allocation and charges based on user requirements. Cloud providers use big data handling techniques for efficient handling of massive data and its storage, processing, and analysis. The IT industry has started providing the cost of big data storage and processing cheaply, creating exponential growth in big data applications.

3.3 Intersection of big data and IoT

Connecting billions of devices plays a vital role in generating big data. Also, big data analytics helps one to improve business models of IoT. The intersection of big

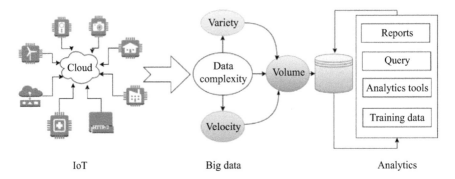

Figure 3.3   Intersection of big data and IoT [4]

data and IoT is illustrated in Figure 3.3. Initially, various sensors and devices are interconnected and communicate with each other such as smart city traffic control units, car sensors for autonomous driving, smart home appliances, and aircraft navigation control units. The data communicated are in a heterogeneous data format that is stored in the cloud. The data are then accessed from the cloud and stored in a big data storage system such as Hadoop distributed file system (HDFS). Finally, decision analytics is performed on stored data using analytic tools such as Apache Spark, MapReduce, and Splunk.

3.4   Big data analytics

Big data analytics is the process of searching the data stores, extracting meaningful information, performing analysis leading to profitable business insights [5]. It also refers to mining hidden correlations, data trends, and patterns [6] from heterogeneous data using nontraditional tools and technologies with the main aim to boost business decisions [7,8]. It requires specific tools and technologies that can transform non-comprehendible data of varied forms (structured, unstructured, and semi-structured) to comprehendible format, as a function of time, to aid business models. Models and algorithms for big data should be designed with the goal of finding latent correlations, patterns, and data trends [9]. The desired outputs are in the form of graphs, tables, or charts to directly transform into well-informed organizational decisions [10].

A naïve way of dealing with enormous amounts of data is to sample data based on trial and error method [11], but its effectiveness is not guaranteed. Visual data analytics, which focuses on visually interpreting the data to gain meaningful insights, is an active area of research by itself. The exploratory data analysis environment [12] provides a visual data analytics platform for complex datasets.

3.4.1   Taxonomy of big data analytics

A wide range of applications of big data is presented in [13]. Various types of big data analytics are as follows:

1. Real-time analytics: It demands to perform faster analytical solutions to time-critical applications such as smart city traffic control, aircraft and navigation control. The data are streamed in an online and dynamic manner that requires high responsive decisions. Example architectures include Greenplum [14] and HANA [15].

2. Offline analytics: It provides relaxation in terms of responsiveness for not so critical applications such as smart home management and offline web analytics. A Hadoop-based architecture [16] is discussed to cut down the data conversion costs. Some of the offline analytics frameworks include SCRIBE [17], Kafka [18], time-tunnel [19], and Chukwa [20].

3. Memory-level analytics: It facilitates performing real-time operations on data that can be sufficiently stored in the clusters of sizes in the range of terabytes. MongoDB [21] is a big data storing database that aids in memory-level operations.

4. Business intelligence (BI) analytics: It deals with data that do not fit memory-level internal databases but require BI units to operate both online and offline. It aims to identify potential business opportunities to enhance market competence. BI operations involve analyzing customer purchase trends, tracking and predicting sales in future, risk analysis, logistic and supply chain management, etc.

5. Massive intelligence: It deals with an enormous amount of data that do not fit BI units but operate offline at a massive scale. It aims to make highly critical business decisions and policies by storing data in the HDFS, and the MapReduce tool is used for data mining.

3.4.2   Architecture of IoT big data

Similar to the generic IoT architecture discussed in Section 3.2, an IoT architecture to handle big data [4] is shown in Figure 3.4. The layer with IoT devices is the same as the perceptron layer in the generic IoT architecture, which consists of the sensors and devices. These sensors are responsible for collecting signals from the places where they are deployed and transmit it to the next layer in the architecture stack. The next higher layer with network devices is the transport layer, which connects the perceptron layer to IoT gateway. The technologies used in this layer are Zigbee, Bluetooth, Wi-Fi, etc. The IoT gateway facilitates storing the gathered big data from sensors using a cloud environment. The data are then transferred to a distributed file system storage for efficient data handling. Big data analytics is performed on the stored data from the cloud and distributed file systems using big data tools such as MapReduce, Hadoop, and Apache Spark. This performs similar functionality to the processing layer in traditional IoT architecture, along with suitable APIs to cater to various IoT applications such as smart city management, smart home control, aircraft navigation, and agricultural monitoring. There are other variants of IoT architecture based on whether its cloud-centric storage or ICN (information-centric networking) based in the literature [22,23].

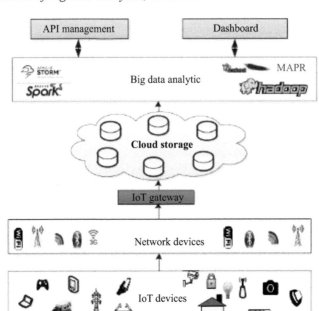

Figure 3.4   IoT architecture for big data [4]

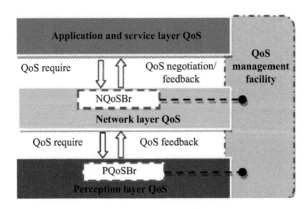

Figure 3.5   QoS architecture for IoT [24]

QoS architecture for IoT [24] is shown in Figure 3.5. At the application level, QoS requirements include service time, service delay, service accuracy, and service priority. Network-level, bandwidth, jitter, delay, and packet loss rate are QoS indicators. Similarly, at the perceptron layer, sampling rate, coverage, time synchronization, and mobility are QoS requirements. Since QoS requirements are to be met at every layer, the required parameters are passed from higher to lower layers and the QoS feedback is then passed in the reverse direction. There are QoS brokers named NQoSBr in the network layer and PQoSBr in the perceptron layer. NQoSBr broker handles QoS requirements from a higher layer and translates it into local QoS requests. Application layer calls NQoSBr with parameters such as L: least time delay, R: service priority, T: application type, and P: parameters to the perceptron layer. The QoS requests are used to handle QoS services based on the QoS mechanism associated with the network, that is, IntServ or DiffServ for the Internet and UMST in the mobile networks. The same parameters are then passed to PQoSBr in the perceptron layer. PQoSBr converts the QoS requirements to local QoS indicators to physical devices in the perceptron layer.

3.5 Security and privacy challenges of big data

The exponential growth of data and facilities of data storage (data centers, cloud) on the Internet support different services. Most of the online applications are doing data mining to provide a better experience to the user. Big data plays a vital role in real-time value-added service to people and industries. Nowadays, IoT devices such as smartwatches, mobile phones, and smart specs collect a rich set of personal information such as personal interest, preference, and behavioral pattern. Hence, privacy and security of big data are very important in all the phases (data acquisition, storage, and analytics). The routing protocols in IoT, security attacks, and solutions in routing are discussed in Sections 3.6 and 3.7. The most common cyberattacks on big data are as follows:

1. Spamming
   Sending a large amount of restricted electronic messages into the network is known as spamming. The person or electronic machine sends a spamming message called a spammer.
2. Search poisoning
   The aim of the attacker is not to stall the data, and the aim is to poison the data. It is happening mainly against financial sectors. The poisoning affects the availability of the system, and the system becomes undetected continuously over time.
3. Botnets
   A computer code that takes the control of a group of computers that are organized like botnets.
4. Denial-of-service (DoS)
   The DoS attack makes the destination system or a network inaccessible to its intended users. The DoS attack can be flooding services or crashing services. In flooding attacks, the node receives too many messages, and that causes a slowdown of the system or eventually stopping the system. The popular attacks are buffer overflow attacks, ICMP flood, and SYN flood. In crashing attack, vulnerabilities cause the target system or service to crash.

5. Phishing

   Correspondence that falsely claims to originate from reputable sources, including trading pages, banks, electronic payment providers, or IT administrators, also tempts consumers and obtains sensitive information from them.
6. Malware

   The software performs malicious activities, including performing and propagating malicious activities, that damage and corrupt data or operating systems, installation of spyware, stealing personal credentials or hard disk space, etc.

The security issues that affect four different areas of the big data are protecting data collection sensors, data analysis, output, and communication. Nowadays, cybersecurity has shifted to monitoring network and Internet traffic for the detection of security attacks. Hackers can easily make technologies such as intrusion detection devices, firewalls, and antivirus software inefficient. Hence, it causes more difficulties in big data networks to store and process petabytes and exabytes of information being transferred between systems. It is very easy for hackers to enter into any network and attack the data.

The BDA can provide help to improve the security dimension to the big data by

1. Monitoring network traffic: Monitor and predict malicious sources and destinations with abnormal traffic patterns.
2. Monitoring web transactions: Detect and predict unauthorized user access patterns, particularly in the usage of critical resources or activities.
3. Monitoring network servers: Detect abnormal patterns such as sudden configuration changes, noncompliance with predefined policy related to server manipulation.
4. Monitoring network source: Monitoring unusual usage patterns of any machine, such as related to the type of data the source transmits, processes, receives, and resource utilization.
5. Monitor user behavior: Detecting anomalies by comparing the normal behavior of a user or a group of users such as access time or transaction amount with the access behavior.

An efficient working of security using big data analytics requires proper monitoring. The main problem in this space is that the different sources and destinations collect, store, and process big data. There is no centralized system to monitor security issues.

3.6   Routing protocols in IoT

Wireless sensor networks and IoT are nearly synonymous. Routing protocols for wireless sensor networks are classified into flat, hierarchical, and location-based routing. Flat routing protocols are used for networks with a flat structure with a huge amount of sensor nodes. Due to the large number of sensor nodes, the receiver node sends a query to the group of sensor nodes and waits for a reply from the intended sensors. Example: SPIN (sensor protocols for information via negotiation) [25]. The flat structure can be considered suitable for IoT applications such as homes, healthcare, smart parking. These IoT applications have less tolerance for packet delay and loss. Hierarchical routing protocols are specifically designed for networks with a hierarchical structure like the Internet. The entire network is divided into various clusters, and each cluster is assigned a cluster head. The nodes of the cluster to communicate with nodes outside the cluster require the cluster head. This routing requires setup time for cluster formation and the election of cluster head, which makes it unsuitable for delay intolerant IoT networks. Example of the hierarchical routing protocol: LEACH (low-energy adaptive clustering hierarchy) [26]. Location-based routing protocols take the geographical location into consideration. The nodes send a packet to a specific geographic location rather than a destination node address. Example: geographic adaptive fidelity [27].

Various IETF (Internet Engineering Task Force) working groups for IoT include 6LoWPAN [28] as a convergence layer, RPL [29] as a routing protocol, and CoAP [30] facilitates low-power wireless networks to be integrated to the Internet. 6LoWPAN (IPv6 over low-power wireless personal area networks) [28] enables the extension of the IPv6 networks to the IoT networks. This is advantageous as the existing IPv6 infrastructures can be reused for IoT. RPL (IPv6 routing protocols for low-power and lossy network) [29] is a routing protocol specifically designed for devices with constrained power, memory capacity, and computational capacity. CoAP (Constrained Application Protocol) [30] is targeted at low-power devices that are to be monitored by Internet hosts. It enables translation to HTTP messages for integration with the web.

3.7 Security challenges and existing solutions in IoT routing

3.7.1 Selective forwarding attacks

Malicious nodes present in the data path between the source and destination selectively forward the packets. That is, they drop the packets randomly, causing network disruption. On the other hand, if a malicious node drops all the packets, then it is said to be a black hole attack. One possible solution would be to create disjoint paths in the network and to enable multipath routing of the same packet over the network.

3.7.2 Sinkhole attacks

A malicious node advertises that it has the best shortest path to the destination. All the other nodes in the network will be attracted to this malicious node to route traffic through it. Generally, this attack is hard to detect because it is highly challenging to verify the routing information provided by a node. An Intrusion Detection System [31] with an end-to-end message security is proposed for detecting sinkhole attacks. End-to-end security is achieved using IPSec, a mandatory feature in IPv6. A lightweight and robust solution [32] is proposed for detecting sinkhole attacks using Received Signal Strength Indicator (RSSI). Another alternative in the detection of sinkhole attacks [33] is based on the CPU usage of the objects or nodes.

3.7.3 HELLO flood and acknowledgment spoofing attacks

When attackers broadcast HELLO messages with strong transmission power, they convince all the nodes in the network to be their neighbor, who is not the actual scenario. Similarly, a malicious node spoofs the acknowledgment packet using overheard traffic. If the transmission power of a legitimate node is lesser compared to the attacker, then it results in a weak link. Packets sent over this weak link help one to launch a selective forwarding attack, eventually, a solution where for each HELLO message [34] the link is to be verified bidirectionally.

3.7.4 Replay attacks

Replay attacks, as shown in Figure 3.6, occur when malicious nodes record the messages sent over the network and replay them later. RPL [29] protocol is specifically designed to counteract this attack by discarding older messages with lower DODAG (destination-oriented directed acyclic graph) version number.

3.7.5 Wormhole attacks

A wormhole attack is launched when a malicious node tunnels the messages received from one part of a network to another malicious node in another part of the network. Figure 3.7 depicts the wormhole attack.

Though node 1 and node 2 do not have a link to each other, they are deceived by the attackers to have a path between them. Wormhole attack, when used along with selective forwarding and sinkhole attack, possibly disrupts the entire network.

3.7.6 Sybil attack

In a Sybil attack, a single attacker poses multiple identities for itself in the network either simultaneously or one at a time. It is an extension of spoofing attacks. One possible solution for the detection of a Sybil attack is to determine the geographical location of the objects/nodes in the network as no two different nodes can have the same location [32,35–40].

Figure 3.6   Replay attacks

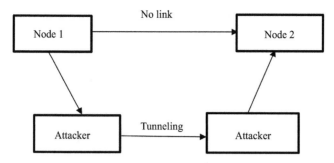

Figure 3.7   Wormhole attacks

3.7.7   Denial-of-service (DoS) attacks

DoS attacks are launched when attackers deplete the bandwidth and the energy resources of the legitimate nodes in the network. It is an attack on availability to the legitimate nodes in the network. Countermeasures to DoS include limiting the traffic rate or isolating nodes sending excess amounts of traffic in the network [41].

Other attacks include the passive eavesdropping attack and active modification attack. Solutions to eavesdropping [41] include implementation of the Advanced Encryption Standard (AES-128) in cipher block chaining-message authentication code: CBC-MAC (CCM) mode for low-power lossy networks [29]. Example: Zigbee uses CCM, PANA (Protocol for Carrying Authentication for Network Access) [42], and EAP-TLS (Extensible Authentication Protocol-Transport Layer Security) [43]. Solutions to modification attacks include implementation of access control policies on storage, data integrity mechanisms such as MAC to the transmitted messages, and inclusion of sequence numbers under integrity protection. Table 3.1 shows the list of routing attacks on IoT and the security goals compromised.

The big data stored in clouds and data centers need to be exchanged and processed on the basis of the service-level agreement (SLA) signed between the cloud providers and the generators of big data. Network resources need to be dynamically allocated to follow the QoS requirements specified in SLA, such as the exchange of data and security. The dynamic resource allocation based on the user requirement during data exchange creates overhead to the routers and routing protocols. The large volume of data generation leads to an increase in data traffic communication in a unicast/multicast/broadcast manner.

3.8   The arrival of SDN into big data and IoT

In the year 2000, a new proposal introduced for efficient handling of the resources by the data center providers while handling big data was SDN. SDN is a new paradigm shift in current computer networking. SDN is aimed at separating the control and the data planes to facilitate programmability in the network. In a non-SDN environment, there are three planes: the management plane, the control plane, and the data plane.

Table 3.1   Possible attacks on IoT routing and the security goals compromised

Attacks	Security goals compromised			
	Confidentiality	Integrity	Availability	Authenticity
Eavesdropping	✓			
Packet modification	✓	✓		
Spoofing				✓
Sybil attack				✓
Replay attack		✓	✓	✓
HELLO flood			✓	
ACK spoofing			✓	✓
Selective forwarding	✓		✓	
DoS			✓	
Sinkhole attack	✓		✓	
Wormhole attack	✓		✓	

The management plane in the application layer monitors the network and coordinates the functions between the control and the data plane. Protocols under the management plane are SNMP, HTTPS, and SSH. The control and data planes are located in the same layer-3 switching device. The control plane is responsible for making routing decisions based on the routing protocols OSPF, BGP, etc.

In traditional switching devices, each device contains a suppurate control plane and data plane. The routing decisions taken by the control plane are transferred to the data plane where the routes get updated in the FIB. Based on the forwarding table entries in the data plane, the packets get forwarded in the network. Figure 3.8 represents traditional routing using normal switching devices.

In SDN, decoupling the control plane from the data plane, the control plane of the switches moved to a centralized controller. The decoupling removes all the control functionality from individual switching devices, and the control functionality moves to an external centralized controller known as the SDN controller. The controller has a global view of the network, and that helps to perform the control functionality and update to all the devices. This decoupling abstracted from the applications that run on top of the controller. Therefore, each switch does not handle the traffic and routing decisions on its own. The individual switching device performs the switching based on updated flow information from the controller. The controller is used to handle the traffic at the switches. It takes control decisions and is responsible for the installation of the configuration rules in the switches connected to it. Figure 3.9 represents the centralized controller-based routing.

3.9   Architecture of SDN

Figure 3.10 shows the conceptual architecture of SDN. In contrast to the existing tightly coupled networking devices, the network intelligence is moved to a

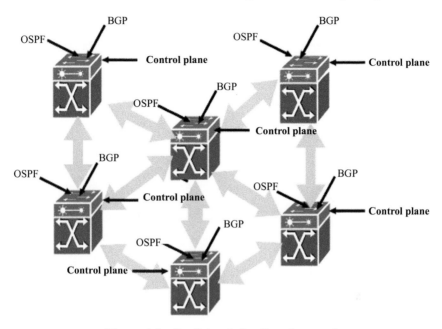

Figure 3.8   Traditional distributed network

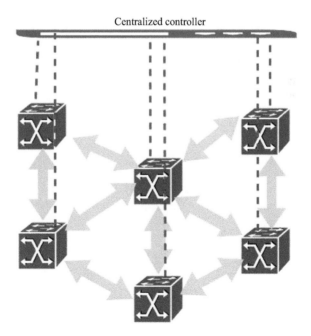

Figure 3.9   Centralized network

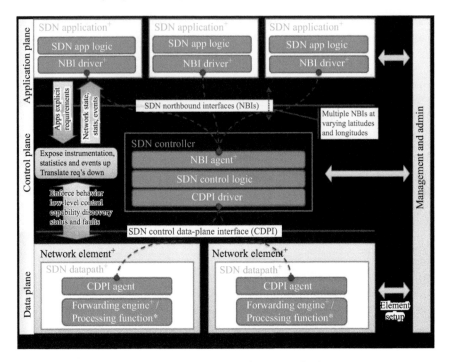

Figure 3.10   SDN architecture [44]

centralized SDN controller. The SDN applications communicate with the controller, their required network behavior via the northbound interface (NBI). It is
said to be an NBI because the SDN controller is interfaced with a component above
it. The SDN application consists of application logic and one or more NBI driver
(s). The SDN controller consists of one or more NBI agents, control logic, and one
or more control data-plane interface (CDPI) driver(s). The control logic of the
controller is responsible for monitoring and controlling the network traffic flow
among the networking devices. On collecting the big data traffic, the SDN controller is responsible for dynamic resource allocation for efficient handling of time-
critical applications. The SDN architecture facilitates network abstraction so that
SDN appears to the applications as a single logical switch.

   This architecture also enables the network operators and administrators, the
flexibility to configure, maintain, manage, and optimize the network resources usage
dynamically. CDPI is a southbound interface that interconnects the controller with
the network elements. The network elements are responsible for collecting data from
various sensors in the field. Conventional big data architecture stores the generated
big data in suitable data centers. Big data applications require dynamic allocation of
resources to meet the SLA signed between the application service provider and the
users on parameters such as QoS, response time, processing time, miss rate, privacy,
fan in, fan out, bandwidth, latency, throughput rate, loss of data, and costs involved in
the transmission. SDN can be integrated into the data centers to enable dynamic

resource allocation meeting the demands of SLAs. On integrating cloud-based data centers to SDN, networking as a service and infrastructure as a service can be well automated by the SDN controller. Different approaches were proposed for integrated big data and SDN architectures such as, cloud-based SDN architecture for dynamic resource allocation of big data and optimal power consumption in big data centers [45], a distributive approach for SDN data centers with optimal subset topology allotment for efficient handling of data traffic load [46], an SDN architecture that abstracts the transport node into a virtual switch operated according to the OpenFlow protocol [47].

The SDN controller is interfaced with the components below it. The network element consists of a CDPI agent and one or more forwarding elements. The network element acts on the basis of the configuration rules installed on the forwarding elements by the controller. However, the differences between them are tabulated as shown in Table 3.2. Physically, the following are the two architectures aiming the separation of control plane and the forwarding plane:

Table 3.2   Differences between ForCES and OpenFlow

Attribute	ForCES	OpenFlow
Goal	To break the closed box (wherein control plane and data plane are coupled together) of networking elements by using either a protocol for the separation of the control elements and network elements or separate boxes for control elements and network elements, while both form a single networking element	To separate the control plane from the network elements and move it to the controller
Architecture	Separation of the control elements and the forwarding elements inside a network element. A network element consists of one or more control element(s) and forwarding element(s)	Network elements retain only the forwarding elements, while the control logic is completely transferred to the central controller
Forwarding model	The building blocks of the forwarding elements are logical functional blocks (LFBs)	The building blocks of the OpenFlow switch (forwarding element) are the flow tables
Protocol interface	ForCES defines two layers of protocols: 1. ForCES Protocol layer defines the protocol to be followed by control elements and forwarding elements 2. ForCES transport mapping layer defines the transport of messages between control and forwarding elements from the protocol layer	OpenFlow protocol for communications between the OpenFlow controller and the OpenFlow switches

1. ForCES [48]
2. OpenFlow [49]

ForCES is aimed at breaking the traditional closed-box network element. ForCES consists of the following two kinds of separation between the control and forwarding elements:

1. Blade level: In blade level of separation, between the control and forwarding elements in traditional closed-box network elements, proprietary interfaces are replaced by a standard protocol [48].
2. Box level: In box level of separation, separate boxes are used for the control element and forwarding element each within a network element.

OpenFlow formulates new network architecture when compared to the existing Internet architecture. OpenFlow, which is both a protocol between the controller and the switches and the architecture specification, is the exact implementation of SDN. The OpenFlow version 1.0 was originally specified in Stanford University. The Open Networking Foundation inherited the specification from Stanford and released its first OpenFlow version 1.2. The control and forwarding elements are logical elements, physically present in the same traditional switches. OpenFlow architecture results in the complete physical separation of the control elements and the forwarding elements. OpenFlow standard is currently adopted for practical implementations of SDN and widely in the research community.

3.10   Routing in SDN

The SDN-enabled routing service application runs on top of the controller. This application is responsible for creating the global topology of OpenFlow island. An OpenFlow island denotes the entire set of OpenFlow switches connected to the same OpenFlow controller. The routing service application consists of the following three modules:

1. Link discovery—discovers and maintains the status of the links between the OpenFlow switches and between the OpenFlow switches and end hosts.
2. Topology Manager—builds and maintains a global topology database and calculates the shortest paths among OpenFlow switches.
3. Virtual routing engine—generates and maintains a virtual networking topology aimed at facilitating interoperability between the SDN controller and traditional non-OpenFlow switches. In environments where both OpenFlow- and non-OpenFlow-enabled switches coexist, non-OpenFlow switches run traditional routing protocols such as BGP and OSPF. The virtual topology consists of virtual machines running traditional routing protocols. Basically, it is for routing between OpenFlow island and traditional non-OpenFlow switches.

In an OpenFlow network, the routing service application performs the link discovery using the Link Layer Discovery Protocol (LLDP), which is used by

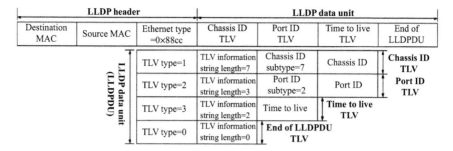

Figure 3.11   LLDP frame format [50]

network devices to enable advertising of their identity, capability, and neighbors. LLDP supports a multi-vendor network, which is advantageous compared to the proprietary protocols such as CDP (Cisco Discovery Protocol), which can be used only by a single vendor. Figure 3.11 shows a typical LLDP frame format. An LLDP frame has the Ethernet type set to 0×88 cm^3.

The link discovery module of the routing service application sends a packet_out LLDP message to all the switches connected to the controller [51]. The immediate neighboring switches of the controller on receiving the packet_out message send the message to all its connected devices. If the devices receiving this message are OpenFlow switches, it looks up to the flow table. If no flow table entry matches, the switch on receiving the packet_out message from the immediate neighbors of the controller sends a packet_in message to the controller. If the neighboring device is a non-OpenFlow switch, then the link discovery is performed by the controller through a broadcast mechanism. The controller directs the OpenFlow switches to broadcast the packet_out message. An OpenFlow switch on the reception of this message will respond with a packet_in message to the controller. The neighbor database is constructed in the controller by using this packet_out and packet_in information received from the link discovery module. The Topology Manager on receiving the information from the neighbor database of the controller makes a connection between the two switches in its topology information table. In the case of link discovery between OpenFlow switches and end hosts, link discovery module performs ARP resolution when unknown traffic enters the OpenFlow island. Based on the ARP resolution, the Topology Manager keeps track of the MAC addresses of the networking elements. This is used in the construction of a global topology database. The global topology database is used by the Topology Manager module to calculate the shortest path between every point-to-point route in the network using Dijkstra's algorithm [51].

Figure 3.12 illustrates the ARP resolution by the link discovery module of the routing service application. The steps are as follows:

1. Host H1 sends a packet with destination IP of Host H2 to S1.
2. The OpenFlow switch (S1) looks up the flow table, and since there are no corresponding entries, S1 sends an OpenFlow request packet to the controller.

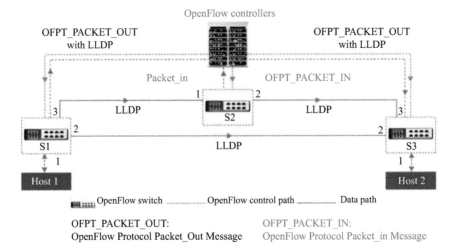

Figure 3.12   SDN route discovery process [51]

The controller directs the OpenFlow switch S1 to send an ARP request to host H2 to resolve its MAC address.
3.   Host H2 responds with its MAC address, and this response is sent to the controller. Now, the controller installs the flow rules to connect host H1 to host H2.

The centralized controller is responsible for the management and maintenance of the global network. It installs configuration rules into the forwarding elements of the networking devices. The building blocks in OpenFlow switches are flow tables because the main functionality of the OpenFlow switches is forwarding. Forwarding in these switches relies on the flow table entries only. Flow tables consist of flow entries, and the flow entries comprise the following:

1.   Match field—the incoming packet header is matched against the matching rules
2.   Counter—maintains statistical packet information such as the number of packets received, number of bytes transmitted, and the duration of the flow. The counter gets incremented each time it receives a packet. It maintains the count of the number of packet lookups, number of packet matches, and flow duration (TTL).
3.   Action—dictates the action to be carried out on encountering a match between the packet header and the matching rules. The following are the list of possible actions taken by an OpenFlow switch:
     (i)   drop the packet,
     (ii)   forward the packet to the controller,
     (iii) forward the packet to the next flow table (OpenFlow supports multiple flow tables and pipeline processing),
     (iv)   modify the packet header (IP address).

The OpenFlow on matching the packet header against a set of matching rules performs the necessary action as per the flow table entry. However, if there is no matching entry pertaining to an incoming packet header, then the following rules are executed on table miss:

- dropping the packet,
- forwarding the packet via the OpenFlow channel to the controller,
- looking up into the next flow table,
- modify the packet header.

It is to be noted that OpenFlow supports multiple flow tables and pipeline processing. In the case of hybrid switches that support both OpenFlow and non-OpenFlow, it consists of ports for connecting itself to the OpenFlow channel and for non-OpenFlow communication. On a table miss in a hybrid switch, the set of rules also includes packet forwarding using non-OpenFlow protocols such as BGP and OSPF. Modifying the packet header action finds application in cloud environments to enable software-controlled load balancing.

SDN is benefited by big data for traffic engineering. The primary objectives of traffic engineering are to increase network utilization and traffic load balancing. SDN controller is used to provide a holistic view of data traffic and loss information. Traffic engineering is facilitated by modifying the flow tables maintained by the controller. Figure 3.13 shows the architecture of SDN for big data with traffic engineering enabled.

Traffic engineering involves monitoring network parameters, especially bandwidth utilization in both fine-grained and coarse-grained levels. This also helps in managing the network, load balancing, and traffic anomaly detection. A counter is maintained and updated when a packet crosses a switch. The counter has to be updated in a streaming manner, and hence big data streaming techniques are useful for maintaining traffic statistics.

A fine-grained approach for SDN traffic monitoring uses big data process techniques [53]. The SDN controller collects the data traffic and data loss information from the servers, switches, and routers through the southbound API. The gathered traffic information is sent from the SDN controller to the big data applications through the northbound API.

Big data analytics is performed on the traffic data and sent to the traffic engineering manager. The manager then updates the SDN controller. As per the updates, the controller modifies the flow tables and switches on/off the respective links through the southbound API. Conventional layered architectural design permits only the sharing of information between subsequent layers. Cross-layer design permits communication between non-subsequent layers, which helps in the improvement of network utilization and performance. SDN controller acts as a medium for enabling communications among cross layers. The cross-layer design architecture [52] is shown in Figure 3.14. The SDN controller has a global view of the data in the physical layer, packet information in the network layer, and the application information in the application layer. The SDN controller and Hadoop cooperate in the network layer. The cross-layer information gathered by

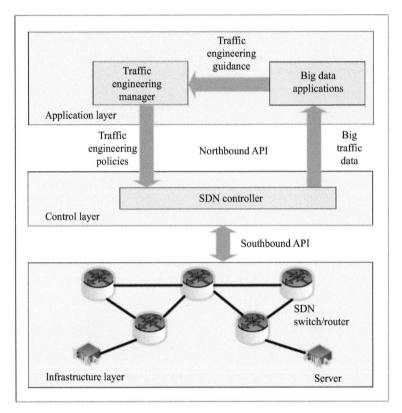

Figure 3.13   SDN architecture for big data enabling traffic engineering [52]

the controller is passed to Hadoop. Hadoop does data processing, and the net-work control strategies are passed to the controller. This information is useful to the controller to make better decisions with respect to updating the flow tables, parameter tuning in physical layer devices, resource allocation, topology con-struction, and routing techniques.

3.11   Attacks on SDN and existing solutions

Figure 3.15 shows the classification of SDN attacks on the basis of the resources that are targeted or affected by them.

3.11.1   Conflicting flow rules

In an SDN environment, SDN applications run on top of the SDN controller. Multiple applications running on top of the controller insert flow entries into the OpenFlow switches dynamically. As a result, the flow entry inserted into the OpenFlow switch by

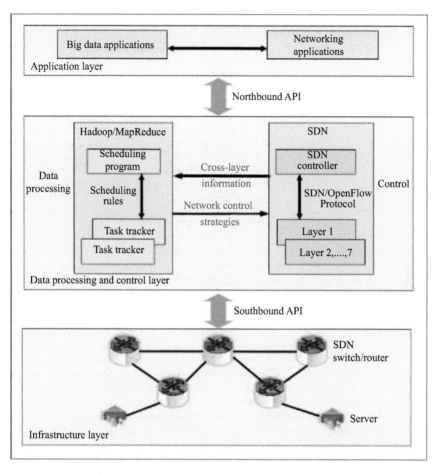

Figure 3.14   Cross-layer SDN architecture for big data [52]

an OpenFlow application possibly conflicts with the existing security flow rules. This scenario of conflicting flow rules is illustrated in Figure 3.16.

1. The firewall blocks the traffic with the source IP address of 10.0.0.2 and destination IP address of 10.0.0.4.
2. The firewall permits the incoming traffic from an external host with an IP address of 10.0.0.2 to an internal host of IP address 10.0.0.3.
3. Meanwhile, another application running on top of the controller creates three flow rules. The first rule modifies the source IP of a packet to 10.0.0.1 if a packet is delivered from 10.0.0.2 to 10.0.0.3 (port 80). The second rule modifies the destination IP of a packet to 10.0.0.4 if a packet is delivered from 10.0.0.1 to 10.0.0.3 (port 80). The third rule allows forwarding of packets from 10.0.0.1 to 10.0.0.4 (port 80).

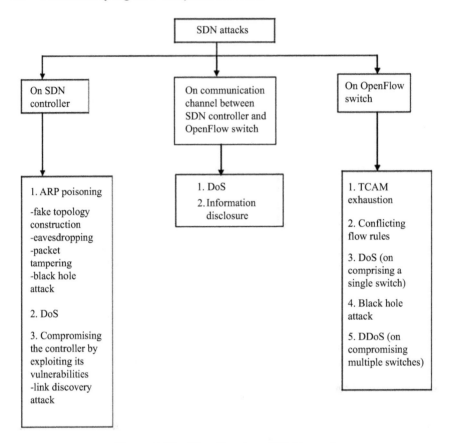

Figure 3.15   Classification of SDN attacks

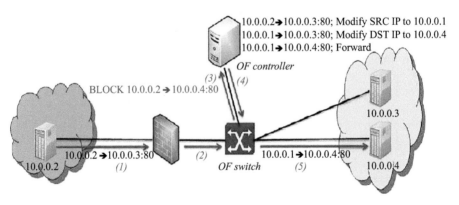

Figure 3.16   Conflicting flow rules [54]

4. The SDN controller inserts the three flow rules into the OpenFlow switch.
5. The packet with source IP of 10.0.0.2 is modified to 10.0.0.1, and destination IP of 10.0.0.3 is modified to 10.0.0.4. This packet is delivered to the internal host with an IP address of 10.0.0.4. This packet's original source is 10.0.0.2, and the traffic from 10.0.0.2 to 10.0.0.4 has been blocked by the firewall application. Yet, due to another application running on top of the controller, a rule conflict has occurred.

The impacts of conflicting flow rules [54] are as follows:

1. permits unauthorized access to the organization's network,
2. paves the way for malicious traffic to enter the organization,
3. compromises OpenFlow switches on unauthorized access,
4. controller DoS can be launched by compromised switches,
5. eavesdropping, spoofing, packet dropping, and tampering sensitive data transmitted to the network, and
6. ARP poisoning on the management information base stored at the SDN controller can be launched via compromised OpenFlow switches.

A security policy enforcement kernel FortNOX [54] has been implemented as an extension to the NOX OpenFlow controller [55]. FortNOX provides role-based authentication for rule insertion into the OpenFlow switches. The highest priority for rule insertion is given to the network administrator. The second highest priority is given to security applications such as firewalls. The least priority is assigned to the non-security-related applications that run on top of the controller. If an application with less priority attempts to insert a rule in conflict with an existing rule inserted by a security application, then FortNOX denies such an attempt. The role-based authentication is enabled using a digital signature wherein the FortNOX is preconfigured with the public keys of the various roles.

3.11.2   TCAM exhaustion

TCAM stands for ternary content associative memory, which stores the flow tables in an OpenFlow switch. Attackers target the TCAM of the OpenFlow switch to perform a DoS attack on the switch. Attackers send packets with arbitrary or fabricated traffic and force the controller to install a large number of fake flow entries into the OpenFlow switch. This results in TCAM exhaustion. Legitimate flow entries cannot be made on the switch until the existing fake entries expire.

The impacts of TCAM exhaustion are as follows:

1. resource depletion (TCAM) on OpenFlow switches
2. causes DoS on SDN controller
3. bandwidth depletion

SPHINX [56] is a policy framework for SDN controllers. It uses flow graphs to model the network topology in an SDN environment. It captures the OpenFlow control and data messages to build the flow graph with the nodes representing switches and edges representing the flow. SPHINX maintains the topological and forwarding metadata using the incoming and outgoing OpenFlow messages and traffic flow statistics messages. The flow statistics messages are communicated by the switch to the controller. Switch to controller communications include FEATURES_REPLY and STATS_REPLY messages other than data packets. FEATURES_REPLY communicates the port details of OpenFlow switches to the SDN controller. STATS_REPLY communicates the traffic statistics at the switch per port, per-flow, and per-flow table. SPHINX continuously monitors and updates the flow graphs and raises the alarm on the identification of deviant behavior. It also provides a policy engine for the network administrators to define security policies. In an attempt for TCAM exhaustion, SPHINX compares the flow rate with the existing flow statistics and administrator policies. On TCAM exhaustion, the flow rate will be higher, and thereby SPHINX detects the TCAM exhaustion attack. The administrator is entitled to take necessary actions on the security alarm made by SPHINX.

3.11.3   ARP poisoning

Compromised OpenFlow switches send forged physical addresses to the SDN controller. As a result, the controller gets a fake topology view and installs fake flow entries into legitimate OpenFlow switches. The impact of ARP poisoning attack is as follows:

1. Fake topology construction by the Topology Manager application running on the SDN controller.
2. Utilizing the fake topology constructed at the controller, attackers can perform passive attacks such as eavesdropping and active attacks such as packet tampering and packet dropping.

SPHINX [56] builds a flow graph that maintains and updates all the MAC-IP bindings in the network. When any deviation is observed in the OpenFlow messages compared to the MAC-IP bindings, SPHINX raises a security alarm.

3.11.4   Information disclosure

This attack is targeted at the communication channel between the SDN controller and the OpenFlow switches. If the communication channel is not secure, attackers can easily perform passive attacks such as eavesdropping the sensitive data transmitted and active attacks such as packet dropping and tampering. Though TLS/SSL is used to establish secure communication, various papers in the literature report the possible vulnerabilities such as fake self-signed certificates, compromised certificate authority, vulnerabilities in TLS/SSL on exploitation to launch man-in-the-middle attacks [57–59]. Possible solutions include oligarchic trust models with multiple trust-anchor certifications, threshold cryptography across the controller replicas n [60]. The switch needs at least k ($k \leq n$) shares from the controllers to get a valid controller message.

3.11.5   Denial-of-service (DoS) attacks

DoS attacks target OpenFlow switches, controller-switch communication channels, and the SDN controller. Attackers send arbitrary packets to OpenFlow switches. The switch spends some time for flow table lookup. When millions of such packets are sent by attackers, then it creates the unavailability of the switch's service to other legitimate hosts in the network for each and every table-miss, OpenFlow switch contacts the controller. As a result, bandwidth depletion occurs. Also, depletion of resources such as memory and processor occurs at the SDN controller.

The impact of the DoS attacks is given as follows:

1.   Bandwidth depletion.
2.   Unavailability of control logic service to legitimate hosts.
3.   Resource depletion at SDN controller and OpenFlow switches.
4.   Insertion of fake flow rules into the OF switches aimed at disrupting the proper functioning of the network.

SPHINX [56] detects DoS by using the flow statistics information such as the flow rate of the PACKET_IN messages and the administrator-specified policies. On observation of deviant behavior, it raises the alarm.

3.11.6   Exploiting vulnerabilities in OpenFlow switches

Exploiting the vulnerabilities in OpenFlow (OF) switches possibly triggers the following attacks:

1.   DoS on compromising one OF switch.
2.   DDoS on compromising multiple OF switches.
3.   A compromised switch serves as a black hole.

Autonomic trust management solutions for software components [61] are possible mitigations.

3.11.7   Exploiting vulnerabilities in SDN controllers

Compromising an SDN controller by exploiting vulnerabilities in the controller is equivalent to compromising the entire network. So, the SDN controllers must be kept secure at any cost. Link discovery attack is another attack that can be performed on SDN controllers by manipulating the LLDP packets during the link discovery process in order to create fake links or relay links for the purpose of eavesdropping. In addition to the aforementioned attacks on various components of SDN architecture, DDoS attacks can be performed on the application layer and the northbound API [62]. Big data analytics could be performed to help one to detect and predict security attacks on SDN architecture. The paper [63] discusses some traditional machine learning algorithms such as regression, BayesNet, decision trees to predict security attacks such as link discovery attack and ARP poisoning attack on SDN controllers.

3.12   Can SDN be applied to IoT?

In an SDN environment, there can be possibly more than one centralized controller [64]. The OpenDayLight controller [65] provides a cluster-based high availability model. This model consists of multiple controllers, each having a partial or complete view of the switches. The controllers have to exchange information with each other. The main aim of this model is to provide fault tolerance and load balancing in SDN. OpenFlow version 1.2 onwards specifies the following two modes of operation when there are multiple controllers in the SDN environment.

1. Equal interaction: All the controllers have a complete view and access to the switches. Synchronization among them is essential in this model. This is required to ensure that one controller does not overwrite rules installed by another controller on the switch.
2. Master/slave interaction: In this mode, there will be a single master controller and multiple slave controllers.

Application of SDN to IoT makes the following assumptions:

1. each IoT object has an embedded OpenFlow switch and an SDN controller (or)
2. IoT objects with lesser resources (no embedded OpenFlow components) are associated with a node having SDN capabilities.

Figure 3.17 shows the application of SDN to IoT. Multiple SDN networks are interconnected. There are two types of nodes in the ad hoc network of IoT devices. The nodes labeled OF-N are embedded with OpenFlow switch and controller. The nodes labeled with S-N are sensors or smart objects that lack OpenFlow switch and

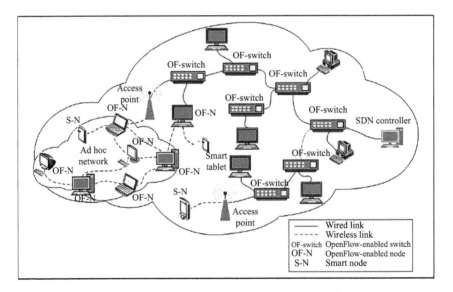

Figure 3.17   Mapping of SDN to IoT [64]

controller. These nodes are connected to a node with SDN capability. A single SDN network may contain one or more controllers that control that particular network/ domain. A domain denotes an organization, or an enterprise, or a data center. SDN, when applied to IoT, requires heterogeneous interconnection among multiple SDN domains. This interconnection is facilitated through the edge controllers of various SDN domains. The various controller implementations are [66–69].

The different hardware in SDN-based IoT architecture and NFV-based IoT architecture on 4G saves different QoS parameters [70]. Cloud-based solutions help one to address the heterogeneity of IoT devices, vendors, communication protocols, language, and data formats. However, the coexistence of traditional IT networks with the new IoT-based networks and dealing with unprecedented network traffic remains as challenges to be addressed. To deal with these challenges, a software architecture solution guarantees the interoperability among the noncompliant industrial devices [71]. The SDN controller is based on OpenDaylight [65] with IoT plugins, which manages and stores data according to the OneM2M standard [72]. Some of the future directions for IoT big data include visualization, integration, security, and data mining. As the data grow in scale, there is a need for dimensionality reduction methods [73,74] conditioned on preserving the pairwise distance and minimal information loss. Data correlations are much easier to observe in a low-dimensional space visually. To come up with a suitable visualization technique, capturing the heterogeneous data is a challenge. This also includes the betterment of big data indexing techniques. For faster response time, there is a need to either store data locally or run parallel visualization queries using clusters depending on the requirement [75]. To address the diversity of data formats, integration of data is a necessity [76]. Identifying structures in various data formats help to generate a unified view. Specifically, entity detection [77], coreference resolution [78,79], building a knowledge base [80], multimodal analysis [81] in the context of big data is another promising direction. With the increasing numbers of devices getting connected to IoT, privacy is another major concern. One promising research direction is to identify suspicious traffic (traffic classification) and ways to tackle zero-day attacks [82] arising due to interoperability issues. Classification [83,84], clustering [85], prediction [86], and rule mining [87,88] are the conventional big data mining algorithms. Parallel K-means [89] and parallel association rule mining [88] are specially designed for the parallel architectures of IoT big data. There is still a lot of scope for modeling data mining algorithms across multiple platforms, multiple vendors, dynamic, and streaming data.

3.13 Summary

IoT is a network of power-limited and cost-sensitive things. IoT demands agile networking capabilities to deal with the increasing traffic generated by the increasing number of devices getting connected to it. SDN promises to be a viable solution to the agility requirement of IoT. SDN architecture decouples the control plane from the data plane, and the data plane is programmatically controlled by the control plane.

SDN dynamically changes network behavior based on the new traffic patterns, policy changes, and security considerations, enabling agility in IoT. SDN helps to achieve the QoS to the IoT tasks in a heterogeneous wireless environment by centralized control logic. The power-limited and cost-sensitive nature of IoT devices make them suitable only for forwarding traffic and not for controlling the network. Also, SDN eliminates the need for huge hardware investments. While being advantageous, the SDN paradigm offers new challenges. The performance of the hardware and software components of SDN needs to be balanced. That is, high-speed processing at the controller and low processing at the switches lead to packet losses in the network. The coexistence of the current network infrastructures and SDN is another challenge. The virtual routing engine module of the OpenFlow protocol in SDN controllers helps to achieve this purpose. Security considerations in the controller-to-controller communications in a multi-controller environment is an open challenge.

In this chapter, the paradigm shift of networking to SDN is discussed. The architecture of SDN is described in detail. Routing in SDN is elucidated, and security on SDN routing is analyzed. Existing solutions and mitigations to the vulnerabilities in SDN routing are also discussed. A generic 5-layer architecture of the IoT is presented. Big data, big data analytics, and the intersection of IoT and big data, along with the IoT architecture for big data, are discussed. Routing protocols used in IoT and the possible attacks on IoT routing is also discussed. Finally, the mapping of SDN to IoT is illustrated, and future directions are discussed.

References

[1] M. Wu, T.-J. Lu, F.-Y. Ling, J. Sun, and H.-Y. Du, "Research on the architecture of Internet of Things," In 3rd international conference on advanced computer theory and engineering (ICACTE), vol. 5, pp. V5-484, Chengdu, China, IEEE, 2010.

[2] A. J. Jara, L. Ladid, and A. Skarmeta, "The internet of everything through IPv6: An analysis of challenges, solutions and opportunities," Journal of Wireless Mobile Networks, Ubiquitous Computing, and Dependable Applications, vol. 4, no. 3, pp. 97–118, 2013.

[3] Gartner, "Gartner says 4.9 billion connected things will be in use in 2015," http://www.gartner.com/newsroom/id/2905717.

[4] M. Marjani, F. Nasaruddin, A. Gani, et al., "Big IoT data analytics: Architecture, opportunities, and open research challenges," IEEE Access, vol. 5, pp. 5247–61, 2017.

[5] O. Kwon and N. B. L. Shin, "Data quality management, data usage experience and acquisition intention of big data analytics," International Journal of Information Management, vol. 34, no. 3, pp. 387–394, 2014.

[6] R. Mital, J. Coughlin, and M. Canaday, "Using big data technologies and analytics to predict sensor anomalies," in Proc. Adv. Maui Opt. Space Surveill. Technol. Conf., Sep. 2014, p. 84.

[7]   N. Golchha, "Big data-the information revolution," International Journal of Advanced Research, vol. 1, no. 12, pp. 791–794, 2015.

[8]   P. Russom, Big Data Analytics. TDWI, 4th Quart., 2011.

[9]   S. Oswal and S. Koul, "Big data analytic and visualization on mobile devices," in Proc. Nat. Conf. New Horizons IT-NCNHIT, 2013, p. 223.

[10] L. Candela and D. P. C. Pagano, "Managing big data through hybrid data infrastructures," ERCIM News, vol. 89, pp. 37–38, 2012.

[11] A. Siddiqa, "A survey of big data management: Taxonomy and state-of-the-art," Journal of Network and Computer Applications, vol. 71, pp. 151–166, 2016.

[12] C. A. Steed, "Big data visual analytics for exploratory earth system simulation analysis," Computers & Geosciences, vol. 61, pp. 71–82, 2013.

[13] C. L. P. Chen and C.-Y. Zhang, "Data-intensive applications, challenges, techniques and technologies: A survey on big data," Information Science, vol. 275, pp. 314–347, 2014.

[14] F. M. Waas, "Beyond conventional data warehousing-massively parallel data processing with Greenplum database," in International Workshop on Business Intelligence for the Real-Time Enterprise. Berlin, Germany: Springer, 2008.

[15] F. Färber, S. K. Cha, J. Primsch, C. Bornhövd, S. Sigg, and W. Lehner, "SAP HANA database: Data management for modern business applications," ACM SIGMOD Record, vol. 40, no. 4, pp. 45–51, 2011.

[16] M. Cheng, "Mu rhythm-based cursor control: An offline analysis," Clinical Neurophysiology, vol. 115, no. 4, pp. 745–751, 2004.

[17] M. Castro, P. Druschel, A. M. Kermarrec, and A. I. T. Rowstron, "Scribe: A large-scale and decentralized application-level multicast infrastructure," IEEE Journal on Selected Areas in Communications, vol. 20, no. 8, pp. 1489–1499, 2002.

[18] J. Kreps, N. Narkhede, and J. Rao, "KAFKA: A distributed messaging system for log processing," in Proc. NetDB, 2011, pp. 1–7.

[19] H. Notsu, Y. Okada, M. Akaishi, and K. Niijima, "Time-tunnel: Visual analysis tool for time-series numerical data and its extension toward parallel coordinates," in Proc. Int. Conf. Comput. Graph., Imag. Vis. (CGIV), Jul. 2005, pp. 167–172.

[20] A. Rabkin and R. H. Katz, "Chukwa: A system for reliable large-scale log collection," in Proc. LISA, Nov. 2010, pp. 1–15.

[21] K. Chodorow, MongoDB: The Definitive Guide. Newton, MA: O'Reilly Media, Inc, 2014.

[22] J. Gubbi, R. Buyya, S. Marusic, and M. Palaniswami, "Internet of Things (IoT): A vision, architectural elements, and future directions," Future Generation Computer Systems, vol. 29, no. 7, pp. 1645–1660, 2013.

[23] Y. Zhang, ICN Based Architecture for IoT. IRTF Contribution, Oct. 2013.

[24] R. Duan, X. Chen, and T. Xing, "A QoS architecture for IOT," in Proc. Int. Conf. 4th Int. Conf. Cyber, Phys. Soc. Comput. (iThings/CPSCom), Oct. 2011, pp. 717–720.

[25]   J. Kulik, W. Heinzelman, and H. Balakrishnan, "Negotiation-based protocols for disseminating information in wireless sensor networks," Wireless Networks, vol. 8, no. 2/3, pp. 169–185, 2002.

[26]   W. Heinzelman, A. Chandrakasan, and H. Balakrishnan, "An application specific protocol architecture for wireless microsensor networks," Wireless Communications, IEEE Transactions on, vol. 1, no. 4, pp. 660–670, 2002.

[27]   Y. Xu, J. Heidemann, and D. Estrin, "Geography-informed energy conservation for ad hoc routing," in Proceedings of the 7th Annual International Conference on Mobile Computing and Networking, ACM, 2001, pp. 70–84.

[28]   Z. Shelby and C. Bormann, *6LoWPAN: The Wireless Embedded Internet*, Vol. 33, Wiley, New Jersey, United States, 2010.

[29]   T. Winter, P. Thubert, A. Brandt, *et al.*, "RPL: IPv6 routing protocol for low power and lossy networks," in Work in Progress, http://tools.ietf.org/html/draft-ietf-roll-rpl-11, 2010.

[30]   Z. Shelby, C. Bormann, and D. Sturek, "Constrained application protocol CoAP," in RFC 7252, 2011.

[31]   E. C. H. Ngai, J. Liu, and M. R. Lyu, "On the intruder detection for sinkhole attack in wireless sensor networks," in Proceedings of the IEEE International Conference on Communications (ICC '06), Vol. 8, IEEE, 2006, pp. 3383–3389.

[32]   Demirbas M and Song Y, "An RSSI based scheme for Sybil attack detection in wireless sensor networks," in Proceedings of the 2006 International Symposium on World of Wireless, Mobile and Multimedia Networks, IEEE Computer Society, 2006, pp. 564–570.

[33]   C. Chen, M. Song, and G. Hsieh, "Intrusion detection of sinkhole attacks in large-scale wireless sensor networks," in IEEE International Conference on Wireless Communications, Networking and Information Security (WCNIS), 2010, pp. 711–716.

[34]   C. Karlof and D. Wagner, "Secure routing in wireless sensor networks: attacks and countermeasures," Ad Hoc Networks, vol. 1, no. 2, pp. 293–315, 2003.

[35]   B. Xiao, B. Yu, and C. Gao, "Detection and localization of Sybil nodes in VANETs," in Proceedings of the 2006 Workshop on Dependability Issues in Wireless Ad Hoc Networks and Sensor Networks, 2006, pp. 1–8.

[36]   B. Yu, C. Z. Xu, and B. Xiao, "Detecting Sybil attacks in VANETs," Journal of Parallel and Distributed Computing, vol. 73, no. 6, pp. 746–756, 2013.

[37]   J.-P. Hubaux, S. Capkun, and J. Luo. "The security and privacy of smart vehicles," IEEE Security and Privacy, vol. 2, no. 3, pp. 49–55, 2004.

[38]   S. Capkun and J.-P. Hubaux, "Secure positioning of wireless devices with application to sensor networks," in Proceedings of INFOCOM, 2005, pp. 1917–1928.

[39]   M. S. Gaur, J. Grover, and V. Laxmi, "A novel defense mechanism against Sybil attacks in VANET," in Proceedings of the 3rd International Conference on Security of Information and Networks, 2010, pp. 249–255.

[40]   J. Grover, M. S. Gaur, V. Laxmi, and N. K. Prajapati, "A Sybil attack detection approach using neighbouring vehicles in VANET," in Proceedings

of the 4th International Conference on Security of Information and Networks, 2011, pp. 151–158.

[41] M. Richardson, A. Lozano, T. Tsao, V. Daza, R. Alexander, and M. Dohler, "A security threat analysis for routing protocol for low-power and lossy networks (rpl)," draft-ietf-roll-security-threats-10, 2013.

[42] D. Forsberg, Y. Ohba, Ed., B. Patil, H. Tschofenig, and A. Yegin, "Protocol for carrying authentication for network access (PANA)," in RFC 5191, May 2008,

[43] D. Simon, B. Aboba, and R. Hurst, "The EAP-TLS authentication protocol," in RFC5216, Mar. 2008.

[44] SDN Architecture Overview. (n.d.). Open Networking Foundation. Retrieved April 5, 2016, https://www.opennetworking.org/images/stories/downloads/sdn-resources/technicalreports/SDN-architecture-overview-1.0.

[45] W. Hong, K. Wang, and Y.-H. Hsu, "Application-aware resource allocation for SDN-based cloud data centers," in Proc. Int'l. Conf. Cloud Computing and Big Data 2013, Fuzhou, China, Dec. 2013.

[46] Y. Han, S. S. Seo, J. Li, J. Hyun, J. H. Yoo, and J. W. K. Hong, "Software defined networking-based traffic engineering for data center networks," in Proc. 16th Asia-Pacific Network Operations and Management Symp., Taiwan, Sep. 2014.

[47] A. Sadasivarao, S. Syed, P. Pan, *et al.*, "Bursting data between data centers: case for transport SDN," in Proc. IEEE 21st Symp. High-Performance Interconnects, Mountain View, CA, Aug. 2013.

[48] L. Yang, R. Dantu, T. Anderson, and R. Gopal, "Forwarding and Control Element Separation (ForCES) Framework," in RFC 3746, Apr. 2004.

[49] N. McKeown, T. Anderson, H. Balakrishnan, *et al.*, "OpenFlow: Enabling innovation in campus networks," ACM SIGCOMM Computer Communication Review, vol. 38, no. 2, pp. 69–74, 2008.

[50] X. Zhang, L. Guo, W. Hou, Q. Zhang, and S. Wang, "Failure recovery solutions using cognitive mechanisms based on software-defined optical network platform," Optical Engineering, vol. 56, no. 1, p. 016107, 2017.

[51] G. Khetrapal and S. K. Sharma, "Demystifying Routing Services in Software-Defined Networking," Aricent, 2013. www.aricent.com/pdf/Aricent-Demystifying-Routing-Services-SDN-Whitepaper.pdf.

[52] L. Cui, F. R. Yu, and Q. Yan. "When big data meets software-defined networking: SDN for big data and big data for SDN," IEEE Network, vol. 30, no. 1, pp. 58–65, 2016.

[53] W. Queiroz, M. A. M. Capretz, and M. Dantas. "An approach for SDN traffic monitoring based on big data techniques." Journal of Network and Computer Applications, vol. 131, pp. 28–39, 2019.

[54] P. Porras, S. Shin, V. Yegneswaran, M. Fong, M. Tyson, and G. Gu, "A security enforcement kernel for OpenFlow networks," in Proceedings of the First Workshop on Hot Topics in Software Defined Networks, 2012, pp. 121–126.

[55]   N. Gude, T. Koponen, J. Pettit, *et al.*, "NOX: Towards an operating system for networks," in Proceedings of ACM Computer Communications Review, Jul. 2008.

[56]   M. Dhawan, R. Poddar, K. Mahajan, and V. Mann, "Sphinx: Detecting security attacks in software-defined networks," in NDSS, 2015.

[57]   R. Holz, T. Riedmaier, N. Kammenhuber, and G. Carle, "X. 509 forensics: Detecting and localising the SSL/TLS men-in-the-middle," In European Symposium on Research in Computer Security, Springer, Berlin, Heidelberg, 2012, pp. 217–234.

[58]   M. Georgiev, S. Iyengar, S. Jana, R. Anubhai, D. Boneh, and V. Shmatikov, "The most dangerous code in the world: validating SSL certificates in non-browser software," in The Proceedings of ACM CCS, 2012.

[59]   C. Soghoian and S. Stamm, "Certified lies: Detecting and defeating government interception attacks against SSL," In Proceedings of ACM Symposium on Operating Systems Principles, New York, United States, 2010, pp. 1–18.

[60]   Y. G. Desmedt. "Threshold cryptography," European Transactions on Telecommunications, vol. 5, no. 4, 1994.

[61]   Z. Yan and C. Prehofer, "Autonomic trust management for a component-based software system," in The Proceedings of IEEE Trans. on Dep. and Sec. Computing, Vol. 8, no. 6, 2011.

[62]   Q. Yan, F. R. Yu, Q. Gong, and J. Li, "Software-defined networking (SDN) and distributed denial of service (DDOS) attacks in cloud computing environments: A survey, some research issues, and challenges," IEEE Communications Surveys and Tutorials, 2015, DOI:10.1109/COMST.2015.2487361.

[63]   E. Unal, S. Sen-Baidya, and R. Hewett, "Towards prediction of security attacks on software defined networks: A big data analytic approach," in 2018 IEEE International Conference on Big Data (Big Data). IEEE, 2018.

[64]   O. Flauzac, C. Gonzalez, A. Hachani, and F. Nolot, "SDN based architecture for IoT and improvement of the security," in Advanced Information Networking and Applications Workshops (WAINA), 2015 IEEE 29th International Conference on, Mar. 2015, pp. 688–693.

[65]   Network Functions Virtualization (NFV), OpenDaylight, https://www.opendaylight.org.

[66]   G. Savarese, M. Vaser, and M. Ruggieri, "A software defined networking-based context-aware framework combining 4G cellular networks with M2M," in Proc. of the 16th International Symposium on Wireless Personal Multimedia Communications, Jun. 2013, pp. 1–6.

[67]   Z. Qin, G. Denker, C. Giannelli, P. Bellavista, and N. Venkatasubramanian, "A software defined networking architecture for the Internet-of-Things," in Proc. of the 2014 IEEE Network Operations and Management Symposium (NOMS), May 2014, pp. 1–9.

[68]   J. Li, E. Altman, and C. Touati. "A General SDN-based IoT Framework with NVF Implementation," ZTE Communications, ZTE Corporation, vol. 13,

no. 3, pp. 42, 2015. wwwen.zte.com.cn/endata/magazine/ztecommunications/ 2015/3/articles/201510/t2 0151021445054.html><hal-01197042>.

[69] N. Omnes, M. Bouillon, G. Fromentoux, and O. Le Grand, "A programmable and virtualized network & IT infrastructure for the Internet of Things: How can NFV & SDN help for facing the upcoming challenges," in Proc. IEEE ICIN, Feb. 2015, pp. 64–69.

[70] M. Alenezi, K. Almustafa, and K. A. Meerja, "Cloud based SDN and NFV architectures for IoT infrastructure," Egyptian Informatics Journal, vol. 20, no. 1, pp. 1–10, 2019.

[71] J. L. Romero-Gázquez and M. Bueno-Delgado, "Software architecture solution based on SDN for an industrial IoT scenario," Wireless Communications and Mobile Computing, vol. 2018, 2018.

[72] One M2M Standard. http://www.onem2m.org/.

[73] A. T. Azar and A. E. Hassanien, "Dimensionality reduction of medical big data using neural-fuzzy classifier," Soft Computing, vol. 19, no. 4, pp. 1115–1127, 2015.

[74] V. L. Popov and M. Heß, "Method of dimensionality reduction in contact mechanics and friction," Springer, Berlin Heidelberg, 2015.

[75] H. Childs, B. Geveci, W. Schroeder, *et al.*, "Research challenges for visualization software," Computer, vol. 46, no. 5, pp. 34–42, 2013.

[76] D. Agrawal, P. Bernstein, E. Bertino, *et al.*, "Challenges and opportunities with big data: A community white paper developed by leading researchers across the United States," in *Computing Community Consortium, White Paper*, 2012.

[77] V. Yadav and S. Bethard, "A survey on recent advances in named entity recognition from deep learning models," in Proceedings of the 27th International Conference on Computational Linguistics, 2018 Aug, pp. 2145–2158.

[78] K. Lee, L. He, and L. Zettlemoyer, Higher-order coreference resolution with coarse-to-fine inference. arXiv preprint arXiv:1804.05392. 2018 Apr 15. 33.

[79] M. E. Peters, M. Neumann, M. Iyyer, *et al.*, Deep contextualized word representations. arXiv preprint arXiv:1802.05365. 2018 Feb 15.

[80] Q. Wang, B. Wang, and L. Guo, "Knowledge base completion using embeddings and rules," in Twenty-Fourth International Joint Conference on Artificial Intelligence, 2015 Jun 24.

[81] Y. Du, C. Raman, A. W. Black, L. P. Morency, M. Eskenazi, Multimodal polynomial fusion for detecting driver distraction. arXiv preprint arXiv:1810.10565. 2018 Oct 24.

[82] K. Steinklauber. Data Protection in the Internet of Things. [Online]. 2014. Available: https://securityintelligence.com/data-protection-inthe-internet-of-things.

[83] C. Bielza and P. Larrañaga, "Discrete Bayesian network classifiers: A survey," ACM Computing Surveys, vol. 47, no. 1, p. 5, 2014.

[84] F. Chen, P. Deng, J. Wan, D. Zhang, A. V. Vasilakos, and X. Rong, "Data mining for the Internet of Things: Literature review and challenges," International Journal of Distributed Sensor Networks, vol. 12, 2015.

[85]   P. Berkhin, *A Survey of Clustering Data Mining Techniques, in Grouping Multidimensional Data*. Berlin, Germany: Springer, 2006, pp. 25–71.

[86]   A. Gandomi and M. Haider, "Beyond the hype: Big data concepts, methods, and analytics," International Journal of Information Management, vol. 35, no. 2, pp. 137–144, 2015.

[87]   A. Gosain and M. Bhugra, "A comprehensive survey of association rules on quantitative data in data mining," in Proc. IEEE Conf. Inf. Commun. Technol., Apr. 2013, pp. 1003–1008.

[88]   X. Wu and S. Zhang, "Synthesizing high-frequency rules from different data sources," IEEE Transactions on Knowledge and Data Engineering, vol. 15, no. 2, pp. 353–367, 2003.

[89]   K. Su, "A logical framework for identifying quality knowledge from different data sources," Decision Support System, vol. 42, no. 3, pp. 1673–1683, 2006.

Chapter 4

Efficient ciphertext-policy attribute-based signcryption for secure big data storage in cloud

Praveen Kumar Premkamal[1,2,3], Syam Kumar Pasupuleti[2] and Alphonse PJA[1]

Due to the huge volume and complexity of big data, outsourcing big data to a cloud is the best option for data storage and access, because the cloud has the capabilities of storing and processing of big data. However, data privacy, access control, and authentication are significant concerns for big data because the cloud cannot be fully trusted. Ciphertext-policy attribute-based signcryption (CP-ABSC) has been an effective cryptographic technique to provide privacy, access control, and authenticity in the cloud environment. However, the following two main issues of CP-ABSC that limits CP-ABSC scheme to deploy for big data in the cloud: (1) suffer from higher computation overheads during signcryption and designcryption and (2) CP-ABSC provides unlimited time data access rights as long as attributes satisfy the access policy which restricts to apply for commercial big data applications. This chapter proposes an efficient ciphertext-policy attribute-based signcryption (ECP-ABSC) for big data storage in cloud to address the previous two issues. ECP-ABSC scheme reduces the required number of exponentiation operations during signcryption and outsources the inflated pairing computation during the designcryption process, which, in turn, reduces the computation overhead of data owner and user. Our scheme also provides flexible access control by giving data access rights to unlimited times or a fixed number of times based on the user. This flexible access control feature increases the applicability in commercial applications. Further, we prove the desired security requirements of our scheme that include data confidentiality, signcryptor privacy, and unforgeability in security analysis. The feasibility and practicality of our scheme are provided in performance evaluation.

[1]Department of Computer Applications, National Institute of Technology Tiruchirappalli, Tiruchirappalli, India
[2]Centre for Cloud Computing, Institute for Development and Research in Banking Technology, Hyderabad, India
[3]Department of Computer Science and Engineering, Kamaraj College of Engineering and Technology, Madurai, India

4.1   Introduction

Big data has the immense potential to add value to the organization's growth. So the organization is required to capture, store, manage, and mine the big data for its productivity. This requirement brings new challenges to the organization in which they could setup an infrastructure to store big data. Setting up the infrastructure locally is an expensive and time-consuming process [1]. The best alternative approach is to outsource the big data into the cloud because it has the advantages of global accessibility, scalability, and a pay-per-user model [2].

Taking financial and health-care big data applications as an example, nowadays, many of these applications are outsourced to the cloud server to enjoy the advantages of the cloud. However, storing sensitive and private financial or health information on an external third-party server (cloud server) always raises the following privacy and security concerns [3]. The issues are (1) how to ensure the privacy of private and sensitive information stored in the cloud, (2) how to restrict the unauthorized data access, and (3) a small change in the data leads to false report which affects decision-making, which raises the question of how to guarantee the stored data authenticity?

Attribute-based signcryption (ABSC) [4] is a promising solution to address the previous issues simultaneously. ABSC is a mixture of attribute-based encryption (ABE) [5] and attribute-based signature (ABS) [6]. ABE is the one-to-many cryptographic primitive, which is mainly used in the cloud environment to provide data confidentiality (privacy and fine-grained access control). The encryption operation is associated with a set of attributes, and the decryption secret key is based on a predicate. The predicate is a policy that consists of attributes and Boolean operators, such as AND, OR, or threshold gate. [(CLOUD or BIGDATA) and FACULTY] are examples for predicate/policy, in which (OR, ARE) are Boolean operators and (CLOUD, BIGDATA, FACULTY) are attributes. This predicate/policy indicates that the faculty from the cloud lab or big data lab can access the data. This approach of ABE is called key-policy ABE (KP-ABE) [7]. In contrast to this approach, the CP-ABE [8–10] is proposed in which the encryption operation is associated with the policy and the decryption secret key on the basis of a set of attributes.

On the other hand, ABS is attracted to the researchers in the recent past, because it provides data authenticity in the cloud environment without revealing the user information, that is, it preserves the privacy of the signer. ABS associated with KP-ABE is called key-policy ABS (KP-ABS) [11,12]. In KP-ABS, the signing key (SK) of the signer is based on policy, and the data signing process is associated with a set of signer–signing attributes. ABS associated with CP-ABE is called signature-policy ABS (SP-ABS) [13,14]. In SP-ABS, the SK of the signer is based on a set of attributes, and the data signing process is associated with the policy, while the signer–signing attribute set satisfies the signing policy.

Key-policy ABSC (KP-ABSC) and (CP-ABSC) are the two variations of ABSC. The KP-ABS and KP-ABE combination is called KP-ABSC [12], and the SP-ABS and CP-ABE combination is called CP-ABSC [15]. In this chapter, we only focus on

CP-ABSC rather than KP-ABSC because CP-ABSC enables the data owners to control over their data by specifying access policy over attributes. There has been considerable attention so far in the literature toward CP-ABSC.

4.1.1 Related work

Gagné *et al.* [4] introduced the ABSC scheme for the first time. In this scheme, the signing attributes are separated from decryption attributes to provide the different access rights. This scheme is based on the threshold gate access structure, and they proved that their scheme is secure in the standard model. However, Wang *et al.* [16] proved that the scheme of Gagné *et al.* [4] suffered from private key forgery attack. Wang *et al.* [17] proposed CP-ABSC scheme, which supports an access tree as an access structure for signcryption. The security of this scheme is proved under the generic group and the random oracle model. Emura *et al.* [18] proposed a dynamic ABSC scheme that supports tree access structure for signature and AND-gate access structure for encryption. In this scheme, the encryptor can update the access structure dynamically, which does not affect the user secret key. This dynamic update improves efficiency, and they proved the security in the standard model. Guo *et al.* [19] realized the ring signcryption for the first time. In this scheme, they constructed the ring with partial attributes to protect the sender's identity. They proved their scheme security in the random oracle model. Liu *et al.* [20] proposed a CP-ABSC scheme for personal health record sharing system to provide the privacy, authenticity, and access control. In this scheme, they introduced the idea of sign then encrypt. Rao [21] improved the scheme of Liu *et al.* [20] for PHR system. He claimed that the security proof is incorrect in Liu *et al.* [20] and also proved that this scheme does not support the public verifiable property. Hu *et al.* [22] proposed a new CP-ABSC scheme for multicast communication that is required in the smart grid, social networks, and body area networks. This scheme supports access tree as an access structure. In their subsequent work [23], Hu *et al.* proposed the CP-ABSC scheme to secure pull-based and push-based multicast communication in the smart grid. However, both these schemes are not formally proved secure. The summary of all the previous related works is shown in Table 4.1.

Although few CP-ABSC schemes exist, not all of them are suitable for practical big data applications in the cloud because of the following reasons: (1) existing CP-ABSC schemes suffer from efficiency issues because they require the number of exponentiation and pairing operations during signcryption and designcryption; (2) all the CP-ABSC schemes provide unlimited data access until the user attributes satisfy the policy. This approach is not suitable for commercial big data applications such as online education, on-demand audio access, on-demand video access, and online software applications because these applications may require data access on the basis of the number of times rather than unlimited data access, while the user attributes satisfy the policy. Also, few commercial applications offer trial access initially to get the experience of that application, which requires few times data access rather than unlimited time access. Thus, it is necessary to design an ECP-ABSC for big data storage in the cloud, which supports flexible access control.

Table 4.1   Summary of related works

Authors	Access structure	Security model	Public verifiability	Signcryptor privacy
Gagné *et al.* [4]	Threshold gate	Standard model	×	×
Chen *et al.* [15]	Monotone Boolean function	Standard model	×	×
Wang *et al.* [17]	Access tree	Generic group and random oracle model	×	×
Emura *et al.* [18]	Access tree and AND-gate	Standard model	✓	×
Guo *et al.* [19]	Access tree	Random oracle model	×	✓
Liu *et al.* [20]	Monotone Boolean function	Standard model	×	✓
Rao [21]	Monotone Boolean function	Standard model	✓	✓
Hu *et al.* [22]	Access tree	Generic group model	✓	×
Hu *et al.* [23]	Access tree	Generic group model	✓	×

4.1.2   Contributions

In this chapter, we propose an ECP-ABSC for big data storage in cloud. The main contributions of this chapter are as follows:

1. **Efficiency:** Our scheme reduces the number of exponentiation operations during signcryption operations, which reduces the burden of the data owner. Our scheme outsources the inflated pairing computation of the signature verification process during designcryption, which reduces the burden of data users. The theoretical and implementation results in performance evaluation prove that our scheme is efficient when compared with other existing schemes.
2. **Flexible access control:** All the users are assigned with data access limit at the registration phase itself. The data access limit is set either "−1" or "$\aleph$," "−1" represents unlimited time access, and "$\aleph$" represents fixed "$\aleph$" time access. Whenever the data user requests the ciphertext from the cloud, the cloud first verifies the data access limit. If it is "−1" or greater than zero, then it provides the data access to the user. This enables our scheme to provide flexible access control, which is an essential requirement for commercial big data applications.
3. **Security:** Our scheme is proven to be secure, and it achieves the desired security goals of data confidentiality, signcryptor privacy, and unforgeability.

4.2   Preliminaries

In this section, we introduce different notations, basic definitions, security assumptions, and security models that are required to design the proposed ECP-ABSC scheme. Table 4.2 introduces the different notations used in the proposed scheme. Notations used in the proposed scheme are as follows.

Table 4.2   Notations used in the proposed scheme

Notation	Meaning
λ	Security parameter
MPK	Master private key
PK	Public key
$\mathbb{UL}$	User list
ID	User identity
SK	Signing key
ω_s	Signing attribute set
DK	Decryption key
ω_d	User attribute set
M	Message
τ_s	Signing policy
τ_e	Encryption policy
$\mathcal{C}$	Ciphertext
$flag$	Signature verification status
$\mathcal{G}$	Group
$\mathfrak{g}$	Generator of $\mathcal{G}$
h_1	Collision-resistant hash function
$\mathbb{U}$	Universal attributes
aL	User's data access limit
$\triangleright$	Comments

Definition 4.1 *Bilinear pairing* [24,25]*: A bilinear pairing* $(\mathfrak{e})$ *is defined as* $\mathfrak{e}$*:* $\mathcal{G} \times \mathcal{G} \rightarrow \mathcal{G}_t$*, where* $\mathcal{G}$ *and* $\mathcal{G}_t$ *are multiplicative cyclic groups of order p. Let p be the large prime number. The bilinear pairing should satisfy the following properties:*

1. ***Bilinear:*** $\mathfrak{e}(\mathfrak{g}^x, \mathfrak{g}^y) = \mathfrak{e}(\mathfrak{g}, \mathfrak{g})^{xy}$*, where* $\mathfrak{g} \in \mathcal{G}$*,* $x, y \xleftarrow{R} Z_p$
2. ***Nondegenerate:*** $\mathfrak{e}(\mathfrak{g}, \mathfrak{g}) = 1$*, where* $\mathfrak{g} \in \mathcal{G}$
3. ***Computable:*** There exists an algorithm to compute $\mathfrak{e}(\mathfrak{g}, \mathfrak{g})$

Definition 4.2 *Decisional Bilinear Diffie–Hellman (DBDH) assumption* [9,26]*: The DBDH problem is to distinguish* $Z = \mathfrak{e}(\mathfrak{g}, \mathfrak{g})^{xyz}$ *from random* $Z = R$ *for the DBDH tuple* $(\mathfrak{g}, \mathfrak{g}^x, \mathfrak{g}^y, \mathfrak{g}^z, Z) \in \mathcal{G}_t$*, where x, y, z* $\in Z_p$*. The probabilistic polynomial time (PPT) algorithm* $\mathfrak{B}$ *has an advantage* ε *in solving the DBDH problem if*

$$|Pr[\mathfrak{B}(\mathfrak{g}, \mathfrak{g}^x, \mathfrak{g}^y, \mathfrak{g}^z, \mathfrak{e}(\mathfrak{g}, \mathfrak{g})^{xyz}) = 0] - Pr[\mathfrak{B}(\mathfrak{g}, \mathfrak{g}^x, \mathfrak{g}^y, \mathfrak{g}^z, R) = 0]| \geq \varepsilon$$

Definition 4.3 *No PPT algorithm has a non-negligible advantage in solving DBDH problem if DBDH assumption holds* [9,26].

Definition 4.4 *q-Computational Diffie–Hellman (q-CDH) problem* [21]*: The q-CDH problem is to compute* $\mathfrak{g}^{z^{q+1}}$ *for the tuple* $\left(\mathfrak{g}, \mathfrak{g}^z, \mathfrak{g}^{z^2}, \ldots, \mathfrak{g}^{z^q}, \mathfrak{g}^{z^{q+2}}, \ldots, \mathfrak{g}^{z^{2q}}\right) \in \mathcal{G}^{2q}$*, where* $\mathfrak{g}$ *is a generator, and z is {2, 3,…, p−1}; p is a large prime number.*

Definition 4.5 *No PPT algorithm has a non-negligible advantage in solving q-CDH problem* [21].

Definition 4.6 *Monotone span program* [21]: *A monotone span program (MSP) is a matrix defined as* $\Upsilon = (\mathfrak{m}, \rho)$, *where* $\mathfrak{m}$ *is a matrix of order* $r \times c$ *over* Z_p *and* ρ *is the row labeling function that maps every row of* $\mathfrak{m}$, *that is,* $\rho : [r] \rightarrow (\vartheta_1, \vartheta_1, \ldots, \vartheta_c)$; $(\vartheta_1, \vartheta_1, \ldots, \vartheta_c)$ *is a set of variables. Let* $\bar{y} = (y_1, y_2, \ldots, y_c) \in \{0, 1\}^c$. $Y_k = \{i \in [r] : \rho(i) = \vartheta_j \wedge y_j = k\}$, *where j=1 to c and k=0 or 1, and it implies that* $Y_0 \cup Y_1 = [r]$.
    If Υ *accepts the input* $\bar{y}$, *then it is denoted by* $\Upsilon(\bar{y}) = 1$, *otherwise it is denoted by* $\Upsilon(\bar{y}) = 0$. $\Upsilon(\bar{y}) = 1$ *implies that* $[\{\exists (a_i : i \in Y_1)\} \in Z_p$ *such that* $\sum_{i \in Y_1} a_i \cdot \mathfrak{m}^i = \bar{1}_c, \{\exists (a_i : i \in Y_0)\} \in Z_p$ *such that* $\sum_{i \in Y_0} a_i \cdot \mathfrak{m}^i = \bar{0}_c]$, *where* $\mathfrak{m}^i$ *is the ith row of* $\mathfrak{m}$, $\bar{1}_c = (1, 0, \ldots, 0)$ *and* $\bar{0}_c = (0, 0, \ldots, 0)$. *Therefore,* $[\exists (a_1, a_2, \ldots, a_r) \in Z_p$ *such that* $\sum_{i \in r} \cdot a_i \cdot \mathfrak{m}^i = \bar{1}_c$ *and* $a_i = 0 \ \forall_i$ *in* $Y_0]$.

Definition 4.7 *Policy* [21]: *A policy* (τ) *is a Boolean function that consists of a set of attributes and AND and OR gates. Let attribute set* $\omega \in \mathbb{U}$ *where* $\mathbb{U}$ *be the universal attributes. If* ω *satisfies a policy* (τ), *then it is denoted by* $\tau(\omega) = 1$, *otherwise* $\tau(\omega) = 0$.
    In our scheme, we use the MSP to represent the policy such that $\tau = (\mathfrak{m}_{r \times c}, \rho)$, *where* $\rho : [r] \rightarrow \omega$ *is a row labeling function of* $\mathfrak{m}$. *Here, the attributes are variables in MSP. From definition 0, satisfying the policy* τ *by the set of attributes* ω *is written as follows:* $Y_1 = \{i \in [r] : \rho(i) \in \omega\}$ *and* $Y_0 = \{i \in [r]; \rho(i) \notin \omega\}$
    $\tau(\omega) = 1 \Leftrightarrow [\exists (a_1, a_2, \ldots, a_r) \in Z_p$ *such that* $\sum_{i \in r} a_i \cdot \mathfrak{m}^i = \bar{1}_c$ *and* $a_i = 0 \ \forall_i \rho_i \notin \omega]$

4.2.1 Security model

In this part, we describe the security models that are used to prove the proposed scheme's security requirements, which include data confidentiality, signcryptor privacy, and ciphertext unforgeability. The description of the notations involved in this security model is as follows: master private key (*MPK*), public key (*PK*), security parameter (λ), binary coin (μ), singing policy (τ_s^*), and encryption policy (τ_e^*).

4.2.1.1 Game I

Definition 4.8 *ECP-ABSC scheme is indistinguishable against chosen-plaintext attack (IND-CPA) if PPT adversaries have at most negligible advantage in the following security game* [24,25].

    The IND-CPA security definition is given in Figure 4.1. There are five phases in this model, such as init phase, setup phase, query phase, challenge phase, and guess phase. The adversary ($\mathscr{A}$) plays a game against the challenger (ζ).
    Init phase: $\mathscr{A}$ requests *PK* from the challenger (ζ).
    Setup phase: ζ sends *PK* to $\mathscr{A}$.
    Query phase I: $\mathscr{A}$ sends the signing attribute set ω_s^* and decryption attribute set ω_d^* and requests signing key *SK** and decryption key *DK** from ζ. ζ serves the same.

$$(MPK, PK) \leftarrow SystemSetup(\lambda); \mu \leftarrow \{0,1\}$$
$$(\omega_s^*, \omega_d^*) \leftarrow \mathscr{A}$$
$$SK^* \leftarrow SignKeyGen(MPK, PK, \omega_s^*)$$
$$DK^* \leftarrow DecKeyGen(MPK, PK, \omega_d^*)$$
$$(M_0, M_1) \leftarrow \mathscr{A}$$
$$\mathscr{C}_\mu^* \leftarrow Signcryption(M_\mu, PK, SK^*, \tau_s^*, \tau_e^*)$$
$$(\mu') \leftarrow \mathscr{A}$$
$$if\ \mu = \mu'\ then\ \mathscr{A}\ wins\ the\ game$$

Figure 4.1   Security game for IND-CPA

$$(MPK, PK) \leftarrow SystemSetup(\lambda)$$
$$(\tau_s, \tau_e, M, \omega_s^1, \omega_s^2); \tau_s(\omega_s^1) = \tau_s(\omega_s^2) = 1 \leftarrow \mathscr{A}$$
$$SK^1, SK^2 \leftarrow SignKeyGen(MPK, PK, \omega_s^1, \omega_s^2)$$
$$\mathscr{C}^\mu \leftarrow Signcryption(M, PK, SK^\mu, \tau_s, \tau_e); \mu \in \{0,1\}$$
$$(\mu') \leftarrow \mathscr{A}$$
$$if\ \mu = \mu'\ then\ \mathscr{A}\ wins\ the\ game$$

Figure 4.2   Security game for signcryptor privacy

Challenge phase: $\mathscr{A}$ outputs the two same size messages M_0 and M_1 and requests the ciphertext. ζ tosses the binary coin and chooses the μ value; $\mu \in \{0, 1\}$. Based on the μ value, ζ generates and sends the ciphertext $\mathscr{C}_\mu^*$ for the message M_μ.

Query phase II: $\mathscr{A}$ may be repeating the query as similar as in query phase I and ζ serves $\mathscr{A}$ as similar in query phase I.

Guess: $\mathscr{A}$ submits the guess μ' for the received ciphertext $\mathscr{C}_\mu^*$. $\mathscr{A}$ wins the game if $\mu = \mu'$. The advantage of $\mathbb{A}$ winning this game is $\Pr[\mu = \mu'] - (1/2)$.

4.2.1.2   Game II

The security definition for signcryptor privacy is given in Figure 4.2. There are four phases in this model, such as setup phase, query phase, challenge phase, and guess phase. The adversary ($\mathscr{A}$) plays a game against the challenger (ζ).

Setup phase: ζ sends *MPK*, *PK* to $\mathscr{A}$

Query phase: $\mathscr{A}$ sends a message M, two signing attribute sets ω_s^1, ω_s^2, signing policy (τ_s) such that $\tau_s(\omega_s^1) = \tau_s(\omega_s^2) = 1$, encryption policy ($\tau_e$) to ζ and requests the ciphertext from ζ.

Challenge phase: ζ first generates two signing key SK^1 and SK^2, and ζ tosses the binary coin μ. Based on the μ value, it chooses the signing key SK^μ and generates the challenge ciphertext $\mathscr{C}^\mu$ which does not reveal any information about μ.

Guess: $\mathscr{A}$ guesses μ' for μ. $\mathscr{A}$ wins this game if the guess is $\mu' = \mu$. The advantage of $\mathscr{A}$ to win this game is $\Pr[\mathscr{A}\ wins]$.

4.2.1.3   Game III

The security definition of existential unforgeability under the chosen message attack (EUF-CMA) is given in Figure 4.3. There are four phases in this model, such as init phase, setup phase, query phase, and forge phase. The adversary ($\mathscr{A}$) plays a game against the challenger (ζ).

$$\tau_s^* \leftarrow \mathscr{A}$$
$$(MPK, PK) \leftarrow SystemSetup(\lambda)$$
$$(\omega_s^*, \omega_d^*) \leftarrow \mathscr{A}$$
$$SK^* \leftarrow SignKeyGen(MPK, PK, \omega_s^*)$$
$$DK^* \leftarrow DecKeyGen(MPK, PK, \omega_d^*)$$
$$(M, \tau_s, \tau_e) \leftarrow \mathscr{A}$$
$$\mathscr{C}^* \leftarrow Signcryption(M, PK, SK, \tau_s, \tau_e)$$
$$(\mathscr{C}^f) \leftarrow \mathscr{A}$$

$\mathscr{A}$ wins the game if Designcryption_Out$(PK, \mathscr{C}^f, \tau_s^*) = 1$ and Designcryption$(PK, flag, \mathscr{C}^f, DK) = M^*$ where $\tau_s^*(\omega_d^*) = 1$ and $\mathscr{C}^f$ was not queried earlier.

Figure 4.3   Security game for EUF-CMA

Init phase: $\mathscr{A}$ chooses and sends the signing policy τ_s^* which will be used for forging the ciphertext. $\mathscr{A}$ requests the *PK* from the challenger (ζ).

Setup phase: ζ generates and submits the *PK* to $\mathscr{A}$.

Query phase: $\mathscr{A}$ sends the signing attribute set ω_s^* and decryption attribute set ω_d^* and requests signing key *SK** and decryption key *DK** from ζ. ζ serves the same. $\mathscr{A}$ outputs the message *M*, singing policy (τ_s), and encryption policy (τ_e) and requests the ciphertext. ζ selects the signing attributes ω_s such that $\tau_s^*(\omega_s) = 1$ and generates the signing key *SK*. Then, ζ generates and sends the ciphertext $\mathscr{C}^*$. This query may be repeated as much as $\mathscr{A}$ required.

Forge phase: $\mathscr{A}$ outputs a forged ciphertext $\mathscr{C}^f$ for the τ_s^*.

$\mathbb{A}$ wins this game if the designcryption of the given ciphertext $\mathscr{C}^f$ returns the message (M^*) with the constraint that the $\mathscr{C}^f$ was not queried in the query phase. The advantage of $\mathbb{A}$ winning this game is Pr $[\mathbb{A}$ wins].

Definition 4.9 *ECP-ABSC scheme is EUF-CMA secure if PPT adversaries have at most negligible advantage in the previous security game* [21].

4.3   System model

In this section, we describe our ECP-ABSC architecture, the formal definition of our ECP-ABSC scheme, and security goals.

4.3.1   System architecture of ECP-ABSC

Our ECP-ABSC scheme architecture is shown in Figure 4.4. Our scheme architecture consists of the following five entities, such as trusted authority, data owner, cloud server, data users, and third-party auditor.

- **Trusted authority** $(\mathbb{TA})$: $\mathbb{TA}$ initially generates the public parameters that are used to generate the *SK*, decryption key (*DK*), and encrypt the data. $\mathbb{TA}$ generates the *SK* for data owners with signing attributes and generates the *DK* for data users with user attributes. $\mathbb{TA}$ registers the new user by issuing the user identity to the user. Then it adds the user identity and data access limit for the concerned user in the user list.

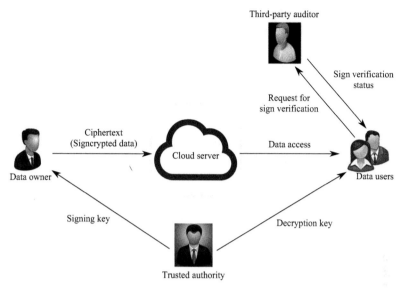

Figure 4.4   Architecture of ECP-ABSC scheme

- **Data owner** ($\mathfrak{DD}$): $\mathfrak{DD}$ defines the signing policy and encryption policy. The signing policy is used for authenticity, and encryption policy is used to decide who can access the data. $\mathfrak{DD}$ signcrypts (encryption and signing) her/his data using the signing policy and encryption policy. Then the signcrypted data (ciphertext) is outsourced into the cloud.
- **Cloud server** ($\mathbb{CS}$): $\mathbb{CS}$ is an untrusted entity. $\mathbb{CS}$ provides the storage space to the $\mathfrak{DD}$ to store the signcrypted data (ciphertext) as a service. $\mathbb{CS}$ stores the user list. $\mathbb{CS}$ allows the $\mathfrak{DU}$ to download the signcrypted data if the user data access limit does not exceed by verifying the data access limit in the user list.
- **Data users** ($\mathfrak{DU}$): $\mathfrak{DU}$ is an untrusted entity. $\mathfrak{DU}$ accesses the signcrypted data from the cloud. $\mathfrak{DU}$ can successfully decrypt the ciphertext if the attributes in the *DK* satisfy the encryption policy.
- **Third-party auditor** ($\mathbb{TPA}$): $\mathbb{TPA}$ is a trusted entity. It performs the outsourced computations. $\mathbb{TPA}$ checks the authenticity of data by verifying the signature on the behalf of $\mathfrak{DU}$.

4.3.2   Formal definition of ECP-ABSC

Our scheme consists of seven algorithms, such as SystemSetup, Join, SignKeyGen, DecKeyGen, Signcryption, Designcryption_Out, and Designcryption. The high-level definitions of all seven algorithms are as follows:

SystemSetup $(\lambda) \rightarrow (MPK, PK)$: This algorithm outputs the *MPK* and *PK* for the input of security parameter (λ). $\mathbb{TA}$ executes SystemSetup algorithm.

Join $(\mathbb{UL}) \rightarrow (ID, \mathbb{UL})$: The join algorithm runs by the $\mathbb{TA}$. It takes the input of user list ($\mathbb{UL}$) and outputs the user identity (*ID*) along with the updated user list ($\mathbb{UL}$).

SignKeyGen $(MPK, PK, \omega_s) \rightarrow SK$: $\mathbb{TA}$ generates the *SK* for the given signing attribute set (ω_s) using *MPK* and *PK* using this algorithm.

DecKeyGen $(MPK, PK, \omega_d) \rightarrow DK$: $\mathbb{TA}$ generates the *DK* for the given user attribute set (ω_d) using *MPK* and *PK* using this algorithm.

Signcryption $(M, PK, SK, \tau_s, \tau_e) \rightarrow \mathscr{C}$: $\mathfrak{DO}$ executes this algorithm with message (*M*), *PK*, *SK*, signing policy (τ_s), and encryption policy (τ_e). It returns the ciphertext $(\mathscr{C})$ as output.

Designcryption_Out $(PK, \mathscr{C}) \rightarrow flag$ or $\perp$: Designcryption_Out algorithm is performed by $\mathbb{TPA}$. The *PK* and ciphertext $(\mathscr{C})$ are the inputs for this algorithm and it outputs *flag* or $\perp$.

Designcryption $(PK, flag, \mathscr{C}, DK) \rightarrow M$ or $\perp$: The execution of designcryption algorithm is performed by $\mathfrak{DU}$. It takes *PK*, signature verification status (*flag*), ciphertext $(\mathscr{C})$, and *DK* as inputs. It outputs the message (*M*) or $\perp$.

4.3.3 Security goals

The following are our ECP-ABSC scheme security goals:

- **Data confidentiality:** It allows only authorized users who have the set of attributes that satisfy the encryption access policy to obtain sensitive information. In other words, it protects sensitive information from unauthorized users who do not have enough attributes to satisfy the encryption policy.
- **Data authentication:** It protects the outsourced content from being altered by unauthorized users.
- **Signcryptor privacy:** The privacy of the signcryptor should be protected from other users. In particular, the data users should not know the exact attributes used by the data owner in the signing process.
- **Unforgeability:** It allows only authorized users who have the set of signing attributes that satisfy the signing policy to create valid signcrypted data (ciphertext). In other words, it prevents unauthorized users from generating valid signcrypted data (ciphertext) that does not have enough signing attributes to satisfy the signing policy.

4.4 Construction of ECP-ABSC scheme

In this section, we explain the detailed algorithmic constructions of the proposed ECP-ABSC scheme, which is based on the scheme of Rao [21]. In the proposed scheme, we have combined two nice features, such as outsourcing the inflated computations and flexible data access with the scheme of Rao [21]. The proposed ECP-ABSC scheme consists of four different phases, such as setup, key generation, signcrypt, and designcrypt. The details of the different phases are as follows.

4.4.1 Setup

The setup phase initializes the system and also registers the new user by using SystemSetup and Join algorithm, respectively. Let $\mathbb{U}$ and $\mathbb{UL}$ be the universal attribute set and user list, respectively. The generator of $\mathscr{G}$ is denoted by $\mathfrak{g}$. Let $h_1 : \mathscr{G} \to Z_p$ be the collision-resistant hash function. SystemSetup algorithm is used to generate the *MPK* and *PK*, *MPK* is required to generate the *SK* and *DK*, *PK* is required in all algorithms. Algorithm 1 describes the SystemSetup algorithm.

Algorithm 1 SystemSetup

    Input: λ
    Output: *MPK, PK*
    1: Compute $v = \mathfrak{e}(\mathfrak{g}, \mathfrak{g})^{\alpha}$; where α is a random number from Z_p.
    2: Pick random number δ, Ψ from $\mathscr{G}$
    3: Choose t_i as a random number from Z_p for all the attributes in the universal attribute set ($\mathbb{U}$).
    4: $MPK = \mathfrak{g}^{\alpha}$ ▷ Master public key
    5: $PK = (\mathfrak{g}, \delta, \Psi, h_1, v, t_i : \forall i \in \mathbb{U})$ ▷Public key
    6: Return *MPK, PK*

Join algorithm generates the user identity (*ID*) for the new user whenever she/he is a part of the system. This algorithm also adds the *ID* and permissible access limit for the user in the user list ($\mathbb{UL}$). Let *aL* be the user's data access limit. $\mathbb{TA}$ assigns *aL* value as either -1 or "$\aleph$," where -1 represents that the user can access the data unlimited times and "$\aleph$" represents that the user can access the data only "$\aleph$" times. The details of the join algorithm is given in Algorithm 2. After execution of this algorithm, $\mathbb{TA}$ stores $\mathbb{UL}$ into the cloud, and issues *ID* to the new user.

Algorithm 2 Join

    Input: $\mathbb{UL}$
    Output: *ID*, $\mathbb{UL}$
    1: Choose *ID* as a random number from Z_p
    2: Let $aL = -1$ or $\aleph$
    3: Add *ID*, *aL* into the $\mathbb{UL}$
    4: Return *ID*, $\mathbb{UL}$

4.4.2 Key generation

The key generation phase is used to create the *SK* and *DK* using SignKeyGen and DecKeyGen algorithms, respectively. Let γ and $\bar{\gamma}$ be the random numbers chosen from Z_p. SignKeyGen algorithm is described in Algorithm 3, and the DecKeyGen algorithm is given in Algorithm 4.

Algorithm 3 SignKeyGen

    Input: *MPK, PK,* ω_s
    Output: *SK*
    1: Compute $SK_1 = \mathfrak{g}^{\alpha} \cdot \delta^{\gamma}$ ▷ Signing key parameters SK_1, SK_2, SK_j
generation
    2: Compute $SK_2 = \mathfrak{g}^{\gamma}$
    3: Compute $SK_j = \mathfrak{t}_i^{\gamma}, \forall i \in \omega_s$
    4: Return $SK = (SK_1, SK_2, SK_i : \forall i \in \omega_s, \omega_s)$ ▷Signing key

---

Algorithm 4 DecKeyGen

    Input: *MPK, PK,* ω_d
    Output: *DK*
    1: Compute $DK_1 = \mathfrak{g}^{\alpha} \cdot \delta^{\tilde{\gamma}}$ ▷ Decryption key parameters DK_1, DK_2, DK_j
generation
    2: Compute $DK_2 = \mathfrak{g}^{\tilde{\gamma}}$
    3: Compute $DK_j = \mathfrak{t}_i^{\tilde{\gamma}}, \forall i \in \omega_d$
    4: Return $DK = (DK_1, DK_2, DK_i : \forall i \in \omega_d, \omega_d)$ ▷ Decryption key

---

4.4.3 *Signcrypt*

First, the data owner defines the signing policy $(\tau_s = (\mathfrak{m}_s, \rho_s))$ and encryption policy $(\tau_e = (\mathfrak{m}_e, \rho_e))$. Here, $\mathfrak{m}_s$ represents the $r_s \times c_s$ matrix and the corresponding row function is ρ_s; $\mathfrak{m}_e$ represents the $r_e \times c_e$ matrix and the corresponding row function is ρ_e. Let $\mathfrak{m}_s^i$ be the *i*th row of $\mathfrak{m}_s$ and $\mathfrak{m}_e^i$ be the *i*th row of $\mathfrak{m}_e$. The $\mathfrak{DD}$ selects the signing policy such that $\tau_s(\omega_s) = 1$ and it should preserve the $\mathfrak{DD}$ privacy. Let *tt* be the present time.

Signcryption algorithm is used to perform encryption, and then to sign the encrypted data. This process is explained in the Algorithm 5. At the end of signcryption, the ciphertext (signcrypted data) is uploaded into the cloud. The ciphertext consists of a data encryption component, components that are relevant to the attributes in the encryption policy, and signature components. The encryption and attribute-relevant components provide privacy and access control (data confidentiality), and signature components provide data authenticity.

Algorithm 5 Signcryption

    Input: *M, PK, SK,* τ_s, τ_e
    Output: $\mathscr{C}$
    1: Pick a random vector $\vartheta = (s, \vartheta_2, \vartheta_3, \ldots, \vartheta_{r_e})$ from Z_p

2: Compute $\overline{\lambda}_i = \mathfrak{m}_e^i \cdot \vartheta$; where $i \in [r_e]$

3: Compute $\mathscr{C}_1 = \mathfrak{g}^s$

4: Compute $\mathscr{C}_2 = M \cdot v^s = M \cdot (\mathfrak{e}(\mathfrak{g}, \mathfrak{g})^\alpha)^S = M \cdot \mathfrak{e}(\mathfrak{g}, \mathfrak{g})^{\alpha S}$ ▷ Data encryption

5: Compute $\mathscr{C}_i = \delta^{\overline{\lambda}_i} . t_{\rho e(i)}^S : \forall i \in [r_e]$ ▷ Policy-attribute-related parameters generation

6: Pick a random number β from Z_p

7: Compute a vector $\bar{a} = (a_1, a_2, \ldots, a_{r_s})$ from Z_p such that $\bar{a} \cdot \mathfrak{m}_s = \bar{1}$, that is, $\sum_{i \in r_s} a_i \cdot \mathfrak{m}_s^i = \bar{1}$, and $a_i = 0 \; \forall i : \rho_s(i) \notin \omega_s$

8: Pick a random vector $\bar{b} = (b_1, b_2, \ldots, b_{r_s})$ from Z_p such that $\sum_{i \in r_s} b_i$. $\mathfrak{m}_s^i = \bar{0}$

9: Compute $\sigma_1 = \mathfrak{g}^\beta$ ▷ Signing parameters $\sigma_1, \sigma_2, \sigma_i$ generation

10: Compute $\sigma_i = \mathfrak{g}^{bi} \cdot (SK_2)^{a_i} = \mathfrak{g}^{b_i} \cdot (\mathfrak{g}^\gamma)^{a_i} : \mathfrak{g}^{b_i} \cdot \mathfrak{g}^{\gamma . a_i} : \forall i \in [r_s]$

11: Compute $\theta = h_1(tt, \tau_s, \tau_e, \mathscr{C}_1, \mathscr{C}_2, \mathscr{C}_i, \sigma_1, \sigma_i)$

12: Compute $\sigma_2 = (\sigma_2 = (SK_1) \left(\prod_{i \in [r_s]} SK_{\rho_s(i)}^{a_i} \cdot t_{\rho_s(i)}^{b_i} \right) \cdot (\Psi^{\beta . \theta}) = (\mathfrak{g}^\alpha \cdot \delta^\gamma)$ $\left(\prod_{i \in [r_s]} SK_{\rho_s(i)}^{a_i} \cdot t_{\rho_s(i)}^{b_i} \right) \cdot (\Psi^{\beta . \theta})$

13: Return $\mathscr{C} = (\tau_s, \tau_e, tt, \mathscr{C}_1, \mathscr{C}_2, \mathscr{C}_i, \sigma_1, \sigma_2, \sigma_i)$ ▷ Ciphertext

---

4.4.4 Designcrypt

The designcrypt phase is used to get the exact plain text from the ciphertext. It consists of two algorithms, such as Designcryption_Out and Designcryption algorithms. First, the data user requests the ciphertext from the cloud with the *ID*. In turn, $\mathbb{CS}$ verifies the data access limit (*aL*) of the user in the user list $\mathbb{UL}$. If the data access limit (*aL*) is either "−1" or ">0," then it provides the ciphertext to the user and subtracts the access limit one ($\aleph = \aleph - 1$) if ">0" and updates the same in the $\mathbb{UL}$. If the data access limit is "0," then it does not provide the ciphertext to the user because the user access limit is exceeded.

After receiving the ciphertext, the data user verifies the ciphertext signature to ensure the authenticity of the data with the help of $\mathbb{TPA}$. The Designcryption_Out algorithm is executed by $\mathbb{TPA}$ to verify the signature of the ciphertext, which is a part of the designcryption process. The outsourced signature verification process does not require a *DK* because our scheme signature has the publicly verifiable property. Let tt' be the current time and let t_l be the time limit for decryption. If Designcryption_Out algorithm returns one, then verification is successful. Otherwise, verification is failed. If Designcryption_Out algorithm returns $\perp$, then the decryption time limit is over. The detailed steps are explained in Algorithm 6.

Algorithm 6 Designcryption_Out

Input: *PK*, $\mathscr{C}$

Output: *flag* or $\perp$

1: **if** $|tt' - tt| \le t_l$ **then**

2: Compute $\theta = h_1(tt, \tau_s, \tau_e, \mathscr{C}_1, \mathscr{C}_2, \mathscr{C}_i, \sigma_1, \sigma_i)$

3: Compute $\Delta_i = (1, r_2, r_3, \ldots, r_{n_s}) \cdot \mathbf{m}_s^i, \forall i \in [r_s]$, where $r_2, r_3, \ldots, r_{n_s} \rightarrow Z_p$

4: Compute $vs = \dfrac{e(\sigma_2, \mathfrak{g})}{\prod_{i \in [r_s]} e\left(\delta^{\Delta_i} \cdot t_{\rho_s(i)}, \sigma_i\right) \cdot e\left(\sigma_1, \Psi^\theta\right)} = e(\mathfrak{g}, \mathfrak{g})^\alpha$ ▷ Signature computation

5: **if** $v = vs$ **then**   ▷Signature verification

6:    Return *flag* $= 1$

7: **else**

8:    Return *flag* $= 0$

9: **end if**

10: **else**

11:    Return $\perp$

12: **end if**

After signature verification by the $\mathbb{TPA}$ using Designcryption_Out algorithm, the user executes the designcryption algorithm to decrypt the ciphertext. First, this algorithm verifies whether signature verification is successful or not. If yes, then it decrypts the ciphertext and returns the message. Otherwise, it returns $\perp$. The user can get the exact plain text only if the user attribute set satisfies the encryption policy. Algorithm 7 explains the decryption algorithm in detail.

Algorithm 7 Designcryption

Input: *PK, flag, $\mathscr{C}$, DK*

Output: *M* or $\perp$

1: *flag* $= 1$ **then**

2: Compute a vector $\bar{a}' = \left(a'_1, a'_2, \ldots, a'_{r_e}\right) \in Z_p$ such that $\bar{a}' \cdot \mathbf{m}_e = \bar{1}$, that is, $\sum_{i \in r_e} a'_i \cdot \mathbf{m}_e^i = \bar{1}$, and $\forall i, a'_i = 0$ when $\rho_e(i) \notin \omega_d$.

3: Compute $A = e(\mathfrak{g}, \mathfrak{g})^{a.s}$

4: $M = \mathscr{C}_2/A = M.e(\mathfrak{g}, \mathfrak{g})^{a.s}/e(\mathfrak{g}, \mathfrak{g})^{a.s}$ ▷ Decryption

5: Return M

6: **else**

7: Return $\perp$

8: **end if**

4.4.4.1 Correctness

The correctness of computing *vs* in Algorithm 6 of step 4 is given as follows:

$$
\begin{aligned}
\sum_{i \in [r_s]} (\gamma \cdot a_i + b_i) \cdot \Delta_i &= \sum_{i \in [r_s]} (\gamma \cdot a_i + b_i) \cdot \left((1, r_2, r_3, \ldots, r_{n_s}) \cdot \mathbf{m}_s^i\right) \\
&= (\gamma, \gamma r_2, \gamma r_3, \ldots, \gamma r_{n_s}) \cdot \sum_{i \in r_s} a_i \cdot \mathbf{m}_s^i + (1, r_2, r_3, \ldots, r_{n_s}) \cdot \sum_{i \in r_s} b_i \cdot \mathbf{m}_s^i \\
&= (\gamma, \gamma r_2, \gamma r_3, \ldots, \gamma r_{n_s}) \cdot (1, 0, 0, \ldots, 0) + (1, r_2, r_3, \ldots, r_{n_s}) \cdot (0, 0, 0, \ldots, 0) \\
&= \gamma.
\end{aligned}
$$

$$vs \ = \ \frac{\mathfrak{e}(\sigma_2, \mathfrak{g})}{\prod_{i\in[r_s]}\mathfrak{e}\big(\delta^{\Delta_i}\cdot t_{\rho_s(i)}, \sigma_i\big)\cdot \mathfrak{e}\big(\sigma_1, \Psi^\theta\big)}$$

$$= \ \frac{\mathfrak{e}\left(\big(\mathfrak{g}^\alpha\cdot\delta^\gamma\big)\cdot\left(\prod_{i\in[r_s]}t_{\rho_s(i)}^{\gamma.a_i}\cdot t_{\rho_s(i)}^{b_i}\right)\cdot\big(\Psi^{\beta.\theta}\big), \mathfrak{g}\right)}{\prod_{i\in[r_s]}\mathfrak{e}\big(\delta^{\Delta_i}\cdot t_{\rho_s(i)}, \mathfrak{g}^{b_i}\cdot\mathfrak{g}^{\gamma.a_i}\big)\cdot\mathfrak{e}\big(\mathfrak{g}^\beta, \Psi^\theta\big)}$$

$$= \ \frac{\mathfrak{e}(\mathfrak{g}, \mathfrak{g})^\alpha\cdot\mathfrak{e}(\mathfrak{g}, \delta)^\gamma\cdot\mathfrak{e}\left(\mathfrak{g}, \prod_{i\in[r_s]}t_{\rho_s(i)}^{\gamma.a_i+b_i}\right)\cdot\mathfrak{e}(\mathfrak{g}, \Psi)^{\beta.\theta}}{\prod_{i\in[r_s]}\mathfrak{e}\big(\delta^{\Delta_i}\cdot t_{\rho_s(i)}, \mathfrak{g}^{\gamma.a_i+b_i}\big)\cdot\mathfrak{e}(\mathfrak{g}, \Psi)^{\beta.\theta}}$$

$$= \ \frac{\mathfrak{e}(\mathfrak{g}, \mathfrak{g})^\alpha\cdot\mathfrak{e}(\mathfrak{g}, \delta)^\gamma\cdot\mathfrak{e}\left(\mathfrak{g}, \prod_{i\in[r_s]}t_{\rho_s(i)}^{\gamma.a_i+b_i}\right)\cdot\mathfrak{e}(\mathfrak{g}, \Psi)^{\beta.\theta}}{\mathfrak{e}(\delta, \mathfrak{g})^{\sum_{i\in[r_s]}(\gamma.a_i+b_i)\cdot\Delta_i}\cdot\mathfrak{e}\left(\prod_{i\in[r_s]}t_{\rho_s(i)}^{\gamma.a_i+b_i}, \mathfrak{g}\right)\cdot\mathfrak{e}(\mathfrak{g}, \Psi)^{\beta.\theta}}$$

$$= \ \frac{\mathfrak{e}(\mathfrak{g}, \mathfrak{g})^\alpha\cdot\mathfrak{e}(\mathfrak{g}, \delta)^\gamma\cdot\mathfrak{e}\left(\mathfrak{g}, \prod_{i\in[r_s]}t_{\rho_s(i)}^{\gamma.a_i+b_i}\right).\mathfrak{e}(\mathfrak{g}, \Psi)^{\beta.\theta}}{\mathfrak{e}(\delta, \mathfrak{g})^\gamma\cdot\mathfrak{e}\left(\prod_{i\in[r_s]}t_{\rho_s(i)}^{\gamma.a_i+b_i}, \mathfrak{g}\right)\cdot\mathfrak{e}(\mathfrak{g}, \Psi)^{\beta.\theta}}$$

$$= \ \mathfrak{e}(\mathfrak{g}, \mathfrak{g})^\alpha$$

The correctness of computing A value in Algorithm 7 of step 3 is given next:

$$A \ = \ \frac{\mathfrak{e}\left(DK_1\cdot\prod_{i\in[r_e]}DK_{\rho_e(i)}^{a_i'}, \mathscr{C}_1\right)}{\mathfrak{e}\left(DK_2, \prod_{i\in[r_e]}\mathscr{C}_i^{a_i'}\right)}$$

$$= \ \frac{\mathfrak{e}\left(\mathfrak{g}^\alpha\cdot\delta^{\bar\gamma}\cdot\prod_{i\in[r_e]}t_{\rho_e(i)}^{\bar\gamma\cdot a_i'}, \mathfrak{g}^s\right)}{\mathfrak{e}\left(\mathfrak{g}^{\bar\gamma}, \prod_{i\in[r_e]}\delta^{\bar\lambda_i\cdot a_i'}\cdot t_{\rho_e(i)}^{s.a_i'}\right)}$$

$$= \ \frac{\mathfrak{e}(\mathfrak{g}, \mathfrak{g})^{\alpha.s}\mathfrak{e}(\delta, \mathfrak{g})^{\bar\gamma.s}\mathfrak{e}\left(\prod_{i\in[r_e]}t_{\rho_e(i)}^{a_i'}, \mathfrak{g}\right)^{\bar\gamma.s}}{\mathfrak{e}(\mathfrak{g}, \delta)^{\bar\gamma\cdot\sum_{i\in[r_e]}a_i'\cdot\bar\lambda_i}\mathfrak{e}\left(\mathfrak{g}, \prod_{i\in[r_e]}t_{\rho_e(i)}^{a_i'}\right)^{\bar\gamma.s}}$$

$$= \ \frac{\mathfrak{e}(\mathfrak{g}, \mathfrak{g})^{\alpha.s}\mathfrak{e}(\delta, \mathfrak{g})^{\bar\gamma.s}\mathfrak{e}\left(\prod_{i\in[r_e]}t_{\rho_e(i)}^{a_i'}, \mathfrak{g}\right)^{\bar\gamma.s}}{\mathfrak{e}(\mathfrak{g}, \delta)^{\bar\gamma.s}\mathfrak{e}\left(\mathfrak{g}, \prod_{i\in[r_e]}t_{\rho_e(i)}^{a_i'}\right)^{\bar\gamma.s}}$$

$$= \ \mathfrak{e}(\mathfrak{g}, \mathfrak{g})^{\alpha.s}$$

4.5 Security analysis

Here, we prove that our ECP-ABSC scheme is secure by proving data confidentiality, signcryptor privacy, and unforgeability, which are defined in Section 4.3.3.

Theorem 4.1 Data confidentiality. No PPT adversary $(\mathscr{A})$ breaches the IND-CPA security of our ECP-ABSC scheme with the non-negligible advantage if the DBDH assumption holds.

Proof: In this proof, we reduce the CPA security of the ECP-ABSC scheme to the DBDH assumption. The security game defined in Section 4.2.1.1 is used to prove that the ECP-ABSC scheme is secure against IND-CPA. This theorem is proved by proof by contradiction method. We can construct a simulator ($\mathbb{S}$) that breaks the DBDH assumption with the advantage of $\varepsilon/2$ if PPT adversary ($\mathscr{A}$) breaks the IND-CPA security of ECP-ABSC scheme with the advantage ε which is against Definition 4.8. The contradictory assumption is proved as follows:

The challenger ζ gives the DBDH tuple $(\mathfrak{g}, \mathfrak{g}^x, \mathfrak{g}^y, \mathfrak{g}^z, \mathbb{Z})$ to $\mathbb{S}$, where x, y, z $\rightarrow^R \mathbb{Z}_p$, $\mathfrak{g}$ is a generator of $\mathscr{G}$, and $\mathbb{Z} = \mathfrak{e}(\mathfrak{g}, \mathfrak{g})^R$ if $\kappa = 1$, $\mathbb{Z} = \mathfrak{e}(\mathfrak{g}, \mathfrak{g})^{xyz}$ if $\kappa = 0$; κ is a binary coin that has the value either zero or one, $R \rightarrow^R \mathscr{G}_t$. Now the challenger for the adversary is $\mathbb{S}$. The simulator for adversary to decide whether $\mathbb{Z} = \mathfrak{e}(\mathfrak{g}, \mathfrak{g})^{xyz}$ or $\mathbb{Z} = \mathfrak{e}(\mathfrak{g}, \mathfrak{g})^R$. The following steps describe the simulation.

Init phase: $\mathscr{A}$ selects and sends the defy encryption policy (τ_e^*) to $\mathbb{S}$ and also requests PK from $\mathbb{S}$.

Setup phase: $\mathbb{S}$ generates MPK and PK using the SystemSetup algorithm. Then, it sends the same to $\mathscr{A}$. The generation of MPK and PK are as follows:

Let $\alpha = xy + \widehat{a}$ where $\widehat{a} \xleftarrow{R} \mathbb{Z}_p$

Compute $v = \mathfrak{e}(\mathfrak{g}, \mathfrak{g})^\alpha = \mathfrak{e}(\mathfrak{g}, \mathfrak{g})^{xy+\widehat{a}} = \mathfrak{e}(\mathfrak{g}, \mathfrak{g})^{xy} + \mathfrak{e}(\mathfrak{g}, \mathfrak{g})^{\widehat{a}}$

Pick $\delta, \Psi \rightarrow^R \mathscr{G}$

Pick $t_i \rightarrow^R \mathbb{Z}_p \forall i \in \mathbb{U}$

$MPK^* = \mathfrak{g}^\alpha = \mathfrak{g}^{xy+\widehat{a}}$

$PK^* = (\mathfrak{g}, \Psi, \delta, h_1, v, t_i : \forall i \in \mathbb{U}).$

Query phase I: $\mathscr{A}$ sends the signing attribute set $\omega_s^* = \{x_i | x_i \in \mathbb{U}\}$ and decryption (user) attribute set $\omega_d^* = \{x_i | x_i \notin \mathbb{U}\}$; $x_i \in \tau_e^*$ to $\mathbb{S}$. Then it requests the signing key SK* and decryption key DK* from $\mathbb{S}$. $\mathbb{S}$ generates the SK* and DK* as follows using SignKeyGen and DecKeyGen algorithms.

Signing key $SK^* = (SK_1, SK_2, SK_i : \forall i \in \omega_s^*, \omega_s^*)$ where

$SK_1 = \mathfrak{g}^\alpha . \delta^\gamma = \mathfrak{g}^{xy+\widehat{a}} . \delta^\gamma, \gamma \xleftarrow{R} \mathbb{Z}_p$

$SK_2 = \mathfrak{g}^\gamma$

$SK_i = \mathfrak{t}_i^\gamma, \forall i \in \omega_s^*.$

Decryption key $DK^* = (DK_1, DK_2, DK_i : \forall i \in \omega_d^*, \omega_d^*)$ where

$DK_1 = \mathfrak{g}^\alpha . \delta^{\widehat{\gamma}} = \mathfrak{g}^{xy+\widehat{a}} . \delta^{\widehat{\gamma}}, \widehat{\gamma} \xleftarrow{R} \mathbb{Z}_p$

$DK_2 = \mathfrak{g}^{\widehat{\gamma}}$

$DK_i = \mathfrak{t}_i^{\widehat{\gamma}}, \forall i \in \omega_d^*.$

Challenge phase: $\mathscr{A}$ outputs two messages of the same size M_0 and M_1 and requests the ciphertext. $\mathbb{S}$ tosses the binary coin and chooses the μ value; $\mu \in \{0,1\}$. Based on the μ value, $\mathbb{S}$ selects the message M_μ and signcrypts the message using signcryption algorithm. Pick $z \xrightarrow{R} Z_p$. Pick $\bar{a} = (a_1, a_2, \ldots, a_{r_s^*})$ from Z_p such that $\bar{a} \cdot \mathrm{m}_s = \bar{1}$, that is, $\sum_{i \in r_s} a_i \cdot \mathrm{m}_s^i = \bar{1}$. Pick $\bar{b} = (b_1, b_2, \ldots, b_{r_s^*})$ from Z_p such that $\sum_{i \in r_s} b_i \cdot \mathrm{m}_s^i = \bar{0}$.

$$\mathscr{C}_1 = \mathfrak{g}^z$$

$$\mathscr{C}_2 = M \cdot v^z = M \cdot \mathfrak{e}(\mathfrak{g}, \mathfrak{g})^{a \cdot z} = M \cdot \mathfrak{e}(\mathfrak{g}, \mathfrak{g})^{(xy + \widehat{a}) \cdot z} = M \cdot \mathfrak{e}(\mathfrak{g}, \mathfrak{g})^{xyz} \cdot \mathfrak{e}(\mathfrak{g}, \mathfrak{g})^{\widehat{a} \cdot z}$$

$$\mathscr{C}_i = \delta^{\overline{\lambda}_i} \cdot t_{\rho_e(i)}^{\vec{z}} : \forall i \in [r_e^*], \vartheta = (z, \vartheta_2, \vartheta_3, \ldots, \vartheta_{r_e^*}) \xrightarrow{R} Z_p, \ \overline{\lambda}_i = \mathrm{m}_e^i \cdot \vartheta \ \forall i \in [r_e^*].$$

$$\sigma_1 = \mathfrak{g}^{\beta^1}, \beta^1 \xrightarrow{R} Z_p$$

$$\sigma_i = \mathfrak{g}^{b_i} \cdot (SK_2)^{a_i} = \mathfrak{g}^{b_i} \cdot \mathfrak{g}^{\gamma \cdot a_i} : \forall i \in [r_s^*]$$

$$\theta^1 = h_1 \left(tt, \tau_s^*, \tau_e^*, \mathscr{C}_1, \mathscr{C}_2, \mathscr{C}_i, \sigma_1, \sigma_i \right).$$

$$\sigma_2 = (SK_1) \left(\prod_{i \in [r_s^*]} SK_{\rho_s(i)}^{a_i} \cdot t_{\rho_s(i)}^{b_i} \right) \cdot \left(\Psi^{\beta^1 \cdot \theta^1} \right)$$

$$\mathscr{C}_\mu^* = \left(\tau_s^*, \tau_e^*, tt, \mathscr{C}_1, \mathscr{C}_2, \mathscr{C}_i, \sigma_1, \sigma_2, \sigma_i \right)$$

After the generation of signcrypted data (ciphertext), the $\mathbb{S}$ sends the same to the $\mathscr{A}$.

Query phase II: $\mathscr{A}$ may be repeating the query as similar as in query phase I with the same condition that $\omega_d^* = \{x_i | x_i \in \mathbb{U}\}; x_i \in \tau_e^*$ to $\mathbb{S}$. $\mathbb{S}$ serves $\mathscr{A}$ as similar in query phase I.

Guess: $\mathscr{A}$ submits the guess μ' for the received ciphertext $\mathscr{C}_\mu^*$.

$$\mathbb{S} \ outputs \begin{cases} \kappa' = 0, \mathbb{Z} = \mathfrak{e}(\mathfrak{g}, \mathfrak{g})^{xyz} & if \ \mu = \mu' \\ \kappa' = 1, \mathbb{Z} = \mathfrak{e}(\mathfrak{g}, \mathfrak{g})^R & if \ \mu \neq \mu' \end{cases}$$

$\mathbb{S}$ provides ideal simulation when $\kappa' = 0$ and it provides exact ciphertext to the $\mathscr{A}$ that is $\mathbb{Z} = \mathfrak{e}(\mathfrak{g}, \mathfrak{g})^{xyz}$. $\mathbb{S}$ does not act as an ideal simulator when $\kappa' = 1$ and it provides random message to the $\mathscr{A}$ that is $\mathbb{Z} = \mathfrak{e}(\mathfrak{g}, \mathfrak{g})^R$. Therefore, the advantage of $\mathbb{A}$ to win this game is

$$\begin{cases} \Pr[\mu = \mu' | \kappa = 0] = \dfrac{1}{2} + \varepsilon & if \ \mu = \mu' \\ \Pr[\mu \neq \mu' | \kappa = 1] = \dfrac{1}{2} & if \ \mu \neq \mu' \end{cases}$$

The advantage of $\mathbb{S}$ is

$$\begin{cases} \Pr[\kappa = \kappa' | \kappa = 0] = \dfrac{1}{2} + \varepsilon & if \ \kappa' = 0 \\ \Pr[\kappa = \kappa' | \kappa = 1] = \dfrac{1}{2} & if \ \kappa' = 1 \end{cases}$$

The overall advantage of $\mathbb{S}$ *is* $\Pr[\kappa = \kappa'] - \frac{1}{2} = \frac{1}{2}\Pr[\kappa = \kappa'|\kappa = 0] + \frac{1}{2}$ $\Pr[\kappa = \kappa'|\kappa = 1] - \frac{1}{2} = \frac{1}{2}\left(\frac{1}{2} + \varepsilon\right) + \frac{1}{2}\left(\frac{1}{2}\right) - \frac{1}{2} = \frac{\varepsilon}{2}.$

This theorem proved the contradictory assumption against Definition 4.3 so that no adversary can have a non-negligible advantage in this game. By Definition 4.8, we conclude that the ECP-ABSC scheme is secure.

Theorem 4.2 Signcryptor privacy. Our ECP-ABSC scheme preserves the signcryptor privacy.

Proof: We have to prove that we can construct the same ciphertext with the use of two different SKs with selecting proper random values. If so, the ciphertext does not reveal any information about signing attributes. Then, the advantage of the adversary to win this game is the probability of just making a random guess about the ciphertext. The proof uses the security game defined in Section 4.2.1.2.

Setup phase: The challenger (ζ) *runs the SystemSetup algorithms to generate the MPK, PK, and sends the same to the adversary* $(\mathscr{A})$.

Query phase: $\mathscr{A}$ *sends a message M, two signing attribute sets* ω_s^1, ω_s^2, *and signing policy* (τ_s) *such that* $\tau_s(\omega_s^1) = \tau_s(\omega_s^2) = 1$, *encryption policy* (τ_e) *to* ζ *and requests the ciphertext from* ζ.

Challenge phase: ζ *first generates signing key* SK^1 *using* ω_s^1 *and signing key* SK^2 *using* ω_s^2. ζ *uses the SignKeyGen algorithm to generate the SK.*

Let $SK^1 = \left(SK_1^1, SK_2^1, SK_i^1 : \forall i \in \omega_s^1, \omega_s^1\right)$
where

$$SK_1^1 = \mathfrak{g}^\alpha . \delta^\gamma$$

$$SK_2^1 = \mathfrak{g}^\gamma$$

$$SK_i^1 = \mathfrak{t}_i^\gamma . \forall i \in \omega_s^1.$$

Let $SK^2 = \left(SK_1^2, SK_2^2, SK_i^2 : \forall i \in \omega_s^2, \omega_s^2\right)$ *where*

$$SK_1^2 = \mathfrak{g}^\alpha \cdot \delta^\gamma$$

$$SK_2^2 = \mathfrak{g}^\gamma$$

$$SK_i^2 = \mathfrak{t}_i^\gamma, \forall i \in \omega_s^2.$$

After that, ζ *randomly chooses* SK^μ, *where* $\mu \in \{1, 2\}$, *and produces the ciphertext* $\mathscr{C}^\mu$. *Then,* ζ *sends the* $\mathscr{C}^\mu$ *to* $\mathscr{A}$.

To prove $\mathscr{C}^\mu$ *does not reveal any information about the signcryptor, we have to show that* $\mathscr{C}^1$ *generated using* SK^1 *and* $\mathscr{C}^2$ *generated using* SK^2 *are equal. Let* $\vartheta^1 = (s^1, \vartheta_2, \vartheta_3, \ldots, \vartheta_{r_e})$ *from* Z_p. *Pick* $\bar{a}^1 = \left(a_1^1, a_2^1, \ldots, a_{r_s}^1\right)$ *from* Z_p *such that* $\bar{a}^1$. $\mathfrak{m}_s = \bar{1}$, *that is,* $\sum_{i \in r_s} a_i^1 \cdot \mathfrak{m}_s^i = \bar{1}$. *Pick* $\bar{b}^1 = \left(b_1^1, b_2^1, \ldots, b_{r_s}^1\right)$ *from* Z_p *such that* $\sum_{i \in r_s} b_i^1 \cdot \mathfrak{m}_s^i = \bar{0}$.

Let $\mathscr{C}^1 = \left(\tau_s, \tau_e, tt, \mathscr{C}_1^1, \mathscr{C}_2^1, \mathscr{C}_i^1, \sigma_1^1, \sigma_2^1, \sigma_i^1\right)$, *where*

$\mathscr{C}_1^1 = \mathfrak{g}^{s^1}$, s^1 *from* Z_p

$\mathscr{C}_2^1 = M \cdot v^{s^1} = M \cdot \left(\mathfrak{e}(\mathfrak{g}, \mathfrak{g})^\alpha\right)^{s^1} = M \cdot \mathfrak{e}(\mathfrak{g}, \mathfrak{g})^{\alpha s^1}$

$\mathscr{C}_i^1 = \delta^{\overline{\lambda_i}} \cdot t_{\rho_e(i)}^{s^1} : \forall i \in [re], \overline{\lambda_i^1} = \mathfrak{m}_e^i \cdot \vartheta$; *where* $i \in [r_e]$

$\sigma_1^1 = \mathfrak{g}^{\beta^1}$, β^1 *from* Z_p

$\sigma_i^1 = \mathfrak{g}^{b_i^1} \cdot (SK_2)^{a_i^1} = \mathfrak{g}^{b_i^1} \cdot (\mathfrak{g}^\gamma)^{a_i^1} = \mathfrak{g}^{b_i^1} \cdot \mathfrak{g}^{\gamma \cdot a_i^1} : \forall i \in [r_s]$

$\theta^1 = h_1\left(tt, \tau_s, \tau_e, \mathscr{C}_1^1, \mathscr{C}_2^1, \mathscr{C}_i^1, \sigma_1^1, \sigma_i^1\right)$

$\sigma_2^1 = \left(SK_1^1\right)\left(\prod_{i \in [r_s]} SK_{\rho_s(i)}^{a_i^1} \cdot t_{\rho_s(i)}^{b_i^1}\right) \cdot \left(\Psi^{\beta^1} \cdot \theta^1\right)$

Now the challenger computes $\mathscr{C}^2$. *Consider the challenger sets* $\overline{\lambda_i^1} = \overline{\lambda_i^2}, s^1 = s^2$, *and* $\beta^1 = \beta^2$ *for computing* $\mathscr{C}^2$. *Since* $s^1 = s^2$, $\overline{\lambda_i^1} = \overline{\lambda_i^2}$, *and* $\beta^1 = \beta^2$,

$\mathscr{C}_1^2 = \mathscr{C}_1^1$

$\mathscr{C}_2^2 = \mathscr{C}_2^1$

$\mathscr{C}_i^2 = \mathscr{C}_i^1$

$\sigma_1^2 = \sigma_1^1$

Compute a vector $\bar{a}^2 = \left(a_1^2, a_2^2, \ldots, a_{r_s}^2\right)$ *from* Z_p *such that* $\bar{a}^2 \cdot \mathfrak{m}_s = \overline{1}$, *that is,* $\sum_{i \in r_s} a_i^2 \cdot \mathfrak{m}_s^i = \overline{1}$ *and set* $b_i^2 = \left(a_i^1 - a_i^2\right)\gamma + b_i^1$; $\forall i \in [r_s]$. *Since* $b_i^2 = \left(a_i^1 - a_i^2\right)\gamma + b_i^1, b_i^2 + a_i^2 \gamma = a_i^1 \gamma + b_i^1$, *which implies that*

$\sigma_i^2 = \mathfrak{g}^{b_i^2 + \gamma \cdot a_i^2} = \mathfrak{g}^{b_i^1 + \gamma \cdot a_i^1} = \sigma_i^1 : \forall i \in [r_s]$

Since $\mathscr{C}_1^2 = \mathscr{C}_1^1, \mathscr{C}_2^2 = \mathscr{C}_2^1, \mathscr{C}_i^2 = \mathscr{C}_i^1$, $\sigma_1^2 = \sigma_1^1, \sigma_i^2 = \sigma_i^1$ *implies that* $\theta^2 = h_1\left(tt, \tau_s, \tau_e, \mathscr{C}_1^2, \mathscr{C}_2^2, \mathscr{C}_i^2, \sigma_1^2, \sigma_i^2\right) = h_1\left(tt, \tau_s, \tau_e, \mathscr{C}_1^1, \mathscr{C}_2^1, \mathscr{C}_i^1, \sigma_1^1, \sigma_i^1\right) = \theta^1$. *Therefore,* $\sigma_2^2 = \left(SK_1^2\right)\left(\prod_{i \in [r_s]} SK_{\rho_s(i)}^{a_i^2} \cdot t_{\rho_s(i)}^{b_i^2}\right) \cdot \left(\Psi^{\beta^2 \cdot \theta^2}\right) = \left(SK_1^1\right)\left(\prod_{i \in [r_s]} SK_{\rho_s(i)}^{a_i^1} \cdot t_{\rho_s(i)}^{b_i^1}\right) \cdot \left(\Psi^{\beta^1 \cdot \theta^1}\right) = \sigma_2^1$.

From the previous descriptions, $\mathscr{C}^1 = \mathscr{C}^2$, *which implies that the ciphertext generated using* SK^1 *can be generated using* SK^2 *by properly assuming the random values and vice versa. Hence, the challenge ciphertext* $\mathscr{C}^\mu$ *does not reveal any information about* μ.

Guess: $\mathscr{A}$ *guesses* μ' *for* μ. *As the challenge ciphertext* $\mathscr{C}^\mu$ *does not reveal any information about* μ, *the* $\mathscr{A}$ *only can make a random guess about the challenge ciphertext. So* $\mathscr{A}$ *wins this game if the guess is correct that is* $\mu' = \mu$. *The advantage* of $\mathscr{A}$ to win this game is $\Pr[\mu = \mu'] = 1/2$. *Thus, our ECP-ABSC scheme preserves signcryptor privacy.*

Theorem 4.3 No PPT adversary $(\mathscr{A})$ breaches the security of our ECP-ABSC scheme under EUF-CMA with the non-negligible advantage if the q-CDH assumption holds.

Proof: In this proof, we reduce the EUF-CMA security of the ECP-ABSC scheme to the q-CDH assumption. The security game defined in Section 4.2.1.3 is used to prove that the ECP-ABSC scheme is secure against EUF-CMA. This theorem is proved by proof by contradiction method. We can construct a simulator $(\mathbb{S})$ that breaks the q-CDH problem if PPT adversary $(\mathscr{A})$ breaks the security of ECP-ABSC scheme under EUF-CMA with the advantage ε that is against Definition 4.3. The contradictory assumption is proved as follows:

The challenger ζ gives the q-CDH tuple $(\mathfrak{g}, \mathfrak{g}_1, \mathfrak{g}_2, \ldots, \mathfrak{g}_q, \mathfrak{g}_{q2}, \ldots, \mathfrak{g}_{2q})$, where $\mathfrak{g}_i = \mathfrak{g}^{z^i}, q = (2, 3, \ldots, p - 1)$; p is a large prime number. Now the challenger for the adversary is simulator $\mathbb{S}$. The following steps describe the simulation.

__Init phase:__ $\mathscr{A}$ chooses and sends the signing policy $\tau_s^* = (\mathfrak{m}_s^*, \rho_s^*)$ which will be used for forging the ciphertext. $\mathfrak{m}_s^*$ represents the $r_s^* \times c_s^*$ matrix and the corresponding row function is ρ_s^* and $c_s^* \leq q$. Let $\mathfrak{m}_s^*(i)$ be the ith row of $\mathfrak{m}_s^*$. $\mathscr{A}$ requests the PK from $\mathbb{S}$.

__Setup phase:__ $\mathbb{S}$ generates and submits the PK to $\mathscr{A}$. Let $\delta = \mathfrak{g}_1$. The following are the steps to generate PK using SystemSetup algorithm.

Choose x_i as a random number from Z_p for all the attributes in $\mathbb{U}$.

Let $t_i = \mathfrak{g}^{x_i} \cdot \sum_{j \in c_s^*} \mathfrak{g}_j^{\mathfrak{m}_s^*(i,j)}$, if $i \in r_s^*$, otherwise $t_i = \mathfrak{g}^{x_i}$.

Let $\alpha = \hat{a} + z^{q+1}$ where $\hat{a} \rightarrow^R Z_p$.

Compute $v = \mathfrak{e}(\mathfrak{g}, \mathfrak{g})^{\alpha} = \mathfrak{e}(\mathfrak{g}, \mathfrak{g})^{\widehat{a + z^{q+1}}} = \mathfrak{e}(\mathfrak{g}, \mathfrak{g})\hat{a} \cdot \mathfrak{e}\left(\mathfrak{g}_q, \mathfrak{g}_1\right)$

Pick $\delta, \Psi \rightarrow^R \mathscr{G}$

Pick $t_i \rightarrow^R Z_p \; \forall i \in \mathbb{U}$

$$PK^* = (\mathfrak{g}, \Psi, \delta, h_1, v, t_i : \forall i \in \mathbb{U}).$$

__Query phase:__ $\mathscr{A}$ sends the signing attribute set ω_s^*, and decryption attribute set ω_d^* and requests the signing key SK* and the decryption key DK^* from $\mathbb{S}$. $\mathbb{S}$ serves the same. Pick a random vector $\bar{l} = (l_1, l_2, \ldots, l_{c_s^*})$ from Z_p where $l_1 = -1$ such that $\mathfrak{m}_s^*(i) \cdot (\bar{l}) = 0 \; \forall i \in \rho_s^*(i) \in \omega_s^*$. Pick $\gamma = \gamma' + \sum_{i \in c_s^*} l_i \cdot z^{q-i+1}$. Let $\bar{\gamma} = \bar{\gamma}' - z^q$. The generation of SK* and DK^* are as follows:

$$SK_1 = \mathfrak{g}^{\hat{a}} \cdot \delta^{\gamma'} \cdot \prod_{i=2}^{c_s^*} \mathfrak{g}_{q-i+2}^{l_i}$$

$$SK_2 = \mathfrak{g}^{\gamma'} \cdot \prod_{i \in [c_s^*]} \mathfrak{g}_{q-i+1}^{l_i}$$

$$SK_i = (SK_2)^{x_i}, \forall i \in \omega_s$$

$$DK_1 = \mathfrak{g}^{\widehat{a}} \cdot \delta^{\vec{\gamma}}$$

$$DK_2 = \mathfrak{g}^{\vec{\gamma}} \cdot \mathfrak{g}_q^{-1}$$

$$DK_i = \mathfrak{t}_i^{\vec{\gamma}} \cdot \mathfrak{g}_q^{-x_i}, \quad \forall i \in \omega_d^*.$$

Signing key $SK^* = (SK_1, SK_2, SK_i : \forall i \in \omega_s^*, \omega_s^*)$.

Decryption key $DK^* = (DK_1, DK_2, DK_i : \forall i \in \omega_d^*, \omega_d^*)$.

Then, $\mathscr{A}$ outputs the message M, singing policy (τ_s), and encryption policy (τ_e) and requests the ciphertext. $\mathbb{S}$ selects the signing attributes ω_s such that $\tau_s^*(\omega_s) = 1$ and generates the signing key SK. Later, $\mathbb{S}$ generates and sends the ciphertext $\mathscr{C}^*$. This query may be repeated as much as $\mathscr{A}$ required. The generation of $\mathscr{C}^*$ using Signcryption algorithm is as follows:

Pick $s' \xrightarrow{R} Z_p$ *and set* $s = s' - z$.

$$\mathscr{C}_1 = \mathfrak{g}^{s'} \cdot \mathfrak{g}_1^{-1}$$

$$\mathscr{C}_2 = M \cdot v^{s1} \cdot \mathfrak{e}(\mathfrak{g}, \mathfrak{g}_1)^{-\alpha} \cdot \mathfrak{e}(\mathfrak{g}q, \mathfrak{g}_2)^{-1} = M \cdot \mathfrak{e}(\mathfrak{g}, \mathfrak{g})^{\alpha \cdot s}$$

Pick a random vector $\vartheta = (s' - z, \vartheta_2, \vartheta_3, \ldots, \vartheta_{r_e})$ *from* Z_p.

Then, $\overline{\lambda}_i = \mathfrak{m}_e^i \cdot \vartheta = (s' - z) \cdot \mathfrak{m}_e^{(i,1)} + \sum_{j=2}^{c_e} \vartheta_j \cdot \mathfrak{m}_e^{(i,j)}$.

$$\mathscr{C}_i = \delta^{\left(s' \cdot \mathfrak{m}_e^{(i,1)} + \sum_{j=2}^{c_e} \cdot \vartheta_j \cdot \mathfrak{m}_e^{(i,j)}\right)} \cdot \mathfrak{g}2^{-\mathfrak{m}_e^{(i,1)}} \cdot \mathfrak{t}_{\rho_e(i)}^{s'} \cdot \mathfrak{g}1^{-x_{pe(i)}} \quad \forall i \in [r_e].$$

$$\sigma_1 = \mathfrak{g}^{\beta^1}, \beta^1 \xrightarrow{R} Z_p.$$

Pick $\overline{a} = (a_1, a_2, \ldots, a_{r_s^*})$ *from* Z_p *such that* $\overline{a} \cdot \mathfrak{m}_s = \overline{1}$, *that is,* $\sum_{i \in r_s} a_i \cdot \mathfrak{m}_s^i = \overline{1}$. *Pick* $\overline{b} = (b_1, b_2, \ldots, b_{r_s^*})$ *from* Z_p *such that* $\sum_{i \in r_s} b_i \cdot \mathfrak{m}_s^i = \overline{0}$. *Pick* $z \xrightarrow{R} Z_p$.

$$\sigma_i = \mathfrak{g}^{b_i} \cdot (SK_2)^{a_i} = \mathfrak{g}^{b_i} \cdot \mathfrak{g}^{\gamma \cdot a_i} : \forall i \in [r_s].$$

$$\theta^1 = h_1\left(tt, \tau_s, \tau_e, \mathscr{C}_1, \mathscr{C}_2, \mathscr{C}_i, \sigma_q, \sigma_i\right).$$

$$\sigma_2 = \mathfrak{g}^{\widehat{a}} \cdot \delta^{\gamma} \cdot \left(\prod_{i \in [r_s]} \mathfrak{t}_{\rho_s(i)}^{\gamma \cdot a_i + b_i}\right) \left(\mathfrak{g}w^1 \mathfrak{g}^1\right) \left(\Psi^{\beta^1 \cdot \theta^1}\right).$$

The ciphertext $\mathscr{C}^* = (\tau_s, \tau_e, tt, \mathscr{C}_1, \mathscr{C}_2, \mathscr{C}_i, \sigma_1, \sigma_2, \sigma_i)$. *Now it sends* $\mathscr{C}$ *to* $\mathscr{A}$.

Forge phase: *$\mathscr{A}$ sends the valid forged ciphertext* $\mathscr{C}^f = (\tau_s^*, \tau_e^*, tt, \mathscr{C}_1^*, \mathscr{C}_2^*, \mathscr{C}_i^*, \sigma_1^*, \sigma_2^*, \sigma_i^*)$ *that never queried in the query phase with the tuple* $(M^*, \tau_s^*, \tau_e^*)$, *Designcryption_Out* $(PK, \mathscr{C}^f, \tau_s) = 1$, *and Designcryption* $(PK, flag, \mathscr{C}^f, DK) = M^*$.

As $\mathscr{A}$ forges the ciphertext correctly, we can construct $\mathbb{S}$ that solves the q-CDH problem. The simulation is as follows:

$$\frac{\sigma_2^*}{\mathfrak{g}^{\widehat{\alpha}} \cdot \left(\prod_{i\in[r_s^*]}(SK_i^*)^{x_{\rho_s^*(i)}}\right) \cdot \Psi^{\beta'} \cdot \theta'}$$

$$= \frac{\mathfrak{g}^{\alpha} \cdot \delta^{\gamma} \cdot \left(\prod_{i\in[r_s^*]} t_{\rho_s^*(i)}^{\gamma.a_i+b_i}\right) \cdot \Psi^{\beta'} \cdot \theta'}{\mathfrak{g}^{\widehat{\alpha}} \cdot \left(\prod_{i\in[r_s^*]}(SK_i^*)^{x_{\rho_s^*(i)}}\right) \cdot \Psi^{\beta'} \cdot \theta'}$$

$$= \frac{\mathfrak{g}^{\widehat{\alpha}} + z^{q+1} \cdot \delta^{\gamma} \cdot \left(\prod_{i\in[r_s^*]}\left(\mathfrak{g}^{x_{\rho_s^*(i)}}\prod_{j\in[c_s^*]}\mathfrak{g}_j^{-m_s^*(i,j)}\right)^{\gamma.a_i+b_i}\right) \cdot \Psi^{\beta'} \cdot \theta'}{\mathfrak{g}^{\widehat{\alpha}} \cdot \left(\prod_{i\in[r_s^*]}(SK_i^*)^{x_{\rho_s^*(i)}}\right) \cdot \Psi^{\beta'} \cdot \theta'}$$

$$= \frac{\mathfrak{g}^{\widehat{\alpha}} \cdot \mathfrak{g}^{z^{q+1}} \cdot \delta^{\gamma} \cdot \prod_{i\in[r_s^*]}\left(\mathfrak{g}^{\gamma.a_i+b_i}\right)^{x_{\rho_s^*(i)}}\left(\prod_{i\in[r_s^*]}\prod_{j\in[c_s^*]}\mathfrak{g}^{z^j-m_s^*(i,j)\left(\gamma.a_i^*+b_i^*\right)}\right) \cdot \Psi^{\beta'} \cdot \theta'}{\mathfrak{g}^{\widehat{\alpha}} \cdot \left(\prod_{i\in[r_s^*]}(SK_i^*)^{x_{\rho_s^*(i)}}\right) \cdot \Psi^{\beta'} \cdot \theta'}$$

$$= \frac{\mathfrak{g}^{\widehat{\alpha}} \cdot \mathfrak{g}^{z^{q+1}} \cdot \delta^{\gamma} \cdot \left(\prod_{i\in[r_s^*]}\mathfrak{g}^{\gamma.a_i+b_i}\right)^{x_{\rho_s^*(i)}}(\mathfrak{g}^{-z\gamma}) \cdot \Psi^{\beta'} \cdot \theta'}{\mathfrak{g}^{\widehat{\alpha}} \cdot \left(\prod_{i\in[r_s^*]}(SK_i^*)^{x_{\rho_s^*(i)}}\right) \cdot \Psi^{\beta'} \cdot \theta'}$$

$$= \frac{\mathfrak{g}^{\widehat{\alpha}} \cdot \mathfrak{g}^{z^{q+1}} \cdot \left(\prod_{i\in[r_s^*]}(SK_i^*)^{x_{\rho_s^*(i)}}\right) \cdot \Psi^{\beta'} \cdot \theta'}{\mathfrak{g}^{\widehat{\alpha}} \cdot \left(\prod_{i\in[r_s^*]}(SK_i^*)^{x_{\rho_s^*(i)}}\right) \cdot \Psi^{\beta'} \cdot \theta'}$$

$$= \mathfrak{g}^{z^{q+1}}$$

Thus, $\mathbb{S}$ solves the q-CDH problem. But this contradicts Definition 4.5, so there is no adversary that can have a non-negligible advantage in this game. By Definition 4.9, we conclude that the ciphertext of ECP-ABSC scheme is not forgeable under EUF-CMA.

4.6   Performance evaluation

In performance evaluation, we compare the performance of our ECP-ABSC scheme with other existing schemes theoretically and experimentally. The functionality comparison of our ECP-ABSC scheme and other CP-ABSC schemes [15,17,18,20–23] is given in Table 4.3. As shown in Table 4.3, our ECP-ABSC scheme is the only scheme that supports limited data access options, which is an essential requirement

Table 4.3   Comparison of existing CP-ABSC schemes

Scheme	Signing AS[a]	Encryption AS[a]	Outsourced design-cryption	Publicly verifiable	Limited data access
[17]	Tree	Tree	✗	✗	✗
[15]	MBF[b]	MBF[b]	✗	✗	✗
[18]	Tree	AND-gate	✗	✓	✗
[20]	MBF[b]	MBF[b]	✗	✗	✗
[22]	Tree	Tree	✗	✗	✗
[21]	MBF[b]	MBF[b]	✗	✓	✗
[23]	Tree	Tree	✗	✗	✗
Our	MBF[b]	MBF[b]	✓	✓	✓

[a]Access structure.
[b]Monotone Boolean function.

for commercial applications, and it outsources the inflated computations of design-cryption to reduce the computation overhead of the data user.

Table 4.4 shows the theoretical computation overhead comparison of our ECP-ABSC scheme and other CP-ABSC expressive schemes [15,20,21] in terms of signcryption overhead, designcryption overhead, and outsourced designcryption overhead. Here, we only consider the pairing and exponentiation operations required because other operations such as multiplication, division, and hashing require negligible computation overhead when compared with pairing and exponentiation operations [27]. As shown in Table 4.4, our ECP-ABSC scheme only requires $(4n_{\tau_s} + 2n_{\tau_e} + 4)E$ operations during signcryption which is less than other schemes. Further, our ECP-ABSC scheme only requires $(2n_{\omega_d})E + 2P$ operations during designcryption, which is less than other schemes because we outsourced the inflated pairing computations that required to verify the signature to TPA. Even, when we combine the computation overhead of designcryption and outsourced computation overhead of our scheme, our scheme only required $(n_{\tau_s} + 2n_{\omega_d} + 1)E + (n_{\tau_s} + 4)P$ which is also comparatively less than the other existing schemes. Thus, we proved that our ECP-ABSC scheme is efficient theoretically.

Then, we implemented the pairing and exponentiation operations over an 80-bit elliptic curve group based on symmetric Type 1 pairing (SS512) using the Charm crypto library [28]. The software and hardware configuration of the laptop used for implementation is shown in Figure 4.5. The computation cost of one pairing operation is 0.62 ms, and one exponentiation operation is 0.30 ms. We compare the computation cost required for the signcryption and designcryption processes of our ECP-ABSC scheme with schemes presented in [15,20,21]. Table 4.5 shows the signcryption computation cost that is overhead of the data owner, and Table 4.6 shows the designcryption computation cost that is overhead of the data user.

From Table 4.5, it is observed that our ECP-ABSC scheme requires less signcryption computation cost, which reduces the overhead of data owners in all experimental conditions. It is also observed from Table 4.6 that our ECP-ABSC scheme

Table 4.4 Comparison of computation overhead

Scheme	Signcryption	Designcryption	Outsourced designcryption
[15]	$(5n_{\tau_s} + 2n_{\tau_e} + 8)E$	$(2n_{\tau_s} + n_{\omega_d} + 3)E + (2n_{\tau_s} + 2n_{\omega_d} + 4)P$	—
[20]	$(2n_{\tau_s} + 2n_{\tau_s}c_s + 2n_{\tau_e} + 6)E$	$(2n_{\tau_s}c_s + 2n_{\omega_d} + 1)E + (n_{\tau_s}c_s + 2n_{\omega_d} + 6)P$	—
[21]	$(6n_{\tau_s} + 2n_{\tau_e} + 7)E$	$(2n_{\tau_s}c_s + 2n_{\omega_d} + 2)E + (n_{\tau_s} + 5)P$	—
Our	$(4n_{\tau_s} + 2n_{\tau_e} + 4)E$	$(2n_{\omega_d})E + 2P$	$(n_{\tau_s} + 1)E + (n_{\tau_s} + 2)P$

n_{τ_s}—number of attributes in the signing policy; n_{τ_e}—number of attributes in the encryption policy; E—cost of performing one exponentiation operation; P—cost of performing one pairing operation; n_{ω_d}—number of attributes in the user attribute set; c_s—number of columns in the singing monotone span program matrix.

Intel core i7 @ 2.50 GHz ← *Processor*
16 GB RAM ← *Memory*
Windows 10 ← *Operatingsystem*
Python 3.2 ← *Software*
Charm crypto 4.2 ← *Library*

Figure 4.5   Hardware and software configuration for implementation

Table 4.5   Comparison of data owner computation overhead (Signcryption cost in ms)

Experimental assumptions	[15]	[20]	[21]	Our scheme
$n_{\tau_s} = 10, n_{\tau_e} = 10$	23.4	73.8	26.1	19.2
$n_{\tau_s} = 10, n_{\tau_e} = 20$	29.4	79.8	32.1	25.2
$n_{\tau_s} = 10, n_{\tau_e} = 30$	35.4	85.8	38.1	31.2
$n_{\tau_s} = 20, n_{\tau_e} = 10$	38.4	259.8	44.1	31.2
$n_{\tau_s} = 20, n_{\tau_e} = 20$	44.4	265.8	50.1	37.2
$n_{\tau_s} = 20, n_{\tau_e} = 30$	50.4	271.8	56.1	43.2
$n_{\tau_s} = 30, n_{\tau_e} = 10$	53.4	565.8	62.1	43.2
$n_{\tau_s} = 30, n_{\tau_e} = 20$	59.4	571.8	68.1	49.2
$n_{\tau_s} = 30, n_{\tau_e} = 30$	65.4	577.8	74.1	55.2

n_{τ_s}—number of attributes in the signing policy; n_{τ_e}—number of attributes in the encryption policy.

Table 4.6   Comparison of data user computation overhead (designcryption cost in ms)

Experimental assumptions	[15]	[20]	[21]	Our scheme
$n_{\tau_s} = 10, n_{\omega_d} = 10$	37.18	144.42	21.9	7.24
$n_{\tau_s} = 10, n_{\omega_d} = 20$	52.58	162.82	27.9	13.24
$n_{\tau_s} = 10, n_{\omega_d} = 30$	67.98	181.22	33.9	19.24
$n_{\tau_s} = 20, n_{\omega_d} = 10$	55.58	510.42	34.1	7.24
$n_{\tau_s} = 20, n_{\omega_d} = 20$	70.98	528.82	40.1	13.24
$n_{\tau_s} = 20, n_{\omega_d} = 30$	86.38	547.22	46.1	19.24
$n_{\tau_s} = 30, n_{\omega_d} = 10$	73.98	1,120.42	46.3	7.24
$n_{\tau_s} = 30, n_{\omega_d} = 20$	89.38	1,138.82	52.3	13.24
$n_{\tau_s} = 30, n_{\omega_d} = 30$	104.78	1,157.22	58.3	19.24

n_{τ_s}—number of attributes in the signing policy; n_{ω_d}—number of attributes in the user attribute set.

requires very less designcryption computation cost because we have outsourced the heavy computation to reduce the overhead of data users while making it convenient to access the data using resource-constrained devices.

Furthermore, we tested the computation time required to signcrypt and designcrypt the 10-GB file of ECP-ABSC scheme. The results are compared with the existing [15,20,21] schemes. These comparisons are shown in Figures 4.6 and 4.7. The following are the observations from Figures 4.6 and 4.7: (1) the signcryption cost grows against the number of attributes in the encryption policy and signing policy, and designcryption cost grows against the number of attributes in the signing policy and user attributes; (2) ECP-ABSC scheme requires less signcryption and designcryption computation cost; (3) ECP-ABSC scheme performs much better when more attributes

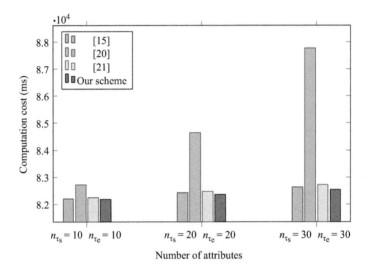

Figure 4.6   Signcryption computation time

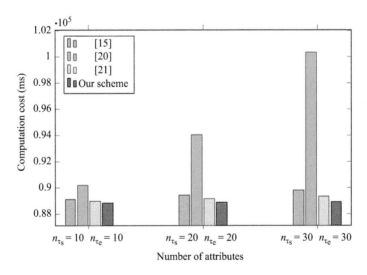

Figure 4.7   Designcryption computation time

involved. Thus, ECP-ABSC scheme is efficient and reduces the computation overhead of data owners and data users.

4.7 Conclusion

In this chapter, we proposed an ECP-ABSC scheme that cuts down the number of exponentiations operations in signcryption to reduce the overhead of data owners. It also outsources the inflated pairing computations of designcryption to reduce the overhead of data users. Also, the ECP-ABSC scheme grants data access in an infinite number of times or the limited number of times, which is essential for commercial applications. Furthermore, our ECP-ABSC attains the required security goals that include data confidentiality, signcryptor privacy, and unforgeability. Our ECP-ABSC scheme achieves the following improvements than the other existing CP-ABSC schemes: (1) more efficient in signcryption, (2) more efficient in designcryption, and (3) flexible access control for commercial applications. These improvements make the ECP-ABSC scheme more appropriate and practical for big data in the cloud environment.

References

[1] Khan N, Yaqoob I, Hashem IAT, *et al.* Big data: survey, technologies, opportunities, and challenges. The Scientific World Journal. 2014;2014. Available from: https://doi.org/10.1155/2014/712826.

[2] Hashem IAT, Yaqoob I, Anuar NB, *et al.* The rise of "big data" on cloud computing: review and open research issues. Information Systems. 2015;47: 98–115. Available from: https://doi.org/10.1016/j.is.2014.07.006.

[3] Gupta B, Agrawal DP, and Yamaguchi S. Handbook of research on modern cryptographic solutions for computer and cyber security. IGI Global, Hershey, PA; 2016. Available from: https://doi.org/10.4018/978-1-5225-0105-3.

[4] Gagné M, Narayan S, and Safavi-Naini R. Threshold attribute-based signcryption. In: International Conference on Security and Cryptography for Networks. Springer; 2010. p. 154–171. Available from: https://doi.org/10.1007/978-3-642-15317-4_11.

[5] Sahai A and Waters B. Fuzzy identity-based encryption. In: Annual International Conference on the Theory and Applications of Cryptographic Techniques. Springer; 2005. p. 457–473. Available from: https://doi.org/10.1007/11426639_27.

[6] Maji HK, Prabhakaran M, and Rosulek M. Attribute-based signatures. In: Cryptographers' Track at the RSA Conference. Springer; 2011. p. 376–392. Available from: https://doi.org/10.1007/978-3-642-19074-2_24.

[7] Goyal V, Pandey O, Sahai A, *et al.* Attribute-based encryption for fine-grained access control of encrypted data. In: Proceedings of the 13th ACM Conference on Computer and Communications Security. ACM; 2006. p. 89–98. Available from: https://doi.org/10.1145/1180405.1180418.

[8] Bethencourt J, Sahai A, and Waters B. Ciphertext-policy attribute-based encryption. In: IEEE Symposium on Security and Privacy, 2007. SP'07. IEEE; 2007. p. 321–334. Available from: https://doi.org/10.1109/SP.2007.11.

[9] Waters B. Ciphertext-policy attribute-based encryption: an expressive, efficient, and provably secure realization. In: International Workshop on Public Key Cryptography. Springer; 2011. p. 53–70. Available from: https://doi.org/10.1007/978-3-642-19379-8_4.

[10] Kumar PP, Kumar PS, and Alphonse P. An efficient ciphertext policy-attribute based encryption for big data access control in cloud computing. In: 2017 Ninth International Conference on Advanced Computing (ICoAC). IEEE; 2017. p. 114–120. Available from: https://doi.org/10.1109/ICoAC.2017.8441507.

[11] Gagné M, Narayan S, and Safavi-Naini R. Short pairing-efficient threshold-attribute-based signature. In: International Conference on Pairing-Based Cryptography. Springer; 2012. p. 295–313. Available from: https://doi.org/10.1007/978-3-642-36334-4_19.

[12] Rao YS and Dutta R. Efficient attribute-based signature and signcryption realizing expressive access structures. International Journal of Information Security. 2016;15(1):81–109. Available from: https://doi.org/10.1007/s10207-015-0289-6.

[13] Herranz J, Laguillaumie F, Libert B, *et al.* Short attribute-based signatures for threshold predicates. In: Cryptographers' Track at the RSA Conference. Springer; 2012. p. 51–67. Available from: https://doi.org/10.1007/978-3-642-27954-6_4.

[14] Rao YS. Signature-policy attribute-based key-insulated signature. IET Information Security. 2016;11(1):23–33. Available from: https://doi.org/10.1049/iet-ifs.2015.0355.

[15] Chen C, Chen J, Lim HW, *et al.* Combined public-key schemes: the case of ABE and ABS. In: International Conference on Provable Security. Springer; 2012. p. 53–69. Available from: https://doi.org/10.1007/978-3-642-33272-2_5.

[16] Wang CJ, Huang JS, Lin WL, *et al.* Security analysis of Gagne et al.'s threshold attribute-based signcryption scheme. In: 2013 5th International Conference on Intelligent Networking and Collaborative Systems. IEEE; 2013. p. 103–108. Available from: https://doi.org/10.1109/INCoS.2013.23.

[17] Wang C and Huang J. Attribute-based signcryption with ciphertext-policy and claim-predicate mechanism. In: 2011 Seventh International Conference on Computational Intelligence and Security. IEEE; 2011. p. 905–909. Available from: https://doi.org/10.1109/CIS.2011.204.

[18] Emura K, Miyaji A, and Rahman MS. Dynamic attribute-based signcryption without random oracles. International Journal of Applied Cryptography. 2012;2 (3):199–211. Available from: https://doi.org/10.1504/IJACT.2012.045589.

[19] Guo Z, Li M, and Fan X. Attribute-based ring signcryption scheme. Security and Communication Networks. 2013;6(6):790–796. Available from: https://doi.org/10.1002/sec.614.

[20] Liu J, Huang X, and Liu JK. Secure sharing of personal health records in cloud computing: ciphertext-policy attribute-based signcryption. Future

Generation Computer Systems. 2015;52:67–76. Available from: https://doi.org/10.1016/j.future.2014.10.014.

[21] Rao YS. A secure and efficient ciphertext-policy attribute-based signcryption for personal health records sharing in cloud computing. Future Generation Computer Systems. 2017;67:133–151. Available from: http://doi.org/10.1016/j.future.2016.07.019.

[22] Hu C, Cheng X, Tian Z, *et al.* An attribute-based signcryption scheme to secure attribute-defined multicast communications. In: International Conference on Security and Privacy in Communication Systems. Springer; 2015. p. 418–437. Available from: https://doi.org/10.1007/978-3-319-28865-9_23.

[23] Hu C, Yu J, Cheng X, *et al.* CP_ABSC: an attribute-based signcryption scheme to secure multicast communications in smart grids. Mathematical Foundations of Computer Science. 2018;1(1):77–100. Available from: http://doi.org/10.3934/mfc.2018005.

[24] Premkamal PK, Pasupuleti SK, and Alphonse P. A new verifiable outsourced ciphertext-policy attribute based encryption for big data privacy and access control in cloud. Journal of Ambient Intelligence and Humanized Computing. 2019;10(7):2693–2707. Available from: https://doi.org/10.1007/s12652-018-0967-0.

[25] Premkamal PK, Pasupuleti SK, and Alphonse P. Efficient revocable CP-ABE for big data access control in cloud computing. International Journal of Security and Networks. 2019;14(3):119–132. Available from: https://doi.org/10.1504/IJSN.2019.101411.

[26] Premkamal PK, Pasupuleti SK, and Alphonse P. Efficient escrow-free CP-ABE with constant size ciphertext and secret key for big data storage in cloud. International Journal of Cloud Applications and Computing (IJCAC). 2020;10(1):28–45. Available from: https://doi.org/10.4018/IJCAC.2020010103.

[27] Li H, Lin X, Yang H, *et al.* EPPDR: an efficient privacy-preserving demand response scheme with adaptive key evolution in smart grid. IEEE Transactions on Parallel and Distributed Systems. 2014;25(8):2053–2064. Available from: https://doi.org/10.1109/TPDS.2013.124.

[28] Akinyele JA, Garman C, Miers I, *et al.* Charm: a framework for rapidly prototyping cryptosystems. Journal of Cryptographic Engineering. 2013;3(2):111–128. Available from: https://doi.org/10.1007/s13389-013-0057-3.

Chapter 5

Privacy-preserving techniques in big data

Remya Krishnan Pacheeri[1] and Arun Raj Kumar Parthiban[1]

Big data is a collection of a massive volume of data from various sources like social networks, the Internet of Things (IoT), and business applications. As multiple parties are involved in these systems, there is an increased chance of privacy breaches in the big data domain. Preservation of privacy plays a crucial role in preventing sensitive information from being visible to others. This chapter gives insights on overview of big data, associated privacy challenges in different phases of the big data life cycle, and focus on various privacy-preserving techniques in big data. This chapter also briefs about the privacy-preserving solutions in resource-constrained devices.

5.1 Introduction

Due to the emergence of the IoT and the use of connected devices, the growth of the data is massively increasing. Data generated by the devices are large and complex and are available in three forms: structured, semi-structured, and unstructured. Structured data are highly organized, easy-to-query, and reliable. An example of structured data would be relational data. Semi-structured data are not well organized, like structured data. It may have some metadata tagging or markers associated with it that make it easier to analyze. Examples of semi-structured data are XML, JSON, etc. Unstructured data are the data that are not organized at all. Examples include word processing documents, videos, photos, etc. In a recent survey, it has been mentioned that 500 million tweets, 3.9 billion emails, and 4 petabytes of Facebook messages are generated per day. It is predicted that the accumulated digital universe of data would be around 44 zettabytes by 2020.

Big data is a term used to describe such a huge collection of data that grow exponentially with time [1]. The properties of big data are characterized by five Vs: volume, velocity, variety, veracity, and value [2]. The volume is related to the size of data. It is the vast amount of data being generated and stored every second from various sources such as human interactions in social media platforms, business

---

[1]Computer Science and Engineering Department, National Institute of Technology Calicut, Kozhikode, India

activities, machines, and networks. Velocity refers to the data generation speed. The speed with which the data are generated and processed to comply with the requirements determines the real potential of the data. Variety defines data diversity. Data come from various sources in varieties of forms, such as documents, emails, social media text messages, video, still images, audio, and graphs. It may be structured or unstructured. Veracity refers to the accuracy of the data. There can be uncertainty of data due to inconsistency, duplication, volatility, etc., removing which improves the accuracy of big data. Value denotes the profitability of big data. The bulk of data having no value is of no use. To extract information, it requires to be converted into something valuable. Figure 5.1 represents the five Vs of big data.

Big data is becoming pervasive and has applications in many fields today. Big data analytics helps companies to interpret a huge amount of data very faster. The sectors benefiting from big data include healthcare, telecommunications, weather forecasting, manufacturing, banking, transportation, media, and entertainment, etc. Some of the challenges confronted while handling of big data are the integration of data from multiple sources, getting relevant content from the big data, ensuring data availability to customers, need of scalable storage, and a sufficient amount of domain knowledge. Big data has the following three major phases in its life cycle [3]:

- data generation and acquisition,
- data storage, and
- data processing.

Data generation and acquisition is the process of generating and gathering data from various sources before storage. It is possible to generate data from domains such as industry, Internet, and science. For example, Facebook alone is creating a 25 TB of new data every day. Data acquisition is made using sensors, log files, network packet capturing devices, etc. Data storage in big data involves massive computation and storage of a large number of data files and objects. Apache Hadoop, NoSQL, PolyBase, etc. are some of the essential tools used to store and analyze big data. And data processing is the process of transmission, preprocessing, and extraction of

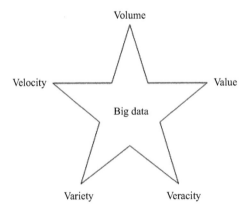

Figure 5.1   Five Vs of big data

useful information from the huge volume of raw data. The big data processing tools include Apache Flink, Apache Storm, etc.

The scalability, immense processing power, and massive storage capacity of cloud computing drove the industries to integrate cloud computing technologies with big data. Analyzing the critical data and reporting on time brought edge computing technologies such as Kubernetes. However, these technologies are boons in terms of customer satisfaction toward the quality of service at the cost of security and privacy issues.

Privacy is the privilege of a person to prevent data about himself becoming available to people other than those they allow to. A significant challenge in big data is to ensure that an individual's personal information is being collected, shared, and utilized correctly. This chapter discusses the privacy challenges and various techniques that exist to guarantee privacy in big data according to the phases of the life cycle of big data.

5.2   Big data privacy in data generation phase

It is the first step in the big data life cycle. Large-scale and highly complex datasets are generated through various sources. The data generation can be active or passive. In the active data generation, the data owner is willing to share the data with a third party, whereas in passive data generation, the data are generated as a result of some online activity by the data owner such as browsing [4]. In such cases, the data owner may not even notice that a third party steals the information. Hence, there is a need for the owner to reduce the chance of privacy breaches in the data generation phase. It is done through either restricting access or falsifying information [4].

5.2.1   Access restriction

If the data owner does not want to disclose the data with a third party as it may reveal some sensitive information, he may refuse to provide such data that are called access restriction [4]. To ensure this, the data owner has to implement access control mechanisms. The data shall be provided by the data owner actively or passively. In an active data collection, the data owner may agree for the data collection by opting for some surveys or registration forms on the website, and he is aware of the data being collected. If the data owner thinks that the data are sensitive and not to be revealed, he can restrict the active data collection by simply removing the permission granted to the data collector. In passive data collection, the data collector records the data from the routine activities of the data owner without his consent. To prevent passive data collection and ensure privacy, the data user makes use of various security tools such as Privacy Badger, and AdBlock, designed for Internet data protection. The three major categories of security tools are as follows.

5.2.1.1   Anti-tracking extensions
When browsing the Internet, the user visits web pages that consist of trackers. These trackers collect information about the user's online activities and then send

them to third-party companies. It is a clear violation of one's privacy. To minimize the existence of these trackers, the user utilizes the anti-tracker extensions [4]. The popular anti-tracking extensions include Do Not Track Me, Disconnect, Ghostery, Privacy Badger, uMatrix, etc.

5.2.1.2   Advertisement and script blockers

This type of extensions is also called Ad-blockers that filter content and block advertisements on a web page. The ads such as pop-ups, banner ads, sticky ads, and auto-playing videos are blocked to allow users to browse the web without distractions. Ad-blockers use filtering rules to block the contents on a web page. The users are allowed to customize these rules and to add exceptions for the web pages that they do not want to block. Smart Pop-up Blocker, AdBlock Plus, NoScript, FlashBlock, etc. are some of the widely used advertisement and script blockers today [4].

5.2.1.3   Encryption tools

Several encryption tools, such as Mailclok and Torchat, are available to enhance privacy protection by keeping sensitive information hidden from malicious users. They encrypt the emails, instant messages, etc. sent between two users to ensure that a third party cannot intercept the communication [4].

Apart from these security tools, the user removes his online activity traces by deleting cookies, emptying cache, etc. that can help to reduce the risk of privacy disclosure.

5.2.2   Data falsification

Another way of protecting privacy in data generation is to falsify the data so that real information is not easily revealed. Data falsification is done using the following methods.

5.2.2.1   Sockpuppets

A sockpuppet is an online identity that is used for misleading purposes. The term "sockpuppet" refers to a puppet created by placing a sock over one's hand. The data generated by an individual user's online activity are taken as data belonging to different individuals with the help of multiple sockpuppets [4]. Hence, the true activities of the user are not quickly revealed. Sockpuppetry is an unethical activity that is sometimes illegal.

5.2.2.2   Fake identity

A fake identity is used to create bogus information about Internet user activities. This fake identifier (ID) is a clone of actual identity but performs online activities that are entirely different from the user's original activities. When a third party collects the data, the true data of the user are hidden under the bogus data generated by the false identity [4].

5.2.2.3   Identity mask

Identity mask is a security tool used to mask one's identity. It hides the personal information of an individual by creating disposable email addresses, secondary phone numbers, and virtual credit cards. When the user performs some online activities such as shopping, he can use these aliases to provide the required pieces of information. In such a way, user privacy is preserved as the websites cannot get real information. An example is MaskMe, which is a browser extension released by Abine, Inc. 2013 [4].

5.3   Big data privacy in data storage phase

The emergence of cloud computing offered ease of storage for a massive volume of data [5]. But, preserving the privacy of such data is a challenging task. If the big data storage system is compromised, it leads to the disclosure of an individual's personal information [6]. It is possible to divide the conventional data protection mechanisms into four categories: file-level data security schemes, database-level data security schemes, media-level security schemes, and application-level encryption schemes [7]. But, these are not directly applicable to the big data analytics platform because of the scalability, availability, and dynamic nature of big data. The big data storage infrastructure should have the ability to be configured dynamically to accommodate diverse applications [3]. Data stored in the cloud must preserve its confidentiality, integrity, and availability [8] that have a direct effect on the user's privacy. The approaches to protect privacy by data storage on the cloud are as follows.

5.3.1   Attribute-based encryption

Attribute-based encryption (ABE) is an encryption technology to ensure the privacy of big data in cloud storage [3]. It is a powerful cryptographic monitoring method that guarantees the data owner's exclusive ownership over big data in public cloud storage. The data are encrypted on the basis of the access policies defined by the data owner. The decryption is only possible for users whose attributes match the access policies of the data owner. The difficulty of this approach lies in the change of access policy. When new organizations outsource their data into the cloud, the data owner may require to change the access frequently [9]. The existing attribute-based access control schemes [10,11] do not allow policy updation because it requires high computational and communication overhead [9] and suggests a method for policy updation where the data owner has to send update requests to the cloud server, and the cloud server updates the policy directly without decrypting the data [3].

Figure 5.2 shows the system model proposed by [9] for policy updation in ABE schemes. The AA represents the authorities responsible for generating the secret-key–public-key pair for each attribute in its domain and the secret key for each user. The server updates the ciphertext from old to new access policies. The owner defines the access policies and uploads them in the server as well as requests the server for policy updations. The user can decrypt the ciphertext, only if his attributes match with the access policy defined in the ciphertext [9].

5.3.2   Identity-based encryption

It is a public-key encryption technique in which the user generates a public key from a known unique ID. A trusted third-party server calculates the corresponding private

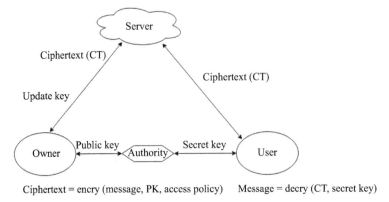

Ciphertext = encry (message, PK, access policy)   Message = decry (CT, secret key)

Figure 5.2   System model for policy updation in ABE schemes [9]

key from the public key. These primitives protect the privacy of data between the sender and the receiver [3]. Identity-based encryption does not require any predistribution of public keys but requires a trusted third party as a private key generator. The scheme does not support the updation of the ciphertext receiver. But there are some approaches proposed for updating the ciphertext recipient such as anonymous identity-based proxy re-encryption [12], which supports one- and multiple times updation of the ciphertext receiver [13].

5.3.3   *Homomorphic encryption*

An encryption scheme is called homomorphic over an operation "*" if it supports the following equation:

$$E(m_1) * (m_2) = E(m_1 * m_2), \forall m_1, m_2 \in M \tag{5.1}$$

where E is the encryption algorithm, and m is the set of all possible messages. Homomorphic encryption is an ideal approach for securing and processing of big data. It provides a solution to solve privacy issues in big data cloud storage. It enables us to perform computations on encrypted data without sharing the secret key required for data decryption. It offers complete privacy, but the computational complexity is very high and challenging to implement with existing hardware [3]. But with sufficient investment in improvisation, homomorphic encryption will be a practical tool for the secure processing of big datasets [14].

5.3.4   *Storage path encryption*

The big data stored on the cloud is classified into public (data accessible to all) and confidential data (restricted from irrelevant accesses). The scheme [15] in which only the storage path is encrypted instead of encrypting the whole big data is called the cryptographic virtual mapping of big data. It ensures fault tolerance by storing the copies for each piece of data on cloud storage. For specific applications, some

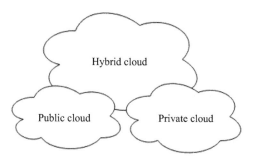

Figure 5.3   Hybrid cloud

parts of the data that are considered confidential can also be encrypted, which improves privacy.

5.3.5   *Usage of hybrid clouds*

Cloud storage can be implemented as three models, public, private, or hybrid. Among these, a hybrid cloud is a cloud computing environment that combines a public and a private cloud by allowing data and applications to be shared between them. Private clouds are secured by themselves, but scalability is limited [3]. The public cloud is highly scalable and easy to access but vulnerable to a privacy breach. Hybrid cloud is a privacy-preserving solution for big data storage in the cloud that has got both the features of the private and public cloud. In the hybrid cloud, the data are separated into confidential and nonconfidential data and are stored in private and public cloud parts, respectively, which ensures privacy protection [3]. Figure 5.3 shows the concept of the hybrid cloud.

Table 5.1 shows merits and demerits of these privacy preserving techniques in big data storage.

5.4   Big data privacy in data processing phase

Big data processing paradigm categorizes systems into batch, stream, parallel, and machine learning processing systems [16]. The two methods of privacy protection in the data processing phase are as follows.

5.4.1   *Protect data from unauthorized disclosure*

Big data storage may contain sensitive information from the data owner. Directly revealing them for processing may violate user privacy. The approach in [17] suggests how to modify data before processing. Mainly anonymization techniques are used to protect data from unauthorized disclosure. The percent of data to be anonymized depends on how much privacy we want to preserve in that data. But, a high level of anonymization may affect the utility of the

Table 5.1   Privacy preserving techniques and its merits and demerits in big data storage context

Technique	Merits	Demerits
Attribute-based encryption (ABE)	• Allows encrypted big data to be kept confidential on an untrusted cloud storage • Partially tolerates compromise attacks • Flexible for big data environment as granular access control is possible [3]	• Fails to achieve de-duplication of encrypted data in big data cloud • High encryption time because of long ciphertext length • Overhead of encryption policy updation in big data environment
Identity-based encryption (IBE)	• Fine-grained access control based on identity for big data storage in cloud • Data privacy is under control of data owners than cloud service providers (CSP) • Provides confidentiality, integrity, and non-repudiation	• Compromise of private key generator (PKG) results in privacy loss of the big data cloud storage • Access permission revocation issues • Time-consuming in big data environment
Homomorphic encryption (HE)	• Ideal for securing big data in remote cloud servers • Libraries can be tailored to address computations of big data analytics • Currently used in big data applications such as secure VOIP and CallForFire [14]	• Insufficient performance for applications using big data analytics • Hardware expansion is required for performing computations in big datasets [14]
Storage path encryption (SPE)	• Improves availability and robustness of big data by storing replicas of data on cloud • Integration of trapdoor function with SPE enhances the big data privacy	• Cost overhead as it requires to maintain several parameters and data structures • Inefficiency in big data environment due to data replication
Hybrid clouds	• Offers both scalability of public cloud and security of private cloud to big data • Reduces communication overhead between private and public cloud • Provides future research targets for analyzing and storing big data	• High initial deployment cost • Compatibility issues of private and public cloud infrastructures in big data environment

data. The balancing of the trade-off between privacy and utility is essential in big data processing. Some privacy-preserving data processing approaches use the greedy algorithm that generates the anonymized table with minimum information loss [3].

5.4.2 Extract significant information without trampling privacy

Another important data processing activity is to extract useful information from big data without a privacy breach. But the traditional data mining techniques cannot be applied to big data as it contains a large volume of dynamic data. Therefore, for mining information from big data along with privacy assurance, these techniques have to be modified. The privacy-preserving data mining techniques widely used for extracting useful information from a large volume of data are classified as follows:

- Privacy preserving clustering:
  The conventional clustering algorithms are not suitable for big data processing. A cloud-computing-based parallel processing was proposed [3], which makes clustering feasible for huge datasets. Privacy preservation in clustering is another major challenge while handling big data. It can be assured by associating the concepts such as probability distribution model, secure multiparty computation, and distributed local clustering, which is efficient for handling decentralized big data.
- Privacy-preserving data classification:
  Classification is the process of determining in which group the new input data belong to. To deal with big data, existing classification algorithms also have to be modified. The use of a quantum-based support vector machine approach [3] for privacy-preserving big data classification reduces the computational complexity and the required training data. Another approach proposed in [18] alters the original big datasets by using random offsets and use the Bayesian formula to reconstruct knowledge from it. But it is suitable only for centralized environment. A random perturbation matrix [19] is another method used to alter the original data, and use a multiattribute joint distribution matrix for reconstruction. Improving the accuracy and privacy of classification algorithms to handle large and complex data is still an open research area.
- Privacy-preserving association rule mining:
  Association rule mining techniques are developed to identify the patterns between the input data. Preserving privacy in association rule mining means preventing sensitive information from being mined from big data. Privacy protection techniques associated with the concepts such as MapReduce, decision trees, and Boolean association rules are used for processing big data with association rule mining.

5.5 Traditional privacy-preserving techniques and its scalability in big data

Privacy in big data has raised severe issues regarding the need for effective techniques for safeguarding privacy. Cryptography alone cannot uphold the privacy requirements of big data. It is because the big data architecture is different from traditional information architectures based on three properties: the velocity, variety, and volume [20].

This section reviews some of the traditional methods used for maintaining privacy in big data. These methods ensure privacy in big data only to a certain extent due to their limitations, and that led to the emergence of new methods.

5.5.1   Data anonymization

Data anonymization, also known as data de-identification [20], is a critical tool in the protection of privacy, which can be adapted to privacy preservation in big data analytics. It helps one to protect privacy in data storage and data processing phases of big data. It is a method to protect private or sensitive data by masking or encrypting personally identifiable information from a database.

In this method, sensitive data segments are obscured in such a manner that maintains data privacy [21]. There are three privacy-preserving methods of de-identification: k-anonymity, L-diversity, and T-closeness. The approaches assume sensitive data to be organized as multiple records with the following four attributes [17]:

- ID—uniquely identifies a record.
- Quasi-identifier (QID)—reidentifies a record by linking it to an external dataset.
- Sensitive attribute—the attribute which a user does not want to disclose.
- Nonsensitive attribute—attributes that can be revealed without compromising privacy.

5.5.1.1 k-Anonymity

A data release is said to have the k-anonymity property if it is not possible to distinguish the information for each person contained in the release, from at least $(k-1)$ individuals whose information also appears in the release [16]. k-Anonymity can be achieved by applying the following operations [3]:

- Generalization
- Suppression
- Permutation
- Perturbation

Generalization is the process of replacing the value of a particular QID attribute with a broader category. In suppression, the attribute values not supposed to be disclosed are replaced with some special characters such as an "*" that ensures privacy. In permutation, the records with sensitive information are rearranged into different groups so that the link between QID and sensitive attributes are removed. And perturbation involves modifying the original data by swapping or generating some synthetic information such that the statistical information generated from the original and modified data remains the same [3]. k-Anonymity and its variants are the widely used privacy models. The anonymized table is called a k-anonymous table. Consider an example of 2-anonymity. Table 5.2 represents a database table for employee details of an organization. Each row of the table represents a record relating to a particular employee with attributes such as Name, Age, Gender, City, and Income. By applying generalization, the individual values of the attribute

Table 5.2   *Non-anonymized table comprising*
employee details of an organization

Name	Age	Gender	City	Income
Priya	25	Female	Kolkata	50,000
Sniya	26	Female	Kolkata	30,000
Angel	22	Female	Kolkata	18,000
Neha	19	Female	Chennai	26,000
Rose	18	Female	Chennai	28,000
Salini	19	Female	Chennai	39,000
John	37	Male	Mumbai	48,000
Roy	33	Male	Mumbai	60,000
Price	32	Male	Mumbai	52,000

Table 5.3   *3-Anonymity table concerning the*
attributes "Age," "Gender," and "City"

Name	Age	Gender	City	Income
*	[21,30]	Female	Kolkata	*
*	[21,30]	Female	Kolkata	*
*	[21,30]	Female	Kolkata	*
*	[10,20]	Female	Chennai	*
*	[10,20]	Female	Chennai	*
*	[10,20]	Female	Chennai	*
*	[31,40]	Male	Mumbai	*
*	[31,40]	Male	Mumbai	*
*	[31,40]	Male	Mumbai	*

"Age" may be supplanted by the intervals [10,20,21,30,31,40], etc. And using suppression, all the values in the "Name" attribute and each of the values in the "Income" attribute is replaced by an "*." Table 5.3 has 3-anonymity concerning the attributes "Age," "Gender," and "City." For any combination of these attributes found in any row of the table, there are always no less than three rows with those exact attributes [16]. *k*-Anonymization is vulnerable to temporal attack, complementary release attack, unsorted matching attack, etc. [22], which lead toward the *L*-diversity method of data anonymization.

5.5.1.2   *L*-Diversity

The *L*-diversity technique of data anonymization tries to bring diversity in the sensitive attribute of data. An equivalence class in a table is the subset of all elements in the table that are equivalent to each other. A *k*-anonymous table is said to be *L*-diverse if each equivalence class in the table has at least "*L*" "well-represented" values for each sensitive attribute S [23]. A table in which all equivalence class is *L*-diverse is called an *L*-diverse table [23]. The term "well-represented" may be clarified by the following principles:

- **Distinct *L*-diversity:**
  A value appears more recurrently than other values within an equivalence class. The drawback of this approach is that the attacker can infer that this value is likely to represent the entity based on the probability of occurrence [24].

- **Entropy *L*-diversity:**
  The entire table must have at least $\log(L)$ as entropy to be able to meet entropy *L*-diversity for every equivalence class. This technique may be too prohibitive in the case of low entropy of the entire table when only a few values are the same [24].

- **Recursive (c, L)-diversity:**
  A table is said to agree to this principle if the sensitive attribute value in each equivalence class does not occur either too frequently or too rarely [24]. This notion is stronger than the previous two notions mentioned earlier [23,24].

L-diversity is an extension of the *k*-anonymity model. It uses the generalization and suppression operations to reduce the granularity of data representation such that each given record maps to at least k different records in the data [16]. Table 5.4 shows an example of *L*-diversity. For example, consider the Income attribute of Table 5.2 as a sensitive attribute and apply a generalization to Age attribute and suppress the Name, Gender, and City attributes. The resulting table, Table 5.4, is a 3-diverse version of Table 5.2 since each equivalence class has at least three different values for sensitive attribute Income. A drawback of this approach is that it relays upon the range of sensitive attributes. To make data *L*-diverse, while sensitive attributes have distinct values less than *L*, it is necessary to insert fictitious data. These fictional data strengthen security but may lead to analytical issues [16]. *L*-diversity method is subject to skewness and similarity attack [25]. It is insufficient to prevent attribute exposure due to the semantic relationship between the sensitive attributes [26,27].

Table 5.4   3-Diverse table with respect to the sensitive attribute "Income"

Name	Age	Gender	City	Income
*	[21,30]	Person	XX	50,000
*	[21,30]	Person	XX	30,000
*	[21,30]	Person	XX	18,000
*	[10,20]	Person	XX	26,000
*	[10,20]	Person	XX	28,000
*	[10,20]	Person	XX	39,000
*	[31,40]	Person	XX	48,000
*	[31,40]	Person	XX	60,000
*	[31,40]	Person	XX	52,000

5.5.1.3   *T*-Closeness

It is an extension of *L*-diversity that is used to preserve privacy in datasets by decreasing the granularity of data representation—such a reduction results in loss of data management adequacy for privacy purposes. The principle of *T*-closeness states that an equivalence class is said to have *T*-closeness if the distance between the distribution of a sensitive attribute in this class and the distribution of the attribute in the whole table is no more than a threshold *T*. A table is said to have *T*-closeness if all equivalence classes have *T*-closeness [23]. The distance between the distributions is measured using earth mover's distance [20]. The main advantage of *T*-closeness is that it prevents attribute disclosure and also identifies the semantic closeness of attributes. The issue with *T*-closeness is that it improves the likelihood of reidentification as the volume and range of data increase. The computational complexity to find an optimal solution is $2O(n)O(m)$ [28].

Big data can also increase the risk of reidentification [16]. Hence, de-identification techniques are feasible for privacy in big data analytics only if privacy-preserving algorithms are modified to avoid the reidentification risks.

5.5.2   *Notice and consent*

Another widely used privacy preservation technique in the data generation phase of big data is the notice and consent [29]. Whenever a user accesses a web service, a notice is displayed that states the policies, and the user must provide the consent before using the service. The user has to read and understand privacy policies clearly as he is responsible for the privacy of his data. But the lack of availability of notices in the local language and the constrained interfaces on mobile screens makes the privacy notices difficult to read [30].

The difficulty of using this approach in the big data environment is that the notice has to be changed frequently on the basis of the requirements, and it becomes a burden for the user to give consent to these changes every time. A solution is to use the support of third parties that offer choices of distinct privacy profiles. The inability to anticipate the consequences of the consent and failure in the "opt-out" of certain services are the other significant issues related to this approach [30].

Modern data analytics can extract useful information from big data but still raises a high risk to the privacy of users. Table 5.5 presents the traditional preserving privacy measures and their scalability in big data.

5.6   Recent privacy preserving techniques in big data

5.6.1   *HybrEx*

The hybrid execution model [31] is a privacy preservation model used in cloud computing. It manages public and private data separately. HybrEx uses its public cloud to handle the nonsensitive data that an organization declares as public, whereas it uses its private cloud for the organization's sensitive data that has to be kept private. Figure 5.4 shows the HybrEx architecture. The HybrEx execution framework partitions and runs the applications that want to access both private and public data.

Table 5.5   Traditional privacy preserving techniques and their scalability in big data

Privacy preservation technique	Scalability in big data
De-identification (data anonymization)	• Reidentification issues in big data – An attacker may get external knowledge assistance for de-identification in big data, which increases the risk of reidentification • Disclosure risk – Attribute and identity disclosures are the two major risks in anonymized data • Requires creation of new anonymization policies and privacy definition for the big data context
Notice and consent	• Overhead of cost – If the use of personal information is not apparent at the time of consent collection, its future uses would require going back to individuals for their amended consent which is costly to undertake • Increased burden for individuals – Big data is collected and processed so often that makes consent a burden for most individuals • Complex relationship between individuals and users of their personal data – In big data, as large datasets are combined and the users change, the relationship between individuals and the users of their personal data become complicated

MapReduce is a programming model coupled with Hadoop file systems to process big data. The HybrEx model can be realized using the Hadoop MapReduce [31]. The four categories that show how HybrEx MapReduce enables new types of applications that utilize both private and public clouds are the following:

• Map hybrid
• Horizontal partitioning
• Vertical partitioning
• Hybrid

The MapReduce applications may have to process both private and public datasets. MapReduce enables this type of application to utilize a public cloud without compromising privacy safely. Such a category is called MapHybrid, shown in Figure 5.5. It executes the map phase in both private and public clouds, whereas it executes the reduce phase in only one of the clouds [31].

In horizontal partitioning, the map phase is executed at public clouds only, while the reduce phase is executed at a private cloud, as shown in Figure 5.6 [31].

The vertical partitioning executes the map and reduce tasks in the public cloud using public data as the input, shuffles intermediate data among them, and stores

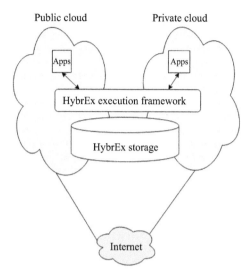

Figure 5.4   HybrEx architecture [31]

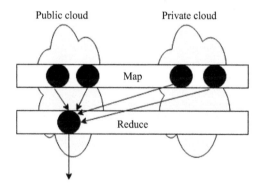

Figure 5.5   Map hybrid [31]

the result in the public cloud. It performs the same job in the private cloud with private data [31]. It is shown in Figure 5.7.

In the hybrid category, as shown in Figure 5.8, the map phase and the reduce phase are executed on both public and private clouds [31].

HybrEx offers secure integration in big data environment but deals only with cloud as an adversary.

5.6.2   Differential privacy

Differential privacy [32] is a method that helps to extract useful information from the database without violating privacy, which is a stronger solution for big data privacy.

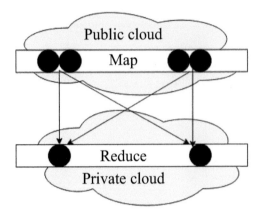

Figure 5.6   Horizontal partitioning [31]

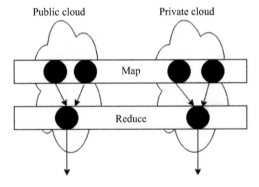

Figure 5.7   Vertical partitioning [31]

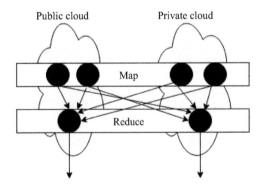

Figure 5.8   Hybrid [31]

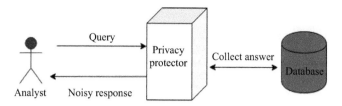

Figure 5.9 Differential privacy mechanism [32]

It is carried out by introducing a minimum distraction in the information provided by the database system [33]. In differential privacy, the analyst is not allowed to access the database directly. There is an intermediate software called "Privacy Protector" between the database and the analyst. Figure 5.9 shows the differential privacy mechanism [33]. The process steps are as follows:

1. The analyst can query the database through the privacy protector.
2. The Privacy Protector assesses this query, evaluates the privacy risks, and sends it to the database.
3. The Privacy Protector then collects the answer from the database.
4. To ensure the privacy of sensitive data from the database, the Privacy Protector adds some noises to data and sends the modified response to the analyst.

Differential privacy does not make any modifications to the original data. It merely distorts the data by adding some noises. The two mainly used noise mechanisms in differential privacy are Laplace Mechanism and Exponential Mechanism [33]. It provides a mathematically precise guarantee to privacy.

Differential privacy has been applied in different contexts concerning big data. Airavat [34] uses the MapReduce paradigm for the implementation of differential privacy. But it has got several limitations and can be used only as an initial step of implementing differential privacy in big data. The GUPT [35] mechanism tries to implement the MapReduce concept in differential privacy. It discusses the impact of block size on noise and accuracy. The size of the block corresponds to the mapper in MapReduce, and it should be optimally chosen to reduce estimation error.

Efforts on the application of differential privacy to big data location services are still in progress. Google uses differential privacy in sharing large-scale traffic statistics [33]. Apple iOS uses differential privacy in its messaging and searching apps [33]. And it is also deployed in telecommunication and e-health big data platforms. Thus, differential privacy is a workable solution in big data scenarios as it ensures privacy without actually altering data. But the modification of differential privacy concepts for applying into big data context is challenging and yet to be explored more.

5.6.3 Hiding a needle in a haystack: privacy-preserving a priori algorithm in MapReduce framework

The MapReduce framework, coupled with Hadoop, is widely used to handle big data. Privacy threat is the major obstacle for data mining using Hadoop. Hiding a needle in a haystack [36] is a privacy-preserving data mining technique in Hadoop that safeguards privacy without utility degradation. The idea behind the technique is that it is difficult to detect a rare information class, such as needles, in a haystack, such as a large volume of data.

The existing privacy-preserving association rule algorithms [37] have to consider the privacy-data utility trade-off before modifying original transaction data through the noise addition, whereas this technique does not have to consider such a trade-off because it can filter out noise using a code. But this incurs additional computation cost. By adding noise into original data, the technique intends that privacy protection is completely guaranteed [36]. Figure 5.10 depicts the hiding of a needle in a haystack concept. The red squares are original association rules, and the empty circles are noised association rules. Original rules are not revealed as there are many noised association rules [36].

Several challenges may arise while implementing the concept in big data context, such as nontechnical staff needs to access data, speed up manual introspection, explore data to design models, a combination of structured and unstructured data.

A privacy-preserving data mining algorithm, proposed in [36], overcomes the drawbacks of existing approaches and decreases the risk of association rule leakage based on an a priori algorithm in MapReduce framework, where the association rules are extracted by adding dummy noise to original data.

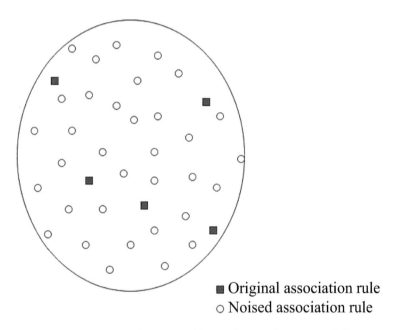

■ Original association rule
○ Noised association rule

Figure 5.10   Hiding a needle in a haystack concept [36]

5.7   Privacy-preserving solutions in resource constrained devices

The IoT comes with lots of benefits to make your daily lives smarter. The role of big data in IoT is to process a large amount of data generated from the IoT devices. Several recent techniques are emerging for privacy preservation in big data due to the rapid development of the IoT. IoT devices are considered as a significant privacy concern as they collect a lot of user's private data that should not be revealed without explicit consent from the user. IoT devices are resource-constrained with restricted size, weight capacities, and network connectivity. Efficient security and privacy algorithms (involving bilinear operations) cannot be directly applied to resource-constrained devices due to high computational complexity [38]. The complex heterogeneity of IoT systems has an impact on the user's privacy. The following are the major privacy threats in IoT:

- **User identification**

    The IoT devices collect a huge amount of user data from various sources security systems, traffic monitoring, online shopping, weather tracking systems, etc. It is possible to identify a person from these collected details. Hence, user identification is a major threat regarding the user's privacy.

- **User tracking**

    It involves tracking the user's location by making use of the data collected from that user using GPS sensors. This may help one to predict the workplace, home, and other visited places of the user which is a clear violation of privacy [38].

- **Profiling**

    Profiling assesses the personal interests of the user from his online activities. It leads to privacy violations if the information used is to determine the behavior of a user such as his online shopping interests, political views [38].

- **Utility monitoring**

    In utility monitoring, the risk is of direct importance for the collection of customer's utility usage. Such information may be used to infer the daily patterns of the user without. In IoT, it is complex to find privacy violations due to its undefined domain boundaries. Therefore, IoT environments must safeguard the user details from the threat of privacy breach. Obtaining the consents of the users is one of the widely used solutions to overcome privacy challenges in IoT environments [38].

In IoT, it is complex to find privacy violations due to its undefined domain boundaries. Therefore, IoT environments must safeguard the user details from the threat of privacy breach. The widely used solutions to overcome privacy challenges in IoT environments are as follows:

- **Authentication of IoT devices**

    It allows the users to authenticate the IoT devices using robust authentication mechanisms such as two-factor authentication, digital certificates, and biometrics, [39]. An encryption method based on XOR operations is used for mutual authentication in the RFID system for IoT applications [40]. In [41], the method implements a fingerprint-based authentication framework where each IoT device has a unique fingerprint to communicate with the cloud infrastructure. The approach in [42] proposes an authentication scheme based on software-defined networking for heterogeneous IoT environments.

- **IoT data encryption**

  It safeguards user privacy and discourages the breach of sensitive IoT data by encrypting the data sent between the IoT devices using conventional cryptographic algorithms and IoT public key infrastructure security methods. Several secure communication protocols have been proposed on the basis of digital signatures and hash values to ensure data privacy in the IoT environment. Lightweight cryptographic techniques such as PRESENT and TWINE are also of extensive use in the IoT environment.

- **Edge computing and plug-in architectures**

  In edge computing, most of the data processing occurs at the network edge that increases the concern of data privacy [38]. A trusted software entity such as a plug-in mediator can be deployed in the data distribution pipeline that executes the user privacy policies [43,44]. The mediator can control the to and from data based on the policy restrictions.

- **Data anonymization**

  It removes the identifiable information from the user data collected by the IoT devices. Image blurring and denaturing mechanisms are commonly used for anonymization in IoT applications [45,46]. Denaturing alters a specific part of the image using image processing techniques to preserve personal privacy. A privacy model based on k-anonymity [47] uses the time-based sliding window technique to manage IoT streams by partitioning the stream tuples based on their description.

- **Data forgetting and data summarization**

  Data forgetting removes all copies of the dataset, whereas data summarization conceals the data by providing a higher level of abstraction [38]. It makes the users comfortable to share their data since the collected data will be removed once the purpose is complete. Data summarization can be temporal summarization or spatial summarization based on whether collected data are a function of time or location. The data forgetting techniques based on cryptography [47] works on the principle that the encrypted data are deleted when the required decryption key is deleted. Data mining techniques [48,49] are widely used to summarize data collected by IoT devices [50].

The IoT applications are extremely flexible and heterogeneous with different requirements [51]. IoT devices should be integrated with privacy and security measures during the manufacture itself to prevent privacy leaks [38]. And the users of IoT must take additional care when permitting access to their personal information [52].

5.8   Conclusion

Big data is a major threat to personal privacy because the data leaks caused by poor data management. Several attack vectors exist at different levels of the infrastructure that collects, stores, and processes the big data. In this chapter, we have investigated the various privacy-preserving techniques in big data. Each phase of the big data life cycle is presented along with the existing solutions for privacy preservation. This chapter also discusses both conventional and latest techniques for protecting the privacy of big data. Since the big data analytics is emerging as a key to analyze the data generated from IoT devices, the chapter presents privacy-preserving solutions for resource-constrained IoT devices as well.

References

[1] Shahin D, Ennab H, Saeed R, and Alwidian J. Big Data Platform Privacy and Security, A Review. IJCSNS International Journal of Computer Science and Network Security. 2019 19;05:24.

[2] Hiba J, Hadi H, Hameed Shnain A, Hadishaheed S, and Haji A. Big Data and Five V's Characteristics. International Journal of Advances in Electronics and Computer Science. 2015 2:2393–2835.

[3] Mehmood A, Natgunanathan I, Xiang Y, *et al.* Protection of Big Data Privacy. IEEE Access. 2016 4:1821–1834.

[4] Xu L, Jiang C, Wang J, *et al.* Information Security in Big Data: Privacy and Data Mining. IEEE Access. 2014 2:1149–1176.

[5] Liu S. Exploring the Future of Computing. IT Professional. 2013 01;15:2–3.

[6] Sokolova M and Matwin S. In: Personal Privacy Protection in Time of Big Data. Cham: Springer. vol. 605; 2016. p. 365–380. Available from: https://doi.org/10.1007/978-3-319-18781-5_18.

[7] Cheng H, Rong C, Hwang K, *et al.* Secure Big Data Storage and Sharing Scheme for Cloud Tenants. China Communications. 2015 12;6:106–115.

[8] Xiao Z and Xiao Y. Security and Privacy in Cloud Computing. Communications Surveys and Tutorials, IEEE. 2013 01;15:843–859.

[9] Yang K, Jia X, and Ren K. Secure and Verifiable Policy Update Outsourcing for Big Data Access Control in the Cloud. IEEE Transactions on Parallel and Distributed Systems. 2015 26;12:3461–3470.

[10] Yang K, Jia X, Ren K, *et al.* DAC-MACS: Effective Data Access Control for Multi-Authority Cloud Storage Systems. In: 2013 Proceedings IEEE INFOCOM; 2013. p. 2895–2903.

[11] Yang K and Jia X. Expressive, Efficient, and Revocable Data Access Control for Multi-Authority Cloud Storage. IEEE Transactions on Parallel and Distributed Systems. 2014 25;7:1735–1744.

[12] Shao J. Anonymous ID-Based Proxy Re-Encryption. Berlin, Heidelberg: Springer; 2012. p. 364–375. Available from: https://doi.org/10.1007/978-3-642-31448-3_27.

[13] Liang K, Susilo W, and Liu JK. Privacy-Preserving Ciphertext Multi-Sharing Control for Big Data Storage. IEEE Transactions on Information Forensics and Security. 2015 10;8:1578–1589.

[14] Hallman R, Diallo M, August M, *et al.* Homomorphic Encryption for Secure Computation on Big Data. SCITEPRESS – Science and Technology Publications, Lda; 2018.

[15] Manogaran G, Thota C, and Kumar M. Meta Cloud Data Storage Architecture for Big Data Security in Cloud Computing. Procedia Computer Science. 2016 12;87:128–133.

[16] Jain P, Gyanchandani M, and Khare N. Big Data Privacy: A Technological Perspective and Review. Journal of Big Data. 2016 12:3.

[17] Fung B, Wang K, Chen R, *et al.* Privacy-Preserving Data Publishing: A Survey of Recent Developments. ACM Computing Surveys. 2010 06:42.

[18] Agrawal R and Srikant R. Privacy-Preserving Data Mining. In: Proceedings of the 2000 ACM SIGMOD International Conference on Management of Data. SIGMOD '00. New York, NY, USA: Association for Computing Machinery; 2000. p. 439–450.

[19] Ge Weiping ZH, Wang W, and Baile S. Privacy Preserving Classification Mining. Journal of Computer Research and Development. 2006 43;1:39.

[20] Gosain A and Chugh N. Privacy Preservation in Big Data. International Journal of Computer Applications. 2014 100:44–47.

[21] Mai JE. Big Data Privacy: The Datafication of Personal Information. The Information Society. 2016 32;3:192–199.

[22] Sweeney L. K-Anonymity: A Model for Protecting Privacy. International Journal of Uncertainty, Fuzziness and Knowledge-Based Systems. 2002 10;5:557–570.

[23] Li N, Li T, and Venkatasubramanian S. t-Closeness: Privacy Beyond k-Anonymity and l-Diversity. In: 2007 IEEE 23rd International Conference on Data Engineering; 2007. p. 106–115.

[24] Machanavajjhala A, Gehrke J, Kifer D, *et al.* l-Diversity: Privacy Beyond k-Anonymity. Atlanta, USA: IEEE. vol. 1; 2006. p. 24.

[25] Rajendran K, Jayabalan M, and Rana ME. A Study on k-Anonymity, l-Diversity, and t-Closeness Techniques Focusing Medical Data. IJCSNS International Journal of Computer Science and Network Security. 2017 17;12.

[26] Chakraborty S, Ambooken JG, Tripathy BK, *et al.* Analysis and Performance Enhancement to Achieve Recursive (c, l) Diversity Anonymization in Social Networks. Transactions on Data Privacy. 2015 8;2:173–215.

[27] Mehta BB and Rao UP. Improved l-Diversity: Scalable Anonymization Approach for Privacy Preserving Big Data Publishing. Journal of King Saud University – Computer and Information Sciences. 2019. Available from: https://doi.org/10.1016/j.jksuci.2019.08.006.

[28] Bredereck R, Nichterlein A, Niedermeier R, *et al.* The Effect of Homogeneity on the Complexity of k-Anonymity. Springer-Verlag Berlin Heidelberg. vol. 6914; 2011. p. 53–64.

[29] Cate F and Mayer-Schönberger V. Notice and Consent in a World of Big Data. International Data Privacy Law. 2013 05;3:67–73.

[30] Tene O. Privacy: The New Generations. International Data Privacy Law. 2010 11;1.

[31] Ko SY, Jeon K, and Morales R. The HybrEx Model for Confidentiality and Privacy in Cloud Computing. In: Proceedings of the 3rd USENIX Conference on Hot Topics in Cloud Computing. HotCloud'11. Portland, OR, USA: USENIX Association; 2011. p. 8.

[32] Microsoft. Differential Privacy for Everyone. New York: Microsoft; 2015. Available from: http://download.microsoft.com/.../Differential_Privacy_for_ Everyone.pdf.

[33] Jain P, Gyanchandani M, and Khare N. Differential Privacy: Its Technological Prescriptive Using Big Data. Journal of Big Data. 2018 12;5.

[34] Roy I, Setty S, Kilzer A, *et al.* Airavat: Security and Privacy for MapReduce. San Jose, CA, USA: Elsevier; 2010. p. 297–312.

[35] Mohan P, Thakurta A, Shi E, *et al.* GUPT: Privacy Preserving Data Analysis Made Easy. In: Proceedings of the 2012 ACM SIGMOD International Conference on Management of Data. SIGMOD '12. New York, NY, USA: Association for Computing Machinery; 2012. p. 349–360.

[36] Jung K, Park S, and Park S. Hiding a Needle in a Haystack: Privacy Preserving Apriori Algorithm InMapReduce Framework. In: Proceedings of the First International Workshop on Privacy and Security of Big Data. PSBD '14. New York, NY, USA: Association for Computing Machinery; 2014. p. 11–17.

[37] Verma A, Cherkasova L, and Campbell R. Play It Again, SimMR!. Austin, Texas, USA: IEEE; 2011. p. 253–261.

[38] Seliem M, Elgazzar K, and Khalil K. Towards Privacy Preserving IoT Environments: A Survey. Wireless Communications and Mobile Computing. 2018 2018:15.

[39] Rapyde. Top 10 IoT Security Solutions for the Most Common IoT Security Issues. rapyde; 2015. Available from: https://www.rapyder.com/top-10-iot-security-solutions-common-iot-security-issues.

[40] Lee J, Lin W, and Huang Y. A Lightweight Authentication Protocol for Internet of Things. In: 2014 International Symposium on Next-Generation Electronics (ISNE); 2014. p. 1–2.

[41] Sharaf-Dabbagh Y and Saad W. On the Authentication of Devices in the Internet of Things. Coimbra, Portugal: IEEE; 2016. p. 1–3.

[42] Salman O, Abdallah S, Elhajj IH, *et al.* Identity-Based Authentication Scheme for the Internet of Things. In: 2016 IEEE Symposium on Computers and Communication (ISCC); 2016. p. 1109–1111.

[43] Davies N, Taft N, Satyanarayanan M, *et al.* Privacy Mediators: Helping IoT Cross the Chasm. In: Proceedings of the 17th International Workshop on Mobile Computing Systems and Applications. HotMobile '16. New York, NY, USA: Association for Computing Machinery; 2016. p. 39–44.

[44] Klonoff DC. Fog Computing and Edge Computing Architectures for Processing Data From Diabetes Devices Connected to the Medical Internet of Things. Journal of Diabetes Science and Technology. 2017 11:647–652.

Handbook of big data analytics, volume 2

[45] Reiter MK and Rubin AD. Crowds: Anonymity for Web Transactions. New York, USA: ACM Transactions on Information and System Security; 1997.

[46] Cirillo F, Wu FJ, Solmaz G, *et al.* Embracing the Future Internet of Things. Sensors. 2019 19:351.

[47] Otgonbayar A, Pervez Z, and Dahal K. Toward Anonymizing IoT Data Streams via Partitioning. In: 2016 IEEE 13th International Conference on Mobile Ad Hoc and Sensor Systems (MASS); 2016. p. 331–336.

[48] Cantoni V, Lombardi L, and Lombardi P. Challenges for Data Mining in Distributed Sensor Networks. In: 18th International Conference on Pattern Recognition (ICPR'06). vol. 1; 2006. p. 1000–1007.

[49] Keller T, Thiesse F, Kungl J, *et al.* Using Low-Level Reader Data to Detect False-Positive RFID Tag Reads. In: 2010 Internet of Things (IOT); 2010. p. 1–8.

[50] Liu Y, Wang YP, Wang X, *et al.* Privacy-Preserving Raw Data Collection Without a Trusted Authority for IoT. Computer Networks. 2018 11:148.

[51] Zhuo G, Jia Q, Guo L, *et al.* Privacy-Preserving Verifiable Data Aggregation and Analysis for Cloud-Assisted Mobile Crowdsourcing. San Francisco, CA, USA: IEEE; 2016. p. 1–9.

[52] Dabbagh M and Rayes A. In: Internet of Things Security and Privacy. Cham: Springer; 2017. p. 195–223.

Chapter 6

Big data and behaviour analytics

Amit Kumar Tyagi[1], Keesara Sravanthi[2] and Gillala Rekha[3]

In today's era of technology (with rapid developments in technology), the data is increasing day by day by billions of devices (connected together as things/devices through Internet). Today it has become essential to analyse this data (after its generation by devices) through modern analytics tools. In some cases, data needs to be analysed at the time of its generation to handle the online real transactions used in real-life applications like banking, airlines, aerospace, military, pharmacy. Note that this generated data is present in structured, semi-structured, and unstructured format. As use of smart devices is increasing day by day, then this data is being produced in massive (large) volume, i.e., it is called big data. Many organizations store and handle the big data from every source they dealt with. The analytical skills used to handle big data include the knowledge of business processes, techniques, methodologies also used to handle the data along with the finding of the optimal solution to enhance the profit of an organization(s) like e-commerce, social media, game-playing. On another side, today's e-commerce, social media platforms, or many games are very much popular in the age of 14–25. The volume and different variety of data generated day by day are increasing every year (via accessing web by millions of users). Most of the data is in unstructured form (not meaningful) created via Blogs, online social networking, e-commerce, websites, etc. As an essential use of big data analytics (BDA), behavioural analytics focused on looking into the actions/activities of people over web (Internet). Several applications like e-commerce, gaming, social media platform, and other applications used behavioural analytics (BA) to identify opportunities to optimize in order to realize specific business results/productivity/outcomes. Behavioural data is the raw data that is generated when users click, swipe, and navigate a site or app.

    User and entity behaviour analytics (or UEBA) is a type of cyber security process that looks/notes normal behaviour of users. Analysis of user's behaviour is done using

[1]School of Computer Science and Engineering, Vellore Institute of Technology, Chennai, Tamil Nadu, India
[2]Department of CSE, VNR Vignana Jyothi Institute of Engineering & Technology, Hyderabad, Telangana, India
[3]Department of CSE, Koneru Lakshmaiah Educational Foundation, Hyderabad, Telangana, India

efficient decision support systems or modern machine learning techniques. The behaviour analysis in big data is being done by using tools like Hadoop and also various other techniques like association rules, liner regression, perceptron (including machine learning and deep learning techniques). Systems detect any anomalous behaviour/instances (track actions of users digitally) when there are deviations from these 'normal' patterns. Note that the technique embedded with the decision support capabilities also adds value to the analysis done for big data. The analysis of such type (unstructured) of data is done by discovering the patterns using clustering, association rule, etc. Not only this analysis is limited to pattern recognition, but also it extends to the behaviour analysis. It also includes the behaviour analysis of an individual (or group of individuals) in the applications/field of e-commerce, online social media, military, malware, etc.

This chapter gives a deep insight into the field of big data and behaviour analytics, i.e., 'How are customers using the product, if at all?' Giving answer to such questions, we move forward to discuss the sections like conceptual description of big data, importance of big data, and behaviour analytics in near future. Further, the tools required for processing and analysing of big data (or tracking every user's action digitally, or experiences of users with the products) are discussed. Next, the behaviour analysis along with its applications like watching movies on Netflix (or any video programme on web), game playing is given in detail. Streaming, Sharing, Stealing, Pausing (i.e., needs and interests), etc. moments are being covered and analysed in the respective examples (or applications) by deep learning tool. Later, this chapter also discusses various algorithms and techniques used for the big data and behaviour analytics with different examples. This chapter will also cover the future trends and needs to design the novel techniques for big data and behaviour analytics using machine learning and deep learning (as future research directions/some research gaps in current) so that the analysis can be done efficiently in terms of computation.

6.1   Introduction about big data and behaviour analytics

The term 'big data' is used to describe the huge collection of data (big data) and yet growing exponentially with time. Such data is so complex and large in size that traditional data management tools are not efficient to store or do processing on it. Apart from the size/volume other characteristics like velocity, variety make it challenging for traditional data management tools to handle it. The three Vs (volume, velocity, and variety) are emerging recently and defined as a common framework to describe big data.

For example, Gartner, Inc. defines big data in similar terms: 'Big data is high-volume, high-velocity and high-variety information assets that demand cost-effective, innovative forms of information processing for enhanced insight and decision making' [1].

Similarly, TechAmerica Foundation defines big data as follows: 'Big data is a term that describes large volumes of high velocity, complex and variable data that require advanced techniques and technologies to enable the capture, storage, distribution, management, and analysis of the information' [2].

The three Vs have been described briefly as follows:

Volume: It refers to the magnitude of data. The size of the data (big data) is reported to be in terabytes and petabytes. As per IBM survey in 2012, over 535 respondents over one terabyte to be big data [3]. But Facebook processes one million photographs per second and requires more than 20 petabytes. So, the volume of big data varies with many factors such as time, type of data, and many more.

Variety: It represents the type of data. The way data is stored, big data supports heterogonous data sets. The data can be in structured, semi-structured, and unstructured form. The structured data basically represented in tabular form such as tables, spreadsheets, or relational databases. The existing data constitutes on 5 per cent in structured form. The unstructured data like audio, video, images, and text which lack structured representation needs to be analysed by the machine, while semi-structured data is not fully structured or unstructured and does not conform to a specific standard – for example, extensible markup language (XML) files, JSON (JavaScript Object Notation) files.

Velocity: It refers to the rate at which data is generated and speed at which it should be analysed. Due to the explosion of smartphones and sensors has led to increase rate of data creation and a growing need to real-time analytics. For example, Wal-Mart processes more than 1 million transactions per hour. The emanation of data from smart devices produces huge real-time information to be analysed and provide personalized offers to the customer – for example, recommendation system by Amazon.

As data generation is increasing in exponential manner from smart devices, retailers need to deal with such huge streaming data to meet the demands of real-time analytics. Traditional data management techniques are not capable of handling such situations and that is where big data come into play. It enables firms to create real-time analytics for huge data.

Certain dimensions of big data were also stated in addition to the three Vs. Those comprise [4] the following:

Veracity: IBM recently introduced the fourth 'V' called Veracity, which is the unreliability inherent in certain data sources. For example, in social media consumer feelings are ambiguous in nature, because they entail human judgement. Nevertheless, they contain precious data. Another dimension of big data, which is tackled by tools and analytics built for the management and retrieval of uncertain data, is the need to deal with unreliable and uncertainty data.

Variability (and complexity): The additional dimensions of big data are variability and complexity which are introduced by SAS. Changes in flow rates of data are known as variability. Big data rate is often not constant and has frequent peaks and troughs. The fact that big data is generated through the use of a variety of sources refers to complexity. This presents a key challenge: linking, matching, cleaning, and transforming of data obtained from various sources.

Value: It is introduced by Oracle to define attribute of big data. Based on the definition by Oracle, big data is often defined by a 'low-value density'. In other words, the originally obtained information typically has a low volume value. Nonetheless, the analysis of large volumes of such data can produce a high value.

Note that many Vs have been discussed in [5]. Hence, the remaining part of this chapter is organized as follows:

- Section 6.2 discusses related work related to big data and behaviour analytics.
- Section 6.3 discusses motivation behind this work, interested/useful facts/ points behind writing this chapter.
- Section 6.4 discusses importance and benefits of big data in current era, i.e., in solving many complex problems (i.e., in present and future).
- Section 6.5 discusses several existing algorithms, tools available for data analytics and behaviour analytics.
- Section 6.6 discusses many critical issues and challenges in area of big data, data analytics, and behaviour analytics.
- Further, Section 6.7 discusses/provides several opportunities for future researchers (with identifying several research gaps in terms like data, big data, BDA, and behaviour analytics, etc.).
- Section 6.8 discusses taxonomy of related terms of analytics, used in current in many applications.
- In last in Section 6.9, this chapter will be summarized, including several useful remarks for future (in brief).

6.2   Related work

BDA and behaviour analytics are two interrelated terms. Behaviour analytics require big data to provide effective decisions. Behaviour analytics may help industries to analyse customer's behaviour, i.e., to increase profit of their business. Similarly, doctors can analyse behaviour of their patients to handle and cure diseases of the respective patients – for example, customer behaviour analysis, the traditional analytical systems [6].

In the mid-1970s, the DBMS (Database Management System) was built with two approaches. In response to enormous information storage needs created by the Apollo special programme, the first approach is created on the hierarchical data model, characterized by IMSs (Information Management Systems) from IBM. The second approach is created to achieve database standards and to resolve problems in hierarchical model, as it is failed to represent complex relationships of DBMSs. This approach is based on network data model. Those two models had however some clear drawbacks; for example, the complex programmes had to be written to answer simple questions. The data autonomy was also limited. Many DBMSs were then put into practice with the first commercial products being introduced in the 1970s and the early 1980s. Relational DBMS was commonly used in the 1980s and the 1990s, as its processes and systems became increasingly complex, were restricted to meeting the company's more complex entities and software requirements. Two new database models, the Object-Relational Database Management Systems (ORDBMSs) and Object-Oriented Database Management Systems (OODBMSs), have come up in response to the increasing complexity of database applications and subscribers to related and object data models, respectively. Third generation of DBMSs is a combination of ORDBMSs and OODBMSs.

Discovery of BDA: When the size, velocity, and variety of data exceed IT-operational system's ability to collect, store, analyse, and process it, then that data transforms to big data. Variety of tools and equipment's are used by most of the organizations to handle unstructured data but fail to achieve, they do not have ability to mine it and derive necessary insights in a given time period because of rapid growth in volume of data. Through the science, projects at companies' big data comes into view to help telecom companies to understand the customer opinion about telecommunication, that is, the users (customers) who all are satisfied with their services, which service causes the dissatisfaction and predicts who all are the users planning to change the service. To obtain that information, billions of loosely structured bytes of data must be processed in different locations until the necessary data is identified. This type of analysis allows management to fix defective processes or people and therefore can reach customers at risk. Big data is becoming one of the most relevant technological trends, which can dramatically change the way companies analyse and make valuable insights into their usage of customer behaviour [7]. Customer analytics' key concepts [8]: a customer analytics' survey reveals the following key concepts:

1. **Venn diagram:** Discover that hidden relationships merge multiple sections to uncover connections, relations, or differences. Discover customers who have purchased various product categories and easily identify the opportunities for cross-sales.
2. **Data profiling:** Customer attributes choose records from your data tree and create customer profiles that show common attributes and behaviours. To guide successful sales and marketing plans, customer profiles are used.
3. **Forecasting:** Forecast time series analysis allows you to adapt to changes, trends, and seasonal patterns. You can forecast monthly sales volume accurately and estimate the expected amount of orders in a given month.
4. **Mapping:** Geographic zones mapping uses colour code to indicate customer behaviour in geographical regions as it changes. A map of geographical regions divided up into polygons shows where the concentration of your churners or specific products is best sells.
5. **Association rules** (cause/effect basket analysis): This technique senses relationships or patterns of affinity through data and creates a set of rules. The rules that are most useful for key business insights are automatically selected: Which products do customers buy at the same time and when? Who do not buy and why? What do you buy? What new opportunities are there for cross-selling?
6. **Decision tree:** Classification and prediction of behaviour, decision trees are one of the most common classification methods for various data mining applications and support decision-making processes. Classification allows you to choose the right product to recommend and to forecast future turnover to individual customers. ID3, C4.5, and CART are the most commonly used decision tree algorithms.

Now some of the data visualization tools can be included as

- **Polymaps:** Polymaps are the free JavaScript library and a SimpleGeo and Stamen joint project. This complex map overlay tool is capable of loading data on a variety of scales, with multi-zoom functions from country to road [9].
- **Flot:** Flot is browser-based software that works with most popular browsers – including Internet Explorer, Chrome, Firefox, Safari, and Opera. It is a JavaScript Plotting Library for jQuery. Flot offers a wide range of visualization features, including data points, interactive diagrams, stacked diagrams, panning and zooming, and other capabilities through a number of plugins for each functionality [9].
- **D3.js:** A JavaScript library to create web standard visualization with the aid of HTML, SVG and CSS; documents are made available by a data-driven approach to DOM manipulation – all with modern browser capabilities and no proprietary frameworks restrictions [9].
- **SAS Visual Analytics:** For more detailed analytics, SAS Visual Analytics is a tool for displaying data sets from all dimensions. SAS Visual Analytics helps even non-technical users to explore the deeper connections behind the data and uncover hidden opportunities, with an intuitive interface and automated forecasting tools [9].

Figure 6.1 shows the evolution of analytics category wise and based on interests of customers/analysts. The author proposed conceptual model to provide cognitive and behavioural process-oriented feedback to learners and teachers for learning [10]. The alarm behaviour analysis and discovery system have been established using flapping and parent–child (P–C) rules to reveal the operation patterns from a large number of alarms in telecom networks [11]. In the paper [12], the author used Map Reduce implementation using C4.5 decision tree algorithm for customer data visualization using Data-Driven Documents. Hence, this section discusses work related to big data, behaviour data, data analytics, and behaviour analytics. Now the next section will discuss about our motivation behind writing this chapter.

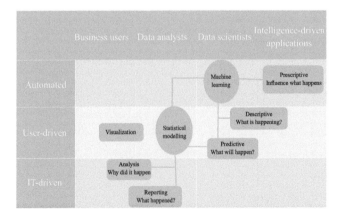

Figure 6.1   Evolution of analytics [13–16]

6.3   Motivation

As discussed in [13], Internet connected devices are generating a lot of data (called big data) in many applications like healthcare, retail, automation, manufacturing, transportation. But this data becomes useful to increase profit for businesses or organizations, based on analysing customer's behaviour, their habits, interests, etc. This data which is used to analyse behaviour of customer/user is called as behavioural data. Behavioural data tells us 'how engagement with our product impacts retention, conversion, revenue, and the outcomes we care about'? For behavioural data, behavioural analytics required to get answer to many unsolved questions, faced in our day-to-day life. Using behavioural data and analytics on it can provide user-level data; based on that, skilled teams can get answer of questions like: What do users click within the product? Where do users get stuck? How do users react to feature changes? How long do users take from first click to conversion? How do users react to marketing messages? Which ads are the most effective? Can the team nudge users to be more successful? And so on. To provide answer to such raised questions, we provide maximum convenient services to his/her door and use behaviour analytics in this current era. Also to increase profits, investment in businesses, we increase the use of technology to a new and large scale.

Hence, this section discusses about our motivation behind writing this chapter. It shows the necessity of big data and data analytics with behaviour analytics with respect to real world's problems (in real world's applications). Now, the next section will discuss about importance and benefits of big data and behaviour analytics in this current and future era/decade.

6.4   Importance and benefits of big data and behaviour analytics

BDA is often a complex process of analysing large and varied data sets or big data, which can help companies to take sensible business choices and discover knowledge, such as hidden patterns, unknown associations, market trends, and consumer preferences. BDA is an advanced form of analytics that involve complex apps with components like predictor models, statistical algorithms, and it is powered by high-performance analytical systems.

6.4.1   Importance of big data analytics

BDA offers various business benefits, guided by expert analytical systems and software, and highly powered computer systems. Few of the business benefits are listed as follows [17]:

- new opportunities of revenue,
- efficient advertising,
- better services to customer,
- increased operational performance in services,
- competitive benefits over competitors.

Some of the benefits of data analytics and behaviour analytics are included here as follows:

For a wide range of reasons, companies plan to implement BDA, including the following [18]:

- **Business transformation:** BDA is generally believed by executives to deliver tremendous potential to revolutionize their organizations. Seventy-eight per cent of people surveyed agreed in the 2016 IDGE Data & Analytics Survey that gathering and analysing big data would radically change the way their companies do business over the next 1–3 years.
- **Competitive advantage:** Fifty-seven per cent of the businesses surveyed said that their use of analysis allows them to gain a competitive advantage, up from 51 per cent of those who said the same in 2015, in the research report of MIT, funded by the company SAS.
- **Innovation:** BDA will assist companies in the development of their customers' products and services and help them identify new revenue generation opportunities. Sixty-eight per cent of respondents accepted that analytics have helped their company to evolve even in the MIT Sloan Management survey. It is a 52 per cent leap in 2015.
- **Lower costs:** Precisely 49.2 per cent of the companies surveyed reported successfully lowering costs as a result of a big data initiative in the NewVantage Partners Big Data Executive Survey 2017.
- **Improved customer services:** BDA is widely used by companies to analyse social media, customer service, sales, and marketing data. This can help them better assess their client feeling and respond in real time to their customers.
- **Increased security:** IT security is also an important area for BDA. Security software creates huge amounts of log data. By using big data analysis methods to this data, companies can sometimes detect and combat cyber-attacks which would have been unknown.

Hence, this section discusses importance and benefits of data and behaviour analytics in several applications like banking, retail, healthcare. Now, the next section will discuss several existing tools, algorithms, or methods used for analysing data and behaviour of customer/consumer or patients.

6.5   Existing algorithms, tools available for data analytics and behaviour analytics

Big data is all about gathering big volumes of data (structured and unstructured data). Big data analysis is the method used to discover trends, patterns, comparisons, or other valuable insights in these large data stores. BDA has been becoming so popular that almost every major technology company is selling a product with the tag 'BDA'. We have several top big data tools in the market for this reason. This software helps in data storage, evaluation, monitoring, and much more [19].

6.5.1   Apache Hadoop

Apache Hadoop is an open-source framework [5] used to handle big data and clustered file system. Using the MapReduce programming model, it processes data sets of big data. It is written in Java programming language and provides cross-platform support. More than 50 companies use Hadoop. IBM, Intel, Amazon Web services, Microsoft, Facebook, Hortonworks are the few big companies using Hadoop. It is free of cost to use under the apache license. HDFS (Hadoop file system) is capable of holding all types of data – video, images, JSON, XML across the same file.

6.5.2   Cloudera

With regard to the core of big data, few companies are closely tied to the core open-source platform Hadoop big data as Cloudera. Hadoop founders started a company. Recently the Hadoop ecosystem has been further influenced by the merger of Hortonworks, the primary rival of Cloudera. To Cloudera, the key differentiator is a deep understanding of Hadoop and its core skills, which includes the Cloudera Enterprise framework, placed on the top of open source CDH (Cloudera Distribution of Hadoop). It allows one to perform multiple operations (collect, process, manage, discover, model, and distribute) on big data. It provides high security on the data. A free software version was released by Cloudera in CDH (note that Cloudera is the distribution of Hadoop). Per-node the licensing cost is expensive.

6.5.3   Cassandra

Apache Cassandra has been developed to manage large volumes of data, spread through various commodity servers, free of charge, and open-source NoSQL DBMS. It employs CQL (Cassandra Structure Language) to interact with the database. This uses CQL to communicate with the database. Accenture, American Express, Facebook, General Electric, Yahoo is few of the IT companies uses Cassandra. It processes a large amount of data very quickly. Organizations can build and process predictive analytics models using a range of integrated tools with Cloudera Enterprise. Big data tools from Cloudera are a good fit for companies requiring a full stack that includes the core Hadoop technology for gathering and creating big data.

6.5.4   Konstanz Information Miner

Konstanz Information Miner (KNIME) is an open-source tool used for Enterprise Reporting, Integration, Research, CRM (Customer Relationship Management), Data Mining, Data Analytics, Text Mining, and Business Intelligence. It supports multiple operating systems (Linux, OS X, and Windows). Comcast, Johnson & Johnson, Canadian Tire, few of the top companies use KNIME. It emerges easily with other technologies and languages.

6.5.5   Data wrapper

Data wrapper is an open-source data visualization platform that helps its users to quickly and accurately generate simple, embeddable charts. The newsrooms are their main customers throughout the world. The Times, Forbes, Mother Jones, Bloomberg, Facebook, etc. are among the titles. It works on all types of devices – smart phones, PC, laptop. It does not require coding. It provides free of cost services and customizable paid options.

6.5.6   *MongoDB*

MongoDB is free of cost; it supports many operating systems like Windows Vista, Solaris, Linux, OS X 10.7 version, FreeBSD, as it is open-source software, NoSQL and document-oriented database written in C, C++, and JavaScript. Aggregation, adhoc-queries, sharding, indexing, replication, server-side execution of JavaScript, uses BSON (term based on JSON and stands for Binary JSON) format, capped collections, load balancing, and file storage. It supports for multiple technologies and platforms. MongoDB's SMB and enterprise versions are paid versions.

6.5.7   *HPCC*

HPCC (high performance computing cluster) provides a highly scalable supercomputing platform. It is also known as Data Analytics Supercomputer. To support data parallelism, pipeline parallelism, and system parallelism, it uses Thor architecture. It is an open-source tool and is a best alternate for big data platforms like Hadoop. The architecture is focused on clusters of high-performance commodity computing. In data processing in parallel, simple, efficient, and scalable, it supports high-performance web search applications and it is comprehensive and effective in terms of cost.

   Hence, this section discusses several existing methods, tools, and algorithms used for data analytics and behaviour analytics. Now, the next section will discuss several open issues and challenges with respect to BDA and behaviour analytics.

6.6   Open issues and challenges with big data analytics and behaviour analytics

Today's data through Internet of Things is being generated at unexpected (uncountable) rate. Analysing this large amount of data of each application is really impossible. Also, conducting behavioural analysis is more complicated than simply running reports in the analytics tool. But using behavioural data and applying efficient analytics tolls on it make us to understand user/customer behaviour. Note that behavioural analytics help us in finding their day-to-day activities also provide us their product decisions and strategy. We face several issues due to complexity, form of data, also not having proper tools or method to analyse it. We provide here some open issues and challenges with big data and behaviour analytics.

6.6.1   *Challenges with big data analytics*

It is not always as easy to implement a BDA approach as businesses expect. In addition, the majority of surveys show that the number of organizations that profit from their big data analysis is below that of the numbers that conduct big data analysis [18,19]. A variety of hurdles can prevent vendors of BDA from achieving the advantages:

1. **Data growth:** The exponential pace of data growth is one of the biggest challenges in big data analysis. According to IDC, every 2 years the amount of data on global servers doubles approximately. By 2020, nearly 44 zettabytes of the digital information are likely to contain in servers. This data is sufficient to put it into perspective to fill a set of iPads stretching 6.6 times between the Earth and the moon. If they are to help companies, BDA tools must be able to perform well on a scale.

2. **Unstructured data:** The data need not remain in structured databases which are stored in an organization system. Actually, it is unstructured data, including email messages, photos, documents, audio files, videos, and other file types. By using advanced artificial intelligence tools, it is easy to search the unstructured data. Vendors continually update their tools in BDA, so that they can analyse and derive information from unstructured data more effectively.

3. **Data siloes:** ERP (Enterprise Resource Planning) solutions, CRM solutions, supply-chain management software, e-commerce solutions, and office productivity programmes are the different applications used for creating enterprise data. One of the tough challenges in the BDA is the integration of data from all of these previous applications.

4. **Cultural challenge:** While BDAs are widespread, corporate culture has not yet been invaded everywhere. In the New Vantage Partners Survey, 52.5 per cent of executives said they did not use big data as widely as they would like to use due to organizational obstacles like lack of harmonization, internal resistance, or a lack of coherent strategy.

6.6.2 Issues with big data analytics (BDA)

Ethical issues with BDA [20] from organization perspective:

1. **Data trading:** To what level companies collect, purchase, compile, exchange, and distribute information from various sources in a way that respects the rights of individuals.

2. **Ethical governance:** The level at which companies, with guidelines, decision rights, and responsibilities (formal government), have principles, norms and shared beliefs (informal governance), encourage the practice of ethical BDA.

3. **Reputation:** To what extent relevant stakeholders, particularly consumers trust that a company can ethically handle and use information on them.

4. **Data quality:** To what extent organizations guarantee the reliability of large data in a way that respects the rights of individuals.

5. **Algorithmic decision-making:** The excessive respect for individual rights in big data analysis and the resulting organizational decisions.

Ethical issues with BDA from individual perspective:

1. **Privacy:** To what extent an individual may limit and control the use and dissemination of personal information by organizations.
2. **Trust:** The degree to which an individual can have certainty that the companies who have access to their information regarding the person's privileges.
3. **Awareness:** To what degree does an individual agree with data agencies to collect their personal information and how they use them.

Hence, this section discusses about several open issues and challenges existing in BDA and behaviour analytics. For example, as customer's behaviour is a dynamic, changes so fast, and depends on various things, thoughts, and emotions. It is really difficult to analyse the behaviour of customer with higher accuracy. Now, the next section will discuss several opportunities or future research directions which will be more useful for future researchers.

6.7   Opportunities for future researchers

There are many questions are to be solved today. Who will buy which stock? Who will move which direction over the road? Who will buy but which product will be available on online market? What next is the market for large-scale data analysis? For providing answer to such questions, a number of predictions are offered by experts [21], which can be listed here as follows:

1. **Open source:** With the rise in traction in BDA, open-source tools that help break down and analyse data. The popular open-source software frameworks (for storing data and running applications on clusters of commodity hardware) are Hadoop, Spark, and NoSQL. Many proprietary platforms now integrate and/or support leading open-source technologies. For the foreseeable future, this seems unlikely to change.
2. **Market segmentation:** Most of these general data analytics solutions have entered the market but expect more niches such as security, advertising, CRM, and application management and hiring to grow. There are also niches that are concentrated on. Analytical techniques are incorporated easily with existing business systems.
3. **Artificial intelligence and machine learning:** As an appetite in AI grew more and more, vendors rushed through their BDA tools to integrate machine learning and cognitive skills. By 2020, Gartner predicts that virtually all new software devices would integrate AI innovations, including BDA. The organization also claims that 'By 2020, over 30 per cent of CIOs will have AI as top five investment goals'.
4. **Prescriptive analytics:** With this rush to artificial intelligence, companies expect more of prescriptive analytics to be interested. Some consider these tools as the 'ultimate' form of big data analysis, not only can they predict the future but also can recommend intervention paths that could lead to organizations

desirable outcomes. Nonetheless, before such approaches can become common place, providers need both hardware and software developments.

Hence, this section discusses several future research directions in brief, i.e., it gives several future research works for future researchers/readers. Now, the next section will provide a complete taxonomy of analytics and its related terms in brief.

6.8 A taxonomy for analytics and its related terms

Data, big data are two different terms. Similarly, BDA and behaviour analytics are two different terms but are interrelated. There should be a clear picture or difference that should be provided as taxonomy among using terms (nowadays). This kind of doubts is clearly discussed in Table A.1 (refer table on next page).

Hence, this section discusses the taxonomy of analytics and its related terms like descriptive, predictive, prescriptive, analytics in brief. Now, the next section will summarize this work in brief.

6.9 Summary

Behavioural analytics are analytics that organizations/businesses use to increase profit of their business, i.e., focusing on consumer trends, habits/patterns, and activities. In general terms, as discussed earlier behavioural analytics is a tool like BDA that identifies the actions that customers/users take within a digital product/over-buying products online/online retailing. Such actions are identified based on behavioural data of users. Behavioural data is the raw (events) data that is generated when users click, swipe, and navigate a website/applications for buying or visiting for its own purpose. Behavioural data reveals how engagement with your product impacts retention, conversion, revenue, and the outcomes you care about. Note that understanding user behaviour is necessary to increase engagement, retention, lifetime value, conversion rates, and ultimately, revenue with respect to business/organizations. Behavioural analytics software provides concrete answers with a visual interface where teams can segment users, run reports, and deduce customers' needs and interests. Business/organizations need behavioural analytics very badly to improve their business or productivity of their products. Hence, this chapter provides a detailed description about BDA, and behavioural analytics, its importance, open issues, and major challenges faced during analysis. Also in last, several future research directions given in this chapter.

Appendix A

Table A.1   Taxonomy for analytics and its related terms

Analytics	Definition(s)	Responsibilities taken by	Characteristics/features	Level of advancement	Incorporates AI and ML	Level of popularity
Data analytics (DA) [22]	Data sets are being examined in order to draw conclusions with the help of specialized systems and software on the information they contain	Data interpretation, statistical analysis, analysis of results, the acquisition and management of databases of primary, or secondary data sources	Reporting feature, fraud management, version control, quick integrations, scalability	Entry level	Regularly	It is used by all companies
Big data analytics [23]	It is a technique to analyse the large amount of data or big data. This large amount of data is gathered from many sources, including social networks, videos, digital images, transaction logs, and sensors	Convert unstructured data into meaningful insights, cover hidden patterns, market trends and consumer preference for organizational benefit	Data processing, predictive analysis, data encryption, single sign-on, real-time reporting, dashboards, location-based insights, quick integrations, scalability	High	Always	Used by all organizations
Behavioural analytics [24]	Behavioural analysis is a recent development in business analysis that offers new perspectives on the behaviour of consumers on e-commerce platforms, online games, web, mobile, and IoT applications	Customer compartment analysis, behavioural evaluation, and behavioural plans development	Manipulate events that regulate a target behaviour, concentrate on the social importance of the behaviour actions, principles systemic, generalization, motivation, optimism, and doability	Predicted	Usually	Used by all commercial organizations

(Continues)

	Description	Purpose	Approach	Complexity	Visualization	Adoption
Descriptive analytics [14]	Descriptive analytics are the interpretation of historical information to better understand the changes in an organization	To define situations, analyse multiple data sets	For comprehensive, accurate, and live data, visualization is effective	Low	Not usually	Almost all organizations are using
Predictive analytics [15]	The method of prediction of business events and market behaviour is known as predictive analytics	To predict future conditions, analyse multiple data sets	Predictive modelling and extended statistics	High	Mostly	Used by smaller but growing group of organizations
Prescriptive analytics [16]	The business analysis (BA) area that aims to find the best approach for a particular situation	Use information to determine the right measures to be taken	Applying advanced analytical techniques to make specific recommendations	Very high	Always	Not yet wide spread

References

[1]   http: www.gartner.comit-glossarybig-data.

[2]   TechAmerica Foundation's Federal Big Data Commission. 2012. Demystifying Big Data: A Practical Guide to Transforming the Business of Government. TechAmerica Foundation's Federal Big Data Commission. Washington: DC.

[3]   Schroeck M, Shockley R, Smart J, Romero-Morales D, and Tufano P. 2012. Analytics: The Real-World Use of Big Data: How Innovative Enterprises Extract Value From Uncertain Data, Executive Report. IBM Institute for Business Value and Said Business School at the University of Oxford.

[4]   Gandomi A and Haider M. 2015. Beyond the hype: Big data concepts, methods, and analytics. *International Journal of Information Management*.

[5]   Tyagi AK and Rekha G. Machine Learning with Big Data (March 20, 2019). Proceedings of International Conference on Sustainable Computing in Science, Technology and Management (SUSCOM), Amity University Rajasthan, Jaipur, India, February 26–28, 2019. Available at SSRN: https://ssrn.com/abstract=3356269 or http://dx.doi.org/10.2139/ssrn.3356269.

[6]   Rispin S. Database Resources. The Institute of Certified Public Accountants, Ireland. Available at https://docplayer.net/6180815-Database-resources-subject-information-technology-for-managers-level-formation-2-author-seamus-rispin-current-examiner.html.

[7]   Floyer D. 2014. Enterprise Big-Data [Online]. Available: http://wikibon.org/wiki/v/Enterprise_Big-data.

[8]   Beaver D, Kumar S, Li HC, Sobel J, and Vajgel P. October 2010. Customer Analytics Turn Big Data Into Big Value. Actuate Corporation. http://birtanalytics.actuate.com/customer-analytics-turn-big-data-into-big-value Finding a Needle in Haystack: Facebook's Photo Storage. In *OSDI* (Vol. 10, No. 2010, pp. 1–8).

[9]   Lurie A. February 2014. 39 Data Visualization Tools for Big Data [Online]. ProfitBricks, The Laas Company. Available: https://blog.profitbricks.com/39-data-visualization-tools-for-big-data.

[10] Sedrakyan G, Malmberg J, Verbert K, Järvelä S and Kirschner PA. 2018. Linking learning behavior analytics and learning science concepts: designing a learning analytics dashboard for feedback to support learning regulation. *Computers in Human Behavior*, p.105512.

[11] Wang J, He C, Liu Y, *et al.* 2017. Efficient alarm behavior analytics for telecom networks. *Information Sciences*, 402, pp. 1–14.

[12] Khade AA. 2016. Performing customer behavior analysis using big data analytics. *Procedia computer science*, 79, pp. 986–992.

[13] Tyagi AK, Sharma S, Anuradh N, Sreenath N. and Rekha G. How a User will Look the Connections of Internet of Things Devices?: A Smarter Look of Smarter Environment (March 11, 2019). Proceedings of 2nd International Conference on Advanced Computing and Software Engineering (ICACSE)

2019. Available at SSRN: https://ssrn.com/abstract=3350282 or http://dx.doi.org/10.2139/ssrn.3350282.

[14] Djunaedi R and Baga LM and Krisnatuti LM. 2015. Efektivitas Implementasi corporate social responsibility PT. ABC. *Jurnal Aplikasi Bisnis dan Manajemen (JABM)*.

[15] De Filippi P. 2014. Big data, big responsibilities. *Internet Policy Review*, *3*(1). Web, 5 Nov 2019.

[16] French S. 2021. Uncertainty and imprecision: modelling and analysis. *Journal of the Operational Research Society*, 46(1), pp. 70–79. doi:10.2307/2583837.

[17] Rouse M. Big Data Analytics. https: //searchbusinessanalytics.techtarget.com/definition/big-data-analytics.

[18] Harvey C. Big Data Analytics. July 2017. Available at www.datamation.com/big-data/big-data-analytics.html.

[19] Top 15 Big Data Tools (Big Data Analytics Tools). Available at www.softwaretestinghelp.com/big-data-tools/.

[20] Someh I, Davern M, Breidbach CF and Shanks G. 2019. Ethical Issues in Big Data Analytics: A Stakeholder Perspective. Communications of the Association for Information Systems.

[21] Cukier K. 2010. Data Everywhere: A Special Report on Managing Information. Economist Newspaper.

[22] www.northeastern.edu/graduate/blog/what-does-a-data-analyst-do/

[23] Marsden V and Wilkinson V. 2018. Big Data Analytics and Corporate Social Responsibility: Making Sustainability Science Part of the Bottom Line. 10.1109/ProComm.2018.00019.

[24] Spencer J and Ritchie J. Qualitative data analysis for applied policy research. Analyzing Qualitative Data, 1st Edition, 1994, Imprint Routledge, pages 22. Available at www.taylorfrancis.com/books/e/9780203413081/chapters/10.4324/9780203413081-14.

Chapter 7

Analyzing events for traffic prediction on IoT data streams in a smart city scenario

Chittaranjan Hota[1] and Sanket Mishra[1]

In this work, we propose a framework for complex event processing (CEP) coupled with predictive analytics to predict simple events and complex events on Internet of Things (IoT) data streams. The data is consumed through a REST service containing the traffic data of around 2,000 locations in the city of Madrid, Spain. This prediction of complex events will help users in understanding the future state of road traffic and hence take meaningful decisions. For predicting events, we propose a framework that uses WSO2 Siddhi as CEP, along with InfluxDB as persistent storage. The data is consumed in the CEP with the help of a high-speed Apache Kafka messaging pipeline. This data is used to build predictive models inside the CEP that helps users to derive meaningful insights. However, in these event analytics engines, the events are created via rules that are triggered when the streaming data exceeds a certain threshold. The calculation of the "threshold" is utmost necessary as it acts as the means for the generation of simple events and complex events in an event analytics scenario. We have proposed a novel 2-fold approach for finding out the thresholds in such large datasets. We have taken the help of unsupervised learning to get the idea of thresholds. The first phase uses Node-RED and serverless computing to create the thresholds and then supply them back to the CEP for prediction. The machine learning models run on a cloud service, and the predictions or thresholds are returned back through REST services into the CEP. In the second phase, it not only creates the thresholds but also uses novel hypothesis testing techniques along with windowing mechanism on data streams to implement clustering and supply the result back into the CEP. This approach leverages on the usage of statistical techniques to understand the change in distribution of data. The changes in the data distributions trigger the retraining of the machine learning models, and the results are given back into the CEP for being used in an event generation scenario. We have also included a section in which we have incorporated a statistical analysis on the dataset used.

[1]Department of Computer Science and Information Systems, BITS Pilani Hyderabad Campus, Hyderabad, India

7.1 Introduction

Democratization of Internet and easy availability of off-the-shelf hardware has driven technology into creating intelligent applications. IoT has been a driving force in the rapid and incremental deployment of intelligent sensing hardware in multitude of areas, such as smart buildings [1,2], intelligent transportation systems (ITS) [3], smart cities [4,5], and thus, generating voluminous data contributing to the characteristics of big data. Most of the works on big data deal with large-scale datasets and predictive analytics are applied on data streams to extract actionable knowledge from it. Efficient techniques and methodologies to handle data streams and inference of higher order knowledge can be substantiated using CEP engine. CEP has been used in a variety of applications ranging from big data analytics [6], supply chain management [7], smart transportation [8], etc.

A myriad of intelligent or cognitive applications process voluminous data to churn insights in real-time scenarios. These applications tend to be distributed in nature so as to process large-scale data and predict outcomes in real time. Such applications should be able to recognize patterns in order to extract interesting information from the results. In real-time systems, data processing takes place and simple events or complex events are identified. For example, in ITS, a congestion is a higher order inference event. In a smart city, there may be thousands of sensors that are collecting the data from the environment. This data might be getting stored in a central repository, such as cloud or on the secondary storage of a server. In such scenarios, the actionable knowledge can be derived using machine learning approaches, but it might detect congestion in a delayed manner. It is because the data persistence and training of the machine learning approaches take significant time which disallows the generation of insights in real time. On the contrary, applications based on traffic data in a smart city scenario should generate predictions with minimum time latency. CEP systems are primarily event-driven frameworks which help in recognizing patterns in streaming data in order to infer higher order, complex scenarios, such as congestion. CEP systems involve investigating the occurrence of patterns in simple events or correlation between two or more simple events in order to create a complex event. The triggering of a simple or complex event is facilitated by a rule created for the same. The rule-based system has different thresholds, which, if exceeded, invokes the CEP to generate events. For example, a car exceeding a certain threshold can produce a "high-speed" event but if the same event is triggered continuously for consecutive time stamps, it can trigger a complex event. The main concern in rule-based systems is the issue of static thresholds which do not evolve with context. This can be a significant issue as a traffic scenario changes at different times of the day, and the congestion is impacted by environmental factors as well as concentration of people at a place. Even the domain expert may not have a global knowledge regarding the traffic patterns across the different street locations in a smart city. The initial rules built on observations by traffic administrators or domain experts may be inefficient in IoT scenarios due to the presence of data drift. An adaptive thresholding technique is necessary that can supply the CEP rules with updated thresholds over the time with a change in the underlying statistical properties of the data.

IoT data can be sourced from various heterogeneous data sources from multiple domains concerning traffic data, weather data and social data [9]. Data streams encompassing a large number of data instances over a long interval of time follow normal distribution. But in IoT, we consider short data intervals to avoid missing important alerts, and thus, the data may or may not follow Gaussian distribution. Also the presence of data drift in IoT streams further contributes to the necessity to adapt and retrain the approaches. Further, IoT data characteristics evolve over a period of time, thus leading to frequent changes in the underlying statistical properties of the data. In IoT applications, data is streamed in real time and there is necessity to develop approaches that can handle the velocity and heterogeneous nature of data streams.

In order to formulate effective predictions on heterogeneous data streams, researchers have investigated the use of supervised [10] and unsupervised procedures [11]. However, classification approaches require ground truth or "label" for evaluating the performance of the approach over data. In real world IoT applications, data may or may not possess labels, thus limiting the implementation of classification approaches. Clustering approaches circumvent this shortcoming and can work in online and offline settings. To address the previous challenges, this chapter proposes an adaptive thresholding technique based on unsupervised learning approaches for creation of appropriate thresholds with a change in context in data. The predictive analytics component predicts and sends the thresholds to a CEP engine. In this research, the CEP engine is augmented with IBM OpenWhisk where the machine learning approaches are hosted. This serverless solution makes the application distributed in nature and allows it to scale according to the requirements and magnitude of data. A real world traffic dataset is undertaken to solve this ITS problem. The novel contributions in this work are as follows:

- We have conceptualized and implemented a distributed framework with CEP for adaptive thresholding that helps in automatic updating of the CEP rules.
- We have developed a serverless solution called IBM OpenWhisk hosted on IBM cloud to host the machine learning approaches.
- We have proposed modified agglomerative hierarchical clustering to adapt to context on raw IoT data streams.

The remainder of the chapter is outlined as follows: Section 7.2 discusses the various works done by researchers in the area of congestion prediction. Section 7.3 outlines the various components that constitute the proposed framework. It explores each component and its functionalities in the proposed architecture. Section 7.4 depicts the proposed methodology used in this work and the working mechanism of the model. Section 7.5 presents the various experimental outcomes to quantify the effectiveness of the proposed approach. Section 7.6 summarizes the work and discusses future directions of this work.

7.2   Related works

Moosavi and Hovestadt [12] have implemented probabilistic models, such as Markov chains on GPS data traces obtained from the taxis to estimate the travel time in traffic. Othman *et al.* [13] have implemented artificial neural networks and augmented it with a linear regressor model to obtain the duration of the congestion. Ghosh *et al.* [14] have presented a Bayesian support vector regression approach and modeled the uncertainty in the traffic data. Using this approach, they were able to associate confidence and probability with the model forecasts for better performance. Rajput *et al.* [15] have proposed unsupervised learning approaches like clustering along with rough set theory for predicting congestion. Kim *et al.* [16] have demonstrated the prediction of traffic flow by intaking macroscopic traffic information and environmental data using a Gaussian mixture model based artificial neural network. Pang and Zhao [17] have used subtractive clustering in conjunction with a fuzzy neural network to predict the traffic flow. They have implemented an optimization approach, such as Genetic algorithm to estimate the radii of the clusters effective in classifying and predicting traffic flow. Pattanaik *et al.* [18] have illustrated the usage of k-means approach in predicting the rank or magnitude of the traffic congestion. This prediction was followed by a Dijkstra algorithm in order to compute alternative, shortest routes during congestion. Asahara *et al.* [19] have presented a work on prediction of the movement of pedestrians using mixed Markov chain models. Table 7.1 outlines some unsupervised learning approaches that have been proposed by various researchers with their suitability in streaming scenarios.

From Table 7.1, we observe that most of the clustering approaches enumerated previously are based on k-means which motivated to use k-means as a baseline approach. We notice that [11] is the only work that uses unsupervised approach for traffic classification and computation of thresholds for CEP queries which is identical to the objective of the proposed approach.

7.3   Research preliminaries

This section sheds light on the various components of the framework and its application in an ITS scenario. The use-case of ITS has been opted for two main reasons. First, the traffic sensors that are scattered throughout a smart city continuously generate the data at periodic intervals, thus forming voluminous, big data. Second, there is necessity to process this big data in order to create meaningful insights in real time.

This section discusses the various components and the datasets that have been used in the work.

7.3.1   *Dataset description*

We have used the traffic dataset of Aarhus in this work. The data has been taken from the city of Aarhus. The data is periodically polled at every 5-min interval. The city has a deployment of 449 sensors that collect data and stream it to a central repository.

Table 7.1 Literature review

Authors	Proposed approach	Explanation	Limitations
Lloyd [20]	*k*-Means	Generic clustering approach. Partitions the data into *k* number of clusters based on random initialization of initial centroids	Suffers from random restarts to prevent suboptimal clustering, unsuitable for streaming data analysis
Arthur and Vassilvitskii [21]	*k*-Means++	Similar to *k*-means in working principle. Initial centroids are considered randomly. Following centroids are selected with weighted probability	Suffers from random restarts, not scalable for large datasets
Guha and Mishra [22]	STREAM	A single phase clustering approach that performs in-memory computation of large-scale datasets as data streams	However, the approach misclassifies on evolving streams, unsuitable for data drifts
Ackermann et al. [23]	STREAM KM++	It is primarily based on *k*-means++[4]. Stream KM++ maintains a core set using divisive clustering. A merge and reduce approach merges the deconstructed or decaying data back into the tree	Unsuitable for data drift
Chiang and Mirkin [24]	ikmeans	An initial number of clusters are chosen based on anomalies and a threshold obtained from Hartigan's technique [33] to eliminate smaller clusters	Unsuitable for streaming scenarios
Akbar et al. [11]	Midpoint-based *k*-means	Proposes a *k*-means clustering that computes thresholds for CEP queries in two phases. In the first phase, it computes the Euclidean distance between the centroids of the clusters. In the second phase, it finds the midpoint between the two centroids of two different clusters and considers it as the new threshold	More number of false positives, more retrainings required, no statistical significance considered to detect change in data distributions
Mishra et al. [3]	Genetic algorithm based clustering	Genetic algorithm is implemented on the aggregation metrics. The approach uses the statistical significance technique as a distance measure to identify similarity between regions in a smart city scenario and proposes a modified Silhouette coefficient to identify optimal number of communities in a smart city	Unsuitable for streaming scenarios, high computational overhead
Zhang et al. [25]	Gray relational membership degree rank clustering algorithm	Employs a Gray optimization approach to identify levels of congestion in a smart city scenario. Uses a maximum relational tree to provide ranks to congestion in a smart city scenario	Unsuitable for streaming scenarios

Each sensor comprises a start point and an endpoint. It computes the vehicle density that passed in last 5 min along with their average speed while they passed over. We collected data with an interval of 1 h that is equivalent to 5,035 data points. The entire dataset consists of 122,787 data points and is collected over a span of 5 months.

Table 7.2 depicts the data and the various traffic characteristics that constitute the data. The important features that have been used in the proposed work are the avgSpeed, vehicleCount, and avgMeasuredTime. The selection of these features was made as it has been found very important for congestion prediction in traffic scenarios.

Figure 7.1 shows the proposed architecture and the components in it. The individual components are explained in greater detail in the following sections.

7.3.2   Data ingestion

Telegraf is an agent or plugin that is coded in Go for the purpose of acquisition of metrics of the system on which it is hosted or from other heterogeneous sources and persisting them into InfluxDB. Due to its low memory footprint, it can be used in resource constrained scenarios. It acts as a store for data that can range from

Table 7.2   Traffic dataset attributes

Attribute	Description
timestamp	The date and timestamp of the captured data in 5-min interval
avgMeasuredTime	Average time taken in computing the speed of a vehicle in last 5 min
avgMedianTime	Median time that is taken in computation of the speed of a vehicle in last 5 min
status	Working state of the sensor (OK or error)
vehicleCount	The density of vehicles or intensity of vehicles that have passed through in last 5 min
avgSpeed	The average speed of traffic of vehicles on the road in last 5 min

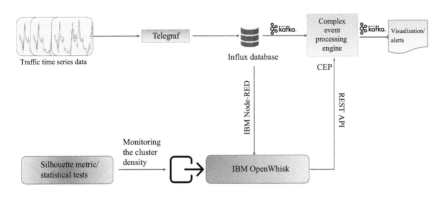

Figure 7.1   Proposed framework

timestamped data to IoT sensor data. Its ability to install with a minimal memory overhead made it a preferred choice in this work.

Apache Kafka is high-speed data pipeline that serves as a broker for the transmission of messages between a sender and a receiver. It is used to simulate the IoT streaming scenario as the messaging broker in Kafka follows a publish–subscribe methodology. It consists of three components in general—Kafka cluster, Kafka producer, and Kafka consumer. Kafka cluster comprises multiple servers that are called as brokers. For enhanced reliability, Kafka uses multiple brokers which serve as a fault-tolerant mechanism. The key advantage in Kafka is the extendibility it offers. Servers can be added or deleted while the cluster is in execution. Kafka is optimized to be as a data pipeline for streaming data.

7.3.3 Complex event processing

A CEP engine [26–28] is created in Node-RED that can intake the data streams and trigger a complex event when the threshold in a rule is exceeded. These rules form the core of the CEP and are written in a certain query language. The CEP has a fast event processor that helps in concatenating heterogeneous data from multiple sources to discover interesting patterns in the data with minimum time latency. The different functionalities of the CEP engine are extended by building apps that serve a particular purpose. The users or domain experts write the rules in these apps that are connected to a predefined source and sink where they intake data and output events, respectively. The rules built on this architecture have static thresholds that are not adaptive in nature. A necessity arises to create dynamic thresholds for these rules as the traffic patterns in a certain location is different from patterns observed in another location.

7.3.4 Clustering approaches

Clustering is a type of unsupervised learning approach for the classification of unlabeled data into groups of data instances called clusters. The data points in individual clusters should be homogeneous in nature. Similarity between data points in a particular cluster and dissimilarity between data points present in different clusters can serve as a yardstick of the quality of the clusters. The succeeding section highlights the various clustering approaches. We also discuss on approaches undertaken to estimate the quality of the clusters. Further, we propose a clustering approach that is extended to work on streaming data. We present two different approaches for adaptive clustering and boundary detection for thresholds estimation. The major highlights that our approach addresses are as follows:

- The approach should be able to work on IoT data streams.
- Adaptive to data drifts in data streams.
- Consistency in forming dense clusters in each iteration.

IoT devices capture data from the environment and store the collected data in a central data repository. Mostly, IoT data is unlabeled and requires the knowledge of a domain expert to assign ground truth or labels to the acquired data. The traffic data collected by the city of Madrid is also unlabeled.

In this work, we are also concerned with the probability distributions of various features of the traffic data and how a change in statistical properties of the data can impact the performance of the model. This characteristic varies on the basis of the spatial and temporal characteristics of the data. For example, a threshold for a certain time of the day may not be the same for another location at the same time. For other regions, a higher threshold may be set up for identifying congestions. In a similar manner, our perception of traffic congestion can change with a change in season. For example, vehicles moving at a slower pace during winters do not mean congestion because of their poor visibility. In this particular phenomenon, despite having similar inputs, there is a chance of different outcomes which are called data drift [29]. If there is a change in data distributions of input features without impacting outputs, then it is called virtual drift. Real data drift represents cases where there is change in outputs with any marked change in data distributions of input features. In IoT, change in output also takes place due to change in data distributions, thus making data drift a significant characteristic in smart city applications.

This motivated us to attempt clustering approaches on the data for classification. Clustering techniques not only help us to classify the data in diverse classes but also ensure an optimal distribution of data instances amongst the classes. Though regression approaches can be used for identifying thresholds, in the presence of data drift in IoT streams, the predictions tend to become insignificant with time. This necessitates the retraining of the approach. The number of retrainings of a regression approach is time-consuming and also increases with the amount of data drifts in dataset. Researchers in [11] have identified k-means as a useful algorithm on traffic prediction. This motivated us to compare the k-means approach with our proposed method.

We have primarily implemented two widely popular algorithms k-means [11] and agglomerative hierarchical clustering. k-Means algorithm [20], also known as the "Lloyd algorithm," works in iterative rounds of partitioning the data by identifying data instances nearer to a certain centroid and grouping them into corresponding cluster. The algorithm starts by initializing random data points as initial center clusters or centroids and successively computing the data points closer to centroids. A problem arises as the convergence of the k-means takes place until it reaches stationary points and the convergence may not be an optimal solution as the convergence may not be global minimum. Agglomerative clustering algorithm [30] conglomerates data instances on the basis of a particular similarity in a "bottom-up" manner. The algorithm initiates by considering each data instance as a microcluster. Similarities are identified between microclusters following which they merge to form a comparatively bigger cluster. These bigger clusters are further merged in each iteration until a final macrocluster is formed.

7.3.5   OpenWhisk

OpenWhisk is a serverless open-source cloud platform that performs the execution of the functions that are triggered by events. These functions are called actions. The source of the events can vary from databases to message queues. Source codes can be hosted on OpenWhisk that can be executed through commands given at the Command

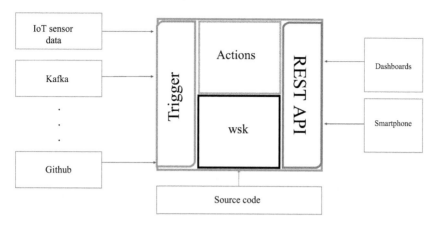

Figure 7.2   OpenWhisk framework

line interface. Once triggered, OpenWhisk can transmit services to a variety of endpoints, such as websites, REST APIs. OpenWhisk executes the user given tasks with the help of functions. Figure 7.2 depicts the OpenWhisk architecture.

OpenWhisk completed the assigned tasks with the help of functions. A function depicts a source code that takes some input and gives a corresponding output. The functions defined in OpenWhisk are generally devoid of any state and are stateless in nature while the back-end web applications are stateful. Maintaining the state of a function can be expensive as scalability is compromised due to the overhead of persisting or check-pointing the state. Synchronization is also expensive as states between various functions need to be in synchrony. In serverless computing paradigm, NoSQL storage can be used for persisting the states, if needed. The OpenWhisk infrastructure anticipates the occurrence of an event. Once the event takes place, a corresponding function can be invoked. This allows for the inclusion of optimized code that gets processed very quickly on an event reception or on arrival of latest data. Actions are stateless functions that contain the function code and are invoked by events or REST API calls. OpenWhisk uses a JSON format for data that is exchanged within the architecture. JSON objects can be easily serialized and, hence, passed as strings that is received by the actions. Once received, actions can process the data and return the result as a JSON object. A trigger is a message invocation. It can instantiate a single or chain of actions, if associated with a rule. Once a trigger is created, it is appended with some action. Once the trigger receives a required set of parameters, which has to be provided by the administrator, it can fire an action.

7.3.6   Evaluation metrics

We have used two standard and widely used metrics to evaluate the usefulness of the clustering approach that has been implemented in this work. In the case of static or offline clustering, cluster validation metrics, such as adjusted rand index, completeness, and homogeneity score, are helpful. But the previous metrics are employed to evaluate the efficiency of clustering approaches on labeled data by comparing predicted labels with ground truth. In IoT scenarios, data drifts tend to change the centroids often which require retraining of the clustering approach. Due to this inherent property, the silhouette coefficient is used to test the effectiveness of the clustering algorithms.

A single evaluation metric is not a sufficient measure for identifying the number of clusters. This is because the underlying mechanism of the evaluation of metrics depends on data characteristics, and strong bias can influence the metric to predict higher values of k. Second, in this work unsupervised learning is used for extracting meaningful insights or knowledge (i.e., congestion). So it should not be restricted under any assumptions that are considered by external cluster validation measures, such as availability of class labels for performance evaluation.

To address the aforesaid issues, we considered using the silhouette coefficient [31] and Calinski–Harabasz (CH) index [32] to identify the optimal clusters in the traffic data as they do not consider any prior assumptions. The silhouette coefficient is effective in evaluating cluster quality over IoT data streams as mentioned in [11].

7.3.6.1   Silhouette coefficient

The silhouette coefficient [31] discovers the possible clustering number by computing the difference between the average intra-cluster distance, i.e., distance within the cluster and the intercluster distance, i.e., distance between two clusters and is defined as follows:

$$\text{Silhouette coefficient } (\theta) = \frac{1}{n} \sum_{j=1}^{n} \left(\frac{y(i) - x(i)}{\max [x(i), y(i)]} \right) \tag{7.1}$$

where i represents the data point, $x(i)$ represents the intra-cluster distance, $y(i)$ represents the intercluster distance.

7.3.6.2   Calinski–Harabasz index

The CH index [32] is a cluster validation metric to identify the degree of dispersion within clusters and amongst different clusters and it can be computed as follows:

$$CH(m) = \frac{a(m)(n - k)}{b(m)(m - 1)} \tag{7.2}$$

where

$$a(m) = \sum_{i=1}^{m} x_m \|a_k - a\|^2 \tag{7.3}$$

$$b(m) = \left(\sum_{i=1}^{m} \sum_{C(j)=m} \|a_j - a_k\|^2 \right) \tag{7.4}$$

where m represents the number of clusters and $a(m)$ represents the divergence noticed at intercluster level. This divergence is otherwise called intercluster covariance.

$b(m)$ stands for intra-cluster covariance and m is the considered samples. Here, a maximum value of CH index represents better and denser clusters.

7.4   Proposed methodology

InfluxDB stores the incoming JSON data. This data can be queried using Chronograf. We have used CEP to derive complex or higher order events from the data streams. For intaking the data, we have used a high speed, open-source messaging broker called Apache Kafka that follows a publish–subscribe mechanism.

A Kafka producer acts a source of data that ingests data from InfluxDB and publishes it to a topic. A Kafka consumer is associated with the CEP that subscribes to the topic and gets the data as and when it arrives. This ensures in-order delivery, message persistence, and high availability of data, and thus minimizing the loss of data during transmission. The CEP engine is primarily a rule-driven system, and simple events are triggered when the data exceeds a certain threshold or falls below a certain threshold. A complex event is the concatenation of such simple events over a period of time. It becomes difficult to decide the thresholds over a period of time as the context changes. For example, a threshold set for triggering a complex event in morning may not be applicable for the afternoon or traffic congestion thresholds on a weekend, which is quite different from the thresholds extracted from traffic data on weekdays. As CEP engines are reactive, i.e., they only fire events when the data arrives, an unavailability of optimized threshold might prove to be a bottleneck for the prediction of interesting scenarios.

By using InfluxDB node in Node-RED, the data is sent to a serverless platform hosted on IBM cloud called as IBM OpenWhisk.

Algorithm 1 Initial clustering

    Input: Initial Static dataset C, Range for number of clusters R
    Output: Optimal Clustering of the dataset
    Initialisation:
    MaxQuality = -1
    BestModel=null
    For *i=n-1 to 1* **do**
        If *Quality=MaxQuality* **then**
            MaxQuality=Quality
            BestModel=Model
        End
        if *I==min(R)* **then**
            break
        end
    end
    Return BestModel

On the contrary, we implemented unsupervised machine learning approaches for the computation of thresholds in the CEP rules. The clustering is initiated as outlined in Algorithm 1. Hierarchical clustering has higher complexity in terms of time and space. The clusters are not regular shaped and have an irregular shape that makes it favorable as in k-means because of the spherical nature of the clusters some useful points might be missed out.

This motivated us to use agglomerative hierarchical clustering. We used pre-processing techniques to remove the outliers. But the concern is the removal of rarely occurring points from the initial data that could be useful "alerts." Such points are clustered at a later point in the clustering process as data is streamed. But if the occurrence of such points is minimal in the data, then this should not affect the clustering process. This is important as it helps in avoiding the loss of useful data that may be alerts by nature.

Though hierarchical clustering does not require the estimation of optimal cluster of clusters, it will be a yardstick for estimation of range of data points present in the possible number of clusters.

Cluster quality plays a pivotal role in unsupervised learning. With time as more data streams are ingested, the clusters become sparse and the cluster quality deteriorates. This can hamper the thresholding procedure. To maintain a consistent cluster quality, we make the process adaptive as presented in Algorithm 2.

Algorithm 2 Adaptive clustering

    Input: Initial Clustering:I, Threshold:P
    Output: Optimal Clusters after entry in the datastream
    Initialisation:
    Model=I
    Quality=SilhouetteScore(I)
    for $d = C[i]$ **do**
        $d = \text{nextPoint}(C')$
        $\text{Model}' = \text{cluster}(\text{Model},d)$
        $\text{Quality}' = \text{SilhouetteScore}(\text{Model}')$
        If $\text{Quality}' \geq P \times \text{Quality}$ **then**
            $\text{Model} = \text{Model}'$
            $\text{Quality} = \text{Quality}'$
    end
    else
        N=NumberofClusters(Model)
        $R' = \text{N-1 to N+1}$
    end
    $\text{Model} = \text{Recluster}(\text{Model, d, } R')$
    $\text{Quality} = \text{SilhouetteScore}(\text{Model})$
    Return Model
  End

Event detection detects whenever a deviation takes place in the attributes of the data streams. This helps in automating the necessary actions to be taken for deviations observed in the data. In IoT data streams, event would indicate change in attributes like traffic velocity and traffic intensity by triggering high speed or high vehicle intensity alerts. For detecting events, we have followed clustering approaches on historical data and the latest or current data. When data instances are grouped into two different clusters, it marks the occurrence of an event. We then compare the change in values of various attributes with the total possible range of that attribute and fire an event if the value crosses a certain threshold.

The previous method can also be performed by directly verifying corresponding data points and checking them with the threshold, and thus skipping the process of clustering. The shortcomings of such an approach are the thresholds that are static and do not evolve with context. Such static thresholds are not able to capture the significant changes in the data distribution. The boundary detection procedure identifies a cutoff value for classifying data instances into various categories. For example, we can split the data into high traffic, moderate traffic, and low traffic depending on the cutoff values for individual features. The boundary values can be further used in action firing rules. Algorithm 3 proposes a method for predicting the threshold values based on the data rather than using constant values throughout. We use the following method for boundary detection.

Algorithm 3 Boundary detection

Input: m × n entries ('m' entries with 'n' features, Clusters of dataset C)
Output: Boundary values for each feature
Step 1: The data points are divided into groups based on clustering.
Step 2: Find the centre of each cluster (M_i)
Step 3: Find the number of points in a cluster (n_i),
    Total number of data points (N),
    Radius of the cluster (longest distance between the centre and a point belonging to the same cluster) (R_i),
    Sum of radii of all clusters (R_{sum})
Step 4: Assign weights to each cluster (W_i) where, $W_i = (R_i/R_{sum}) * (n_i/N)$
Step 5: For each feature in the data: Extract the values of the feature from the respective centroids along with its weight. Sort the values of the feature.
Step 6: The weighted average between two sorted values gives the boundary value between those clusters.

Additionally, if the clusters contain labels they can be retained along with the weights while extracting the values of each feature from respective centroids. For example, in an IoT data stream, while considering the boundaries for traffic intensity if we retain the label for congestion, we can directly construct rules for predicting congestion using only intensity values. Thus, from the clusters, we can obtain boundary conditions for each feature and can create rules for classifying data based on these boundaries.

We query the NoSQL database and then format the data as it is in a JSON format. We store the formatted data into a flat file. Once the data is parsed and is in a proper format, we send the data to the OpenWhisk through the OpenWhisk node. The OpenWhisk is hosted on IBM cloud where it is invoked through Node-RED. In OpenWhisk, we created a "Cloud Foundry" app, where we inserted the Python codes for clustering. Once done, we generate the cloud functions in the OpenWhisk portal. Cloud functions encompass actions, triggers, and rules. Triggers can be invoked by users in an explicit manner. It can be fired on behalf of another user from an external event source that can be a message hub or Kafka queue. Once messages are received, they are sent to user defined actions. Python actions can also consume from high-speed Kafka queues. The entry point for the action is main by default. It can be explicitly specified during the action creation. Algorithms 1–3 are coded as different actions in the OpenWhisk. A rule is created to initiate the app on the dashboard and starts it so that it listens for any API calls. In Node-RED, we provide the URL of our particular account and the app address, API Key, and the name to the node. The thresholds can be stored in a flat file too which can be later used. We update the node and connect it to a node called "set globals" which is a function node. This function node is responsible for the globalization of the computed thresholds that can be used in the framework. Functions are connected to event sources in OpenWhisk using triggers and rules.

Figure 7.3 represents the second Node-RED flow that pulls the data from the InfluxDB and parses the data and sends to the CEP engine and also visualizes it on the debug terminal of Node-RED. The streaming rate can be controlled as we have set one message per 12 s. This value has been tested experimentally as a lot of events will result in a lot of redundant events. The events are pushed into the functions present in OpenWhisk to decide which cluster they belong to on the basis of Algorithms 1–3 mentioned in the preceding sections. The algorithms were implemented using Python 3.6 environment and the codes were embedded in the functions that can be invoked whenever new data is acquired through Kafka to create new thresholds for CEP queries. The proposed framework has pretrained

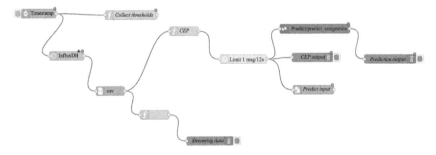

Figure 7.3   Sending of computed thresholds to CEP

clustering approaches trained using historical data on a set of 500 data points. The output is fetched after computing the result over OpenWhisk on IBM cloud and the thresholds are pushed onto the CEP rules that trigger the higher order complex events, i.e., congestion events. The computation takes place on the IBM cloud with minimal time latency. The algorithms were also modified to adjust to the real-time scenario and multiple restarts on the basis of the silhouette coefficient might be a computational overhead that can deter the timely occurrence of congestion events. To address this issue, we took the help of using statistical significant windows. Figure 7.4 depicts the interactions between the various modules of the proposed framework. The next section describes the process of traffic classification and threshold computation in real-time settings using the proposed approach.

7.4.1   *Statistical approach to optimize the number of retrainings*

Rather than intaking the entire data as a whole, data is taken in batches with the help of windows. Kafka allows the intake of data in batches by making some configurations at the runtime of broker. The cluster quality degradation is an important factor in the triggering of the retraining of the formed clusters. But clusters reformation takes place only when there is significant change in the statistical properties, i.e., the probability distributions of the data. We use the concepts of overlapping windows for the detection of significant change underlying statistical properties in the data. Two windows ingest data with a difference in 300 data points, i.e., the first window intakes data from 1 to 500 while the second window consumes from 200 to 700. It is clearly noticed that there is an overlap of 300 data points that is common in both the windows. A Wilcoxon signed-rank test [33] is

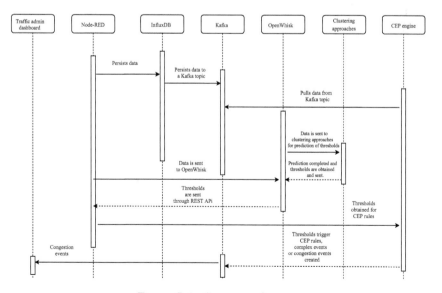

Figure 7.4   Sequence diagram

implemented on windows 1 and 2 at 95% confidence interval with a *p*-value set at 0.05. The null hypothesis (H_0) considered here is the probability distributions in both the windows are similar and the retraining of the formed clusters is not needed. This result is also compared with the evaluation metric values and the retraining is accordingly considered. The alternate hypothesis (H_a) is that there is a significant change in the distribution of data points in the two windows, and this might lead to loosely formed, sparse clusters from which extraction of thresholds for CEP rules is cumbersome. This also addresses data drift in the traffic data which, if not attended, may lead to false alarms causing inconvenience to the traffic administration.

7.5   Experimental results and discussion

As the traffic data is unlabeled, there is a necessity to identify the possible number of clusters in the data. We have used two popular evaluation metrics, silhouette coefficient and CH index, to find the clusters in the data. The silhouette coefficient provides a value between -1 and $+1$. Silhouette values that are near to 0 indicate overlapping clusters while negative values indicate that the data points are allocated to a cluster wrongfully, i.e., the clustering is erroneous. In the CH index, $b(m)$ represents the all-inclusive within cluster variance whereas $a(m)$ represents the all-inclusive between cluster variance. Generally, $a(m)$ represents the variance of the cluster centroids from the centroid mean of the data. A larger value of $a(m)$ depicts that the centroid of individual clusters will be sparse and data points would not be in close proximity to each other. $b(m)$ decrements proportionately to the increase in the number of clusters. Thus, clusters with high CH index indicate better clusters. From Figure 7.5, it cannot be determined whether the possible number of clusters on the data is 2 or 3. It can be clearly seen that according to the CH index, the number of clusters feasible is 2 while according the silhouette coefficient, the number of clusters that the data can be divided into is 3. It is difficult to conclude

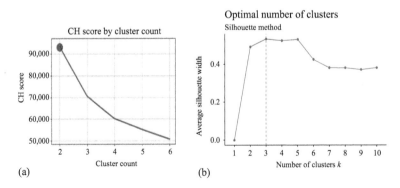

Figure 7.5   (a) Silhouette coefficient to find the optimal clusters and (b) CH index to find the optimal clusters

from these results that into how many clusters the dataset can be divided. We used multiple evaluation criteria to estimate the optimum number of clusters. This procedure of finding optimal clusters has to tackle the problems of quality of clusters, the extent to which clustering scheme fits the specific data set. Validation indices provide a better way to evaluate the clustering approach with a different number of clusters and return the optimal clusters required. Each index aims for a specific goal of clustering. Twenty-nine indices, namely, CH, Duda, Pseudot2, Cindex, Gamma, Beale, CCC, Ptbiserial, Gplus, DB, Frey, Hartigan, Tau, Ratkowsky, Scott, Marriot, Ball, Trcovw, Tracew, Friedman, McClain, Rubin, Silhouette, Dunn, KL, gap, Dindex, Hubert, SDbw, are used. Then, that cluster number, which is indicated by maximum indices, is taken as an optimal number. Figure 7.6 depicts the statistics of number of indices accepting a particular number of clusters as optimal, indicating that 3 is the optimal number of clusters as predicted by a majority of indices. Further, we analyze the cluster quality or cluster density formed by *k*-means and hierarchical clustering approaches. Figure 7.7 exhibits that clusters formed by *k*-means are of superior quality as compared to hierarchical clustering. But the difference in quality of clusters formed is minimal as both the approaches produce a peak of optimal clusters at 3.

From this observation, we can conclude that both the approaches produce clusters of similar quality. But the high peaks or deviations in hierarchical approach depict that as the cluster size varies, the deviation is significant. This can be important in the prediction of data drifts or useful events in the data.

The plot in Figure 7.8 depicts the amount of time consumed in clustering the data instances using *k*-means and hierarchical clustering approaches. This figure illustrates the time taken by the clustering techniques from initial stage to the formation of required number of clusters. It can be noticed that the time consumed

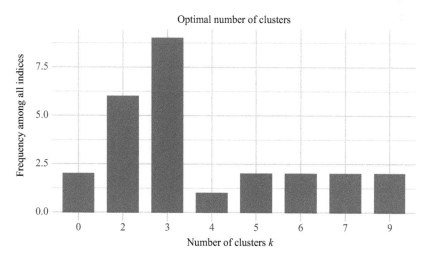

Figure 7.6   Optimal number of clusters across 29 validation metrics on varying cluster sizes

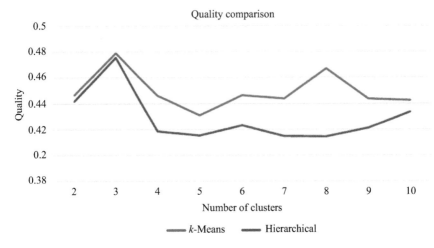

Figure 7.7   Clustering results of baseline and proposed approach

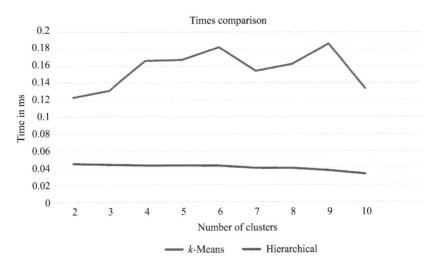

Figure 7.8   Clustering time of baseline and proposed approach

by hierarchical clustering is much less than the time taken by *k*-means to form the same number of clusters. This contradicts the claim that hierarchical clustering possesses higher time complexity than *k*-means. This is mainly attributed to the fact that *k*-means consumes a lot of time in the random initialization of the centroids. Due to this random initialization, the centroids of *k*-means restart iteratively to discover an optimal cluster size whereas hierarchical cluster accomplishes the same result in fewer iterations.

Figure 7.9 exhibits a radial plot showing the clusters formed on the three features considered. It can be seen that the clusters are more evenly distributed and

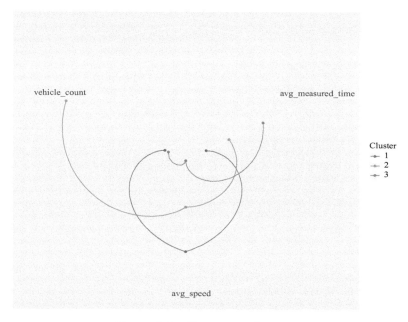

vehicle_count

avg_measured_time

Cluster
- 1
- 2
- 3

avg_speed

Figure 7.9   Cluster visualization

Table 7.3   Computed thresholds for different times of the day

Time of day	Feature	Thresholds	Threshold (mean)
Morning	Vehicle count	4,598	4,642.5
	Vehicle count	4,687	
	avgSpeed	73	75.5
	avgSpeed	78	
Night	Vehicle count	3,607	3,230.5
	Vehicle count	2,854	
	avgSpeed	74	70
	avgSpeed	66	

better formed when the number of clusters are 3 as predicted in the sections earlier. The boundary points between these clusters give us the required thresholds that are necessary for the CEP rules. The thresholds that are computed are represented in Table 7.3.

It is noticed that the thresholds for the day are quite different from the thresholds that we get for the night time. It is because of the adaptive capability of the algorithm and its ability to retrain itself in the presence of data drifts or change in statistical properties of the data. We acquire two thresholds as we consider two boundaries between three clusters. So, our proposed boundary detection algorithm proposes two thresholds signifying the bounds. The mean of these computed

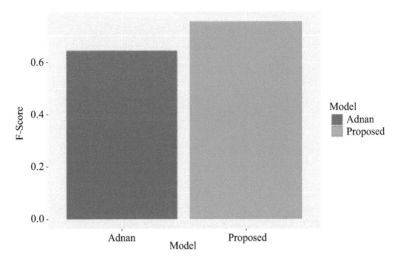

Figure 7.10   Performance comparison between proposed and baseline [11] on the basis of F-score

thresholds for a particular feature is taken as the final threshold that is sent to CEP. These thresholds, if exceeded, can fire simple events. By inferring the pattern and amalgamation of multiple simple events, complex events can be created.

We invoked a TomTom API* to collect actual congestion labels for a particular location. It is a necessary step to evaluate the accuracy of the congestion events predicted by our approach with real congestion events. Figure 7.10 compares the performance our proposed method against a baseline approach [11] on a location in the traffic dataset. It is noticed that our approach performs significantly better with an *F*-score of 75% while the baseline approach records a relatively less *F*-score of 64.1%.

A higher recall of 80% noticed in our proposed model exhibits the optimal thresholds of hierarchical clustering that performs better in detecting congestions over *k*-means clustering approach [11].

7.6   Conclusion

This chapter presents an adaptive clustering approach that is based on agglomerative clustering technique. The silhouette coefficient serves as a yardstick to measure the cluster quality. The clustering approach was implemented on historical data and gradually it was adapted for a streaming scenario. The clustering algorithm was implemented in a streaming manner using Node-RED and OpenWhisk which hosted the algorithms and sent the computed thresholds to the CEP rules using which the rules became adaptive to context. The traffic dataset of Aarhus was

*https://developer.tomtom.com/traffic-api

taken in this work, and the clustering approaches have been evaluated in terms of time and quality. We proposed to use a serverless architecture to accommodate the large-scale traffic data of a smart city scenario. We introduced modularity in the framework that can be extended and scaled as per the requirements of the particular data. We found the optimal clusters through a range of evaluation metrics and gave a statistical solution to optimize the retraining of the proposed clustering approach for adapting to data drifts. We also compared the performance of our proposed approach with a baseline approach in terms of F-score.

Acknowledgment

The authors would like to thank TCS Research for funding this research through TCS PhD fellowship to the second author.

References

[1]   Jie Y, Pei JY, Jun L, *et al.* Smart home system based on IoT technologies. In: Computational and Information Sciences (ICCIS), 2013 Fifth International Conference on. IEEE; 2013. p. 1789–1791.

[2]   Serra J, Pubill D, Antonopoulos A, *et al.* Smart HVAC control in IoT: Energy consumption minimization with user comfort constraints. The Scientific World Journal. 2014;2014.

[3]   Mishra S, Hota C, Kumar L, *et al.* An evolutionary GA-based approach for community detection in IoT. IEEE Access. 2019;7:100512–100534.

[4]   Liu Y, Yang C, Jiang L, *et al.* Intelligent edge computing for IoT-based energy management in smart cities. IEEE Network. 2019;33(2):111–117.

[5]   Rathore MM, Paul A, Hong WH, *et al.* Exploiting IoT and big data analytics: Defining smart digital city using real-time urban data. Sustainable Cities and Society. 2018;40:600–610.

[6]   Zhang P, Shi X, and Khan SU. QuantCloud: Enabling big data complex event processing for quantitative finance through a data-driven execution. IEEE Transactions on Big Data. 2018.

[7]   Nawaz F, Janjua NK, and Hussain OK. PERCEPTUS: Predictive complex event processing and reasoning for IoT-enabled supply chain. Knowledge-Based Systems. 2019.

[8]   Wang Y, Gao H, and Chen G. Predictive complex event processing based on evolving Bayesian networks. Pattern Recognition Letters. 2018;105: 207–216.

[9]   Akbar A, Kousiouris G, Pervaiz H, *et al.* Real-time probabilistic data fusion for large-scale IoT applications. IEEE Access. 2018;6:10015–10027.

[10] Quadri NS and Yadav K. Efficient data classification for IoT devices using AWS Kinesis platform. In: 2018 21st Saudi Computer Society National Computer Conference (NCC). IEEE; 2018. p. 1–5.

[11] Akbar A, Carrez F, Moessner K, *et al.* Context-aware stream processing for distributed IoT applications. In: 2015 IEEE 2nd World Forum on Internet of Things (WF-IoT). IEEE; 2015. p. 663–668.

[12] Moosavi V and Hovestadt L. Modeling urban traffic dynamics in coexistence with urban data streams. In: Proceedings of the 2nd ACM SIGKDD International Workshop on Urban Computing. ACM; 2013. p. 10.

[13] Othman MSB, Keoh SL, and Tan G. Efficient journey planning and congestion prediction through deep learning. In: 2017 International Smart Cities Conference (ISC2). IEEE; 2017. p. 1–6.

[14] Ghosh B, Asif MT, and Dauwels J. Bayesian prediction of the duration of non-recurring road incidents. In: 2016 IEEE Region 10 Conference (TENCON). IEEE; 2016. p. 87–90.

[15] Rajput D, Singh P, and Bhattacharya M. An efficient and generic hybrid framework for high dimensional data clustering. In: Proceedings of International Conference on Data Mining and Knowledge Engineering, World Academy of Science, Engineering and Technology; 2010. p. 174–179.

[16] Oh SD, Kim YJ, and Hong JS. Urban traffic flow prediction system using a multifactor pattern recognition model. IEEE Transactions on Intelligent Transportation Systems. 2015;16(5):2744–2755.

[17] Pang M and Zhao X. Traffic flow prediction of chaos time series by using subtractive clustering for fuzzy neural network modeling. In: 2008 Second International Symposium on Intelligent Information Technology Application. vol. 1. IEEE; 2008. p. 23–27.

[18] Pattanaik V, Singh M, Gupta P, *et al.* Smart real-time traffic congestion estimation and clustering technique for urban vehicular roads. In: 2016 IEEE Region 10 Conference (TENCON). IEEE; 2016. p. 3420–3423.

[19] Asahara A, Maruyama K, Sato A, *et al.* Pedestrian-movement prediction based on mixed Markov-chain model. In: Proceedings of the 19th ACM SIGSPATIAL International Conference on Advances in Geographic Information Systems. ACM; 2011. p. 25–33.

[20] Lloyd S. Least squares quantization in PCM. IEEE Transactions on Information Theory. 1982;28(2):129–137.

[21] Arthur D and Vassilvitskii S. K-Means++: The advantages of careful seeding. In: Proceedings of the Eighteenth Annual ACM-SIAM Symposium on Discrete Algorithms. SODA'07. Philadelphia, PA, USA: Society for Industrial and Applied Mathematics; 2007. p. 1027–1035.

[22] Guha S and Mishra N. Clustering data streams. In: Data stream management. Berlin, Heidelberg: Springer; 2016. p. 169–187.

[23] Ackermann MR, Märtens M, Raupach C, *et al.* StreamKM++: A clustering algorithm for data streams. Journal of Experimental Algorithmics (JEA). 2012;17:2–1.

[24] Chiang MMT and Mirkin B. Intelligent choice of the number of clusters in k-means clustering: An experimental study with different cluster spreads. Journal of Classification. 2010;27(1):3–40.

[25] Zhang Y, Ye N, Wang R, *et al.* A method for traffic congestion clustering judgment based on grey relational analysis. ISPRS International Journal of Geo-Information. 2016;5(5):71.

[26] Dávid I, Ráth I, and Varró D. Foundations for streaming model transformations by complex event processing. Software & Systems Modeling. 2018;17(1):135–162. Available from: https://doi.org/10.1007/s10270-016-0533-1.

[27] Cugola G and Margara A. Processing flows of information: From data stream to complex event processing. ACM Computing Surveys (CSUR). 2012;44(3):15.

[28] Wu E, Diao Y, and Rizvi S. High-performance complex event processing over streams. In: Proceedings of the 2006 ACM SIGMOD International Conference on Management of Data. ACM; 2006. p. 407–418.

[29] Wang YL and Han QL. Modelling and controller design for discrete-time networked control systems with limited channels and data drift. Information Sciences. 2014;269:332–348.

[30] Bouguettaya A, Yu Q, Liu X, *et al.* Efficient agglomerative hierarchical clustering. Expert Systems with Applications. 2015;42(5):2785–2797.

[31] Aranganayagi S and Thangavel K. Clustering categorical data using silhouette coefficient as a relocating measure. In: International Conference on Computational Intelligence and Multimedia Applications (ICCIMA 2007). vol. 2. IEEE; 2007. p. 13–17.

[32] Maulik U and Bandyopadhyay S. Performance evaluation of some clustering algorithms and validity indices. IEEE Transactions on Pattern Analysis and Machine Intelligence. 2002;24(12):1650–1654.

[33] Taheri S and Hesamian G. A generalization of the Wilcoxon signed-rank test and its applications. Statistical Papers. 2013;54(2):457–470.

Chapter 8

Gender-based classification on e-commerce big data

Chaitanya Kanchibhotla[1],
Venkata Lakshmi Narayana Somayajulu Durvasula[1]
and Radha Krishna Pisipati[1]

Platforms such as social media, e-commerce, mobile phones, and email communications generate every data at big data scale. All this data is stored either in structured or unstructured format in large databases. Data mining is a process of analyzing these large databases and discovering hidden patterns from them. Some of the essential functionalities in data mining include finding associations, correlations, patterns, and classifying the data. Classification is a process in which several rules are identified from training data instances, and the same can be used for predicting or labeling the unlabeled data. The classification problem has a number of applications in vast areas, out of which e-commerce is one of the critical platforms which belongs to the worldwide web.

Existing classification techniques over e-commerce data are mainly based on the users' purchasing patterns. However, gender preferences significantly improve in recommending various products, targeting customers for branding products, providing customized suggestions to the users, etc. In this chapter, we explain three methods for gender-based classification. All the methods are two-phased in which the features are extracted in the first phase. Classification of Gender is done in the second phase based on the features identified in the first phase. The first technique exploits the hierarchical relationships among products and purchasing patterns. In the first phase, dimensionality is reduced from data by identifying the features that well describe the browsing pattern of the users. The second phase uses these features to classify gender. The second technique extracts both basic and advanced features. It uses the random forest to classify the data based on features identified. The third approach extracts behavioral and temporal features along with product features, and classification is done using gradient-boosted trees (GBTs). Experiments were also conducted on the state-of-the-art classification algorithms.

To handle the volume and variety of big data that is generated through e-commerce platforms, experiments are carried out on Apache Spark clusters

[1]Department of computer science and Engineering, National Institute of Technology, Warangal, India

created on Azure HDInsight with two head clusters along with variable node clusters. The dataset is related to clickstream data (provided by FPT group) consisting of browsing logs (with the list of products formed as a hierarchy), session start time, and session end time.

8.1 Introduction

With the increase in Internet usage day by day, social media, and e-commerce became an essential part of daily activity. These elements are accessed in multiple devices such as desktops, laptops, smartphones, tablets, and smart devices, and generating data at big data scale. Out of 7.6 billion total population across the globe, there are 4.38 billion Internet users and 3.4 billion active social media users [1]. This is a significant change when compared to Internet usage at the time of inception as the majority of the Internet users were young, male, better educated, more affluent, and urban [2]. With this enormous usage, Internet and online shopping has become a new platform for roles such as retailers, agents, dealers, and marketers to showcase and promote their goods. One of the crucial challenges for online retailers these days is not only to attract the customers to their online platforms but also to convert them as purchasers. One possible way to make this happen in e-commerce platforms is to analyze the users' behavior from extensive data of e-commerce transactions along with their demographics such as age, gender, place, and decide on the advertising strategies that can promote the business.

Particularly in e-commerce websites, user's behavior can be studied by analyzing the customer data, which mainly contains their browsing and purchase patterns. From the customers browsing data/logs of an e-commerce website within a given period, it is possible to extract essential rules that can help in decision-making. One distinguished standard measure in Internet usage is the gender of the user who is browsing [2]. Identifying and suggesting products based on gender is vital for customized product personalization and can show adverse effects on business if it is identified incorrectly. Gender for an Internet user plays a vital role in advertising, information processing, and online shopping [3]. Gender difference is the most interesting aspect of the advertising and marketing companies for decades. Several research studies exist in the literature, which mainly concentrates on identifying the role of gender in online shopping. Some studies have found that men and women behave differently during online shopping [4], and some studies identified that there are no differences [5]. The study conducted by Zhang *et al.* [6] finds the role of gender in bloggers' switching behavior and concluded that bloggers' intention to switch their blog services was related to three factors: satisfaction, sunk costs, and attractive alternatives. Their study also revealed that females had more sensitivity to satisfaction and fewer tendencies to attractive alternatives than males. Abraham *et al.* [7] showed that men have more preferred online products than women. On the relationship between gender and web design perspective, Tuch *et al.* [8] showed that men are particular to the symmetry of a website when compared to women. Hoffman *et al.* [9] showed that men were more likely to browse and purchase a product than women. According to Tracy [10], male users are 2.4 times more likely than women to shop online. Bernard *et al.* [11] found that men are more likely to explore all the features in the website, such as videos customized views of products, and women are more interested in website communication features such as promotional information. From all these examples, it can be concluded that the gender of the person who is browsing the website plays a considerable role in any e-commerce website.

Gender prediction from e-commerce big data can be modeled as a classification technique in data mining. Classification is one of the most interesting problems in the fast-evolving fields such as e-commerce and web-based businesses in which the data grows exponentially. Various data mining/machine learning techniques are implemented to predict the gender of users based on features identified. The notable techniques are Bayesian logistic regression, support vector machine (SVM), and AdaBoost decision tree [12]. According to Cheng *et al.* [12], identifying the correct set of features for gender identification is still one of the challenging tasks. Bhaskar *et al.* [13] examined weblogs to identify purchase patterns of users to find if users are buying the products that they are familiar with, or they are purposefully shopping. Ketul *et al.* [14] used data mining techniques such as association rules, clustering, sequential patterns, and classification on e-commerce data to identify unusual patterns in the data to improve the service to customers and to increase the success of e-commerce sites. Similar work was also done by Zhang *et al.* [6] to identify buying patterns using the association rule mining technique on web pages. They also designed a model that can predict gender for potential customers.

8.1.1   e-Commerce and big data

Big data refers to extremely large datasets (usually exceeding exabytes) that are analyzed to reveal patterns and trends in users' behavior. The usage of the e-commerce platform is tremendously increasing day by day. According to [15], there are 300 million active users on Amazon, more than 80 million users in Walmart, and eBay. The data generated by these users is also humongous. At a very high level, e-commerce data is classified into usage data, content data, and user data. Usage data consists of user sessions. The content data in a site refers to the collection of objects and their relationships. User data may include information related to registered users and their reviews [13]. Following are some of the benefits that big data can bring in the e-commerce field:

- **Make better strategic plans to improve business**

    Big data analytics can help in understanding customer behavior in shopping, which can help in better strategic planning. Using big data and analytics, aspects such as brands, time of access, and increase in business demands can be assessed.

- **Better understand users**

    Big data can be useful in analyzing the user's shopping patterns, such as the type of products they access, the products that are accessed more by the user, and the sequence in which the products are accessed to suggest the most relevant goods to the users.

- **Provide better projections**

  A customized forecasting system can be developed, which can retrieve the data from multiple data sources and analyze it and provide better projections on the best sellers based on time of day or year. Doing this can project the optimal quantity of goods that are required, along with revenue growth. This will also improve the overall operational process.

- **Improve the services by providing personalized offers and recommendations**

  With big data, users' preferences can be studied, and they can be sent personalized communications through emails or messages related to customized discounts and special offers along with personalized product recommendations.

- **Improve security in aspects like payments and user information**

  According to [16], most e-commerce websites are accessed from mobile phones, and more than 50% of the payments are made from mobile phones. Hence, the online payment system should be secure enough to prevent activities such as unethical hacking and data loss. Big data analytical models can read, analyze the data, and identify fraud-related activities by recognizing suspicious patters. Also, with big data architecture, a centralized database system can be developed with added security so that all the payments can be monitored.

- **Better management of orders and logistics**

  Maintaining the right stock is important for online retailers. Maintaining less stock will result in a miss of opportunity to sell in case if there is a demand, and maintaining too much stock will result in investing more toward the goods. Big data techniques, like predictive analytics, can generate trend forecasting and suggest the right quantities of stock.

  In this chapter, we discuss various ways to predict the gender of users in e-commerce using a classification approach based on analyzing the purchasing patterns of customers in-line with the approach discussed in [17]. As e-commerce websites generate a huge volume of data every minute, analyzing it leads to big data classification problems. It contains all structured, semi-structured, and unstructured data. Handling this data growth, analyzing it, and bringing out the value is practically not possible on a regular framework as they require more time and more infrastructure. Hence to handle the velocity and variety of data, there is a strong need to use big data platforms like Apache Spark and Hadoop. The presented approaches are implemented in Apache Spark, which leverages in-memory computing. Apache Spark was developed at the University of California in 2009 and has become vital for large-scale computations due to its high performance and flexible APIs. The key component of Spark is resilient distributed data (RDD). RDD represents a read-only collection that is partitioned across nodes of the cluster that can be operated in parallel. Our approach identifies a set of features that are useful for the classification.

  In addition to our earlier work [17], our main contributions in this chapter are as follows:

- Performed experiments on the big data platform Apache Spark to test the effectiveness and suitability of the approach presented in [17].

- The procedure is executed on four, six, and eight worker nodes, and the event timelines are analyzed to find the time taken for each step in the process.
- Two other gender prediction approaches proposed in [18,19] for the same dataset are discussed along with their implementations using Apache Spark.
- Performed experiments with the state-of-the-art classification algorithms on the dataset and analyzed the classification results.

Following is the overview of how the spark programs run on a cluster node. Each spark application executes as an independent process on the cluster. This is coordinated by spark context, which is created through the main program. In the spark terminology, the main program is called the driver program. On the cluster, spark context should connect to the cluster manager, as shown in Figure 8.1. The cluster manager is responsible for allocating resources to the application running in the cluster. Once the spark context is connected to the cluster manager, the spark context can also connect to all the executors in the worker nodes, which executes all the application code. Once the connection is established, all the tasks are executed by the executor.

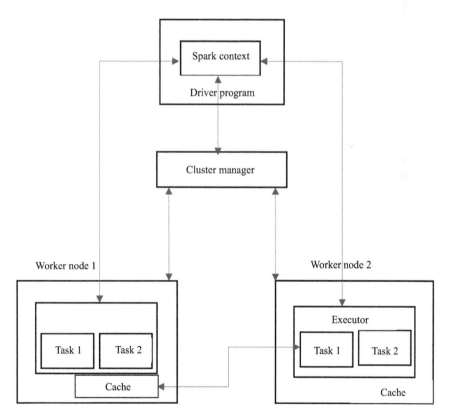

Figure 8.1 Spark cluster overview

8.2   Gender prediction methodology

8.2.1   *Gender prediction based on gender value*

The classification model in this approach is two-phased [18]. In the first phase, the training data is read sequentially and preprocessed to remove unnecessary data. Post-preprocessing features, namely, product category feature, category feature, product prefix feature, are identified. In the second phase, gender is predicted based on features identified in the first phase. Gender is predicated based on gender values calculated for both male and female users. In this work, we considered log data related to purchasing patterns of users per session. The dataset is provided with both training data and testing data. Each record X in the training dataset is a 5-tupled, as shown in the following:

$$X = \{S_{id}, G_{M|F}, S_{Start}, S_{End}, D\} \tag{8.1}$$

where S_{id} is session ID, $G_{M|F}$ is the gender of the person who can be either "Male" or "Female," S_{Start} is the session start time, S_{End} is the session end time, and D is the detail of the products.

Product details in a session can be represented as a hierarchy starting from the category at the highest level followed by subcategory (which can be up to m levels) and finally ending with the product ID. Also, the product details for a session may have data related to one or more products and can be represented as

$$\{C_1/SC_1/SC_2/\cdots SC_m/\text{Pid}_1; C_2/SC_1/SC_2/\cdots SC_m/\text{Pid}_2; C_n/SC_1/SC_2/\cdots SC_m/\text{Pid}_n\}$$

where C_n is the category of nth product in a session, SC_1 is the subcategory of level 1, SC_2 is the subcategory of level 2, SC_n is the subcategory of level m, and Pid_n is the product ID of nth product in a session.

Using the previous convention, typically male data can be represented as

$$X_{Male} = \{S_{id}, G_{Male}, S_{Start}, S_{End}, D\} \tag{8.2}$$

and the female data can be represented as

$$X_{Female} = \{S_{id}, G_{Female}, S_{Start}, S_{End}, D\} \tag{8.3}$$

where the value of G_{Male} is the string "Male," and the value of G_{Female} is the string "Female."

8.2.1.1   Data preprocessing

The main aim of the data preprocessing step is to improve the quality of data, which, in turn, increases accuracy and efficiency. As part of the preprocessing step, the session end time for every session is examined, and the sessions whose logged out time is NULL are omitted. In this case, the assumption is that the user has forgotten to log out. We also calculate the time difference between the start time and end time for each session. We omit the records that have more than 10 h with

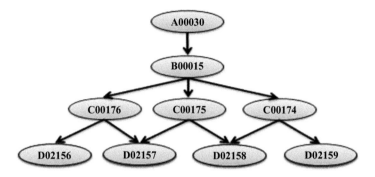

Figure 8.2   Concept hierarchy representation of a product

minimal activity, which is impractical and indefinite. An example in this category is a session with a time gap of more than 10 h for browsing two products. Sessions like this are removed from the data.

8.2.1.2   Feature extraction

Three features based on product category, category, and product ID are extracted. The data (both test and training) is organized in the form of hierarchy starting from the category, subcategory level 1, subcategory level 2, till subcategory level m, and finally, the product ID. The association between the products and categories can be better depicted as a tree starting with category ID as root, subcategory level 1 is the first level node, subcategory level 2 is the second level node, and the product ID as a leaf node. This arrangement is analogous to the concept of concept hierarchy [21], where each product can have more than one subcategory as a parent. Figure 8.2 shows an example tree for one record from session data.

8.2.1.3   Feature extraction based on product category

The input data of a session can be arranged into separated sets, which serves as a feature, as shown in the following:

$$\{\{C_i\}, \{C_i, S_1\}, \{C_i, S_1, S_2\}, \{C_i, S_1, S_2, S_3\}, \ldots, \{C_i, S_1, S_2, S_3, \ldots, S_n, \text{PID}\}\};$$
$$\{\{C_j\}, \{C_j, S_1\}, \{C_j, S_1, S_2\}, \{C_j, S_1, S_2, S_3\}, \ldots, \{C_j, S_1, S_2, S_3, \ldots, S_n, \text{PID}\}\}$$
$$(8.4)$$

where C_i, C_j are the categories, S_1 is level 1 subcategory, S_2 is the level 2 subcategory, and S_n is level n subcategory, and PID is the product ID related to the product. By following a similar approach, the session data for all the sessions can be partitioned and formed as a larger set. Timestamps are also considered, which will help in classifying the records that show ambiguity while classifying records.

8.2.1.4   Feature extraction based on category level

In e-commerce data, it is common that products related to males are contained in male categories, and products related to females are contained in female categories.

Following this rule, features can be extracted from the data by taking the session detail product information D and grouped into a set where the data that are the same across the products in session as explained later.

Consider category level features related to two products. The generic form where the category and subcategories for the two products are the same except the product ID, as shown later:

$$\{\{S_{\text{Start}}, S_{\text{End}}, \ C_i, S_1 : S_n\}, \{P_1, P_2\}\} \tag{8.5}$$

where $S_1{:}S_n$ denote subcategories from S_1 to S_n. The generic form is where the only category is the same with different subcategories and product IDs:

$$\{\{S_{\text{Start}}, S_{\text{End}}, C_i \ \}, \{S_1 : S_n\}, \ \{ P_1, P_2 \}\} \tag{8.6}$$

Feature data is identified for both male and female as they are stored in separate lists, which can be used for classification in the next subsequent steps.

8.2.1.5   Feature-based on the product ID

Logically, data in e-commerce websites are arranged in sequential fashion categorized by gender. If P_i is a product related to males, then it is reasonable that product P_{i+1} is also a product related to males. Hence, all products viewed by males may have sequential product IDs. Similarly, all products viewed by females have their product IDs in sequence. Hence, a common prefix feature is found by scanning all product IDs sequentially across all the sessions and finding its length, which is common, which can be considered as a feature. That is, the average length till which the product IDs are the same in product ID string is taken as the prefix length (p_{ln}).

The whole training data is scanned to identify features that are in the form shown in (8.4)–(8.6).

8.2.1.6   Gender prediction

In this phase, gender is identified in two levels. In the first level, the data is read sequentially and is classified using the category level feature. The feature data is extracted, which matches (8.5) or (8.6). The values are compared against the training data list values that are identified previously. If a match is found, we can consider that gender is identified. All the matched records are removed from the test dataset, which can be considered as the pruning process. Continually removing the identified products information has two advantages:

1.   Reduce the search space.
2.   Decrease the search time.

Even after the previous steps, there will be cases where gender is not identified. Gender is identified in the next level using the product category feature.

8.2.1.7   Operations using the product category feature

In this level, the frequency of each element in the feature set is computed from the training data and tabulated, as shown in Table 8.1.

Table 8.1   Generic table format for product category feature

Element in feature set	Frequency of male	Frequency of female	Total
C_i	X	Y	$(X+Y)$
$\{C_i, S_1\}$	$X1$	$Y1$	$(X1+Y1)$
$\{C_i, S_1, S_2\}$	$X2$	$Y2$	$(X2+Y2)$
.	.	.	.
$\{C_i, S_1, S_2, \ldots, C_i, S_1, S_2, S_3, \ldots, S_n, \text{PID}\}$	(X_n)	(Y_n)	(X_n+Y_n)

Element values for male, $EV_{en}(\text{Male})$, is calculated as

$$EV_{en}(\text{Male}) = \frac{\text{Male}(en)}{\text{Male}(en) + \text{Female}(en)}$$

Element value for female, EV_{en} (Female), is calculated as

$$EV_{en}(\text{Female}) = \frac{\text{Female}(en)}{\text{Male}(en) + \text{Female}(en)}$$

where Male(en) is the frequency of males containing the element *en*, and Female (en) is the frequency of females containing the element *en*.

The element values for each element are summed up to get the gender value of Male ($GV_{(M)}$). The value can be calculated with the following formula:

$$GV_{(M)} = \frac{\sum_{k=1}^{n} EV_{ek}(\text{Male})}{n}$$

Similarly, the gender value of female can be calculated as

$$GV_{(F)} = \frac{\sum_{k=1}^{n} EV_{ek}(\text{Female})}{n}$$

where *n* is the number of elements that are extracted from a record, and EV is the element value of each element. Classification is done based on gender values. If the male gender value is greater than the female gender value, then the product can be classified as male. The records are classified as a female in case the female gender value is greater than the male gender value. In the case of unclassified cases (where the gender score for both male and female are either the same or zero), the product ID feature is applied to determine if the gender is male or female.

8.2.1.8   Experimental results

In this work, Spark clusters are created on Azure HDInsight. Azure HDInsight is the platform offered by Azure to execute open-source frameworks such as Apache

Hadoop, Spark, Kafka. It also offers monitoring along with features such as authentication and authorization with Azure active directory when deployed as an enterprise-grade. The clusters are created consists of 2 head nodes and the variable number of worker nodes starting from 4 and later upgraded to 6 and 8. The clusters use Azure storage as the cluster storage. The head nodes are 4 Cores with a 28-GB RAM, and the worker nodes are 8 Cores with a 56-GB RAM. The clusters are created with Linux as the operating system. The cluster manager used in the approach is YARN. Apache Spark MLlib library was also used during code implementation. The code is implemented in python Jupyter Notebook using PySpark Kernel. The kernel uses the PySpark module on which is an abstraction module over PySpark core.

The dataset that is used in the experiments is provided by the FPT group and was published in the Pacific-Asia Conference on Knowledge Discovery and Data Mining (PAKDD) competition [16]. The total number of records in training data is around 1,500,000, which are the logs related to the products. As the distribution of unique product IDs in the dataset is sparse, the IDs contain additional information regarding the product category hierarchy. Each product ID can be decomposed into four different IDs. The IDs starting with the letter "A" are the most general categories, starting with *D*, correspond to individual products, and *B* and *C* are associated with subcategories and sub-subcategories, respectively. While formulating the approach for gender classification, we assume the following:

1. Every record pertaining to a session in the log file contains all the information as specified in (8.1).
2. Distribution of labels across the training data is not balanced.
3. Labels for the Gender are already provided for training data.
4. Training data consists of both male and female.

The input data is supplied in a CSV format, which is stored in the storage account associated with the Spark cluster. Spark context is created on YARN, which has a unique application ID. As the raw data is in a CSV format, we used the Spark context to load the input CSV file into unstructured text. A new RDD is created to import the raw data and to parse the input CSV file. An input DataFrame (df) is created with all columns, such as gender, session ID, duration, and data. Next, all the features mentioned earlier are extracted from the training set. Table 8.2 shows the total count of the features that are identified as category wise. From the training set, it is observed that the majority of the product IDs have the same values until the

Table 8.2   Total feature count

Feature	Subcategory	Total count	Male features	Female features
Features based on product and category		2,426,621	433,592	1,993,020
Features based on product category	Till second subcategory	69,421	42,323	27,098
	Till first subcategory	11,263	6,542	4,721

fourth position. Hence, the prefix length is taken as 4. The approach is explained on a sample record given as follows (taken from the test data): We first extract the features for the sample record.

Category level features:

11/14/2014 17:15	11/14/2014 18:09	A00002/B00003/C00046/D01169/ A00002/B00003/C00014/D01478/ A00002/B00003/C00046/D01153/

1. {{11/14/2014 17:15, 11/14/2014 8:09} {A00002/B00003/C00046}, {D01169, D01153}}
2. {{11/14/2014 17:15, 11/14/2014 8:09} {A00002/B00003}, {C00046, C00014}, {D01169, D01478, D01153}}

In the previous text, feature 1 is extracted till second level subcategory and feature 2 is extracted till first level subcategory. The element weights of the features are shown in Table 8.3.

Product category level features:
{{A00002, A00002/B00003, A00002/B00003/C00046, A00002/B00003/C00046/D01169}, {A00002, A00002/B00003/A00002/B00003/C00014, A00002/B00003/C00014/D01478}}

The product ID feature is taken into consideration for the elements whose element weight is 0. Since the product's prefix length is taken as 4, the first four digits of the product ID is taken into consideration for concluding the gender. Referring to our example, since the element value of A00002/B00003/C00046/D01169, A00002/B00003/C00046/D01153 is 0, the prefix of length 4 is looked upon, and the frequencies of such product IDs are identified in the training set. The frequency of D0116 in the male set is 3, and the frequency in the female set is 2. The frequency of D0115 in the male dataset is 1, whereas the frequency in the female dataset is 11. Element values of the previous features are shown in Table 8.4.

The Gender values of male and female are as follows:

$$GV(M) = 1.07/7 = 0.15 \text{ and } GV(F) = 5.88/7 = 0.84$$

Table 8.3   Element weights of the features

Element	Male count	Female count	Total
A00002	1,707	12,360	14,067
A00002/B00003	337	2,537	2,874
A00002/B00003/C00046	32	305	337
A00002/B00003/C00046/D01169	0	0	0
A00002/B00003/C00014	51	594	645
A00002/B00003/C00014/D01478	0	1	1
A00002/B00003/C00046/D01153	0	0	0

2131ago2sok

Table 8.4   Element values for the sample record

Element	EV$_{Male}$	EV$_{Female}$
A00002	0.12	0.87
A00002/B00003	0.11	0.88
A00002/B00003/C00046	0.09	0.90
A00002/B00003/C00046/D01169	0.6	0.4
A00002/B00003/C00014	0.07	0.92
A00002/B00003/C00014/D01478	0	1
A00002/B00003/C00046/D01153	0.08	0.91

Command finished at 10-26-2019 18:04:58.930 +01:00, execution took 9s 318ms

Jobs: 12 COMPLETED   Spark: 6 EXECUTORS 15 CORES

Job ID	Job Name	Status	Stages	Tasks	Submission Time	Duration
21	treeAggregate	COMPLETED	1/1		23 minutes ago	2s
22	treeAggregate	COMPLETED	1/1		23 minutes ago	0s
23	treeAggregate	COMPLETED	1/1		23 minutes ago	0s
24	treeAggregate	COMPLETED	1/1		23 minutes ago	0s
25	treeAggregate	COMPLETED	1/1		23 minutes ago	0s
26	treeAggregate	COMPLETED	1/1		23 minutes ago	0s
27	treeAggregate	COMPLETED	1/1		23 minutes ago	0s
28	treeAggregate	COMPLETED	1/1		23 minutes ago	0s
29	treeAggregate	COMPLETED	1/1		23 minutes ago	0s
30	treeAggregate	COMPLETED	1/1		23 minutes ago	0s
31	treeAggregate	COMPLETED	1/1		23 minutes ago	0s
32	treeAggregate	COMPLETED	1/1		23 minutes ago	0s

Figure 8.3   Jobs created on training set for four worker nodes

Since the gender value of female is higher than the gender value of male, the record can be considered as the product is viewed by a female. The approach has generated 70% accuracy according to the submission system published in [17]. The procedure is executed on a varying number of worker nodes in the cluster to observe the performance and impact of adding multiple worker nodes with respect to time. Initially, the cluster is created with four worker nodes, then the numbers of worker nodes are increased to 6 and 8. Detailed results are presented next.

Results on 4, 6, 8 worker nodes

Twelve jobs are created in spark context during the execution of the program for the entire process. Figure 8.3 shows the details about the jobs that are created along with their statuses and the duration in which they are executed. It can be observed that maximum time is taken for job ID 21, which took 2 s to complete. The entire command operation is completed in 9 s, 318 ms. Figure 8.4 shows the status of all the jobs, along with their execution times. The yellow line specifies the total number of executor cores, and the blue line specifies the active tasks. The green line specifies the start time and end time of jobs. For example, the first and second green vertical lines specify the start time and end time of the first job. Figure 8.5 shows the event timeline, which shows total workload distribution across all the jobs, stages, and all the tasks in all the spark executors in the cluster.

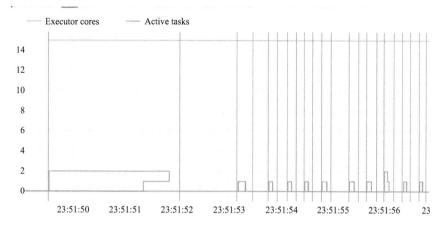

Figure 8.4 Job execution on 4-cores

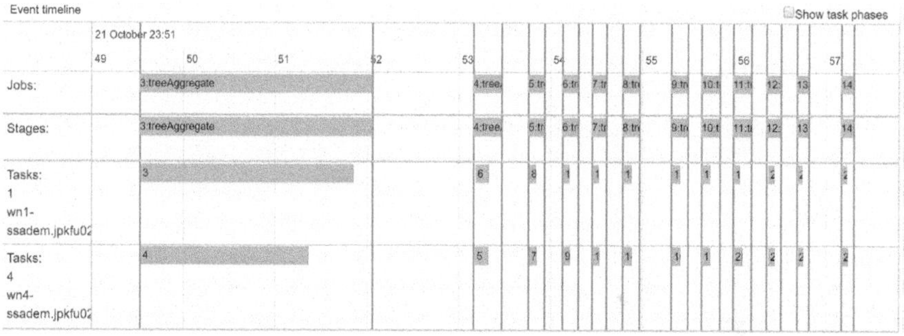

Figure 8.5 Event timeline 4-cores

Cluster performances using 6 and 8 worker nodes are presented in Figures 8.6 and 8.7. The overall command execution time is decreased as we increase the number of worker nodes. The execution time using six worker nodes is 5 s, 771 ms, as shown in Figure 8.6, and the command execution time using eight worker nodes is 3 s, 272 ms, as shown in Figure 8.7. Figures 8.8 and 8.9 show the job execution timings for six and eight worker nodes. It can be observed that there is an improvement in the individual job execution time when the number of worker nodes is increased. Figures 8.10 and 8.11 show the even timeline for six and eight worker nodes. Even in this case, it is observed that overall execution time is decreasing when we increase the number of worker nodes in all the stages and task executors in the cluster.

Execution time

Average execution for all the steps is captured and shown in Table 8.5. The time is captured on a cluster having two head nodes and four worker nodes. In the following

Command finished at 10-26-2019 01:00:19.773 +01:00, execution took 5s 771ms

Jobs: 12 COMPLETED   **Spark:** 6 EXECUTORS 1

Job ID	Job Name	Status	Stages	Tasks	Submission Time
44	treeAggregate	COMPLETED	1/1	————————————————	a few seconds ago
45	treeAggregate	COMPLETED	1/1	————————————————	a few seconds ago
46	treeAggregate	COMPLETED	1/1	————————————————	a few seconds ago
47	treeAggregate	COMPLETED	1/1	————————————————	a few seconds ago
48	treeAggregate	COMPLETED	1/1	————————————————	a few seconds ago
49	treeAggregate	COMPLETED	1/1	————————————————	a few seconds ago
50	treeAggregate	COMPLETED	1/1	————————————————	a few seconds ago
51	treeAggregate	COMPLETED	1/1	————————————————	a few seconds ago
52	treeAggregate	COMPLETED	1/1	————————————————	a few seconds ago
53	treeAggregate	COMPLETED	1/1	————————————————	a few seconds ago
54	treeAggregate	COMPLETED	1/1	————————————————	a few seconds ago
55	treeAggregate	COMPLETED	1/1	————————————————	a few seconds ago

Figure 8.6   Jobs on six worker nodes

Command finished at 10-21-2019 23:52:03.098 +01:00, execution took 3s 272ms

Jobs: 12 COMPLETED   **Spark:** 6 EXECUTORS

Job ID	Job Name	Status	Stages	Tasks	Submission Time
3	treeAggregate	COMPLETED	1/1	————————————————	9 minutes ago
4	treeAggregate	COMPLETED	1/1	————————————————	9 minutes ago
5	treeAggregate	COMPLETED	1/1	————————————————	9 minutes ago
6	treeAggregate	COMPLETED	1/1	————————————————	9 minutes ago
7	treeAggregate	COMPLETED	1/1	————————————————	9 minutes ago
8	treeAggregate	COMPLETED	1/1	————————————————	9 minutes ago
9	treeAggregate	COMPLETED	1/1	————————————————	9 minutes ago
10	treeAggregate	COMPLETED	1/1	————————————————	9 minutes ago
11	treeAggregate	COMPLETED	1/1	————————————————	9 minutes ago
12	treeAggregate	COMPLETED	1/1	————————————————	9 minutes ago
13	treeAggregate	COMPLETED	1/1	————————————————	9 minutes ago
14	treeAggregate	COMPLETED	1/1	————————————————	9 minutes ago

Figure 8.7   Jobs on eight worker nodes

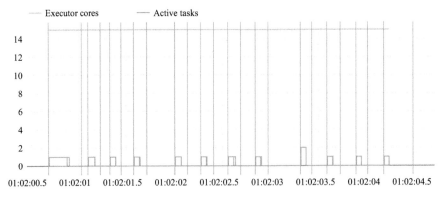

Figure 8.8   Job execution time on six worker nodes

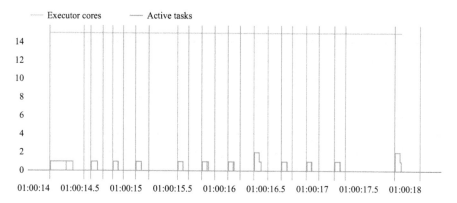

Figure 8.9   Job execution time on eight worker nodes

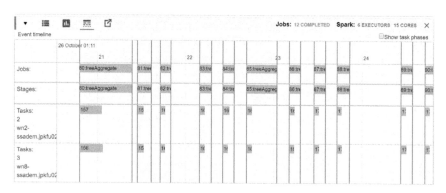

Figure 8.10   Event timeline for six worker nodes

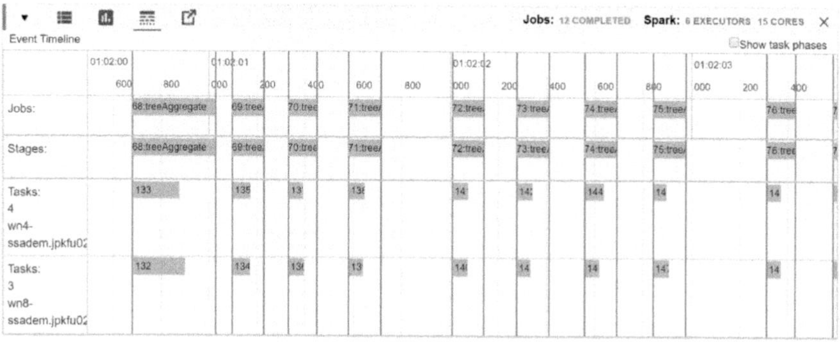

Figure 8.11   Event timeline for eight worker nodes

Table 8.5   Execution time

S. no.	Step	Execution time (in ms)
1	Creating spark context	36
2	Read input data and create RDDs	245
3	Create and load DataFrames	44
4	Extract features	245
5	Read test data and create RDDs	253
6	Create and load DataFrames on test data	760
7	Classify data	244

Table 8.6   Number of products browsed during a session

Number of products	Total female count	Total male count
>5	72,356	11,291
>6	49,808	17,550
>7	21,337	8,131
>8	23,240	16,307

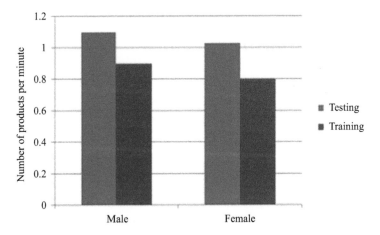

Figure 8.12   Avg. number of products browed per minute

we present the analysis and findings on both test data and training data. Table 8.6 shows the total number of users (both male and female) and the number of products browsed during a session. Figures 8.12 and 8.13 show the relationship between the product viewing percentage (i.e., scaling to the number of products viewed by 100 users) and the number of products browsed during the session. This is captured for both test data and training data, respectively. From Figure 8.12, it can be concluded

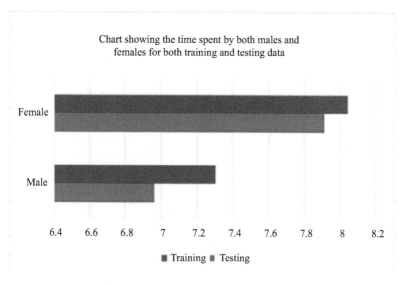

Figure 8.13   Avg. time spent by users

that males browse a higher number of products than females before coming to any conclusion. For example, in the training set, men have browsed as high as 33 products in a single session before ending the session. Following are some of the important conclusions that are observed:

1. Male users browse 22% faster than female users.
2. Female users browse a greater number of products and switches between the categories and products when compared to male users.
3. Female spend more time (average 10.5% more) when compared to men on the Internet for browsing the data (see Figure 8.13).

Figure 8.14 shows the Ambari dashboard showing the metrics such as HDFS disk usage, CPU usage, cluster load, YARN memory, and network usage when the cluster size is six worker nodes. It can be observed that maximum CPU usage is 7.384%, which shows that the method does not consume more CPU. The total average memory occupied for the process is 36 GB.

8.2.2   Classification using random forest

Duong *et al.* [19] described a classification technique that uses both basic and advanced features for the same PAKDD competition dataset. Basic features include start time, end time, total time spent in a session along with individual products/ categories that are viewed in the session. Advanced features include information related to the relation between products and categories in a session. Since the labels in the training dataset are unbalanced, they used techniques such as resampling and cost-sensitive learning to improve the overall prediction.

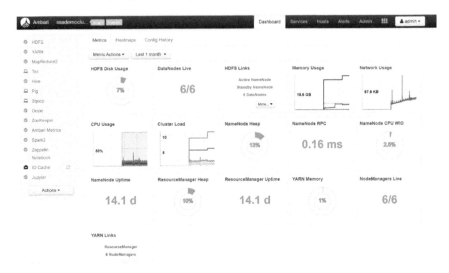

Figure 8.14   Ambari dashboard

Table 8.7   Total feature count

Feature	Description	Feature count
Day	Day in a month	31
Month	Month in a year	12
Day of week	Day in a week	7
Start time	Hour in start time	24
End time	Hour in end time	24
	Total	98

Table 8.8   Total feature count

Feature	Description	Feature count
Duration	Session length	1
Number of products	Number of products	1
Average time per product	Average viewing time of a product	1
	Total	3

8.2.2.1   Basic features

Basic features include the features related to timestamp and the total number of products viewed during the session. A total of 98 distinctive and 3 numeric features are identified. Tables 8.7 and 8.8 show details of all the basic features that are identified. Along with these, all the categories and features that are contained are considered as product and category features. The number of times the product or category is viewed is taken as a feature value.

8.2.2.2 Advanced features

The relation between the products and categories are explored and then stored in a list and a tree data structure similar to Figure 8.2. From the tree representation, the authors explored the following features:

1. The number of nodes at each level of the tree.
2. Node sequence at each level. Most frequent *k*-grams are considered.
3. Node transfer pairs. This is usually calculated between the categories at different levels. This feature generally gives an idea about the browsing patterns of users.

For the training dataset, in total, there are 4 nodes at each level, 1,100 node sequences, and 300 node transfer pairs.

8.2.2.3 Classification

This phase classifies the test data based on features identified in the previous step. Duong *et al.* [19] applied resampling methods to address the class imbalance problem. In the resampling method, instances are added (called oversampling) or removed (called undersampling) from the dataset to make it more balanced. The potential problem with under sampling is that the critical data may be removed from the input dataset [19], and oversampling can add more execution cost. Hence, the authors suggested a class balance technique in which all the instances in the dataset are assigned new weights for both the classes so that the overall consolidated class weight remains the same for a class. The total number of features on the training dataset is 3,500. As the number is huge, the concepts of information gain are applied to select 2,500 features from the input training dataset. Finally, random forest is used to classify the data. This method is evaluated using the balance accuracy measure as the input dataset is not balanced. Balanced accuracy in binary problems deals with imbalanced datasets. It is defined as the average of correct values in each class when calculated individually. Balanced accuracy is calculated as follows:

$$\frac{0.5 * tp}{tp + fn} + \frac{0.5 * tn}{tn + fp}$$

where *tp* is true positive, *tn* is true negative, *fp* is false positive, and *fn* is false negative.

Here, the results are greatly improved when both basic features and advanced features are combined. Studies were also made to identify the relation between the number of features and accuracy. The predictions results were maximum when the number of features is 1,500 from the total 3,500 features [19].

The same model is tested on Apache Spark from the big data perspective. The model was executed for the random forest classifier. The model was executed on the same spark cluster containing two head nodes and four worker nodes. The model was implemented using spark MLlib library, which is the machine learning library offered by Spark. It contains standard machine learning algorithms that can implement classification, regression, clustering as well as other techniques such as dimensionality reduction and collaborative filtering.

The input file for the process is stored in Windows Azure Storage Blob (WASB). Table 8.9 outlines the steps, along with the time taken to execute the step.

Figure 8.15 shows the event timeline for four worker nodes showing total workload distribution across all the jobs, stages, and all the tasks in all the spark executors in the cluster. Figure 8.16 shows the prediction results that are captured from the Jupyter Notebook showing columns session ID, duration, and data from testing data. Label value 0 denotes the female category, and 1 denotes the male category.

8.2.3   Classification using gradient-boosted trees (GBTs)

Lu *et al.* [20] presented a classification model based on GBTs. GBTs are ensembles of decision trees. They execute in iterations by training the decision trees to constantly

Table 8.9   Execution time

S. no.	Step	Time (in ms)
1	Load required spark libraries	23
2	Creating the spark context	252
3	Ingest data	245
4	Create input DataFrame	43
5	Basic feature extraction	296
6	Advanced feature extraction	512
7	Create RDD for features	242
8	Load RDD data into models	75
9	Classify using random forest library	975
10	Save output to Azure blob	63
	Total time	2,726

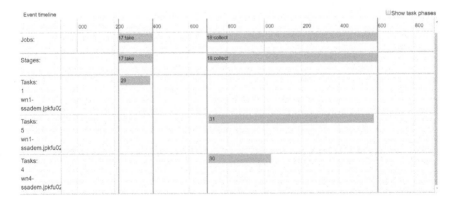

Figure 8.15   Event timeline for random forest

```
+---------+--------+--------------------+-----+
|sessionid|duration|                data|label|
+---------+--------+--------------------+-----+
|sessionid|duration|                data|    2|
|   u10232|00:09:43|A00001/B00009/C00...|    0|
|   u10233|00:08:16|A00001/B00009/C00...|    0|
|   u10240|00:03:43|A00001/B00001/C00...|    0|
|   u10241|00:06:15|A00001/B00001/C00...|    0|
|   u10246|00:08:31|A00001/B00001/C00...|    0|
|   u10253|00:05:26|A00001/B00009/C00...|    0|
|   u11192|00:09:23|A00002/B00002/C00...|    0|
|   u11193|00:12:31|A00006/B00059/C00...|    0|
|   u11196|00:07:20|A00002/B00002/C00...|    0|
|   u11201|00:09:12|A00003/B00004/C00...|    0|
|   u11204|00:10:03|A00001/B00009/C00...|    0|
|   u11211|00:05:25|A00001/B00015/C00...|    0|
|   u11225|00:09:03|A00001/B00001/C00...|    0|
|   u11342|00:04:17|A00002/B00003/C00...|    0|
|   u11345|00:04:45|A00001/B00009/C00...|    0|
|   u11364|00:08:41|A00001/B00021/C00...|    0|
```

Figure 8.16 Prediction results

minimizing the loss function. This model introduced is two-phased in which the features are identified in the first phase, and classification is done in the second phase based on features identified in the first phase. The features in this method are categorized into three categories, namely, behavior features, temporal features, and product features. In the behavior features, the number of products viewed in the session, along with the duration of the session, is studied for both the genders. In the temporal features category, temporal features such as hour and day from the session are studied. In the third category, features based on most general categories, categories appearing in at least five sessions, a category that is viewed first in the session are studied. The following are the main observations from the training set, which are found during feature extraction from the training dataset.

- The distribution between the product frequency and the number of users viewing the products is similar for both male and female.
- From the temporal aspects, it is found that females concentrated more during the day time, and males concentrated more during the evening times.
- It is also found that males spend more time during weekends than females.
- Female browsed category A2 more than male.
- Male preferred category A1 more than females.

Since the male records are less in the dataset, the cost is taken as four for male class and one for female class because the total number of female records is four times the male records. All the features that are extracted in phase one are passed to the second phase, where GBTs do the classification. Along with this classification, the label updating approach is also used to improve the efficiency of the model by taking the product viewed information by both male and female users. For each product in the training dataset, the total male count and female count of users who viewed the product is calculated. Based on the counts, the probability that the male views a product is calculated by using the following formula:

$$PmaleP_{male}(P_i) = \frac{\beta * num\_male(P_i) + 1}{\beta * num\_male(P_i) + num\_female(P_i) + 2}$$

where *num_male* is the number of males that viewed the product P_i and *num_female* is the number of females that viewed the product P_i, and β denotes the weight of male samples. The value of β is assigned 2.5 as the classes are imbalanced. The probability that the female views the product is calculated using $P_{female}(P_i) = 1 - P_{male}(P_i)$.

For each record for the test dataset, the probability score returned by the GBT model is combined with the score that is calculated earlier (say *score(u_i)*). A new score called score^l (u_i) is calculated as given next, which is based on score (u_i) and product information to predict the gender of the user:

$$score^l(u_i) = \alpha * score(u_i) + (1 - \alpha) \cdot \frac{2\Sigma(P_{female}(P_i) - 0.5)}{|D|}$$

where $|D|$ is the number of products viewed in session and $\alpha \in [0,1]$. Setting α value as 0 represents score using the product information and setting α as 1 represents the scores from the GBT model.

From the big data perspective, we executed the model on the same spark cluster containing two head nodes and four worker nodes. The model was implemented using the **Spark MLlib** library. The input file for the process is stored in WASB. Table 8.10 outlines the steps, along with the time taken to execute the step.

8.2.4   *Experimental results with state-of-the-art classifiers*

Experiments are carried out to compare the results of the proposed method with the following six state-of-the-art classification algorithms:

- Decision tree
- Random forest
- SVM
- Logistic regression
- *K*-nearest neighbors (*K*NNs)
- Naïve Bayes (GNB)

We split the total training dataset into three parts: training data (80% of the total data), validation data (10%), which is used for adjusting the classification model's accuracy, and test data (10%). To compare the classifiers' accuracy in multiple

Table 8.10   *Execution time*

S. no.	Step	Time (in ms)
1	Load required spark libraries	23
2	Creating the spark context	252
3	Ingest data	245
4	Create input DataFrame	43
5	Behavior feature extraction	113
6	Temporal feature extraction	206
7	Category feature extraction	313
7	Create RDD and loading data into RDD for features	256
9	Classify using GBT	975
10	Compute gender score	53
11	Compute hybrid gender score	21
	Total time	2,500

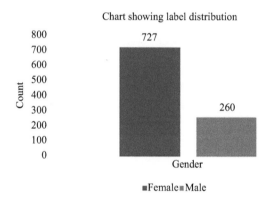

Figure 8.17   *Chart showing the distribution of class labels in the training dataset*

dimensions, we divided the training set into five different possible sets to have a different combination of records. All the executions are done on the machine having Intel i7-8665U CPU@ 1.90 GHz and 16 GB memory.

We do the following two modifications to the dataset before proceeding with the classification.

- **Class balancing**

Figure 8.17 shows the distribution of gender labels in the training dataset. It can be observed that the training dataset is highly skewed as the labels, i.e., gender values are not uniformly distributed having a skew of approximately 3:1.

As the balanced dataset is essential for implementing the classification algorithms to avoid the misclassification or accurate classification results, we first convert the unbalanced dataset into the balanced dataset. Following are some of the approaches that are available in the literature to convert the unbalanced dataset into the balanced dataset.

- **Undersampling:** In this approach, we select the exact number of female records that matches the size of male records, since the male is a minority class having a smaller number of records.
- **Oversampling:** In this approach, the records in the minority class are increased so that the proportion of records in both minority and majority classes reaches 50% in each.

In this chapter, we use synthetic minority oversampling technique (SMOTE) [22] which is one of the oversampling procedures available in the literature. SMOTE generates synthetic samples from the training data. Post applying SMOTE, the number of records for each class is 727.

- **Encoding**

Since the training dataset contains nonnumerical data in some columns such as session ID, product ID, we need to convert them into numerical data for fitting into the model since the classification models require numerical data for classification. This transformation is done by using "label encoding."

Table 8.11 shows the time taken for training the model on the training dataset. It is observed that, in terms of execution time, the decision tree is the quickest algorithm, whereas the logistic regression is the slowest. Our approach consumed more time when compared to other algorithms because of steps such as feature extraction and calculating the length of a prefix length (see Section 8.2.1.5).

Figure 8.18 shows the highest model accuracy values for all the methods calculated for all the five possible training sets. The values are calculated in ten independent runs. It can be observed that both the decision tree and the random forest have the highest accuracy values. In contrast, the logistic regression model has shown the lowest percentage. Our approach has shown a decent performance (with the highest value being 0.9 out of 1) on both testing and training data. The accuracy is calculated by counting the number of true positives for ten randomly chosen records.

Table 8.11   Time taken for training the model

S. no.	Algorithm	Time taken (s)
1	Decision tree	0.12
2	Random forest	0.22
3	Support vector machine	0.17
4	Logistic regression	0.72
5	Naïve Bayes	0.23
6	KNN	0.28
7	Our approach	1.8

Chart showing highest accuracy values of training set and test set

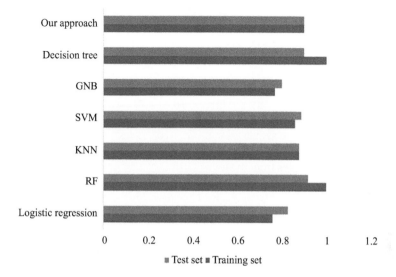

Figure 8.18   Chart showing the distribution of class labels in the training dataset

Table 8.12   Classification accuracy on test dataset

S. no.	Algorithm	Average accuracy score
1	Decision tree	0.66
2	Random forest	0.72
3	Support vector machine	0.77
4	Logistic regression	0.82
5	Naïve Bayes	0.77
6	KNN	0.82
7	Our approach	0.79

Table 8.12 lists the average classification accuracy scores for all the algorithms on the test dataset. The average is calculated for 25 iterations. It can be observed that both logistic regression and KNN have the best accuracy scores when compared to the other algorithms. Our approach has an average accuracy score of 0.79 and has returned better results than decision tree, random forest, SVM, and naïve Bayes classifiers. One of the potential reasons behind KNN's better performance is that the records in the data are not easily separable using a decision plane that SVM uses. Also, since the number of dimensions in the training dataset is not large, KNN dominated all other classifiers in terms of accuracy [23].

Similarly, both logistic regression and our method performed better than random forest classifier because of the presence of a high percentage of explanatory variables,

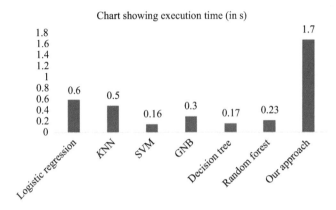

Figure 8.19   Execution time

i.e., the variables which relates to the outcome of the classification [24]. Recall that all the products and its categories, subcategories in the dataset belong to either male or female category that relate to the class prediction. Figure 8.19 shows the overall execution time (which includes training and testing of data). For the dataset provided, SVM has the least execution time. It is fastest, whereas our approach consumed considerably more execution time for classification, which is because of individual times for extracting all the three features, namely, product, category, product ID.

To show the importance of extracting features based on products and sub-categories for e-commerce data, we have chosen a *product ID* from the training dataset, which is present in only male and female categories, respectively. The product ID "*D*18162" is present in only records that are marked as *male* and do not exist in records marked as *female*. Similarly, the product ID "*D*23732" belongs to an only *female* category and does not exist in any of the *male* categorized records. We examine the class labels returned by all the classifiers for the records having these product IDs. For the session data "*A*00001/*B*00009/*C*00038/*D*18162/," all the classifiers returned correct labels (i.e., *male*) except logistic regression and random forest classifier even though the random forest classifier has returned the highest accuracy. Similarly, session data "*A*00003/*B*00012/*C*00028/*D*23732/" is categorized as "male" by a decision tree, naïve Bayes, and SVM classifiers even though they have shown more than 87% accuracy. Hence, considering the details such as product, category can play a significant role in decision-making.

8.3   Summary

Technology advancements such as social media, e-commerce, mobile phones, and email communications generate humongous data. Analyzing this data is essential and forming rules in predicting, labeling, classifying the unlabeled data. Existing classification techniques over e-commerce data are mainly based on the users' purchasing patterns. However, gender preferences play a significant role in targeting customers for branding products, providing customized suggestions to users, etc. In this chapter, we described three methods for gender-based classification. All the methods are two-phased in which the features are extracted in the first phase, whereas the classification of gender is done in the second phase. The first technique is mainly based on hierarchical relationships among products and purchasing patterns. The second technique extracts both basic features and advanced features and uses the random forest to classify the data. The third approach extracts behavior features, temporal features along with product features, and classification is done using GBTs. Experiments are carried out on Apache Spark clusters created on Azure HDInsight with two head clusters along with variable node clusters to handle the data volume. The dataset is related to clickstream data (provided by FPT group) consisting of browsing logs (with the list of products formed as a hierarchy), session start time, and session end time. Experiments are also done on the state-of-the-art classification techniques, and the results are presented.

References

[1]   Simon, K. Digital trends 2019: Every single stat you need to know about the internet, 2019. Available at https://thenextweb.com/contributors/2019/01/30/digital-trends-2019-every-single-stat-you-need-to-know-about-the-internet/.

[2]   Ono, H. and Zavodny, M. Gender, and the Internet. Social Science Quarterly, Vol. 84, No. 1, 2003, pages 111–121.

[3]   Jansen, B. J., Kathleen, M., and Stephen, C. Evaluating the performance of demographic targeting using gender in sponsored search. Information Processing & Management, Vol. 49, No. 1, 2013, pages 286–302.

[4]   Chang, M. K., Cheung, W., and Lai, V. S. Literature derived reference models for the adoption of online shopping. Information and Management, Vol. 42, No. 4, 2005, pages 543–559.

[5]   Ulbrich, F., Christensen, T., and Stankus, L. Gender-specific online shopping preferences. Electronic Commerce Research, Vol. 11, 2011, pages 181–199.

[6]   Zhang, K. Z. K., Matthew, K. O., Leeb, M. K. O., Christy, M. K., Cheung, C. M. K., and Chend, H. Understanding the role of gender in bloggers' switching behavior. Decision Support Systems, Vol. 47, No. 4, 2009, pages 540–546.

[7]   Abraham, L., Morn, M., and Vollman, A. Women on the web: How women are shaping the internet, Comscore Whitepaper, 2010. (www.comscore.com/WomenOnTheWeb).

[8]   Tuch, A. N., Bargas-Avila, J. A., and Opwis, K. Symmetry and aesthetics in website design: It is a man's business. Computer on Human Behaviour, Vol. 26, No. 6, 2010, pages 1831–1837.

[9]   Hoffman, D. L., Kalsbeek, W. D., and Novak, T. P. Internet and web use in the U.S. Communications of the ACM, Vol. 39, No. 12, 1996, pages 36–46.

[10] Tracy, B. "Seasoned Users Lead in E-commerce", 1998 Crain Communications Inc. (https://adage.com/article/news/opinion-seasoned-users-lead-e-commerce/790).

[11] Bernard, J. J., Kathleen, M., and Stephen, C. Evaluating the performance of demographic targeting using gender in sponsored search. Information Processing & Management, Vol. 49, No.1, 2013, pages 286–302.

[12] Cheng, N., Chandramouli, R., and Subbalakshmi, K. P. Author gender identification from text. Digital Investigation, Vol. 8, No. 1, 2011, pages 78–88.

[13] Bhaskar, V., Satyanarayana, P., and Sreeram, M. Analyzing target customer's behavior by mining eCommerce data. International Journal of Information Sciences and Computing, Vol. 4, No. 1, 2010, pages 27–30.

[14] Ketul, B. P., Jignesh, A. C., and Jigar, D. P. Web mining in E-commerce: Pattern discovery, issues, and applications. International Journal of P2P Network Trends and Technology, Vol. 1, No. 3, 2011, pages 40–45.

[15] Smith, C. Amazon statistics, facts and history (2021) | By the numbers, 2019. Available at https://expandedramblings.com/index.php/amazon-statistics/.

[16] Constantine, N. M. 5 ways big data and analytics will impact E-commerce in 2019, 2018. Available at https://medium.com/@constantinenmbufung/5-ways-big-data-and-analytics-will-impact-e-commerce-in-2019-e127d53ac13c.

[17] The 19th Pacific-Asia conference on knowledge discovery and data mining, 2015. Available at https://pakdd.org/archive/pakdd2015/index.php/technical-program/contest.html.

[18] Chaitanya, K., Somayajulu, D., and Krishna, P. R. "A Novel Approach for Classification of E-Commerce Data," Proceedings of Compute '15, 2015, pages 129–134.

[19] Duong, D., Tan, H., and Pham, S. "Customer gender prediction based on E-commerce data," Proceedings of 2016 Eighth International Conference on Knowledge and Systems Engineering (KSE), Hanoi, 2016, pages 91–95.

[20] Lu, S., Zhao, M., Zhang, H., Zhang, C., Wang, W., and Wang, H. "Gender Predictor: A Method to Predict Gender of Customers from E-commerce Website," Proceedings of 2015 IEEE/WIC/ACM International Conference on Web Intelligence and Intelligent Agent Technology (WI-IAT), Singapore, 2015, pages 13–16.

[21] De, S. K. and Krishna, P. R. Mining web data using clustering technique for web personalization. International Journal of Computational Intelligence and Applications (IJCIA), World Scientific, Vol. 2, No. 3, 2002, pages 255–265.

[22] Chawla, N. V., Bowyer, K. W., Hall, L. O., and Kegelmeyer, W. P. SMOTE: Synthetic minority oversampling technique. Journal Of Artificial Intelligence Research, Vol. 16, 2002, pages 321–357.

[23] Adeniyi, D. A., Wei, Z., and Yongquan, Y. Automated web usage data mining and recommendation system using K-Nearest Neighbor (KNN) classification method. Applied Computing and Informatics, Vol. 12, No. 1, 2016, pages 90–108,

[24] Kirasich, K., Smith, T., and Sadler, B. Random forest vs logistic regression: binary classification for heterogeneous datasets. SMU Data Science Review, Vol. 1, No. 3, Article 9, 2018.

Chapter 9

On recommender systems with big data

*Lakshmikanth Paleti[1,2], P. Radha Krishna[3] and
J.V.R. Murthy[2]*

Recommender systems (RSs) have gained popularity due to their explosive use in social networking and e-commerce. Various techniques have been proposed to handle the issues and challenges associated with RSs. In the contemporary world of big data, it is important to derive real-time insights and recommendations to provide useful choices to the customers and to reduce their browsing time. Relevant and more effective recommendations can be provided by analyzing big data such as browsing history, trends and opinions (in one or more forms of text, audio and video) along with the data related to past purchases and ratings. In addition to the traditional approaches, a diversified new cohort of approaches has been evolved to handle the big data scenario.

Modern RSs have to deal with the advent of big data that is mostly characterized by 5Vs, volume, velocity, variety, value and veracity. On one side, it addresses the challenge to have adequate data for RSs to derive useful insights; and it brings out few challenges such as data sparsity, and skewness on the other side. Efficient RSs can be developed by augmenting unstructured data such as reviews, opinions, product summaries, product images and videos along with the structured data such as user profile data and ratings. The e-marketing sites such as Amazon and eBay place thousands of the products resulting in millions of transactions as well as ratings, thereby generating data at big data scale. Existing research outcomes support big data in different dimensions to extend the algorithms with parallel constructs and parallel computing paradigms. Present methodologies and approaches use big data infrastructure such as Hadoop and Spark and support one or more big data characteristics, etc. The challenge for the recommendation system lies in the fact that these characteristics of big data have to be handled appropriately in order to build efficient predictive models and generating effective recommendations, with the underlying big data.

[1]Department of Computer Science and Engineering, Kallam aranadhareddy Institute of Technology, Guntur, India
[2]Department of Computer Science and Engineering, Jawaharlal Nehru Technological University, Kakinada, AP, India
[3]Department of Computer Science and Engineering, National Institute of Technology, Warangal (NITW), Warangal, Telangana, India

This chapter introduces taxonomy of RSs in the context of big data and covers the traditional RSs, namely, collaborative filtering (CF)-based and content-based methods along with the state-of-the-art RSs. We also present a detailed study on (a) state of the art methodologies, (b) issues and challenges such as cold start, scalability and sparsity, (c) similarity measures and methodologies, (d) evaluation metrics and (e) popular experimental datasets. This survey explores the breadth in the field of RSs with a focus on big data to the extent possible and tries to summarize them.

9.1   Introduction

The rapid proliferation of the Internet and social media brought about increased and easier access to information, via a variety of methods and different channels. With the advent of online communication, RSs have evolved.

Recommender (or recommendation) systems mainly focus on helping individual users in finding items that they are interested in. The problem addressed in RSs is *to estimate scores for entities that have not yet been viewed/evaluated by a user*. The assessment is usually based on scores given by a user to other items. Here, there are two possibilities while estimating scores for the items that are not yet evaluated:

- For each user, look at all the items and evaluate.
- For each item, evaluate them with respect to all the users.

So, both the number of items and the number of users are important in estimating the scores. Algorithms or techniques used in RSs usually learn to rank the recommendable items based on their assumed relevance for each user. Usually, the top-k items with the highest scores are recommended to the user.

RSs help in:

- improving the user experience and customer satisfactions by suggesting most likely consume items to users,
- leading in shift of reading patterns of the consumers,
- changing in the purchase behavior,
- stimulating higher engagement on a media streaming platform or a social network and
- making search and decision processes easier or by helping them discover new things.

RSs mainly comprise three components: item (or resource), user and a recommendation algorithm. By analysis of the user's interests and activity and behavioral history, a user model is created by the RS. In a similar manner, the model for the item resource is established by analyzing the items' feature. A comparison is set up between the characteristics of the user and those of the items, for predicting which items the user might like by applying the recommendation algorithm [1]. Predicted results are conveyed to the user as recommendations. Among the various components, the recommendation algorithm is the most important part of RS [2,3]. The algorithmic performance impacts the overall performance of the RS. Consequently, research is focused mainly on the design and implementation of the algorithms.

Primarily, an RS converts the users' historical preferences and behavior for items into future predictions for the most likely preferred item. An item could be anything from books, movies, Web information, etc. RSs are widely used in many existing e-commerce platforms such as Amazon, social networks such as Facebook and Twitter. For instance, Netflix selects 60% of its DVDs based on recommendations provided by RS. In case of e-commerce platforms, the systems suggest new items that might be of interest to the user by analyzing their profiles, purchase history and in social networks, the system suggests persons by analyzing the user's relationships. Other example areas that use RSs are information retrieval, digital information content services, e-tourism, digital libraries, etc.

9.1.1 Big data and recommender systems

With the increase in usage of Internet, methods of accessing and connecting to the content present in the World Wide Web have also increased tremendously. Some of the potential consequences of this are (a) increase in data generation, (b) increase in storage requirements, (c) increase for computing resources to analyze and process the generated data and (d) challenges in usual activities such as accessing the available content, providing a better user experience to users. Many of the traditional tools and systems show some limitations to handling and managing big data. One such traditional technique is the RS.

Big data, a term coined with the massive generation of data, is the information asset that requires specific technology, databases, architectures and analytical methods to store and manage such large and transformation it into *Value*. Big data is mainly characterized by 5Vs, namely, volume, variety, velocity, value and veracity:

- Volume   Refers to the size of the data
- Variety   Refers to the type of the data such as normal data, text, image, audio and video; classified into structured, semi-structured and unstructured data
- Velocity   Refers to speed (or frequency) of data at which it is generated, captured and shared in real time
- Value   Refers to the transformation of data into information asset that may generate economic value for an organization
- Veracity   Refers to the reliability (noise or ambiguity) associated with the source of the data when it is generating

---

Note that there are several other characteristics of big data such as viscosity and virality exist in the literature. However, this chapter mainly covers the RSs with respect to big data characterized by one or more first 5Vs.

Enterprises and individuals use RSs to construct models by analyzing historical behavior, activity and trends. As a result, they recommend items to users which best match their interests and needs [4,5]. Communication on social media was established using blogs, Twitter, Facebook, forums, photo and video sharing portals, etc. There are several categories of social media that include digital libraries, social media, and social reviews. Over the last decade, companies such as Amazon and eBay have introduced several social media RSs. Surveys on this topic have been published by several researchers. Moreover, many companies adopt social recommendation systems (SRSs) to attract and satisfy customers through personalized recommendations, including personalized product recommendation, streaming content recommendation, ads recommendation, news and article recommendation. Big data provides value addition to the RSs and resulting in effective recommendations by way of analyzing a *variety* of data, that is, structured (e.g., past purchases, ratings), semi-structured (e.g., browsing patterns) and unstructured (e.g., feedback such as text, audio and video) in *real time*. The success of RSs depends on the *volume* and value of data available.

9.2   Recommender systems challenges

Literature in RS have centered in various regions, for example, system structures, outline and techniques for RS from a progressively customary, methodological viewpoint [6]. For example, Adomavicius and Tuzhilin introduced the general field of RS and depict content-based, CF-based techniques. A review by Cassisi *et al.* [7] summarizes major challenges with respect to dimensionality reduction techniques and similarity-based approaches. Tang *et al.* [8] stated the definitions of social recommendations and discussed the feature of social recommendation and its ramifications. Yang *et al.* [9] presented a brief, holistic overview of traditional approaches and also discussed the adoption of social network information for RS. Table 9.1 shows the state-of-the-art methodologies and their advantages for RS.

Over the years, researchers (e.g., [20]) have identified that some of the challenges still need to be addressed, such as:

- storing massive amounts of data,
- integrating a variety of data,
- data transmission,
- handling data in different forms and languages.

Along with the challenges posed by big data, the recommendation systems also have other challenges inherently. With the augmentation of the volume of data, the data types become richer. The application environment tends to get increasingly complicated and consequently the algorithms are confronted with the major well-known problems of usage of slangs, data sparsity, cold start, scalability and independent and identically distributed (IID) [21,22].

Data sparsity: A considerably large fraction of the user–item matrix has unknown ratings, and the sparsity exceeds 99%. Such excessive sparsity gives rise to common ratings between too few objects or none and a large deviation results in the similarity computation affecting the quality of the recommendation. Hence, an effective recommendation algorithm must take data sparsity into account.

Table 9.1   Methodologies and advantages of recommendation systems

Paper details	Methodology	Advantages
Ponnam *et al.* [10]	Relationship discovered between different items is compared to a user–item rating matrix, to identify similarities. A new recommender item list is generated for this user and novelty and diversity problems are solved	Better recommendations are derived as the user similarity is projected than item similarity
Kumar *et al.* [11]	The two-class structure of binary matrix factorization is constructed. Maximum margin matrix factorization (MMMF) is used successfully in CF	Accurate rating matrix completion is generated than the ordinal matrix
Dev and Mohan [12]	MapReduce technique is utilized to delete repeated computation overhead. High performance gain compared to other ordinal algorithms	Solves scalability and accuracy of the movie recommender system
Ghazanfar and Prugel-Bennett [13]	All recommender system techniques are combined. Applied to eliminate redundant problems with the recommendation system. Described cascading hybrid recommendation approach by combining the rating, feature and demographic information about items	Improved recommendations
Halder *et al.* [14]	A movie swarm mining concept is proposed. This algorithm used two pruning rules and frequent item mining	Handled cold-start problem
Panigrahi *et al.* [15]	Developed a new hybrid algorithm using *k*-means and dimensionality reduction techniques such as alternating least square (ALS)	Problems of scalability and sparsity are solved
Wang *et al.* [16]	Combined the item demographic information with searching for a set of neighboring users who have the same interests and using a genetic algorithm	Improved system scalability
Zeng *et al.* [17]	Used spark to implement ALS matrix factorization to be compared by using MLlib to generate SGD matrix factorization	Improved accuracy and efficiency
Gomez-Uribe and Hunt [18]	Developed a single global recommender system that is a confluence of different algorithms to help Netflix member retention and member engagement	Improves member retention
Lakshmikanth *et al.* [19]	Constructed user–item–opinion tripartite graph to predict the recommendations	Improves coverage, quality of recommendations and addresses cold-start problem

Cold start: When a new item enters the system, it lacks historical information with regard to the users or lack thereof, as a result of which the user cannot be provided with recommendations for that item, or it presents difficulty in recommending the item to the user. Solutions to such problems are based on hybrid recommendation techniques, combining ratings and content information.

Scalability: In online social networks, data is growing almost exponentially on the face of which recommendations must still be provided efficiently managing the time complexity. Hence, computational cost becomes important and crucial. To tackle such cases, the model-based methods are employed to train model parameters offline, in order to improve the efficiency of online prediction such similarity calculating, features extracting and user modeling.

Independent and identically distributed: Most often, recommendations are received by users which are for irrelevant, duplicate or uninteresting items. A critical reason for those bad recommendations is the intrinsic assumption that recommended users and items are IID in existing theories and systems [6].

Overspecialization: Items recommended to users are based on previously known items or those that are considered as per user profile only. No new items are discovered or other options are not explored.

Serendipity: It is also the objective to present the user with some items that the user may not have heard or thought of before pleasantly surprising the user. Serendipity is often defined as finding unplanned and valuable items by accident. For example, the invention of X-ray, penicillin, and the rediscovery of the Americas are all examples of serendipitous discoveries in science and history [23]. Serendipity constitutes three main components, which are novelty, surprise or unexpectedness and value. In the RS literature, the definition of novelty focuses on two aspects—unknown and different items [24]. Unknown items are those which have not been consumed before by users. Different items are those that are consumed by other users different from the profile of the user in contention.

Shilling attacks: This type of attack occurs typically when a malicious user starts to assign false ratings to items in order to increase or decrease their popularity. Such attacks have attack profiles biasing the RS's results to their benefits. They are divided into two categories, nuke attack and push attack. In nuke attack, attacker gives the lowest score to target items in order to demote them whereas, in push attack, attacker gives the highest score to target items in order to promote them. Constructing attack profiles is the motive of an attacker using attack models having high influence and minimum knowledge. Four types of attack models that can be used are random, average, segment and bandwagon attacks [25,26].

Gray sheep: It is assumed that the CF approach generates recommendations that are consistent for all users. However, there are a fraction of users, who have unusual preferences and such consistency in preference do not apply to those users. Such users are known as grey-sheep users.

9.2.1   Big-data-specific challenges in RS

The 5Vs of big data change the way the traditional RSs build and deployed (Table 9.2):

Table 9.2   Influence of big data characteristics on RSs

Big data characteristic	Leading to
Volume	Handling scalability and sparsity
Velocity	Making recommendations in real-time and right-time
Variety	Analyzing different types of data such as text, image, video and audio for providing qualitative recommendations
Value	Providing effective recommendation that impacts the business strategy and thereby improve sales, revenue, etc.
Veracity	Few online data sources, for instance, social media data, generate biased information such as misinformation, hate speech and fake news, which affects the recommendations. This necessitates the development of Harnessing recommender systems

The RSs face the following challenges while dealing with big data:

1. **Scalability:** When the traditional RSs are used with big data, overall computational time increases when the number of users and user data is increased due to which there is a degradation in the overall systems/application performance.

2. **Sparse data:** In existing systems such as e-commerce, users rate only a small set of products. Moreover, this data is present in multiple sources that are distributed which makes the process of finding similarities and suggesting recommendations extremely difficult.

3. **Cold-start problem:** This is a consequence is due to the presence of sparse data where new users cannot get recommendations unless they rate a minimum number of items/products. Similarly, new items cannot be recommended to the users without a minimum number of required ratings. With the rate of adding new users and products, traditional RSs suffer from cold-start problem where recommendations cannot be generated.

4. **Incorrect recommendations for similar products:** Traditional systems are not capable of deciding similar products if they are present with different names. The systems consider the products are two different products. This problem is more if more data is present and there is a chance that a large number of products will remain unrated.

5. **Gray-sheep problem:** Recommendations cannot be made for the users whose profile is not similar to any of the existing users. When using big data systems with traditional recommender systems (usually collaborative filtering-based recommender systems) have a lot of sparsity in terms of user preferences for items. Such applications usually have a high number of gray sheep users.

6. **Shilling attack:** This problem occurs if a malicious user provides false ratings/reviews to the products that are available in the system to increase the ratings of a product. Such actions will decrease the efficiency and performance of the system. From the context of big data, due to the velocity and volume of data, it is almost impossible for traditional RSs to find such attempts/attacks.

7. **Latency problem:** Traditional RSs provide recommendations to only products that are available and cannot rate any newly added products. In the big data context as new items are added very frequently, it becomes almost impossible for traditional collaborative-based recommendation systems to provide recommendations.

8. **Context-based recommendations:** In the current systems as data comes from multiple sources such as computers, mobile phones and tablets. it is a challenge for existing traditional RSs to provide context-based recommendations that are based on user preferences and context.

9.3   Techniques and approaches for recommender systems

RSs are software tools that aim at making informed decisions about the services that a user may like. Given a list of users, items and user–item interactions (ratings), RS predicts the score/affinity of item j for user i and thereby helps in understanding the user behavior which in turn can be used to make *personalized recommendations*. Classic recommendation tasks include recommending books, movies, and music as well as new Web-based applications such as predicting preferred news articles and websites. The two most commonly used traditional approaches for generating recommendations are **content-based recommenders** and **CF recommenders**.

Figure 9.1 shows the taxonomy covering state-of-the-art RSs. At higher level, the RSs are categorized into three systems:

- Early RSs—systems developed based on the traditional approaches such as CF and content based.
- Big-data RS—systems that support big data in terms of one or more of its characteristics such as volume, variety, velocity, value and variety.

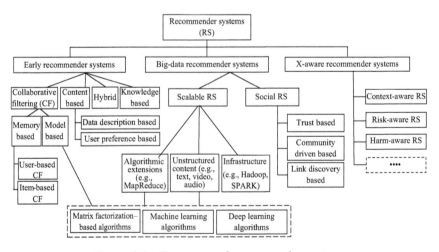

Figure 9.1   Taxonomy of recommender systems

- X-aware RSs—systems that focus on one or more specific aspects such as context, risk and harm that are important in the organizations where the RSs are deployed.
- In the next subsections, we describe these RSs in detail.

9.3.1   Early recommender systems

Early RSs can be broadly classified into two categories of approaches: **CF and content-based filtering**. In CF, the user–item association is obtained based on the preferences of the user given so far and the preference information of other users. In the case of content-based filtering, users and items are represented using a set of features (profile) and an item is recommended by finding the similarity between the user and the item profile.

9.3.1.1   Collaborative-filtering-based recommender systems

CF is the most widely adopted and successful technique used to build RSs in academic research as well as commercial applications. CF is based on the assumption that people who purchased a product in the past will also like the product in the future. The system generates recommendations using only information about rating profiles for different users or items. CF approaches can be further subdivided into **memory-based** (neighborhood-based) and **model-based** approaches.

- Model-based approaches—Use learning models (e.g., machine learning, deep learning) to find user ratings of items that are not yet evaluated.
- Memory-based approaches—Find similar users using a similarity measure such as cosine similarity or Pearson correlation and then consider weighted average of ratings.

Note that model-based approaches are more scalable than memory-based approaches of CF.

Model-based CF approaches

Collaborative methods work with the interaction matrix (also called the rating matrix). Matrix is typically massive, very sparse, and most of the values are missing. It factorizes the user–item rating matrix into two low-rank matrices: user and item matrices. A most commonly used CF-based recommendation method is the **latent factor model** (LFM), which is based on a *low-dimensional* factor model with respect to users and items where user–item affinity modeling is possible. One of the LFM variations is the matrix factorization.

Matrix factorization is a set of *model-based techniques* that have recently gained much popularity because of their scalability and accuracy as well as their successful application in the Netflix Prize competition. Given a user–item rating matrix with partially observed entries, matrix-factorization-based techniques learn low-dimensional user latent factors (U) and item latent factors (V) to simultaneously approximate the observed entries under some loss measure and predict the unobserved entries. We accomplish prediction by determining $U \times V$.

One of the problems with RSs approaches is the **data sparsity**. Matrix factorization can relieve data sparsity using dimensionality reduction techniques such as singular value decomposition (SVD) and generate accurate recommendations compared to memory-based CF methods. That is, researchers employed SVD method as an alternative for matrix factorization for decomposing the rating matrix to identify the hidden factors that affect the user's preferences. SVD methods significantly reduce the memory requirements and computational complexity [27].

There have been numerous approaches for matrix factorization, and these vary among themselves in defining the objective function and regularization term and constraints that they impose. Several matrix factorization techniques have been proposed in the literature such as nonnegative matrix factorization (NMF), incremental SVD-based matrix factorization, weighted low-rank approximation, regularized matrix factorization, maximum margin matrix factorization (MMMF), hierarchical MMMF, proximal MMMF and conformal matrix factorization.

CF-based recommendations have been widely applied in e-commerce and social networks and established itself as one of the most pervasively used technologies in RSs. CF techniques have been facing challenges such as data sparsity, cold start and scalability problems with the emergence of the big data era. This new phenomenon is worsening the performance of RS as it is not able to handle big data and alarms the sparsity problem also. Many machine learning and data mining techniques have been proposed in the literature in order to address these problems and improve the performance of RSs. Examples are probability matrix factorization (PMF), NMF [28,29] and clustering [30–32]. To address the challenges posed by big data, various big data frameworks like Hadoop and Spark are also employed for RSs [33].

Machine learning algorithms like k-nearest neighbor (kNN) algorithm, artificial neural network and naïve Bayes classifier are used for model-based CF.

kNN algorithm is a classification technique that finds the class of a new sample by calculating the distance between a subset of neighboring instances. The algorithm can also be seen as a ranking problem where the different items get different scores. These scores represent the distance between the different items and are grouped into the different features. The kNN also belongs to the classical methods to solve complex classification problems [34]. A case is classified by a majority vote of its neighbors, with the case being assigned to the class most common amongst its kNNs measured by a distance function. If $K = 1$, then the case is simply assigned to the class of its nearest neighbor. The Euclidean distance between the neighbors is calculated as:

$$E(N) = \sqrt{\sum_{x=1}^{z} N + (P_x - Q_x)^2}$$

where N is the total neighbors, P and Q are instant node and its neighbor. kNN is a supervised machine learning algorithm useful for classification problems. It calculates the distance between the test data and trained data and gives the prediction. Figure 9.2 shows the kNN neighbor representation.

Social factors have been recently taken into consideration to deal with the issues of data sparsity and cold start, such as reliability-based trust-aware collaborative filtering (RTCF) [30], matrix factorization model for recommendation in

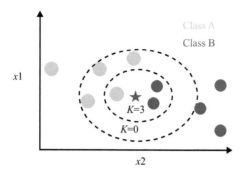

Figure 9.2 kNN neighbor representation with calculated costs

social rating networks (SocialMF) [24], a neighborhood-aware unified probabilistic matrix factorization, a recommendation with social trust ensemble [25] and a personalized recommendation model based on user attributes clustering and rating filling [35].

Traditional systems are suffering from information overloading due to the rapid increase of data at big data scale on the Web. RSs need to handle such data and automatically suggest the most suitable items depending on user needs. Social networks help to overcoming the cold-start problems. Considering the time factor and trust relationship among the friends, collaborative recommendations improved the system accuracy and customer's satisfaction. Recent studies indicated that a variety of hybrid CF-based recommendation algorithms have been emerged. In most traditional RSs, CF is used, but they suffer from *complete cold (CC) start* and *In-CC start* problem. Self-adaptive differential evolution, a deep-neural-network-based model, was used to extract the product's content characteristics [36]. Using these content features, cold-start items are ranked. The integration of tight CF coupling and deep neural work was a viable way of overcoming the problem of cold start.

The extensions of collaborative and hybrid recommender algorithms showed improvement of understanding of users and items and incorporated the contextual information into the recommendation process and supported multi-criteria ratings [6].

Memory-based CF approach

In memory-based CF approach, similar relationships are obtained based on the user–item rating matrix, and the recommendations of the items are made based on high ratings assigned by similar users, similar to the active user [37]. Such ratings from the past are used to directly predict hitherto unknown ratings for new items. Memory-based CF approach can be further subdivided into two distinct bifurcations, the *user-based CF* and the *item-based CF*.

User-based CF: The main idea of user-based CF is that similar users will unquestionably assign similar ratings for the same set of items. Then it becomes feasible to predict the active user's missing ratings on the same set of items based on historical ratings provided by similar users. Initially, the similarities of the other users with the active user are computed. Thereafter, the neighbors of the active user are selected based on the similarities. Finally, the ratings from the historical information of similar neighbor users are utilized to predict the ratings for the same set of items, for the active user [2,3].

Calculate the similarity between users: The rating vector of a user is typically how the ratings are expressed. Similarity is obtained by comparing rating vectors of two users. Classical measures to compute similarity include the cosine similarity and the Pearson correlation coefficient (PCC) [3].

Cosine similarity
The user's ratings are expressed as an *n*-dimensional vector, and similarity is obtained from the user-rating vector angle. In general, smaller the angle, higher will be the similarity. Cosine vector similarity is computed as:

$$\text{sim}_{uv} = \cos\left(\vec{r}_u, \vec{r}_v\right) = \frac{\vec{r}_u \cdot \vec{r}_v}{\|\vec{r}_u\|_2 \times \|\vec{r}_v\|_2} = \frac{\sum_{i \in I_{uv}} \vec{r}_{ui} \cdot \vec{r}_{vi}}{\sqrt{\sum_{i \in I_u} \vec{r}_{ui}^2 \sum_{i \in I_v} \vec{r}_{vi}^2}}$$

where sim_{uv} represents the similarity between users u and v, $\vec{r}_u$ and $\vec{r}_v$ are the rating vectors of users u and v, respectively, $\|\vec{r}_u\|_2$ and $\|\vec{r}_v\|_2$ are the L2 norms of the rating vectors u and v, respectively. $\vec{r}_{ui}$ and $\vec{r}_{vi}$ are the ratings of users u and v on item i. I_u and I_v represent the sets of items rated by users u and v, respectively. I_{uv} is the set of items rated by both u and v.

Pearson correlation coefficient
The similarity using PCC can be computed as

$$\text{sim}_{uv} = \frac{\sum_{i \in I_{uv}} \left(\vec{r}_{ui} - \bar{r}_u\right)\left(\vec{r}_{vi} - \bar{r}_v\right)}{\sqrt{\sum_{i \in I_{uv}} \left(\vec{r}_{ui} - \bar{r}_u\right)}\sqrt{\sum_{i \in I_{uv}} \left(\vec{r}_{vi} - \bar{r}_v\right)}}$$

where $\bar{r}_u$ and $\bar{r}_v$ are the average ratings from u and v, respectively.

Finding the nearest neighbors: There are two methods for finding the nearest neighbors. One is the kNNs while the other is the threshold method. The kNN method finds the first k candidates with the closest similarity to the active user. The threshold method establishes a threshold δ and an user v is selected as the nearest neighbor, depending on whether the similarity between user v and active user u is greater than δ.

Predicting ratings: The two methods that are commonly used in making recommendations to an active user are (a) predicting the ratings and (b) top-N recommendation list. The predicted rating is computed as follows:

$$\hat{r}_{ui} = \bar{r}_u + \frac{\sum_{v \in N_u} \text{sim}_{uv}\left(\vec{r}_{vi} - \bar{r}_v\right)}{\sum_{v \in N_u} |\text{sim}_{uv}|}$$

where N_u represents the nearest neighbor set of the user u.

Item-based CF approach: The item-based CF recommendation algorithm also executes in three steps: (a) compute similarity between items based on user–item rating matrix, (b) identify similar neighbor items based on similarity and (c) predict unknown ratings on active item based on neighboring items and list them.

Compute the similarity between the items: Traditionally, there are two distinct measures between items that are the PCCs [3] and the adjusted cosine vector. The adjusted cosine vector is calculated as follows:

$$\text{sim}_{ij} = \frac{\sum_{u \in U_{ij}} (\vec{r}_{ui} - \vec{r}_u)(\vec{r}_{uj} - \vec{r}_u)}{\sqrt{\sum_{u \in U_i} (\vec{r}_{ui} - \vec{r}_u)^2} \sqrt{\sum_{u \in U_j} (\vec{r}_{uj} - \vec{r}_u)^2}}$$

where sim_{ij} represents the similarity between items i and j. U_i and U_j represent those who rated items i and j. U_{ij} are users who rated both items i and j. PCC method is calculated as

$$\text{sim}_{ij} = \frac{\sum_{u \in U_{ij}} (\vec{r}_{ui} - \vec{r}_i)(\vec{r}_{uj} - \vec{r}_j)}{\sqrt{\sum_{u \in U_i} (\vec{r}_{ui} - \vec{r}_u)^2} \sqrt{\sum_{u \in U_j} (\vec{r}_{uj} - \vec{r}_j)^2}}$$

where $\vec{r}_i$ and $\vec{r}_j$ represent the average ratings on i and j in U_{ij}, respectively.

Find the nearest neighbors: Two methods exist for finding the neighbors in the item-based CF identical to the user-based CF, kNNs and setting threshold.

Prediction of ratings: The ratings are predicted as

$$\hat{r}_{ui} = \vec{r}_i + \frac{\sum_{j \in N_i} \text{sim}_{ij} \times (\vec{r}_{uj} - \vec{r}_j)}{\sum_{j \in N_i} |\text{sim}_{ij}|}$$

where N_i is the similar neighbor set of item i.

Top-N recommendations are generally used in scenarios such as shopping in websites which lack rating information. In this case, a list of items with possible interest to the user is recommended to him or her utilizing implicit feedback information. Relevant data is extracted to create a user–item matrix, where each element is a "0" or "1." The user's preferences are modeled point-wise, each item rating for each user is predicted and rated items sorted in a descending order. Finally, top-N items are recommended to users.

9.3.1.2 Content-based filtering recommendation systems

Content-based filtering RSs match the user profile data such as gender, age and location, and the rated items on the user's list in the user's account to similar items that have a common specification. Content-based filtering methods are based on the description of the item and profile of the user's tastes [38].

The content-based recommendation processes use three steps: (a) content analyzer, (b) profile learner and (c) filtering component. The primary objective here is to present the content of items like documents, web pages, descriptions of products, news and others. Feature extraction methods analyze the data items shifting the item representation of the original information space to the target. The profile learner collects user preference data and attempts to construct the model by generalizing the data. The generalization is learned by applying machine learning techniques. The filtering component utilizes the user data profile to find matching items related to the item list and tries to present new items to the user. The matching is achieved by cosine similarity computation between the prototype and the item vectors.

The most straightforward methodology for relegating a load to a specific tag (or term) in a user profile is by checking the occasions such tag has been utilized by the user or the occasions the tag has been utilized by the network to explain the user behavior. In this way, the principal profile model for user $\mathbf{u}_m$ comprises a vector

$$\mathbf{u}_m = (u_{m,1}, \ldots, u_{m,l})$$
$$\text{where } u_{m,l} = tf_{u_m}(t_l)$$

where tf is the tag frequency.

Similarly, the profile of item i_n is defined as a vector $\mathbf{i}_n = (i_{n,1}, \ldots, i_{n,l})$ where $i_{n,l} = tf_{i_n}(t_l)$

TF cosine-based similarity
The weights of both user and item profiles are exploited by calculating the cosine between their vectors as a similarity measure.

$$g(u_m, i_n) = \cos{}_{tf}(u_m, i_n) = \frac{\sum_l tf_{u_m}(t_l) \cdot tf_{i_n}(t_l)}{\sqrt{\sum_l (tf_{u_m}(t_l))^2} \sqrt{\sum_l (tf_{i_n}(t_l))^2}}$$

TF–IDF cosine-based similarity
The TF–IDF (term frequency—inverse document frequency)-based similarity is given by Cantador *et al.* [39] and it is as follows:

$$(u_m, i_n) = \cos{}_{tf-idf}(u_m, i_n) = \frac{\sum_l tf_{u_m}(t_l) \cdot iuf(t_l) \cdot tf_{i_n}(t_l) \cdot iif(t_l)}{\sqrt{\sum_l (tf_{u_m}(t_l) \cdot iuf(t_l))^2} \sqrt{\sum_l (tf_{i_n}(t_l) \cdot iif(t_l))^2}}$$

TF-based similarity
Cantador *et al.* [39] proposed a personalized similarity measure based on the user's tag frequencies,

$$g(u_m, i_n) = tf_u(u_m, i_n) = \frac{\sum_{l:i_{n,l}>0} tf_{u_m}(t_l)}{\max_{u \in U, t \in T}(tf_u(t))}$$

The model exploits the user's usage of tags that appear in the item profile, without taking into account their weights. For measuring the impact of personalization in Noll and Meinel's approach [40], a similarity measure based on the tag frequencies in the item profiles is given as [39]

$$g(u_m, i_n) = tf_u(u_m, i_n) = \frac{\sum_{l:u_{m,l}>0} tf_{i_n}(t_l)}{\max_{i \in I, t \in T}(tf_i(t))}$$

9.3.1.3 Hybrid recommendation systems

Hybrid recommendation systems combine both CF and content-based filtering approaches to provide effective recommendations in terms of user satisfaction and recommendation accuracy and also address the problems of RS such as cold start, scalability and data sparsity. More recently, with the proliferation of the online social networks, users are more encouraged to study. These algorithms make recommendations for an active user based on the ratings assigned by users who have social relationships with this active user. The accuracy of the recommendation is improved and the problem of cold start is also alleviated considerably. RTCF methods fuse trust relationships between the users. Other methods that fuse trust relationships are trust aware RS method based on confidence and Pareto dominance and context-aware social recommendation via individual trust [30]. Neighbor relationships and time decay factors are utilized to enhance similarity measures. MF methods like SVD, NMF and PMF are integrated with context relationships, and multiple improved algorithms have been proposed in recent years [11,41].

There is likely to be an overestimation using cosine similarity and PCC measures, when the number of common items is too small. Enhanced similarity measures based on structural similarity and time decay solves the problem [3]. Following is a brief discussion of two such measures that are based on structure and time decay.

Similarity measure based on structure
Experimental results show that with increased number of neighbors rating an item, a higher expectation precision is acquired dependent on the decision of those neighbors. In this way, based on the balanced cosine closeness, Salton factor of similitude is brought into the comparability measure. The Salton factor can be portrayed as follows:

$$f_s(u, v) = \frac{|I_{uv}|}{|I_u| + |I_v|}$$

$$f_s(i, j) = \frac{|U_{ij}|}{|U_i| + |U_j|}$$

where $f_s(u, v)$ and $f_s(i, j)$ are the Salton factors dependent on clients and things, respectively. U_i and U_j characterizes folks who valued items i and j. U_{ij} are users who rated both items i and j. I_u and I_v signify the sets of objects rated by users u and v, respectively. I_{uv} is the set of items rated by both u and v.

Similarity measure based on time decay

$$f_t(u, v) = \frac{1}{1 + \exp(\lambda|t_{ui} - t_{vi}|)}$$

$$f_t(i, j) = \frac{1}{1 + \exp(\varphi|t_{ui} - t_{uj}|)}$$

where t_{vi} represents the time of the item i rated by the user v. λ and φ represent parameters of time decay for users and items respectively and t_{ui}, t_{uj} represent the time of the items i and j rated by the user u.

9.3.1.4   Knowledge-based recommendation systems

Knowledge-based RS uses specific domain knowledge, specifying the extent of usefulness of an item to a user. They are in general model the user profile so as to find the connection between user inclinations and existing items, administrations or substance by utilizing derivation algorithms [42]. These systems commonly depend on information provided by human specialists, encoded in the system, and applied so as to create recommendations. A quantitative substance of an information base is combined with a recommendation system that includes a likeness measure. There two main components of knowledge-based RSs: knowledge-base and user profile components. Knowledge-base is one of the essential parts. Knowledge-base can be as a straightforward database or it might contain space philosophy, formalized master information, or probably the information may likewise add up to a case base [43]. The idea of the knowledge-base and the recommendation procedure are firmly connected and impact one another. Since knowledge-based system provides recommendations to a user, a user profile becomes mandatory. The contents of such a profile may include preferences, interests, requirements and others. Information required for the identification of the user requirements, related to the particular recommendation problem, is collated in the profile, implicitly or explicitly.

9.3.2   Big-data recommender systems

Huge amount of information is being generated rapidly for every second all over the world with the use of Internet. The generated information is in a variety of forms like structured, semi-structured and unstructured. The previous information consists of many data related to user profiles, interests, item descriptions, etc. Traditional RSs may not support to analyze huge amount of data. Hence big data RSs are used to address previous problem for giving recommendations.

The RSs driven by big data have several challenges such as storing massive amounts of data, handling shifts in social media platforms and handling data in different forms and languages [38]. Further, sparsity is the greatest challenge in big data where most of the users share their views on fewer items only.

Yang and Yecies [44] presented a novel big data processing framework to investigate user-generated popular cultural content on Douban, a well-known online social network in the Chinese language. They used asynchronous scraping crawler to capture large data samples and employed content mining techniques to manipulate extract heterogeneous features from Douban user profiles and applied improved Apriori algorithm. Quality-aware big-data-based movie recommendation system was proposed by Tang *et al.* [45] that is aimed at parallelizing the item-based CF algorithm to handle the big data scenario for recommendations. They have developed a distributed item-based algorithm by constructing a co-occurrence matrix, which shows the strength of the association of a pair of items in a user's list of preferences. Here, users' preferences are modeled as n-dimensional vectors and

MapReduce routines are developed to process the big data and finally recommendations are drawn. Over the last decade, companies have introduced several social media RSs. Researchers are challenged to develop a social recommendations system that allows users to find relevant products or services. Many companies adopt SRSs to attract and satisfy customers through personalized recommendations. There are commercially available big data RSs such as GroupLens film, Tripadvisor and Amazon.

Big-data-specific RSs can be broadly categorized into two: scalable RSs and social RSs.

9.3.2.1 Scalable recommender systems

Scalable RSs mainly address the scalability issue, which deals with the problem of handling large datasets in the big data. The data includes both structured and unstructured data. Scalable RSs can be developed mainly into three dimensions: (a) algorithm-specific extensions (e.g., parallel algorithms and MapReduce-based algorithms), (b) analyzing unstructured content such as opinions, reviews and posts and (c) use of big-data-specific infrastructure such as Hadoop and Spark frameworks. There are several extensions available in the literature that spans matrix factorization, machine learning and deep learning techniques for building big-data-specific RSs. Table 9.3 shows the works related to big data RSs.

Livinus *et al.* [46] presented an RS that analyzes the big data. This work uses a pseudonymous CF solution along with the content-based approach and k-means for clustering. This work also compares the results from item-based CF and user-based CF. The experiments on Million Song Dataset depicted that the recommendations are derived faster using kNN than by using CF on any number of cores. Dahdouh *et al.* [47] presented an approach to discover relationships between student's activities using parallel FP-growth algorithm to recommend appropriate learning material to the student. In particular, uses the concept of frequent item sets to determine the interesting rules from the transaction database. The extracted rules are used to determine the course catalog, according to the learner's behavior and preferences. The RS is deployed using big data technologies and techniques. The experimental results show the effectiveness and scalability of the proposed system. Finally, the performance of Spark MLlib library is compared to traditional machine learning tools, including Weka, and Dwivedi and Roshni [48] use big data analytic techniques to analyze the educational data and generate different predictions and recommendations for students, teachers and schools. CF-based recommendation techniques are used to recommend elective courses to students depending upon their grade points obtained in other subjects. Item-based recommendation of Mahout machine learning library is used on top of Hadoop to generate the recommendations. Similarity log-likelihood is used to discover patterns among grades and subjects. This work is useful for schools, colleges or universities to suggest alternative elective courses to students.

Verma *et al.* [49] proposed a recommendation system to analyze the large amount of data and provide recommendations. Examples include online ratings, reviews, opinions, complaints, remarks, feedback and comments about any item or

Table 9.3 *Recommender systems that support big data*

Publication details	Proposed method	Big data support	Methodology	Advantages	Limitations
Livinus et al. [46]	GroupLens research system	Hadoop	Provides a pseudonymous collaborative filtering solution for Usenet news and movies	Scalable for large datasets	High processing time
Dahdouh et al. [47]	Parallel FP-growth algorithm	Spark framework on Hadoop ecosystem	Distributed recommender system that encompasses historical data analysis along with the log information	Improved performance in terms of execution time. Scalable to larger datasets	Require higher network bandwidth
Dwivedi and Roshni [48]	Collaborative filtering on a scalable execution environment	Spark framework on Hadoop ecosystem	Item-based recommendation technique from Mahout machine learning library	Good quality recommendations	Accuracy is limited
Verma et al. [49]	Recommendation system with Hadoop framework	Mahout and Hive with Hadoop framework	Analyzed different size files on Hadoop framework	Better execution times even when the data file size is increased	Moderate accuracy
Lalwani et al. [50]	A community-driven social recommendation system	MapReduce framework	A scalable collaborative filtering and community-based social recommendation system	Performed better than item-based CF, in terms of item coverage, cold-start problem and running time	User ratings alone are considered
Chen et al. [51]	Big data mining (clustering and association rules) over cloud computing infrastructure	MapReduce version of random forest algorithm	Presented a density-peaked clustering analysis algorithm. Apriori algorithm is introduced for the association analysis of the D–D rules and the D–T rules, respectively	Achieves high robustness using Gaussian kernel function	Security and privacy of the individual is not addressed
Sunny et al. [52]	Self-adaptive real-time recommendation system	Spark machine learning libraries (Spark MLlib)	Analyzes the events from click stream data generated from user views. Uses stochastic gradient descent for recommendations to new users	Addresses cold-start problem	Accuracy depends on specific machine learning algorithm used
Sahoo et al. [53]	Collaborative filtering-based recommendation system using big data analytics	Big data tools such as data cleaner, Hadoop and Cassandra	Differential privacy is used to safeguard private information of the users	Privacy is preserved	No support for cold-start problem

service. Hadoop framework and Mahout interfaces are used for analyzing the review and rating for movies. Lalwani *et al.* [50] proposed a scalable CF-driven recommendation system, which uses social interactions to derive insights and thereby apt recommendations. Friendship relations are extracted using the community detection algorithm, by analyzing user–user social graph and user–item-based CF for rating prediction. The approach is developed using MapReduce framework. Experiments are carried out on MovieLens and Facebook datasets, to predict the rating of the movie and produce top-k recommendations for new user. The results are compared with traditional CF-based recommendation system. Sunny *et al.* [52] presented a television channel recommendation system for the processing of real-time data streams originating from set-top boxes. It is implemented as a real-time recommendation system using Apache Spark. It recommends the appropriate channels to the viewers based on the recent history and user interests. The proposed system effectively uses distributed processing power of Apache Spark to make recommendations in real time and is highly scalable to withstand the load in the real time. Lambda architecture is leveraged for processing the large amount of data in the system.

Deep learning is another important technique that is leveraged in RSs. Feature characterization with the help of a deep neural network learns from the data and captures the implicit relationships among products and customers, where a Bayesian probabilistic model for matrix ranking performs a collaborative classification [54]. This method is expanded to acquire features of products from diverse groups and customer properties based on their search query log and Web browsing history. The diverse high-dimensional sparse features like high-dimensional customer feedback, etc. are mapped by the neural structure into low-dimensional dense features such as real value vector that retains primary factors, within a combined semantic space. Feature interactions with low-dimensional characteristics are better generalized by deep neural networks. A methodology that combines CF with deep learning calculates more precisely the latent characteristics by improving the standard matrix factorization algorithm to predict the ranking values.

9.3.2.2 Social recommender systems

With the advent of social media sites online such as Facebook, Flickr, Twitter and YouTube, billions of users are creating online content that is in more than terabytes of size. Such an increase in online information generates a huge amount of information overload. SRSs attempt to reduce the amount of information presented by recommending the most relevant and attractive content. SRSs analyze the huge amount of data from social network sites to suggest recommendations to the end users by targeting the data of social media domain. The activity of tagging has been recently identified as a potential source of knowledge about personal interests, preferences, goals and other attributes known from user models [55]. The tags are hence being used for discovering personalized recommendations for items, because it is possible to identify individual and common interests between unknown users, through them. An example of a simple tag-based recommendation mechanism is as follows. Knowledge tags are used to recommend knowledge items. Five main components make up the implementation architecture. They are the set of users, set of interaction with knowledge items, set of new or unvisited knowledge items, set of tags from new or unvisited knowledge items and set of users' knowledge tag. We assume that there are N_u users and N_k knowledge items in a knowledge management system (KMS).

Let U be the set of user's containing all users in the KMS. $U = \{u_1, u_2, \ldots, u_n\}$, $K = \{k_1, k_2, \ldots, k_m\}$ is the set of all items in the knowledge corpus. Let X_{uk} be the association matrix between user and knowledge items. $X_{uk}(u_x, k_y)$ will equal 1 whenever user u_x bookmarks knowledge item k_y. Each row given by U_{ki} in X_{uk} denotes user interaction with knowledge items. Added to this, let UTK_x be a set of users' knowledge tag that was derived from X_{uk}. $UTK_x = \{<u_x, t_p> | u_x \in U \wedge t_p \in T \wedge X_{uk}(u_x, k_y) = 1\}$ and $NTK_y(u_x)$ be a set of tags from the new or unvisited knowledge items, derived from X_{uk}. $NTK_y = \{<u_x, t_p> | k_y \in \wedge t_p \in T \wedge X_{uk}(u_x, k_y) = 0\}$. Cosine similarity scores between UTK_x and $NTK_y(u_x)$, denoting content of new or unvisited knowledge items of user x is computed in order to recommend knowledge items to each user in the KMS [56].

Social media platforms provide new forms of communication and interaction and allow their users to share information and opinions in the form text, image, video, audio, emojis, etc. on a large scale. These platforms also promote the formation of links and social relationships. One of the most valuable features of social platforms is the potential for the dissemination of information on a large scale. RSs play an important role in the information dissemination process as they leverage on the massive user-generated content to assist users in finding relevant information as well as establishing new social relationships (*link discovery*). SRSs can be categorized into three: (a) trust-based, (b) community-driven (c) link-discovery-based systems.

Trust-based systems
Studies on the connection between trust and rating practices may give experiences into the arrangement of trust with regards to online network and lead to potential markers for the powerful utilization of trust in recommendations [57]. Trust conduct shows itself as the dependence on one individual or element by another. Individuals by and large force their trust on those having a decent notoriety. A trust relationship having been set up, the individual being trusted can impact the conduct of the individual who is forcing the trust. Numerous computational trust models have been created to foresee which operators are dependable and they will in general lighten the issues of "data sparsity" and "cold-start" [14,57].

Trust-based recommendation systems provide recommendations based on trust data between the users and items. A connected trust graph is to be established between users and items for knowing the strength of trust level. These systems work better than the RSs that use user or item similarities in their process.

Community-driven systems
Community-driven RSs provide recommendations by considering user communities data from social networking sites. The communities are first established using community detection techniques, and recommendations are provided that are

most relevant to each community. User's community data is collected by observing users' past interaction history from social networking graph. They provide quick recommendations to the community groups that are in online social networks. To address the cold-start problem, these systems first find the community that the new user belongs to and then provide recommendations that are most relevant to that particular community.

Link-discovery-based recommender systems

Link-discovery-based recommendation systems provide recommendations in the form of links that are likely to be formed in future in the social networks. These systems analyze user interaction and item attribute association structure from social networking graphs. These recommendation systems are often used to understand very complex social networking systems.

9.3.3 X-aware recommender systems

Recently, researches and industries are building recommendation systems with a focus on specific aspect (X). Examples of such RSs are (a) context-aware RSs, (b) risk-aware RSs and (c) harm-aware RSs.

9.3.3.1 Context-aware recommendation systems

Context-aware recommendation systems provide recommendations for a particular context situation of a user. The context may be related to location of a person, time of a geographical region or a user's personal situations like lunch and dining out situations, etc. These recommendation systems are very much useful to make decisions depending on a particular context. Examples are music RSs, holiday package RSs, etc.

Context-aware recommendations utilize the circumstance about the user, organization or communication to produce recommendations to users. A specific user may have appraised things as indicated by the unique circumstance, and the user will likewise require recommendations dependent on the setting also. Setting can be current time, circumstance or an area, or other data. The unique circumstance, alongside other data can be, for example, client and thing profile, can be applied to expand the importance and precision of the recommendation [56]. The context information actually characterizes an event or a situation. For example, in the context of age, old people may prefer old music whereas young users may prefer the latest or very recent music. It is therefore obvious that the contextual information greatly influences the shopping preferences of individuals in an e-commerce application. Context-aware recommendation is carried out in a sequence of three steps. They are pre-sifting, post-separating and logical displaying. Pre-sifting utilizes the setting to channel the data of the user/organization before the utilization of any recommendation strategy. Post-sifting attempts to lessen or channel the subsequent created recommendation list. Logical displaying brings the setting data into the recommendation system.

9.3.3.2 Risk-aware recommendation systems

Risk-aware RSs provide recommendations to predict good quality and low-risk applications or bad quality and high-risk applications. A user can choose applications depending upon his requirement with the help of these systems. These RSs give feel-good experience to users not to waste their time when doing their activities in their personal life by assessing risk factor. Examples are malware detection RSs and permission warning RSs.

9.3.3.3 Harm-aware recommendation systems

Sometimes, RSs affect by the spread of low-quality content in social media, hate speech and other channels of misinformation dissemination. This will (a) hinder the RS capacity of achieving accurate predictions and (b) harm the users with the unintended means, amplification and massive distribution. Due to these issues, recommender algorithms are prone to introduce biases in the process of recommending relevant contents/items.

Harm-aware RSs enable mechanisms to mitigate the negative effects of the diffusion of misinformation and unsolicited content and also improve the quality of recommendations. Strategies for building harm-aware RSs include diversification of recommendations, bias mitigation, counter measures, model-level disruption, explainability and interpretation of models.

9.4 Leveraging big data analytics on recommender systems

RSs not only impact the customer purchasing behavior, but it also affects the business parameters, such as sales, revenue and churn rates, either directly or indirectly. Thus, most of the industrial research on RSs focused on personalization and recommendation algorithms and their performance in a real-world environment.

9.4.1 Healthcare

Health-care systems leverage big-data-based recommendations systems to mine entire DNA strings in minutes to possibly discover, monitor, improve health aspects of everyone and derive predictions on disease patterns. For instance, Sharma and Ahuja [58] described an approach for providing accurate treatments for patients using content-based matching. The approach initially stores patient details such as personal data, past medical history and problem symptoms. Later, the patients are arranged into groups according their personal data and medical history. Next, the rules and constraints are formed based on their problem symptoms for each patient group. Now the training is done for each patient group. Substantially, recommendations are drawn for new patients to make perfect treatments. Medicinal services recommender frameworks are intended to give precise and applicable forecasts to the patients. It is exceptionally hard for individuals to investigate different online sources to locate helpful suggestions according to their ailments.

Chen *et al.* [51] proposed a disease–diagnosis (D–D) and treatment recommendation system (DDTRS) to enhance the use of the superior medical technology of advanced hospitals and the rich medical knowledge of experienced doctors. When a new disease affects an individual or a group with typical symptoms, it could cause difficulty for inexperienced doctors to diagnose accurately. First, a density-peaked clustering analysis algorithm is used to successfully identify disease symptoms more accurately. Additionally, association analyses on D–D rules and disease–treatment (D–T) rules are conducted by the Apriori algorithm separately. Extensive experimental results demonstrate that the proposed DDTRS performs effectively and derives D–T recommendations intelligently and accurately. Sahoo *et al.* [53] proposed a health RS that uses CF. It brings out valuable information to users based on the item profile. Based on user preferences and items profile, the recommendation system anticipates whether a person would like to purchase a product. Before buying any product over e-marketing sites, users search for reviews to know and understand the efficacy of the product. Therefore, a recommendation system provides a platform to recommend products that are valuable and acceptable to people. Various approaches are made to efficiently retrieve large quantities of data because there are a lot of unstructured and unprocessed data that needs to be processed and used in various applications. Big data tools, such as data cleaner for data processing, Apache Hadoop and Cassandra for storage and querying of data, are used.

9.4.2   Education

Recommendation systems have become prominent in education sector and yielded benefits in various ways. For example, to recommend elective courses to students, depending upon their grade points obtained in other subjects, to recommend a learning path to the students based on their educational background and interests and recommending the resources/institutions that are best in the industry to offer the courses chosen by the students, etc. are a few use cases for big-data-based recommendation systems in educational sector. A CF method was used to recommend elective courses to students based on their marks obtained in the subjects [59]. This system was developed on Mahout using machine learning library to recommend elective courses to the students based on the grade points obtained in different subjects.

9.4.3   Banking and finance

Banking sector has been using recommendation systems enormously in recent times. Especially it uses recommendations for sanctioning loans to their customers. Sanctioning a loan consists of a sequence of steps like collecting customer personal information, checking creditworthiness of a customer, etc. Getting support from recommendation systems eases task for banks to sanction loans. The recommendation systems suggest a number of alternative loan plans depending on the creditworthiness of a customer by analyzing his financial status. Felfernig *et al.* [60] implemented a recommendation model for loan processing system in banking sector. Kanaujia *et al.* [61] presented a recommendation model for a person to give suggestions on how to maximize his/her wealth by proper money saving, reducing expenditure and showing investment opportunities. Their work uses Apache Hadoop and Mahout for distributed processing and analyzing data, respectively.

9.4.4 Manufacturing

Manufacturing industry is also getting huge positive results with the use of RSs. RSs help in identifying the making of good quality products. These systems can also be used in cloud sector. Alinani *et al.* [62] presented an approach for cloud manufacturing. Cloud manufacturing process is a very difficult and challenging task as it includes mainly selection of cloud service and cloud task scheduling with respect the dynamic client requirements. The authors presented a recommender system for the decentralized cloud manufacturing model for decentralized approach that provides recommendations to clients to better choose their cloud services on their own.

Recently, researchers are developing cross-domain RSs, which aim to generate or improve recommendations for a particular field by exploiting user profiles (or any other data/information) from other fields.

9.5 Evaluation metrics

Accuracy, coverage and diversity metrics are evaluated using several different approaches. The mean absolute error (MAE) is a pervasively used metric, to compute the recommender's prediction [63]. MAE is computed as

$$MAE = \frac{\sum_{(u,i) \in T} |r_{ui} - \widehat{r_{ui}}|}{|T|}$$

where T represents an item set. For a given RS, lower the MAE, higher the prediction, better the performance of the algorithm. The root-mean-squared error (RMSE) is a frequently used metric, which is given by the following:

$$RMSE = \sqrt{\frac{\sum_{(u,i) \in T}(r_{ui} - \widehat{r_{ui}})^2}{|T|}}$$

Recommendation accuracy is also evaluated using *precision* (*prec*) and *recall* (*rec*). The percentage of items in the final recommended list that match the user–item-rating records is known as *precision*. The percentage of items in the user–item rating list that match those in the recommendation list is known as *recall*. *Precision* and *Recall* are defined as follows,

$$\boldsymbol{prec} = \frac{\sum_u (|R(u) \cap T(u)|)}{\sum_u |R(u)|}$$

$$\boldsymbol{rec} = \frac{\sum_u (|R(u) \cap T(u)|)}{\sum_u |T(u)|}$$

where $R(u)$ denotes the number of items recommended to user u and $T(u)$ denotes the user u's liking of the collection of items on the test set. A different evaluation metric for mean recommendation accuracy is the mean reciprocal rank (MRR). It is the mean of the reciprocal of the user's actual response in the recommended list. It is defined as follows:

$$MRR = \frac{1}{|U|} \sum_{u \in U} \frac{1}{\min_{i \in T(u)} p}$$

where p is the rank in the recommended list.

9.6 Popular datasets for recommender systems

Various datasets are used for recommendation systems. Some of the datasets that are popularly used are (Table 9.4) as follows:

(a) MovieLens dataset
(b) Netflix dataset
(c) Million Song Dataset
(d) Book-Crossing dataset
(e) YOW dataset
(f) Jester dataset

(a) MovieLens dataset
MovieLens dataset is one of the mostly downloaded datasets for industry, research and education. The releasing year of MovieLens dataset was in 1998. The dataset consists of attributes like user, item (movie name), rating and timestamp. The ratings are given within the range from 0 to 5. There were more than 7,500 references made by Google scholars. A total four major versions made to dataset right from its launch [64,68].

(b) Netflix dataset
Netflix dataset is the most commonly used dataset for research purposes. There are 2,649,430 users and 17,770 movies in the dataset. Ratings are given for the users and movies list from the range of 1 to 5 and 0 is recorded for missed or empty entries. Movie data attributes are movie ID, movie title and movie released year. Movie year values are from 1896 to 2005 [65,66].

(c) Million Song Dataset
Million Song Dataset is the widely used dataset in the music information retrieval search industry. The dataset consists of nearly 1,000,000 songs. These are taken from 44,745 music artists. Each user in the dataset is supplied tags. There are 2,321 social tags in the dataset. The total dataset comprises audio features with metadata amounting to nearly 300 GB data. Million Song Dataset was launched mainly for commercial scales from the use of music information retrieval search [65,67,68].

(d) Book-Crossing dataset
Book-Crossing dataset is commonly used for book recommendation systems. The dataset was launched through BookCrossing website in the year 2004. It consists of a total of 278,858 users. Nearly 1,149,780 ratings were provided on the books of 271,379 size. The ratings start from range 1 to 10. The dataset consists of attributes like book publisher name, book author name and cover images [65].

Table 9.4 Comparison of different datasets for recommendation systems

Dataset	Domain	Size			Feedback	
		Items	Users	Ratings	Explicit	Implicit
MovieLens 100k [64,65]	Movie	1,682 movies	943	100,000	Ratings from 1 to 5	–
MovieLens 1M [64,65]	Movie	3,900 movies	6,040	1,000,209	Ratings from 1 to 5	–
MovieLens 10M [64,65]	Movie	10,682 movies	71,567	100,000,054	Ratings from 1 to 5	–
Netflix (training) [65,66]	Movie	17,770 movies	480,189	100,480,507	Ratings from 1 to 5	–
Million Song [65,67,68]	Music	1,000,000 songs	44,745	–	–	–
Jester v1 [65,69]	Joke	100 jokes	73,421	4,000,000	Ratings from −10.00 to +10.00	–
Jester v2 [65,69]	Joke	150 jokes	59,132	1,700,000	Ratings from −10.00 to +10.00	–
Book-Crossing [65]	Book	271,379 books	278,858	1,149,780	Ratings from 1 to 10	–
YOW [65]	News	383 articles	25	7,000+	Ratings from 1 to 5	Mouse, keyboard and scroll activities

(e) YOW dataset

The Carnegie Mellon University released YOW dataset for YOW-now news filtering system that is an information filtering system used to provide news articles. Each user nearly rated 383 articles in this dataset. Ratings are given from range 1 to 5. The YOW dataset works well for CF compared to content-based filtering as it does not store news content [65].

(f) Jester dataset

It is an online joke recommender framework that has three distinct renditions of freely accessible communitarian separating dataset. The main adaptation of Jester dataset contains more than 4 million nonstop appraisals gathered from 73.451k clients. There are 100 jokes in the dataset and it is gathered from 1999 to 2003. The subsequent variant contains over 1.69 million consistent evaluations of 150 jokes from 59,132 clients and it is gathered between 2006 and 2009. Additionally there is a refreshed form of the second dataset with over 5M new appraisals from 7.9M complete clients. The evaluations of Jester dataset is in run somewhere in the range of -10.00 and $+10.00$ as a skimming number. The dataset contains two documents where the first incorporates the thing ID and the jokes, and the other one incorporates client ID, thing ID and appraisals [65,69].

9.7 Conclusion

In this chapter, we discussed various techniques and methods for developing RSs, besides evaluation datasets and metrics for RSs. We also discussed the enhancement of RSs with big data and analytics support. CF techniques have been widely used for a long time to generate groups of users with similar interests. However, there is a strong need of incorporating friends' behavior while providing recommendations, as users prefer recommendations from friends compared to those coming from third parties. Further, there is a mutually symbiotic relationship between social media and personalized RSs, which leads to developing SRSs. New types of metadata and public data, for example, ratings, comments, tags and explicit people relationships, provide added value to RSs for improved and enhanced recommendations.

References

[1] Hernando, Antonio, Jesús Bobadilla, and Fernando Ortega. 'Anon negative matrix factorization for collaborative filtering recommender systems based on a Bayesian probabilistic model.' Knowledge Based Systems 97 (2016): 188–202.

[2] Cao, Longbing. 'Non-IID recommender systems: A review and framework of recommendation paradigm shifting.' Engineering 2, no. 2 (2016): 212–224.

[3] Chen, Rui, Qingyi Hua, Yan-Shuo Chang, Bo Wang, Lei Zhang, and Xiangjie Kong. 'A survey of collaborative filtering-based recommender systems: From traditional methods to hybrid methods based on social networks.' IEEE Access 6 (2018): 64301–64320.

[4] Champiri, Zohreh Dehghani, Seyed Reza Shahamiri, and Siti Salwah Binti Salim. 'A systematic review of scholar context-aware recommender systems.' Expert Systems with Applications 42, no. 3 (2015): 1743–1758.

[5] Jugovac, Michael, and Dietmar Jannach. 'Interacting with recommenders – Overview and research directions.' ACM Transactions on Interactive Intelligent Systems 7, no. 3 (2017): 1–46.

[6] Adomavicius, Gediminas, and Alexander Tuzhilin. 'Toward the next generation of recommender systems: A survey of the state-of-the-art and possible extensions.' IEEE Transactions on Knowledge and Data Engineering 17, no. 6 (2005): 734–749.

[7] Cassisi, Carmelo, Placido Montalto, Marco Aliotta, Andrea Cannata, and Alfredo Pulvirenti. 'Similarity measures and dimensionality reduction techniques for time series data mining.' In Advances in Data Mining Knowledge Discovery and Applications, pp. 71–96. InTech, Rijeka, Croatia, 2012.

[8] Tang, Jiliang, Xia Hu, and Huan Liu. 'Social recommendation: A review.' Social Network Analysis and Mining 3, no. 4 (2013): 1113–1133.

[9] Yang, Xiwang, Harald Steck, and Yong Liu. 'Circle-based recommendation in online social networks.' In Proceedings of the 18th ACM SIGKDD International Conference on Knowledge Discovery and Data Mining, pp. 1267–1275. 2012.

[10] Ponnam, Lakshmi Tharun, Sreenivasa Deepak Punyasamudram, Siva Nagaraju Nallagulla, and Srikanth Yellamati. 'Movie recommender system using item based collaborative filtering technique.' In 2016 International Conference on Emerging Trends in Engineering, Technology and Science (ICETETS), pp. 1–5. IEEE, 2016.

[11] Kumar, Vikas, Arun K. Pujari, Sandeep Kumar Sahu, Venkateswara Rao Kagita, and Vineet Padmanabhan. 'Collaborative filtering using multiple binary maximum margin matrix factorizations.' Information Sciences 380 (2017): 1–11.

[12] Dev, Arpan V., and Anuraj Mohan. 'Recommendation system for big data applications based on set similarity of user preferences.' In 2016 International Conference on Next Generation Intelligent Systems (ICNGIS), pp. 1–6. IEEE, 2016.

[13] Ghazanfar, Mustansar Ali, and Adam Prugel-Bennett. 'A scalable, accurate hybrid recommender system.' In 2010 Third International Conference on Knowledge Discovery and Data Mining, pp. 94–98. IEEE, 2010.

[14] Halder, Sajal, AM Jehad Sarkar, and Young-Koo Lee. 'Movie recommendation system based on movie swarm.' In 2012 Second International Conference on Cloud and Green Computing, pp. 804–809. IEEE, 2012.

[15] Panigrahi, Sasmita, Rakesh Kumar Lenka, and Ananya Stitipragyan. 'A hybrid distributed collaborative filtering recommender engine using Apache Spark.' In ANT/SEIT, pp. 1000–1006. 2016.

[16] Wang, Qian, Xianhu Yuan, and Min Sun. 'Collaborative filtering recommendation algorithm based on hybrid user model.' In 2010 Seventh

International Conference on Fuzzy Systems and Knowledge Discovery, vol. 4, pp. 1985–1990. IEEE, 2010.

[17] Zeng, Xuelin, Bin Wu, Jing Shi, Chang Liu, and Qian Guo. 'Parallelization of latent group model for group recommendation algorithm.' In 2016 IEEE First International Conference on Data Science in Cyberspace (DSC), pp. 80–89. IEEE, 2016.

[18] Gomez-Uribe, Carlos A., and Neil Hunt. 'The Netflix recommender system: Algorithms, business value, and innovation.' ACM Transactions on Management Information Systems (TMIS) 6, no. 4 (2015): 1–19.

[19] Paleti Lakshmikanth, P. Radha Krishna and J. V. R. Murthy. 'User opinion driven social recommendation systems.' International Journal of Knowledge-Based and Intelligent Engineering Systems 25, no. 1 (2021): 21–31.

[20] Kaisler, Stephen, Frank Armour, J. Alberto Espinosa, and William Money. 'Big data: Issues and challenges moving forward.' In 2013 46th Hawaii International Conference on System Sciences, pp. 995–1004. IEEE, 2013.

[21] Zhu, Bo, Remigio Hurtado, Jesus Bobadilla, and Fernando Ortega. 'An efficient recommender system method based on the numerical relevances and the non-numerical structures of the ratings.' IEEE Access 6 (2018): 49935–49954.

[22] Khusro, Shah, Zafar Ali, and Irfan Ullah. 'Recommender systems: Issues, challenges, and research opportunities.' In Information Science and Applications (ICISA) 2016, pp. 1179–1189. Springer, Singapore, 2016.

[23] Abbas, Fakhri. 'Serendipity in recommender system: A holistic overview.' In 2018 IEEE/ACS 15th International Conference on Computer Systems and Applications (AICCSA), pp. 1–2. IEEE, 2018.

[24] Jamali, Mohsen, and Martin Ester. 'A matrix factorization technique with trust propagation for recommendation in social networks.' In Proceedings of the fourth ACM conference on Recommender systems, pp. 135–142. 2010.

[25] Si, Mingdan, and Qingshan Li. 'Shilling attacks against collaborative recommender systems: A review.' Artificial Intelligence Review 53, no. 1 (2020): 291–319.

[26] Zhang, Fuguo. 'A survey of shilling attacks in collaborative filtering recommender systems.' In 2009 International Conference on Computational Intelligence and Software Engineering, pp. 1–4. IEEE, 2009.

[27] Parhi, Prateek, Ashish Pal, and Manuj Aggarwal. 'A survey of methods of collaborative filtering techniques.' In 2017 International Conference on Inventive Systems and Control (ICISC), pp. 1–7. IEEE, 2017.

[28] Hernando, Antonio, Jesús Bobadilla, and Fernando Ortega. 'A non negative matrix factorization for collaborative filtering recommender systems based on a Bayesian probabilistic model.' Knowledge-Based Systems 97 (2016): 188–202.

[29] Luo, Xin, Mengchu Zhou, Yunni Xia, and Qingsheng Zhu. 'An efficient non-negative matrix-factorization-based approach to collaborative filtering for recommender systems.' IEEE Transactions on Industrial Informatics 10, no. 2 (2014): 1273–1284.

[30] Moradi, Parham, and Sajad Ahmadian. 'A reliability-based recommendation method to improve trust-aware recommender systems.' Expert Systems with Applications 42, no. 21 (2015): 7386–7398.

[31] Patibandla, R. S. M. Lakshmi, and N. Veeranjaneyulu. 'Performance analysis of partition and evolutionary clustering methods on various cluster validation criteria.' Arabian Journal for Science and Engineering 43, no. 8 (2018): 4379–4390.

[32] Patibandla, R. S. M. Lakshmi, and N. Veeranjaneyulu. 'Survey on clustering algorithms for unstructured data.' In Intelligent Engineering Informatics, pp. 421–429. Springer, Singapore, 2018.

[33] Almohsen, Khadija Ateya, and Huda Kadhim Al-Jobori. 'Recommender system in the context of big data: Implementing SVD-based recommender system using Apache Hadoop and Spark.' In Effective Big Data Management and Opportunities for Implementation, pp. 231–246. IGI Global, 2016.

[34] Moldagulova, Aiman, and Rosnafisah Bte Sulaiman. 'Using KNN algorithm for classification of textual documents.' In 2017 8th International Conference on Information Technology (ICIT), pp. 665–671. IEEE, 2017.

[35] Liji, U., Yahui Chai, and Jianrui Chen. 'Improved personalized recommendation based on user attributes clustering and score matrix filling.' Computer Standards & Interfaces 57 (2018): 59–67.

[36] Wei, Jian, Jianhua He, Kai Chen, Yi Zhou, and Zuoyin Tang. 'Collaborative filtering and deep learning based recommendation system for cold start items.' Expert Systems with Applications 69 (2017): 29–39.

[37] Yang, Zhe, Bing Wu, Kan Zheng, Xianbin Wang, and Lei Lei. 'A survey of collaborative filtering-based recommender systems for mobile internet applications.' IEEE Access 4 (2016): 3273–3287.

[38] Lops, Pasquale, Marco De Gemmis, and Giovanni Semeraro. 'Content-based recommender systems: State of the art and trends.' In Recommender Systems Handbook, pp. 73–105. Springer, Boston, MA, 2011.

[39] Cantador, Iván, Alejandro Bellogín, and David Vallet. 'Content-based recommendation in social tagging systems.' In Proceedings of the Fourth ACM Conference on Recommender Systems, pp. 237–240. 2010.

[40] Noll, Michael G., and Christoph Meinel. 'Web search personalization via social bookmarking and tagging.' In The Semantic Web, pp. 367–380. Springer, Berlin, Heidelberg, 2007.

[41] Koohi, Hamidreza, and Kourosh Kiani. 'A new method to find neighbor users that improves the performance of collaborative filtering.' Expert Systems with Applications 83 (2017): 30–39.

[42] Carrer-Neto, Walter, María Luisa Hernández-Alcaraz, Rafael Valencia-García, and Francisco García-Sánchez. 'Social knowledge-based recommender system. Application to the movies domain.' Expert Systems with Applications 39, no. 12 (2012): 10990–11000.

[43] Tarus, John K., Zhendong Niu, and Ghulam Mustafa. 'Knowledge-based recommendation: A review of ontology-based recommender systems for e-learning.' Artificial Intelligence Review 50, no. 1 (2018): 21–48.

[44] Yang, Jie, and Brian Yecies. 'Mining Chinese social media UGC: A big-data framework for analyzing Douban movie reviews.' Journal of Big Data 3, no. 1 (2016): 3.

[45] Tang, Yan, Mingzheng Li, Wangsong Wang, Pengcheng Xuan, and Kun Geng. 'Quality-aware movie recommendation system on big data.' In Proceedings of the Fourth IEEE/ACM International Conference on Big Data Computing, Applications and Technologies, pp. 273–274. 2017.

[46] Livinus, Udeh Tochukwu, Rachid Chelouah, and Houcine Senoussi. 'Recommender system in big data environment.' International Journal of Computer Science Issues (IJCSI) 13, no. 5 (2016): 1.

[47] Dahdouh, Karim, Ahmed Dakkak, Lahcen Oughdir, and Abdelali Ibriz. 'Large-scale e-learning recommender system based on Spark and Hadoop.' Journal of Big Data 6, no. 1 (2019).

[48] Dwivedi, Surabhi, and VS Kumari Roshni. 'Recommender system for big data in education.' In 2017 5th National Conference on E-Learning & E-Learning Technologies (ELELTECH), pp. 1–4. IEEE, 2017.

[49] Verma, Jai Prakash, Bankim Patel, and Atul Patel. 'Big data analysis: Recommendation system with Hadoop framework.' In 2015 IEEE International Conference on Computational Intelligence & Communication Technology, pp. 92–97. IEEE, 2015.

[50] Lalwani, Deepika, Durvasula VLN Somayajulu, and P. Radha Krishna. 'A community driven social recommendation system.' In 2015 IEEE International Conference on Big Data (Big Data), pp. 821–826. IEEE, 2015.

[51] Chen, Jianguo, Kenli Li, Huigui Rong, Kashif Bilal, Nan Yang, and Keqin Li. 'A disease diagnosis and treatment recommendation system based on big data mining and cloud computing.' Information Sciences 435 (2018): 124–149.

[52] Sunny, Bobin K., P. S. Janardhanan, Anu Bonia Francis, and Reena Murali. 'Implementation of a self-adaptive real time recommendation system using spark machine learning libraries.' In 2017 IEEE International Conference on Signal Processing, Informatics, Communication and Energy Systems (SPICES), pp. 1–7. IEEE, 2017.

[53] Sahoo, Abhaya Kumar, Sitikantha Mallik, Chittaranjan Pradhan, Bhabani Shankar Prasad Mishra, Rabindra Kumar Barik, and Himansu Das. 'Intelligence-based health recommendation system using big data analytics.' In Big Data Analytics for Intelligent Healthcare Management, pp. 227–246. Academic Press, 2019.

[54] Mahout. http://mahout.apache.org/users/basics/algorithms.md (accessed April 20, 2017).

[55] Durao, Frederico, and Peter Dolog. 'A personalized tag-based recommendation in social web systems.' arXiv preprint arXiv:1203.0332 (2012).

[56] Baltrunas, Linas, Marius Kaminskas, Bernd Ludwig, *et al.* 'InCarMusic: Context-aware music recommendations in a car.' In International Conference on Electronic Commerce and Web Technologies, pp. 89–100. Springer, Berlin, Heidelberg, 2011.

[57] Mei, Jian-Ping, Han Yu, Zhiqi Shen, and Chunyan Miao. 'A social influence based trust model for recommender systems.' Intelligent Data Analysis 21, no. 2 (2017): 263–277.

[58] Sharma, Mugdha, and Laxmi Ahuja. 'A data mining approach towards healthcare recommender system.' In International Conference on Next Generation Computing Technologies, pp. 199–210. Springer, Singapore, 2017.

[59] Dwivedi, Surabhi, and VS Kumari Roshni. 'Recommender system for big data in education.' In 2017 5th National Conference on E-Learning & E-Learning Technologies (ELELTECH), pp. 1–4. IEEE, 2017.

[60] Felfernig, Alexander, Klaus Isak, Kalman Szabo, and Peter Zachar. 'The VITA financial services sales support environment.' In Proceedings of the National Conference on Artificial Intelligence, vol. 22, no. 2, p. 1692. AAAI Press; MIT Press, Menlo Park, CA; Cambridge, MA; London, 1999, 2007.

[61] Kanaujia, Pradeep Kumar M., Naliniprava Behera, Manjusha Pandey, and Siddarth Swarup Rautaray. 'Recommendation system for financial analytics.' In 2016 International Conference on ICT in Business Industry & Government (ICTBIG), pp. 1–5. IEEE, 2016.

[62] Alinani, Karim, Deshun Liu, Dong Zhou, and Guojun Wang. 'Recommender system for decentralized cloud manufacturing.' In International Conference on Dependability in Sensor, Cloud, and Big Data Systems and Applications, pp. 170–179. Springer, Singapore, 2019.

[63] Sarwar, Badrul, George Karypis, Joseph Konstan, and John Riedl. 'Item-based collaborative filtering recommendation algorithms.' In Proceedings of the 10th International Conference on World Wide Web, pp. 285–295. 2001.

[64] Harper, F. Maxwell, and Joseph A. Konstan. 'The MovieLens datasets: History and context.' ACM Transactions on Interactive Intelligent Systems (TIIS) 5, no. 4 (2015): 1–19.

[65] Özgöbek, Özlem, Nafiseh Shabib, and Jon Atle Gulla. 'Data sets and news recommendation.' In UMAP Workshops. 2014.

[66] Garcia, Cyril, and Luca Rona. 'The Netflix Challenge.' https://www.researchgate.net/publication/326694752_The_NetflixChallenge.

[67] Liang , Dawen, Haijie Gu, and Brendan O'Connor. 'Music genre classification with the million song dataset.' (2011). In Machine Learning Department, CMU, 2011. www.ee.columbia.edu/~dliang/files/FINAL.pdf.

[68] Bertin-Mahieux, Thierry, Daniel PW Ellis, Brian Whitman, and Paul Lamere. 'The million song dataset.' In International Society for Music Information Retrieval. University of Miami, 2011: 591–596.

[69] Ken Goldberg. http://eigentaste.berkeley.edu/dataset/archive/.

Chapter 10

Analytics in e-commerce at scale

Vaidyanathan Subramanian[1] and Arya Ketan[2]

This chapter focuses on the challenges of architecting for scale in an e-commerce setup, more specifically, the challenges of architecting distributed and analytical systems for scale, to handle more than a billion online visits per month in India's largest e-commerce company, Flipkart.[*] The chapter explains how Flipkart evolved its technology, functions and analytics over time, with Internet users increasingly resorting to the e-commerce market year-on-year. With the business and system metrics gaining paramount importance, data monitoring became more of a necessity in bringing out the best from the e-commerce platform.

The chapter then goes into detail of how Flipkart Data Platform (FDP), the big data platform in Flipkart handles the ingestion, storage, processing, analytics, queries, and reporting of the petabytes of data every day, and of how the Data Sciences and machine learning (ML) department provide inferences that power various business workflows in the Flipkart systems. With due importance given to the data landscape—producers, consumers, freshness, and governance, the chapter then concludes with a summary of how data processing has evolved over the years in Flipkart ensuring that the engineered information is as close to accurate as it should be.

10.1 Background

India's Internet revolution that started in the early 2000s coupled with the emergence of smartphones around the same time resulted in an explosion of Internet users. The estimated number of Internet users for the year 2019 was about 450+ million—roughly the population of the United States.

Flipkart was one of the earliest e-commerce companies that seized this growing Internet usage as an opportunity to enable online shopping in the Indian consumer market enabling millions of Indians to shop physical products online, eventually building trust with innovations in every step of the process.

[1]SDE4 at Flipkart, Bengaluru, India
[2]Architect at Flipkart, Bengaluru, India
[*]Flipkart is an Indian e-commerce company established in 2007.

The systems that powered Flipkart also had to scale exponentially like the business itself—and the company hence adopted SoA—service-oriented architecture with hundreds of microservices to power multiple parts of the website, app, order-management, and supply chain systems. The company then adopted the practice of being a data-driven technology business by thoroughly analyzing various metrics around this complex ecosystem to ensure that the existing system was working as expected both in terms of business and tech. And in order for this to happen, Flipkart invested in a home-grown big data platform that was to power all the data needs of the organization.

We shall delve into this ecosystem by first analyzing the need and then into how the architecture was built to serve the need.

10.2   Analytics use cases

All successful businesses rely on strong analytics to power their strategy, and to power these analytics, two things are mandatory—first, a lot of data on various aspects of the business and second, a way to make sense out of them. e-Commerce has a lot of moving parts because there are a lot of microservices in the systems that work in tandem to ship a package from a warehouse all the way to a customer's doorstep and thus, a lot of data gets generated for every single order.

10.2.1   Business and system metrics

There are two kinds of metrics common across most systems—the business and the system.

We classify business metrics according to their requirements—from weekly reporting to understand the trend of various business metrics to almost real-time requirement of metrics to monitor peak sale periods and take immediate actions if needed. Business analysts rely on this data to make insights of the trends and make suggestions to leadership, which then takes its due course.

Some examples of such business metrics are—tracking how many people came to a product page but left without purchasing the product, tracking the top selling products in a certain category, analyzing the results of AB experiments, capturing the rate of various metrics such as order placement rate, return rate, fulfillment rate, comparison of one sale with an older sale, and so on. Metrics like out-of-stock spikes need more of a real-time perspective to it, given there is an immediate action to take when such a situation happens. Shown next is a warehouse in-scan metric that the warehouse team closely monitors and takes actions when needed (Figure 10.1).

Besides reporting, we use metrics for various purposes such as generating a heat-map of the product page, tracing the user-journey to provide the customer support with the relevant context when providing support, powering product-recommendations, detecting fraud, visualizing the warehouse capacity, and so on. The list is endless.

Most tech systems today use a host of monitoring tools that push various metrics in a near real-time manner to a centralized system, typically a time-series

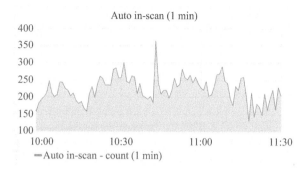

Figure 10.1   A warehouse in-scan graph captures the rate of inwarding products by scanning them in a timeline view

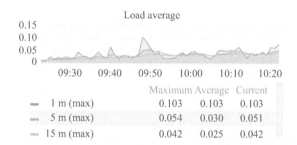

Figure 10.2   A load average graph that shows the maximum, average, and current values of load of a specific machine with 1, 5, and 15 min facets in a timeline view

database that then is used to power multiple such dashboards. Gone are the days when engineers had to keep monitoring logs to get visibility on key functional metrics of a system.

Some examples of such technical metrics are throughput, latency graphs of systems, 5XX, 4XX response measurements, network traffic, data growth, and so on, with a capability to measure the maximum, average, and other aggregation operations on them (Figure 10.2).

During peak sale times when the traffic is exceptionally high, we monitor the internal messaging queue and systems closely that are producing data into the queue and systems consuming this data tweak their scalability accordingly, increasing the server instances behind the load-balancer when the message-queue is quickly filling up and decreasing the same once the load is consumed so that we can use the server instances for other purposes. We monitor the database closely for data-growth rates to plan for adequate disk space. Systems also need to scale up adding more memory or compute as and when the need arises—again this is achieved by monitoring the aggregated load averages over all the servers in a time-series fashion.

With enough graphs on various metrics, we do a lot of the debugging, actually just by looking at the graphs and analyzing them before looking into the logs. Most systems today have enough graphs on their dashboards that they can both predict the load to some extent and debug issues more quickly by correlating patterns in the graphs at specific intervals.

For example, a spike in the 5XX responses from a server at a certain time can be correlated with a drop in QPS of MySQL at that instant which can again be correlated with a drop in TCP packets in the networking dashboard for that particular mothership on which the MySQL VM was being hosted—eventually pointing to a blip in the network traffic because of a malfunctioning switch.

10.2.2   Data sciences

Data is the new oil today, and the best use of data is to learn from it and use it to power various business flows. Also, business intelligence is a key driver in all e-commerce applications today and is the most important differentiating factor. In Flipkart the data collected from various sources in a multitude of AI/ML algorithms powers use-cases such as fraud risk management, personalization of shopping experience, and increasing efficiency in logistics operations.

While the previous section talked about analytics that are done by merging data from various systems or aggregating the same in order to understand the larger picture, data sciences provide the next level of analytics by running algorithms over this data to create models out of the same and comparing more complex behavior in a more palatable way besides figuring out new relationships in data.

One of the most common AI/ML use-cases is the product recommendation module where algorithms can analyze shopping behavior of a user, compare it to known models, and recommend products to enhance the shopping experience. Based on how correct the recommendation was, the model learns or unlearns new factors influencing the decision-making.

A common workflow pattern seen in this analysis is collecting data, filtering out bad data, and training of data to create ML models. These models are used to enhance the efficiency in handling business use-cases. The main challenge is the large volume of data that needs training on existing models and creating relevant new models. This typically translates to optimizing for compute resources to keep the costs low and enabling complex data-science algorithms to make sense of the data.

Given that data and algorithms power data sciences, the FDP was the pivotal piece in making this happen. We shall next go into more detail about the actual data landscape to understand the challenges faced by this platform.

10.3   Data landscape

To understand the complexity of the problem, it is important to understand the data landscape—Who is the producer? Who is the consumer? Is this data relevant? How is this data governed? Each of these is independent topic that poses its own challenges.

10.3.1 Data producers

An e-commerce system is classifiable into two subsystems. The first is the user path system that caters to the user's shopping journey, from the time a user enters an e-commerce website to browse and search for products to eventually placing an order. The second is the order path system that aims to fulfill the order placed by the user via its supply chain.

A typical order is processed by multiple microservices, each solving one piece of the larger puzzle—each of these systems produces data specific to its own processing workflows. All this data needs to be tied to each other to look at the larger picture of the supply chain.

For example, the order-management system ingests the order-information with the primary column *order_id* (among many other attributes), and then the planning system that computes the *dispatch_time*, *shipping_time*, and *delivery_time* ingests the planning data along with the same *order_id* key besides its own key, say the *fulfillment_id*. The next system, like the warehouse, then ingests its own information and ties it either to the *order_id* or the *fulfillment_id* and generates its own *shipment_id* which would be the lingua franca for downstream systems. Eventually all data is joined using common columns to create processable data for supply-chain processes, something meaningful at a supply-chain level.

The producers themselves are microservices that communicate to each other via message-queues to serve very different scale requirements, which often results in nonlinear ingestion—many a time the downstream systems ingest their information before the upstream systems. The joining of data fails for many entities because a dependent system has not been able to ingest its information yet.

Given this asynchronous communication, many systems have "at-least-once" guarantees as opposed to "exactly-once" guarantees. Hence, idempotency is also a key requirement in the data pipeline.

10.3.2 Data consumers

The main motivation for designing the data-pipeline was to empower the analysts or data scientists with sufficient data to make strategic decisions, to create ML models or to monitor the business's various metrics regularly. Further, these requirements extend into the domain of how easy, configurable, and modular it is for them to come up with the most complex of reports and publish the same reports regularly in a variety of formats. However, the most challenging aspect of this would be to empower the users with a way to query this data in a very simple way—for this purpose, SQL is used as a language.

Time is the next most important pivot in the analyst's world—for example, there might be a report on the number of television sets shipped and delivered to the customer in a specific set of pincodes from a specific warehouse in July. For this reason, we process data on time slices—for example, at a day level, a month level and a year level. By arranging data in this format, most of the queries need not go over a huge set but be limited to a much smaller set, decreasing the query times translating into quicker reports.

10.3.3   Data freshness

Data freshness is a key requirement for most Analytic Systems because data is only good if it is relevant and fresh. For example, if a warehousing system, that is, monitoring dispatch breaches, gets information about the breach after 24 h, then the delay in processing directly affects fixing the problem. Essentially, any actionable report cannot have a significant delay in processing. This class of requirements of near-real-time reporting hence requires a different architecture.

10.3.4   Data governance

With so many types of data being generated from a multitude of systems and a very high scale, it is equally important that there is a governance model for the data. There are multiple aspects to data governance in big data systems. Some aspects are that of data availability, usability, integrity, quality, and security. Mostly these aspects are covered by internal data standards and policies of the organization and the governing laws of the land.

In an e-commerce system like Flipkart, there are multiple use-cases that enjoy having a strong data governance model. Mostly the producers and consumers of data are different teams and have different business metrics to track, so establishing trust over the data becomes a very common challenge. Data quality metrics transparently available to producers and consumers help in quickly triaging to data quality issues and establishing trust. Similarly, there is a plethora of personal and confidential data generated which needs sufficient security guardrails. Data governance solutions help in establishing authentication, authorization, and auditory on such data.

10.4   Architecture

At Flipkart, to tackle all these requirements, we created the big data platform called Flipkart Data Platform (FDP). FDP ingests billions of events each day, performs large computations on this data, and generates thousands of business metrics/ reports driving daily decisions. It also provides hundreds of streaming metrics in near real-time to manage sale events (like Big Billion Day—the yearly sale event) and the Flash sales. ML platform (built on top of data platform) enables data scientists to build, deploy, and operate models at scale in production and use ML to solve complex e-commerce problems. Insights platform (built on top of ML platform) generates hundreds of insights about our users each day—such as their predicted gender, age range, price and brand affinity, and income range. Different services use these services within Flipkart to personalize user experiences—such as targeting merchandizing to the right users and personalizing search results based on user price affinity.

Figure 10.3 describes a high-level architecture of FDP system.

In any big data system, primarily there is a data ingestion interface for ingestion data into the system, then a preprocessing layer which prepares the data for

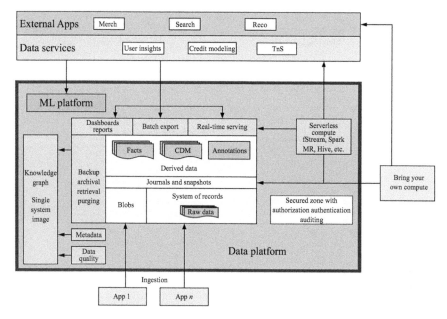

Figure 10.3   High-level architecture of the Flipkart Data Platform

consumption. We can do processing of data in a streaming or batch mode, and finally there is an egress layer to visualize the data via reports or systemically export into other systems. The following sections describe each component of the architecture and the tech stack choices made.

10.4.1   Data ingestion

FDP has taken an opinionated view of building the data-processing pipelines over known structured data. Each ingested payload has a fixed schema which the team creates using a self-serve UI. This design enables a rich catalog of schema and data validation at ingestion. In addition, it helps discard bad data before any consumption, manage schema versioning, and create data lineage.

Flipkart's ingestion services see peak scales of millions of events per second. It uses unique hybrid architecture to scale to such high numbers. This enables ingestion via http-based rest APIs and daemon-based agents that act as local collector buffers before sending the bulk messages to the back-end message queues (Figure 10.4).

The workflow for ingesting data into the data platform starts with the data producer actor (typically data engineers) creating a schema with schema details via the self-serve UI, after which it creates a corresponding message queue. Then, using the daemon end-point or the http end-point, the producer system ingests data to FDP. The schema may also contain pre-ingestion validations. In the event of validation failures, the payload goes to a sideline queue, which the owner team then

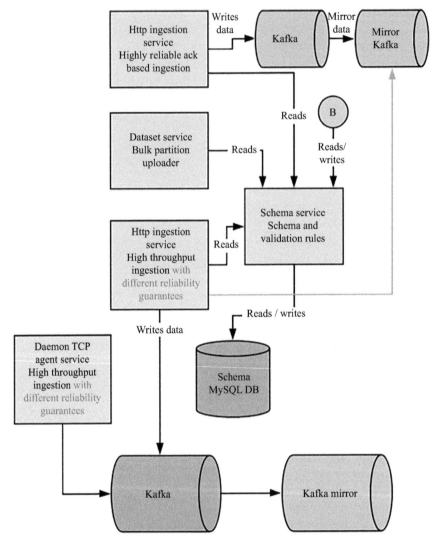

Figure 10.4   System architecture of the Flipkart Ingestion Services

revisits, fixes the errors, and re-ingests. We have designed the APIs with synchronous and asynchronous callbacks, a "200" response showing a successful ingestion or the failure reason.

10.4.2 Data preprocessing

Preprocessing is a batch data processing step wherein the events are bundled into time partitions and are made into journals and snapshots for further consumption. Journal is a concept wherein the raw data is sorted by time and de-duplicated so that only each unique mutation of data is retained. It discards all other entries. Snapshot is a concept wherein the raw data is sorted by time and only the latest mutation of the record is retained. These preprocessing steps are executed so that downstream consumption can be orchestrated faster and efficiently.

10.4.3 Batch data processing

The journal or raw data now goes through the processing stage where users may define Hive over MapReduce/TEZ or Spark jobs to *transform/join* data with other datasets (which could again be other Hive tables or HDFS partitions). We expect that the output of this data is again to fit a structured schema predefined by the team, called as a Fact (comprising multiple dimensions). These facts and dimensions are eventually used to generate reports or exported to the respective team's HDFS clusters for further systematic consumption (Figure 10.5).

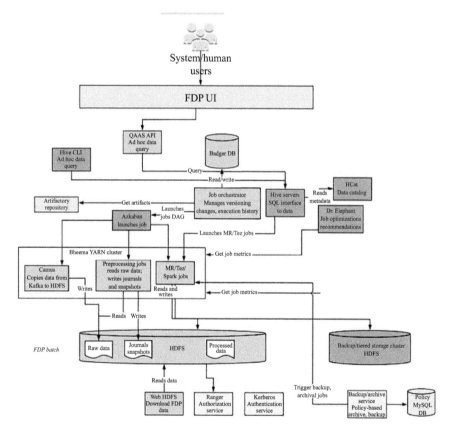

Figure 10.5 System architecture of the Flipkart batch processing services

While the teams own the Hive/Spark[†] Jobs, we give the schema versioning and managing of these jobs as a platform capability. The jobs are run as per a pre-configured schedule, and all failures/alerts over a team's jobs are directly sent over to them. The platform also provides isolation guarantees so that both failure and overutilization of one team's job do not affect any other team's jobs.

The Hadoop[‡] cluster runs about 1,500+ nodes to store and process over 100 PB of data.

10.4.4   Streaming processing

Stream processing is a data-processing paradigm that allows users to analyze continuous data streams and compute within a small time window of receiving the data. The time window may vary from a few seconds to minutes. Analysis and decisions are faster, and businesses can respond much better. That said, an inherent issue with stream processing is that data may never arrive on time. Few reasons are network latency, cached data, or performance issues of the data ingestion system. This leads to incorrectness in data computation and thus incorrect decisions/ analyses. To counter this, there are several stream-processing paradigms/concepts that are evolving to ensure correct results are observed. Watermarking and event triggers are examples of these concepts.

In Flipkart, the real-time ingested data that is generated via the ingestion services can also be directly consumed via their respective Kafka[§] topics. Flipkart streaming platform (fStream) is a managed streaming processing platform that provides higher level abstractions of reading data from sources, applying transformations or joining data streams, aggregating data into generating rolling window aggregations, i.e., 5 min, 1 h, 1 day or historic for each of the metrics and then sinking the results into a data store or message queue.

The streaming-processing consumes lesser resources compared to the batch processing, is more efficient, and so the stream pipeline is being preferred over batch-processing pipelines.

While the team owns the fStream[¶] Jobs, schema versioning and managing of these jobs are platform capabilities. The jobs are run continuously on the stream (whenever data is available) and do not wait for a fixed schedule like the batch variant. The platform also provides isolation guarantees so that both failure and overutilization of one team's job do not affect any other team's jobs.

10.4.5   Report visualization

Once the analyst has created the facts and dimensions, the platform creates boilerplate reports on top of the data using an in-house self-serve UI. Analysts can then select the various *columns*, *filters*, and *group-by* dimensions and define a report.

[†]https://towardsdatascience.com/write-clean-and-solid-scala-spark-jobs-28ac4395424a
[‡]https://hadoop.apache.org/docs/r3.2.1/
[§]https://kafka.apache.org/documentation/
[¶]https://tech.flipkart.com/fstream-comparing-stream-processing-engines-e86e439b0f66

This report is then refreshed either on a scheduled basis or on an ad hoc basis and represented in various visualizations (pie charts, graphs, tables, etc.).

The query results on the chart are then cached for a predetermined amount of time to avoid computation every time the result is viewed, in the absence of new data. Teams also have the option subscribe to the result of the report and get notified via a scheduled email.

10.4.6 *Query platform*

As mentioned earlier, while the data is available, it is equally important to have an interface to query this data in a semantic way—the Query platform solves this problem. In order for Analysts to fetch and experiment with the data in FDP, the platform supports a Hive command-line-interface and a query-as-a-service web UI and ODBC connectors to serve ad hoc querying use-cases.

Users can trigger a Hive query (using Hive-QL) from the Query UI interface and download the output as a CSV file among many other options.

10.4.7 *Data governance*

Data governance in simple terms is to govern or manage the data. A widespread, data-intrinsic business such as ours processes petabyte of data every day, explaining the need to have an effective data governance wrapper around the FDP. Effective analysis of the data helps channelize our functions—technical product, marketing, business, and operational, toward a data decision driven organization.

In Flipkart, we have architected a knowledge graph for all metadata generated from data using RDF[||] and SPARQL[**] to power data governance features which include the following:

* data discovery,
* enable data annotations like TAGS, COMMENTS, Q&A,
* data lineage with table level and column level lineage, and
* data-processing life cycle.

In Flipkart, we use Apache Jena,[††] an open-source semantic web framework to write and read from RDF graphs via SPARQL queries. All meta-data collected about the data and governing policies are queried via the Jena framework to enable the use-cases.

10.5 Conclusion

Flipkart's data platform has really evolved over the years and today its systems are architected and provisioned to handle scale, be resilient to failures and provide multi-tenancy constructs to guarantee availability and reliability of data-processing

---

[||] https://www.w3.org/RDF/
[**] https://www.w3.org/TR/rdf-sparql-query/
[††] https://jena.apache.org/

needs at Flipkart. It has a very complex and highly distributed tech stack that comprises over 30 plus technologies. Most of the technology stack is built over open-source technologies like Hadoop, Kafka, spark, and the team has gained expertise by tuning the cluster as per requirements.

Chapter 11

Big data regression via parallelized radial basis function neural network in Apache Spark

Sheikh Kamaruddin[1,2] and Vadlamani Ravi[1]

Among many versatile neural network architectures, radial basis function neural network (RBFNN) is one that is used to address classification and regression problems. The supervised and unsupervised parts of the RBFNN are not able to handle a large volume of data. The proposed work overcomes this drawback; it has implemented a parallel distributed version of RBFNN implemented with Apache Spark. Henceforth, we will refer to this version of RBFNN as PRBFNN. Incorporating K-means|| or parallel bisecting K-means in-between the input and the hidden layer, and the employment of parallel least square estimation (LSE) with an outer product of matrices is a novel contribution in the work. The PRBFNN employed Gaussian as well as logistic activation functions (AFs) in the hidden layer for nonlinear transformation. The efficacy of the PRBFNN was analyzed with two real-world datasets under 10-fold cross-validation (10-FCV) setup for a regression problem. Here, we want to make a point of presenting the PRBFNN to handle regression in the big data paradigm.

11.1 Introduction

Regression is one of the basic tasks of data mining that has been applied on a vast range of applications in multiple domains. A variety of machine learning techniques and statistical methods, including decision tree, support vector machine, and feed-forward neural networks, have been implemented for regression. Various neural network architectures were proposed for regression, viz., MLP, RBFNN [1], GRNN [2], and GMDH [3].

RBFNN has been used for regression in several domains in literature. Mignon and Jurie [4] used it for face reconstruction. Hannan *et al.* [5] used it for heart disease diagnosis. Taki *et al.* [6] employed RBF for predicting energy consumption in producing wheat.

[1]Centre of Excellence in Analytics, Institute for Development and Research in Banking Technology, Hyderabad, India
[2]School of Computer and Information Sciences, University of Hyderabad, Hyderabad, India

It is important to indicate that the proposal of presenting a distributed and parallel version of RBFNN to make it amenable for big datasets is the main objective of this chapter, thus making it incomparable with any of its competitors with a parallel version.

The remaining portion of the chapter is organized in the following manner: motivation is discussed in Section 11.2, and contribution is presented in Section 11.3. The study of the existing literature is presented in Section 11.4. The approach in the proposal is discussed in Section 11.5. The setup to carry out experimental work is described in Section 11.6, and the details about the datasets used for analysis are presented in Section 11.7. The results of experiment and the discussion thereof are presented in Section 11.8. Section 11.9 discusses the conclusion part along with the future directions.

11.2   Motivation

RBFNN is an amalgamation of unsupervised (from input to hidden layer) and supervised (hidden to output layer) learning where both are incapable of dealing with voluminous data. This has led us to the proposed method, PRBFNN that can handle large volumes of data in a parallel and distributed computational environment. The LSE, the supervised learning, from the hidden layer to the output layer is having a simple estimation and is implementable in a parallel manner.

11.3   Contribution

The current work implemented a parallel distributed version of K-means++ [7] clustering method, also known as K-means|| [8] as the unsupervised learning part of the training data. The experimental work also implemented parallel bisecting K-means [9] as another alternate for unsupervised learning in PRBFNN. The embedding of the K-means|| and parallel bisecting K-means clustering algorithm into the architecture of traditional RBFNN, resulting in PRBFNN is a novelty. The RBFNN involves LSE as its supervised learning part that is parallelized by implementing the outer product of matrices. The PRBFNN is implemented with Gaussian as well as logistic AFs. The efficacy of the PRBFNN is presented on structured and unstructured datasets for regression problems.

11.4   Literature review

The RBFNN has been implemented in multiple domains with different applications. But it is found that the literature depicts a scanty presence of implementation of RBFNN in the parallel environment. De Souza and Fernandes [10] have implemented a parallel version of RBFNN in field-programmable gate array. The parallelism achieved here through the programming of arrays of combinatorial circuit gates and flip-flops. This is parallelism through hardware. We did not find any other work where a parallel version of RBFNN has been implemented through software. This absence of software-based parallelism is the prime motivation for the current piece of work.

We investigated clustering in a parallel mode of implementation. The research community has contributed a lot for several variants of K-means and parallel version of them. A parallel K-means implemented with a MapReduce framework is proposed by Zhao *et al.* [11]. Liao *et al.* [12] have proposed an enhanced version of parallel K-means using MapReduce. The K-means++ [7] is an optimized version that is implemented with the process of initial cluster center or seed selection. The K-means|| is proposed by Bahmani *et al.* [8] which is the parallel version of K-means++. Another approach for clustering is bisecting K-means [9], which is a combination of hierarchical clustering and K-means clustering.

11.5 Proposed methodology

The current work presents the implementation of a parallel version of RBFNN where either the K-means|| or the parallel bisecting K-means is employed for the unsupervised learning part of RBFNN. A parallel version of LSE is implemented with the outer product of matrices that represents the supervised learning part of RBFNN. A brief introduction to K-means++, K-means||, parallel bisecting K-means, and PRBFNN is presented as follows.

11.5.1 Introduction to K-means++

The vanilla version of K-means clustering algorithm is implemented by randomly selecting K cluster centers initially and then the cluster centers are updated like the vanilla version of the K-means algorithm. However, it suffers from drawbacks such as (i) the worst-case execution time of the algorithm is a superpolynomial of input size and (ii) thus clusters generated may not be optimal according to the objective function.

In the K-means++, the initial cluster center selection has addressed the deficiency of optimal clustering. Arthur and Vassilvitskii [7] proposed a novel approach of initial cluster center selection. The algorithm details can be referred to in [13].

11.5.2 Introduction to K-means||

The K-means|| is the parallel version of K-means++. Let us assume that we have n data points and we select k initial seeds. The K-means++ executes k number of passes for sampling one initial cluster center in each pass, whereas K-means|| performs uniform random sampling for the selection of first center. Then, the further cluster centers will be selected in a nonuniform manner with a given probability that is randomly biased by the previously selected centers. The previous cluster center selection is implemented in a parallel manner throughout the partitions. Thus, the obtained $O(k \log n)$ points are ultimately, clustered again into the required k initial centers for the standard K-means iterations.

11.5.3   Introduction to parallel bisecting K-means

Bisecting *K*-means [9] is an approach that combines the best features of *K*-means and hierarchical clustering, i.e., divisive clustering. Here, instead of partitioning the data into *K* clusters in each iteration, it splits one cluster into two subclusters at each step (by using *K*-means) until *K* clusters are obtained. Its algorithm is as follows:

Bisecting K-means: the algorithm

1. Select a cluster to be split.
2. Find two subclusters using the basic *K*-means algorithm (bisecting step).
3. Repeat step 2, the bisecting step, for a fixed number of times and take the split that produces the clustering with the highest overall similarity.
4. Repeat steps 1, 2, and 3 until the desired number of clusters is reached.

Bisecting *K*-means has shown higher efficiency when *K* is high. For the *K*-means algorithm, the computation includes every data point of the dataset and *K* centroids. But, in bisecting *K*-means, only the data points of one cluster and two centroids are involved in the computation in each bisecting step making it computationally cheaper. Bisecting *K*-means produces clusters of similar sizes, while *K*-means is known to generate clusters of widely different sizes [14].

The parallel bisecting *K*-means has been implemented in a parallel and distributed computational environment by Spark MLlib library [15]. The algorithm starts from a single cluster that contains all points. Iteratively it finds divisible clusters on the bottom level and bisects each of them using *K*-means until there are *K* leaf clusters in total or no leaf clusters are divisible. The bisecting steps of clusters on the same level are grouped to increase parallelism. If bisecting all divisible clusters on the bottom level would result in more than *K* leaf clusters, larger clusters get higher priority.

11.5.4   PRBFNN: the proposed approach

In the proposed approach, *K*-means‖ or parallel bisecting *K*-means is employed for clustering the training data. Thus, the cluster centers represent the data points that are present in the cluster in an effective manner. After the clustering process, the quality of the clusters is measured with the Dunn-like index (a modified version of the Dunn index suitable for parallel implementation) which is a cluster validity index.

The Dunn index [16] presents the method for figuring the cluster quality which is based on the presence of high compactness and high separation among the clusters. This unique feature is calculated by the ratio of minimum intra-cluster distance to the maximum intercluster distance. The Dunn index is formulated as

$$Dunn\ index(D) = \min_{1 \leq i \leq M} \left\{ \min_{i+1 \leq j \leq M} \left(\frac{dist(c_i, c_j)}{\max_{1 \leq l \leq M}(diam(c_l))} \right) \right\}$$

where *M* is the count of the clusters under consideration, $dist(c_i, c_j)$ is the intercluster distance, and $diam(c_l)$ is the maximum intra-cluster distance or the largest diameter among all the clusters.

Dunn index calculates maximum intra-cluster distance, which is nothing but the diameter of the cluster under consideration; it is not feasible for voluminous data as it has significant computational overhead. Furthermore, it has the effect of noise and outliers. So, the proposed work has employed a Dunn-like index [17] for measuring the cluster validity. In this method, the diameter is calculated by finding the radius using the distance from each data point present in the cluster to its cluster center, i.e., $d(x, \overline{c_j})$, where $x \epsilon c_j$ cluster and $\overline{c_j}$ is its center. Further, it is immune to noise or outliers present in the data. The Dunn-like index is formulated as

$Dunn - like\ index(DL)$

$$= \min_{1 \le i \le M} \left\{ \min_{i+1 \le j \le M} \left(\frac{dist(c_i, c_j)}{\max\limits_{1 \le l \le M} \left(2 * \frac{1}{|c_l|} \sum_{x \in c_l} d(x, \overline{c_l}) \right)} \right) \right\}$$

The obtained cluster centers, by the previous method, form the nodes in the hidden layer of PRBFNN. Next to that, every test data point is fed to the nodes (neurons) present in the hidden layer either with Gaussian or logistic AFs. The AF computes a value closer to 1 if the neuron has a significant similarity to the test data point else it is closer to 0. The Gaussian AF can be presented as

$$\frac{1}{\sqrt{2\pi\sigma^2}} e^{\left(-(x-\mu)^2/2\sigma^2\right)}$$

where μ is the mean of the distribution and σ^2 is the variance.

The PDF for logistic distribution is presented as

$$\frac{e^{\left(-\frac{(x-\mu)}{\sigma}\right)}}{\sigma \left(1 + e^{\left(\frac{-(x-\mu)}{\sigma}\right)}\right)^2}$$

where σ is the standard deviation, and μ is the mean of the distribution.

The architectural design of PRBFNN is the same as the RBFNN apart from the existence of the cluster centers (obtained through K-means‖ or parallel bisecting K-means) occupying the hidden layer. The architecture of PRBFNN is presented in Figure 11.1.

The LSE presents the supervised learning part in RBFNN. A parallel version of LSE is employed with the outer product of matrices that makes it amenable for large sized dataset.

The unsupervised learning in PRBFNN has been employed with parallel clustering method, i.e., implementing K-means‖ or parallel bisecting K-means. Then the clusters are validated with a parallel implementation of Dunn-like index, and finally, a parallel version of the outer product of matrices is employed for LSE, the supervised learning of PRBFNN. So, the proposed approach presents an end-to-end parallel implementation of RBFNN.

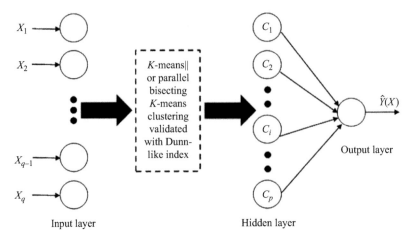

Figure 11.1   *Architectural design of PRBFNN*

11.6   Experimental setup

The experimental work was carried out with standalone Spark cluster 2.2.0 that is the computing environment setup with HDFS as the distributed storage using Hadoop 2.7.3. The code was developed with Apache Zeppelin 0.7.3 as the IDE with the programming language Scala 2.11.8. The standalone Spark cluster comprises a master node and seven worker nodes. The master node also hosts two worker daemons. The resource allocated to driver program is 14 GB of memory. Each one of the seven worker nodes hosts four worker daemons. A memory of 7 GB is allocated to each worker. All seven worker nodes have the same configuration. The total memory allocated amounts to 28 GB in each system.

We figured out that the best execution time is achieved by tweaking the allocated memory to the executors and with the optimal data partitions.

11.7   Dataset description

In the proposed PRBFNN, we have analyzed (i) the collected data from a range of gas sensors detecting the concentration of different gas mixtures and (ii) the Amazon movie review (AMR) dataset that includes movie reviews from different users for the regression problem.

The gas sensor dataset [18] was obtained from UCI repository [19]. It includes the readings received from 16 sensors exposed to varying concentrations of gas mixtures. The dataset contains sensor readings of two different mixtures of gases in air, viz., ethylene with methane and ethylene with CO, which are made into two different datasets. We have analyzed the data for prediction of the concentration of ethylene, methane, and CO in air.

There are 19 features in both datasets. The first field in the dataset is the time of sensor reading, the second field represents CO and methane concentration in ppm in their respective dataset, and the third field represents the ethylene concentration in ppm. The next 16 fields represent the sensor readings from 16 chemical sensors (see Tables 11.1 and 11.2). The ethylene–CO dataset is of size 643 MB, including 4.2 million samples. The ethylene–methane dataset is of size 638 MB, which includes 4.17 million samples.

For the current work of regression problem, we have not included the first field as it contains time-series values. In different experiments, the dependent variable was selected either from the second or third field. We chose the fields from the fourth to the last as independent variables.

The AMR dataset [20] is collected from Stanford Network Analysis Project data repository [21]. It includes 7,911,684 reviews. The reviews contain the product and user, movie ratings, and a plaintext review. The structural details of the dataset can be referred to in [13].

In the current work, the review score or ratings has been selected as our dependent variable. The review in the plain text was preprocessed in which the removals of special characters, HTML tags, emojis, and the acronyms were performed. Next to that, the stop words removal was performed and the tokens were generated. After the completion of preprocessing, the tokens were used to generate a hashing document–term matrix with feature-length of 20 and 100. Then, its TF–IDF value was calculated. Thus, two datasets were generated one with 20 TF–IDF values and the other with 100 TF–IDF values. These TF–IDF values were considered as independent variables for the regression model.

Table 11.1   Details of ethylene–CO gas sensor array dataset

Field name	Details
Time (s)	Time when the sensor reading is performed
CO conc. (ppm)	The concentration of CO (ppm)
Ethylene conc. (ppm)	The concentration of ethylene (ppm)
Sensor readings (16 channels)	Readings from 16 sensors collected into 16 columns

Table 11.2   Details of ethylene–methane gas sensor array dataset

Field name	Details
Time (s)	Time when the sensor reading is performed
Methane conc. (ppm)	The concentration of methane (ppm)
Ethylene conc. (ppm)	The concentration of ethylene (ppm)
Sensor readings (16 channels)	Readings from 16 sensors collected into 16 columns

11.8   Results and discussion

The PRBFNN analyzed the datasets discussed previously. The results are not comparable with any other ML technique since we did not find any work conducted by the research community in the same domain and employing a hybrid architectural technique.

The experiment was performed with min–max normalized data under 10-FCV. The unsupervised learning was carried out with the K-means$\|$ where k has a range of 2–10, and parallel bisecting K-means. Then, the Dunn-like index was used for cluster validation. Next, the cluster centers of the optimally selected clusters validated through Dunn-like index are considered as the neurons present in the hidden layer. Then, with the selected cluster centers, PRBFNN was executed with sigma (σ) values ranging from 0.01 to 1.0 with an increment of 0.01.

The efficiency of the proposed model is figured out with an average mean squared error (MSE) of 10-FCV. The PRBFNN employed the Gaussian and logistic AFs in the hidden layer of PRBFNN that capture the features of a test data point. Hence, it enables the architecture to predict the value.

We have reported an average MSE of 10-FCV for PRBFNN$_1$ (i.e., K-means$\|$+ PRBFNN), which is presented in Table 11.3, and the average MSE of 10-FCV for PRBFNN$_2$ (i.e., parallel bisecting K-means+PRBFNN) that is presented in Table 11.4. The bold values in Table 11.3 and Table 11.4 indicate the better performance of the respective Activation Function.

11.9   Conclusion and future directions

In the current work, we have proposed a PRBFNN. It has an unsupervised learning part that is implemented through clustering in a parallel manner employing either K-means$\|$ or parallel bisecting K-means. The clustering process is validated through a parallel Dunn-like index. The LSE is the supervised learning part of the architecture that is implemented through parallel outer product of matrices. Thus, an end-to-end parallel version of RBFNN, i.e., PRBFNN is implemented with parallel distributed

Table 11.3   Mean MSE for 10-FCV of PRBFNN$_1$ (K-means$\|$+PRBFNN)

Dataset	Prediction of	Gaussian activation function (AF)	Logistic AF
Gas sensor dataset	Ethylene concentration from ethylene–CO dataset	0.07146	**0.064223**
	CO concentration from ethylene–CO dataset	**0.0721126**	0.0735805
	Ethylene concentration from ethylene–methane dataset	0.079	**0.0728**
	Methane concentration from ethylene–methane dataset	0.0604	**0.0554**
Amazon movie review dataset	Review ratings with TF–IDF values of 20 features	1.634948746	**1.6296084**
	Review ratings with TF–IDF values of 100 features	1.64273374	**1.6329117**

Table 11.4   Mean MSE for 10-FCV of PRBFNN$_2$ (parallel bisecting
K-means+PRBFNN)

Dataset	Prediction of	Gaussian activation function (AF)	Logistic AF
Gas sensor dataset	Ethylene concentration from ethylene–CO dataset	0.07147	**0.064224**
	CO concentration from ethylene–CO dataset	**0.0721127**	0.0735807
	Ethylene concentration from ethylene–methane dataset	0.078	**0.072**
	Methane concentration from ethylene–methane dataset	0.0606	**0.0555**
Amazon movie review dataset	Review ratings with TF–IDF values of 20 features	1.63494874	**1.6296085**
	Review ratings with TF–IDF values of 100 features	1.64273379	**1.6329115**

computational framework of Apache Spark, along with HDFS, where the data is stored in a distributed manner. The PRBFNN is coded with Scala.

The proposed PRBFNN has addressed regression problem, which is capable of handling voluminous data. The PRBFNN presents a semi-supervised learning architecture and presented results under 10-FCV. The novelty of the proposed architecture can be enlisted as the implementation of (i) the parallel distributed *K*-means‖ or the parallel bisecting *K*-means as unsupervised learning, (ii) the cluster validity measure, a parallel Dunn-like index, and (iii) LSE as the outer product of matrices in a parallel manner that is the supervised learning of PRBFNN. Future directions include invoking parallel evolving clustering method (PECM) for performing clustering task. The advantage is that PECM performs one-pass clustering. In addition, we adopt parallel stochastic gradient method for the supervised learning part of the network. Thus, the new architecture can be used for solving streaming big data regression. Further, Cauchy AF will be used in place of Gaussian and logistic functions. One could also use the new architecture for time-series forecasting.

References

[1]   Moody J and Darken CJ. Fast learning in networks of locally-tuned processing units. Neural Computation. 1989;1(2):281–94.

[2]   Specht DF. A general regression neural network. IEEE Transactions on Neural Networks. 1991;2(6):568–76.

[3]   Ivakhnenko AG. The Group Method of Data of Handling; a rival of the method of stochastic approximation. Soviet Automatic Control. 1968;13:43–55.

[4]   Mignon A and Jurie F. Reconstructing faces from their signatures using RBF regression. In: Proceedings of the British Machine Vision Conference 2013. Bristol, UK: British Machine Vision Association; 2013. p. 103.1–11.

[5]   Hannan SA, Manza RR, and Ramteke RJ. Generalized regression neural network and radial basis function for heart disease diagnosis. International Journal of Computer Applications. 2010;7(13):7–13.

[6]   Taki M, Rohani A, Soheili-Fard F, and Abdeshahi A. Assessment of energy consumption and modeling of output energy for wheat production by neural network (MLP and RBF) and Gaussian process regression (GPR) models. Journal of Cleaner Production. 2018;172:3028–41.

[7]   Arthur D and Vassilvitskii S. k-Means++: The advantages of careful seeding. In: Proceedings of the Eighteenth Annual ACM-SIAM Symposium on Discrete Algorithms. 2007. p. 1027–35.

[8]   Bahmani B, Moseley B, Vattani A, Kumar R, and Vassilvitskii S. Scalable K-means++. Proceedings of the VLDB Endowment. 2012;5(7):622–33.

[9]   Steinbach M, Karypis G, and Kumar V. A comparison of document clustering techniques. In: KDD Workshop on Text Mining. 2000. p. 525–6.

[10]   De Souza ACD and Fernandes MAC. Parallel fixed point implementation of a radial basis function network in an FPGA. Sensors. 2014;14(10):18223–43.

[11]   Zhao W, Ma H, and He Q. Parallel K-Means Clustering Based on MapReduce. In: MG Jaatun and Gansen Zhao CR, editor. Cloud Computing. Beijing, China: Springer Berlin Heidelberg; 2009. p. 674–9 (Lecture Notes in Computer Science; vol. 5931).

[12]   Liao Q, Yang F, and Zhao J. An improved parallel K-means clustering algorithm with MapReduce. In: 2013 15th IEEE International Conference on Communication Technology. IEEE; 2013. p. 764–8.

[13]   Kamaruddin S and Ravi V. A parallel and distributed radial basis function network for big data analytics. In: IEEE Region 10 Annual International Conference, Proceedings/TENCON. Kochi, India: Institute of Electrical and Electronics Engineers Inc.; 2019. p. 395–9.

[14]   Patil RR and Khan A. Bisecting K-means for clustering web log data. International Journal of Computer Applications. 2015;116(19):36–41.

[15]   Clustering – RDD-based API – Spark 2.2.0 Documentation [Internet]. [cited 2019 Feb 14]. Available from: https://spark.apache.org/docs/2.2.0/mllib-clustering.html#bisecting-k-means.

[16]   Dunn JC. A fuzzy relative of the ISODATA process and its use in detecting compact well-separated clusters. Journal of Cybernetics. 1973;3(3):32–57.

[17]   Bezdek JC and Pal NR. Some new indices of cluster validity. IEEE Transactions on Systems, Man, and Cybernetics-Part B: Cybernetics. 1998;28(3):301–15.

[18]   Fonollosa J, Sheik S, Huerta R, and Marco S. Reservoir computing compensates slow response of chemosensor arrays exposed to fast varying gas concentrations in continuous monitoring. Sensors and Actuators B: Chemical. 2015;215:618–29.

[19]   Gas Sensor Array Under Dynamic Gas Mixtures Data Set [Internet]. 2015 [cited 2018 Jul 2]. Available from: https://archive.ics.uci.edu/ml/datasets/Gas+sensor+array+under+dynamic+gas+mixtures.

[20]   McAuley JJ and Leskovec J. From amateurs to connoisseurs: modeling the evolution of user expertise through online reviews. In: Proceedings of the 22nd International Conference on World Wide Web. 2013. p. 897–908.

[21]   SNAP. Web Data: Amazon Movie Reviews [Internet]. [cited 2018 Nov 10]. Available from: https://snap.stanford.edu/data/web-Movies.html.

Chapter 12

Visual sentiment analysis of bank customer complaints using parallel self-organizing maps

Rohit Gavval[1,2], Vadlamani Ravi[1], Kalavala Revanth Harsha[1,3], Akhilesh Gangwar[1] and Kumar Ravi[1]

Social media has reinforced consumer power, allowing customers to obtain more and more information about businesses and products, voice their opinions as well as convey their grievances. On the flipside, this provides businesses a treasure trove of customer-interaction data that has powerful customer relationship management (CRM) applications. Analyzing data on customer complaints is paramount as their timely non-redressal would lead to reduce profits as a result of customer churn. In this chapter, we introduce a descriptive analytics system for visual sentiment analysis of customer complaints using the self-organizing feature map (SOM). The network eventually learns the underlying classification of grievances that can then be visualized using different methods too. Executives of analytical customer relationship management (ACRM) will derive valuable business insights from the maps and enforce prompt remedial measures. We also propose a high-performance version of the CUDASOM (Compute Unified Device Architecture (CUDA)-based self-organizing function Map) algorithm implemented using NVIDIA®'s parallel computing platform, CUDA, which accelerates the processing of high-dimensional text data and produces fast results. The effectiveness of the proposed model has been demonstrated on a dataset of customer complaints about the products and services of four leading Indian banks. CUDASOM recorded an average speedup of 44 times. Our technique can expand studies into smart grievance redressal systems to provide the complaining consumers with quick solutions.

12.1 Introduction

Businesses embarking on the CRM journey are progressively making use of customer data to drive business decisions. The banking, financial services and insurance

[1]Center of Excellence in Analytics, Institute for Development and Research in Banking Technology, Hyderabad, India
[2]School of Computer and Information Sciences, University of Hyderabad, Hyderabad, India
[3]Indian Institute of Technology (Indian School of Mines) Dhanbad, Dhanbad, India

industry also depends heavily on data analytics for its everyday functions such as fraud detection, credit scoring, risk analysis or cross-selling/up-selling, which fall within the scope of ACRM. In addition to huge quantities of data gathered by these companies from different customer touchpoints, vital customer feedback data is now accessible from social media platforms, which are the most preferred channels for consumers to express their opinions/grievances about the products and services.

Efficient customer feedback analysis will help companies improve the channels of communication with their customers and solve their problems quickly, transforming dissatisfied customers into loyal repeat customers [1,2]. Essentially, the non-resolution of complaints leads to churning of customers and reduced sales. Yet it would be time-consuming to go through the possibly large amounts of complaints and affect the turnaround time. In most cases, a purely manual solution would be impractical. Alternative methods such as text mining and NLP techniques will greatly help here, by offering an automated way to generate insights from a large amount of text. Classification of the sentiments conveyed by the customer in their respective feedback document is the most common activity carried out on customer feedback data. This task involves classifying the sentiments into either positive or negative classes to extract the customers' overall perception of a product or service. Classification of sentiments is carried out at various levels, including document, sentence and aspect. Opinion summarization is another class of customer feedback analysis that generates a summary of the feedback from a large corpus of feedback documents for a target (product or service). Before a full-fledged sentiment analysis of the complaints is conducted, visualization of the complaints by product and severity category significantly decreases the time and effort for the bank executives.

Any tool developed to this end must have the following capabilities—it should be able to segment the complaints in an unsupervised manner, it should be able to adjust itself to the varying landscape of complaints and it should be suitable for processing text data that is high dimensional and it should provide strong visualization capabilities. SOMs are unsupervised and nonlinear neural networks with excellent topology preservation properties that help them to project the inherent structure in the data onto a two-dimensional map of neurons. These neural networks have been shown to be effective in processing large amounts of text data. Also, a rich ecosystem of visualization techniques is available for SOMs making them an effective visualization tool. These traits make SOM an apt choice for analyzing customer feedback.

Since their introduction, SOMs have been widely utilized in business, linguistics, finance and bioinformatics for a range of data analysis tasks such as clustering and data visualization. It is a type of artificial neural network trained using unsupervised learning to generate low-dimensional representations of the input variables, allowing high-dimensional data to be visualized.

We present an unsupervised learning model in this chapter that effectively addresses the need to better evaluate customer complaints in order to extract actionable insights. We examine four datasets of customer complaints linked to four leading Indian commercial banks using SOMs and demonstrate the effectiveness of the proposed method in analyzing and visualizing this data. Since text data is high dimensional, it is computationally expensive and slow to process. We also propose CUDASOM, a parallel version of the model implemented on CUDA, which is parallel computing architecture developed by NVIDIA, in order to increase the speed of computation.

This chapter is structured as follows. First, in Section 12.2 we present the motivation behind this work. Section 12.3 summarizes the essential contributions of our research and a summary of the literature review is provided in Section 12.4. Section 12.5 includes an overview of the techniques. The specifics of our method and of the experimental setup are discussed respectively in Sections 12.6 and 12.7. The results are discussed in Section 12.8, and the final comments are presented in Section 12.9.

12.2   Motivation

Performing a sentiment classification task on a dataset of complaints would logically classify all the documents as negative and performing an opinion summarization on this dataset would result in summaries that are neither meaningful nor useful. Although the aforementioned tasks are therefore common in the field of sentiment analysis and are significantly useful in obtaining knowledge about consumer perception, they are ineffective in evaluating a set of grievances if the main objective is to draw actionable insights quickly. In addition, both of these techniques are supervised learning techniques that require time and effort to label the data and develop a relatively well-performing model. While several authors in the past have approached the task of sentiment analysis using unsupervised learning methods [3,4], they have been able to demonstrate the results on datasets containing both negative and positive sentiments whereas the focus of our study is a complaints dataset that contains documents only with negative sentiments. On the other end of the spectrum are niche unsupervised techniques such as clustering that can produce swift output but impose an overhead of painstakingly detailed analysis in terms of choosing a number of clusters and understanding the nature of grievances within a cohort. Considering that text data is high dimensional, cluster visualization requires help from auxiliary tools to learn about potential interrelationships in the data. Ideally, a tool for analyzing customer complaints would help service executives define the complaint landscape so that they can easily draw actionable insights from it as well as prioritize complaints for rapid resolution. If the tool presents such observations in a visual format, the advantages of such tool would be pronounced. For instance, a service manager with an access to a picture of the complaint landscape can look at the product-wise composition and prioritize action accordingly or can quickly identify a sudden outburst of issues for a particular product and alert the concerned team for immediate action. An SOM efficiently addresses these requirements owing to the following characteristics: (a) it operates on unlabeled data; (b) it automatically performs dimensionality reduction making visualization possible; and (c) owing to its topology preservation properties, it helps to visualize the data landscape together with its topological relationships, which is of paramount importance and also indispensable to this task. So, with SOM at its heart, we have built a platform for visual sentiment analysis that can help banks manage customer complaints efficiently. The proposed method, by virtue of being an unsupervised solution, will easily paint an estimated picture for operational CRM professionals to begin action. As such, this method may serve as an effective precursor before conducting an in-depth analysis using the supervised methods.

12.3   Contribution

As per our survey of the literature, none of the previous works have employed SOMs for the visualization of consumer grievances from a prioritization and redressal standpoint and this is the first attempt. The following are the noteworthy contributions of our work:

- We introduce an approach for conducting visual sentiment analysis of consumer grievances, which is capable of substantially enhancing and speeding up grievance resolution systems. Four real-world datasets comprising customer complaints against Indian banks were used to establish the efficiency of the model.
- We then introduce CUDASOM, a new implementation of CUDA accelerated SOM. This algorithm is devised with a focus on text data with a large number of dimensions in contrast with previous works that addressed problems of a larger number of output nodes (map sizes) or a number of data points. The proposed implementation of CUDA resulted in significant speedup compared to its counterpart of the CPU.

12.4   Literature survey

This work focuses on sentiment analysis of customer complaints and accelerating the analysis with a CUDA-based implementation of SOM. Therefore, we review previous efforts made by researchers in each of these aspects.

SOMs have been predominantly known for their visualization aid. Owing to this ability, they have been widely applied in domains like bioinformatics [5], geosciences [6] and finance [7]. In sentiment analysis research as well, SOMs have been applied for studying tourist sentiments [8], movie reviews [9], sentiments about varieties of wine [10] and in automatically detecting bullying in social networks [11]. Reference [12] proposed an SOM-based approach for studying the sentiments of users registered on a forum focused on the treatment of cancer. Reference [13] conducted studies on the performance of SOMs for supervised and unsupervised sentiment analysis tasks. They observed that the performance is equivalent to the performance of other algorithms commonly employed for sentiment analysis.

Some works have employed SOM for visualizing consumer feedback to gain knowledge about their interests. Reference [14] proposed to use SOM for visually comparing consumer feedback from a geospatial standpoint while [15] proposed an approach to visualize customer feedback and also calculate scores.

SOM is inherently amenable for parallelism. A version of a parallel SOM appeared in [16]. Thereafter, several parallel implementations were reported using OpenGL [17], MapReduce-MPI [18], OpenCL [19] and supercomputers and VLSI chips [20].

Following the introduction of CUDA, several implementations of CUDA-based SOM were proposed by researchers. Reference [21] reported a graphics processing unit (GPU)-accelerated batch-SOM for high-dimensional data. The authors claimed a speedup of $15\times$–$40\times$ vis-à-vis CPU implementation. Reference [22] reported a parallel implementation of batch SOM by using network and data-partitioning methods. They reported gains up to $20\times$ on 10-dimensional data and the gains dropped significantly with increasing dimensions.

A CUDA-based SOM with a three-step implementation on a 1,000-dimensional synthetic data was reported in [23].

Recently, [24] proposed a CUDA-based implementation of sequential SOM by leveraging the cuBLAS library. Datasets with vectors of length 16 and 64 were tested. Table 12.1 presents a summary of the articles reviewed in this section.

12.5 Description of the techniques used

12.5.1 Self-organizing feature maps

Kohonen proposed the SOMs in the 1980s [25,26]. SOMs are unsupervised artificial neural networks that adopt vector quantization and neurobiology principles to produce accurate low-dimensional representations (feature maps) from high-dimensional data. For example, most real-world data, text data or bioinformatics data, is high-dimensional and SOMs prove to be excellent tools for reducing dimensions and assisting in the analysis of such data. This is achieved by SOM's self-organizing property, which generates a set of prototype vectors such that vectors matching with similar points in the input space are topographically nearer on the feature map and those matching with significantly different points are more distant. For a detailed explanation of SOM and guidelines on tuning it for better results, interested readers are referred to [25].

12.5.2 Compute Unified Device Architecture

GPUs are large, parallel-operating processor arrays. While computationally weaker than CPUs, their low cost makes it is possible to bundle a large number of GPU

Table 12.1 Summary of literature review

No.	Topic	References
1	Applications of SOM	[5–11]
2	Application of SOM for sentiment analysis	[12,13]
3	Customer feedback analysis using SOM	[14,15]
4	Non-CUDA parallel implementation of SOM	[16–20]
5	CUDA-based parallel implementation of SOM	[21–24]

cores together to conduct parallel operations much more quickly by increasing the throughput. Originally introduced to accelerate graphics processing, GPUs later found applications in other domains. CUDA is a parallel computing architecture developed by NVIDIA for interacting with its graphic cards.

A program implemented using CUDA is usually structured as follows:

1. Copy the data to be processed into the host memory (main memory) of the machine.
2. Allocate memory for the data in the device memory (global memory of GPU).
3. Load the data into device memory from host memory.
4. Run the kernel functions on the GPU to process the data.
5. Retrieve the results from device memory by copying them to host memory.
6. Copy the results to main memory and return the results to the user.

A set of instructions that run on the GPU at any single time is defined as a kernel. Kernels are executed on the GPU through an array of GPU threads, so that each thread runs the same kernel on the basis of the data allocated to it. Threads are organized in blocks, and blocks are assembled into one grid. Every thread block has access to fast memory called shared memory and each thread has its own local memory.

12.6   Proposed approach

The proposed approach is divided into four phases as follows. A block diagram of the proposed methodology is depicted in Figure 12.1.

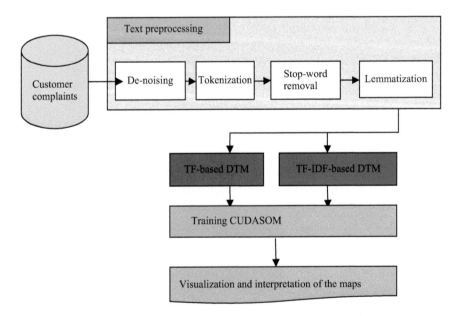

Figure 12.1   Schematic of the proposed approach

12.6.1 Text preprocessing

The standard Python library NLTK was employed for preprocessing the data. On the whole corpus, standard text preprocessing like lemmatization, tokenization and noise reduction have been performed. Estimating the similarity between the complaints forms the backbone of the algorithm, and it is crucial to enrich the complaints so that they depict the dimensions along which we intend to measure similarity. In this analysis, the occurrence of words naming the product, the words related to the product/service and the words in relation to the grievances associated with the product are critical in estimating the similarity. In order to enrich the complaints with this information, we have eliminated unrelated and insignificant words using stop word removal.

To encode the text data into numerical form, we considered two commonly used feature representations, namely, term frequency (TF)-based document-term matrix (henceforth referred to as DTM) and TF–inverse document frequency (TF–IDF)-based DTM.

12.6.2 Implementation of CUDASOM

Many implementations of CUDA-based SOMs were proposed in the literature. Most recent proposals, though, have focused on the batch version. The GPU-based implementation of standard SOM in [24] shows promising performance. In their proposal, the dimension of input vectors defines the second dimension of the block size. Although this leads to dimension-level parallelism and can contribute to significant gains, this design cannot automatically accommodate high-dimensional input since it is constrained by the maximum number of threads allowed by a block based on the architecture on which the system is being implemented.

We propose a novel scheme to parallelize the standard CUDASOM, with a focus on high-dimensional text data. The block size in this scheme is independent of the length of the data vectors, which makes it ideal for working with DTMs. Our implementation assumes a two-dimensional map and therefore uses a three-dimensional data structure to describe the map and its weight vectors. We initially convert the multidimensional data and map structures into single-dimensional arrays to improve GPU memory accesses. All the data transformations are performed within the GPU-related memory (hereafter referred to as the device memory) and the results are then ported back to the main memory. This strategy results in a significant elimination of delays due to memory transfers and synchronizations. In addition to global memory, we also make use of shared memory on the GPU wherever constant data is frequently used for comparisons. The training is carried out by three kernels.

- **getDistances kernel:** An input sample is selected randomly on the host in each iteration and the corresponding index is passed to this kernel call. This kernel distributes a subset of map units in each row, and the threads represent the map units in each block. For each block, the input vector is copied to the shared memory to minimize access to the global memory. The distance between the input vector and the map units represented by the threads in that block is measured within each block and stored in the shared memory. In an array called bmu, the minimum distance and the index of the corresponding map unit are stored on the global memory using a parallel reduction within the kernel. For the corresponding input, therefore, each of the blocks stores a possible candidate for the best matching unit.

- **reduceMin kernel:** This module attempts to determine the bmu by employing a parallel reduction technique. To ensure that the reduction is proper, while launching the kernel, the number of blocks is set to a power of 2.
- **updateWeights kernel:** This kernel uses the corresponding matrix coordinates to compute the distances between the map units. Since hexagonal maps are more accurate and better suited for visualization, we implemented CUDASOM with hexagonal neighbors, and hexagonal coordinates were calculated before the distances were calculated. The updated weights are written directly to the device memory weights array without copying them to the main memory. The weights are copied to the main memory after the completion of all the iterations.

12.6.3   *Segmentation of customer complaints using SOM*

We trained CUDASOM in this process separately with each of the datasets. The heuristics implemented in the SOM Toolbox [27] inspired the estimation of the number of iterations and the map size for each dataset. The method for calculating the number of iterations and the map size is illustrated in Figure 12.2. As per the guidelines in [25], we initialized the prototype vectors using the regular, two-dimensional sequence of vectors taken along a hyperplane spanned by the two largest principal components of the DTM. We performed multiple experiments on standard dataset [28] such as the Iris dataset and the Breast Cancer Wisconsin dataset to select the initial learning rate, and fixed the value at 0.1. The Gaussian decay was used to smooth the learning rate and neighborhood radius.

Cosine similarity, which is built on dot product, has been demonstrated to be a strong measure of similarity for text documents [29]. According to [25], for high-dimensional vectors normalized to constant length (as in our case), the choice of similarity measure—Euclidean distance or cosine similarity does not make a difference in the performance of SOM. As Euclidean distance was employed as the similarity measure in our implementation, we normalized the input data before presenting to SOM.

An outline of the procedure for calculating the map dimensions and a number of iterations is depicted in Figure 12.2. We trained CUDASOM with the TF and TF-IDF-based DTMs separately for each dataset and then visualized the trained prototype vectors with a similarity coloring scheme [30]. The quantization error and speed were computed for each experiment. We conducted experiments on all the datasets with a CPU implementation of SOM configured similarly, to ensure that CUDASOM is generating the correct results.

12.7   Experimental setup

We selected a dataset comprising customer complaints on four leading Indian banks to demonstrate the efficacy of the proposed algorithm. The complaints from

Input: *dataset = m, number of records in the dataset = d, number of dimensions = n*

Output: *number of rows in output layer = nrows, number of columns in output layer = ncols, number of iterations = numItr*

1. Compute the number of neurons in the output layer as *dunits* = $5 \times \sqrt{d}$
2. Compute the principal components from *m* and sort them in descending order of their corresponding eigen values
3. Extract the first two principal components, pc_1 and pc_2
4. **if** $pc_1 = 0 \parallel pc_2 \times munits < pc_1$ **then**
5. $r = 1$
6. **else**
7. $r = \sqrt{\dfrac{pc_1}{pc_2}}$
8. Compute $size_1 = \min\left(dunits, \sqrt{\dfrac{dunits}{r \times \sqrt{\frac{3}{4}}}}\right)$
9. Compute $size_2 = \left\lceil \dfrac{dunits}{size_1} \right\rceil$
10. Compute $nrows = \min(size_1, size_2)$
11. Compute $ncols = \max(size_1, size_2)$
12. Compute $nn = nrows \times ncols$
13. Compute $mpd = \frac{nn}{m}$
14. Compute $numItr = [50 \times mpd] \times d \times 4$
15. Return *nrows, ncols, numItr*

Figure 12.2   Algorithm to calculate map dimension and number of iterations

consumers were published on an online public feedback website. The following are descriptions of the datasets and the experimental setting.

12.7.1   Dataset details

All the real-world datasets employed in the experiments were sourced from [31]. The authors crawled the web and collected consumer complaints and bank executive responses from www.complaintboard.in on four banks. These complaints were raised during the timeframe October–December 2014. Details of the datasets are presented in Table 12.2. As seen in the table, after converting these datasets into the aforementioned feature representations, the average length of the resultant vectors was ~4k. Due to the high dimensionality of these vectors, these datasets can be considered as big social data.

12.7.2   Preprocessing steps

The preprocessing carried out is as follows. First, we filtered out uninformative documents, responses from bank staff/employees, duplicates and all non-complaint data (like customer requests) to ensure that customer complaints are represented uniformly by the dataset. Second, the data was cleaned to eliminate noisy features

Table 12.2   Details of datasets

Bank name	No. of documents	Complaints considered	Features generated
Axis Bank	749	513	3,917
HDFC Bank	1,108	637	4,545
ICICI Bank	758	440	4,268
SBI Bank	1,123	676	4,470

such as special characters, email metadata, contact information and words less than 3 in length. The misspelled terms were also corrected. After the preprocessing, Axis, HDFC, ICICI and SBI banks each had 513, 637, 440 and 676 complaints, respectively.

12.7.3   CUDA setup

All the experiments have been performed on a computer equipped with Intel® Xeon® E5-2640 v4 CPU clocked at 2.4 GHz, 32 GB RAM and an NVIDIA Quadro® P5000 GPU with a 16-GB RAM. The GPU is powered by the NVIDIA Pascal architecture and is equipped with 20 microprocessors holding 128 CUDA cores each. We used CUDA v8.0 with NVIDIA-384 drivers installed on Ubuntu v16.04 operating environment.

Implementation of models and experiments has been performed in Python v3.5.2 and for GPU programming, the PyCUDA [32] module that is a Python interface to CUDA API has been used.

Several implementations [33,34] of SOM employing industrial-grade machine learning frameworks like Tensorflow are available on the open-source platform. These software offer SOM's vanilla implementations and do not adopt the heuristics recommended in the literature for SOM's proper training. Moreover, they do not provide visualization features such as similarity coloring that are more intuitive for visualizing a customer complaints dataset. Also, since machine learning frameworks are placed on top of several abstraction layers, they leave very little scope for tuning SOM's core architecture. Consequently, these implementations were not readily suitable for this study. As a result, we selected PyCUDA as the base platform and developed the architecture from scratch, incorporating the required heuristics and visualization software suitable for this application.

12.8   Results and discussion

The results of each of the two ideas proposed in this work are discussed separately in this section.

12.8.1   Segmentation of customer complaints using CUDASOM

To evaluate CUDASOM's ability to perform the segmentation of customer complaints, two soft criteria have been adopted. The first criterion is topology preservation of the complaint (data) landscape, i.e., similar grievances are mapped to the same or neighboring nodes and dissimilar complaints are mapped to nodes that are farther away. The second criterion is the visualization capabilities of the algorithm.

First, we tried to discern the winning strategy for representing the text features. For this, we compared the maps generated using the two different feature representations adopted. Figure 12.3 depicts the map generated by the TF-based DTM of HDFC dataset and the map generated by the TF–IDF-based DTM of the same dataset.

- The map obtained by the TF feature representation shows broken, scattered regions organized nonuniformly making interpretation difficult. The TF–IDF feature representation on the other hand shows clearly distinct, uniformly arranged regions depicting a clear picture of different segments in the data.
- TF–IDF representation demonstrated a better performance not only in terms of visual distinction of complaints but also in terms of strongly preserving the inherent topology of the data. The purple region that is in the bottom-right section homogeneously represents loan-related complaints. Additionally, within this region, all the car loan grievances are mapped to connected nodes. The map generated using the TF representation did not demonstrate this property. In this map, the purple nodes are not connected and the individual nodes do not represent complaints related to the same product. Even for the other three datasets, these two statements are valid. Hence, it is concluded that TF–IDF is a more suitable representation for this task, and this could be attributed to the fact that TF–IDF encodes richer information as compared to TF.

Figure 12.3   Maps obtained using TF and TF–IDF representations of HDFC bank dataset respectively

Second, we elaborately analyzed the maps generated using TF–IDF representation of each of the datasets. The objective of the analysis was to evaluate CUDASOM along the following dimensions: (a) its ability to segment the complaints on the basis of the product categories they belonged to and (b) its ability to segment the complaints on the basis of the severity. To perform the evaluation, we mapped all the documents (TF–IDF vectors of the complaints) to the corresponding bmus on the trained map. The product-wise segmentation ability was evaluated by studying the positions and distribution of the documents on the map. If complaints related to a single product were mapped to the same or neighboring nodes, CUDASOM was considered to be able to perform product-wise segmentation. To evaluate the ability of the algorithm to perform severity-based segmentation, the following steps were performed. Each of the complaints in the dataset was manually labeled "moderate" or "severe" (symbolically as 1 or 2, respectively). The labeling task was carried out independently by three human annotators—the first author and two volunteers. To determine the final label, a majority voting scheme was applied on the available labels. After training CUDASOM with unlabeled data and obtaining the feature map, we programmatically marked the severity labels on the neuron to which the corresponding complaints are mapped. Broadly, it was noticed that CUDASOM was able to achieve product-wise arrangement of the complaints along with the corresponding severity tagged thereof. The following is a detailed note on the observations made:

- Three separate regions are depicted in the map corresponding to the HDFC dataset (see Figure 12.4)—violet, green and yellow. For certain accounts, banks require their customers to maintain an average balance failing which penalties are collected accordingly. The green area represents all the grievances about such charges that are usually not known to the customers and are seen as *unexplained deductions*. The region in yellow refers to *credit card* related complaints and the region in violet refers to *loan* grievances. Within the nodes in the violet region, complaints of a moderate nature, like customers not receiving a no objection certificate or customer service providing incorrect information, are distinctly separated from complaints of a severe nature like irate customers who are awaiting loan disbursal. This showcases CUDASOM's ability to segregate complaints on the basis of severity in addition to product-wise segmentation. Also, regions colored with different shades of a color depict different aspects of the same product. The two bright yellow nodes in the map's bottom-right section refer to concerns about a disapproval of credit cards. In the intersection, the three regions are complaints that pertain to less frequent products/services like dissatisfaction with *customer service*.
- Four distinct regions are depicted in the map corresponding to Axis dataset (Figure 12.5). The pink colored region on the top-left section of the map represents complaints related to *loans*. The green colored section toward the right is a striking representation of a single issue–all the complaints mapped to this region are about a *login* issue that multiple customers have reported. The following is a region in orange that represents complaints related to *credit cards*. Similar to HDFC dataset, clearly segregated subclusters can be noticed within this region

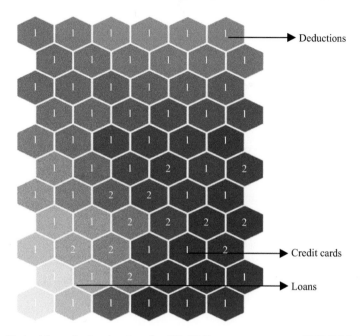

Figure 12.4   Map obtained using the TF–IDF representation of HDFC bank dataset

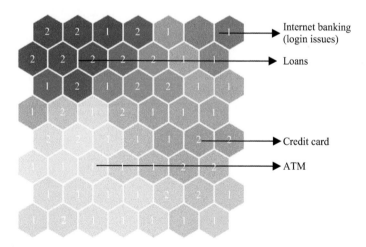

Figure 12.5   Map obtained using the TF–IDF representation of Axis Bank dataset

representing a single product. CUDASOM was able to distinguish between complaints of a moderate nature like customers receiving an incorrect card and severe complaints like harassing recovery calls or billing errors. *ATM*-related complaints are mapped to the region in the bottom-left section.

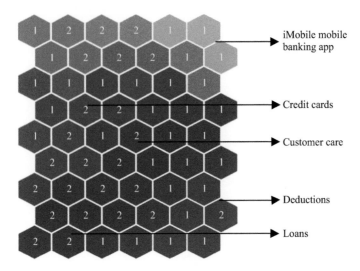

*Figure 12.6   Map obtained using the TF–IDF representation of ICICI bank
dataset*

- The map corresponding to the ICICI bank dataset (see Figure 12.6) depicts approximately four to five separate regions. Three of these regions are clearly distinct; however, the rest of the nodes cannot be separated into visually distinct regions. The section in the top-right represents complaints about *prepaid recharge failure* from the bank's *mobile banking app*. The blue region at the bottom-right refers to *bank accounts charges* and *deductions*. In this area, connected to separate nodes on the map were moderate complaints like inquiries about *uninformed deductions* and extreme complaints threatening to leave the bank due to the same cause. The area corresponding to light pink and dark pink refers to *credit card* issues and specifically fraud calls or regarding harassing calls from recovery agents. *Loan*-related complaints are mapped to the bottom-left while customer service complaints are mapped to the central section of the map. It is important to note that although product-wise visual distinction is absent in some regions of the map, like the region toward the left, the complaints have been grouped correctly in a topology-preserving manner, even in this region. Because of identical wording in the sentences, the regions may be indistinguishable in color.
- Four distinct regions are depicted in the map corresponding to SBI dataset (Figure 12.7). The pink-colored region seen in the top-right section of the map corresponds to complaints on *ATM transactions*. *Internet and mobile banking* complaints are represented by the yellow-colored nodes seen on the top-left region of the map. Within this region is a subcluster (represented by the bright yellow nodes) that corresponds to customers complaining about the failed *prepaid phone recharges* made from the *mobile banking app*. This is a remarkable segregation as it will help identify trending issues suddenly affecting a significant customer base. The region below it in purple widely maps complaints related to *loans*. It also represents few infrequent classes of complaints, for example, complaints about the

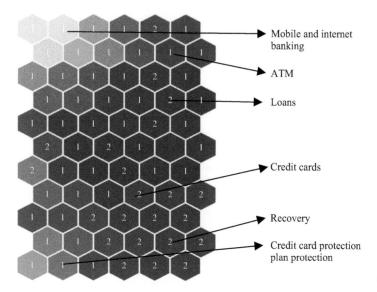

Mobile and internet banking

ATM

Loans

Credit cards

Recovery

Credit card protection plan protection

Figure 12.7   Map obtained using the TF–IDF representation of SBI dataset

behavior of employees at the *branch, pension* deposits. The blue section at the bottom of the maps homogenously maps complaints related to *credit cards*. CUDASOM clearly separates severe complaints from moderate complaints in this region. On the left side are complaints of a moderate nature like the *credit card* shipment getting delayed or failure to generate a PIN number. The green region in this section, present on the bottom-left corner, is specifically related to *Credit card Protection Plan*, a credit and debit card protection service and mostly moderate complaints are associated with this product. On the other hand, more severe complaints like instances of harassment by recovery team and credit card fraud are mapped to the nodes on the right that are labeled as severe.

Hence, descriptive analytics of consumer complaints in the proposed manner offers the benefits of recognizing the various services/products that the consumer is facing issues with, the size of the consumer base affected, or a trending customer issue. It will allow the bank executives in charge of the department of CRM to prioritize complaint redressal.

12.8.2   Performance of CUDASOM

Unlike conventional programs, CUDA programs are not sequential and factors such as synchronization issues can cause errors in the results. Therefore, it is essential to verify the results of CUDA implementations and the best way is to make sure that they match the results of the serial implementations. As mentioned in Section 12.6, the implementation of CUDASOM was verified by matching the quantization errors and visually comparing the maps generated in the respective experiments.

Table 12.3 shows that the differences in the implementations are insignificant and hence validating the GPU implementation. Such minimal differences

Table 12.3 *Quantization errors and execution times*

	Dataset	Dataset dimensions	Quantization error (GPU)	Quantization error (CPU)	Time (GPU) (s)	Time (CPU) (s)	Speedup
Term frequency-based DTM	Axis	513×3,917	0.80627	0.80996	22.12	915.08	41.37
	HDFC	637×4,545	0.80653	0.81383	32.57	1,380.82	42.40
	ICICI	440×4,268	0.81625	0.82011	19.94	837.02	41.98
	SBI	676×4,470	0.82042	0.82578	27.25	1,194.57	43.84
TF–IDF-based DTM	Axis	513×3,917	0.91366	0.91651	22.63	960.74	42.45
	HDFC	637×4,545	0.91562	0.92056	31.48	1,412.07	44.86
	ICICI	440×4,268	0.91467	0.92026	23.66	985.47	41.65
	SBI	676×4,470	0.91769	0.92182	26.73	1,254.52	46.93

are noticed even in iterations of the same experiment owing to the differences in weight initialization and the sequence of presentation of samples to SOM.

Due to the same reason, the map generated using the parallel version (seen in Figure 12.5) and the map generated using the serial implementation (seen in Figure 12.8) also differ, although minimally. CUDASOM was observed to be faster over the serial version by 41–47 times with an average speedup of 43 times. The gains achieved by a GPU implementation have been traditionally demonstrated by comparing with a CPU-based implementation of SOM. However, we believe this is unfair as the optimal CPU implementation of SOM is subjective and debatable [23].

As compared to [23], CUDASOM demonstrated higher peak speedup on data with dimensions larger by 3-fold and the validation has been performed using real-world data. It has also been established that CUDASOM also adopts well with bigger maps; we performed experiments alike [24] and studied the effect of increase in the dimensions of the map on the time taken for the SOM to be trained. The dimensions of input data and number of iterations were maintained the same, and the 64-dimensional weight vectors were considered. As seen in Table 12.4, our implementation demonstrates a gradual increase in the ratio of time taken with an exponential increase in map size as compared to [24].

- The device memory size poses as one of the limiting factors for the proposed algorithm in the following manner. The data matrix and the weight vectors that

Figure 12.8   Map obtained using the TF–IDF representation of Axis bank dataset with standard SOM

Table 12.4   Execution time ratios with increasing map sizes

		Map size					
		16×16	*32×32*	*64×64*	*128×128*	*256×256*	*512×512*
Reference	Time (s)	15.50	31.20	92.30	331.00	1,270.00	4,900.00
[24]	Ratio of increase in time	–	2.01	2.96	3.59	3.84	3.86
CUDASOM	Time (s)	34.25	32.81	33.37	38.40	111.03	431.38
	Ratio of increase in time	–	0.96	1.02	1.15	2.89	3.89

are the core data elements reside on the device memory throughout the execution of the training phase. They are loaded on to the device memory before the start of the training phase, and the trained weights are unloaded to the main memory only after the training phase is complete. This method significantly reduces the data transfer overhead between CPU and GPU and also synchronization, contributing to the speed of the algorithm. However, it constrains the amount of the data that is processed. We plan to work on this limitation in our future works.

12.9   Conclusions and future directions

In this study, we introduce a framework for visual sentiment analysis of customer complaints using SOMs. Two common methods of feature representation, i.e., TF and TF–IDF representation were used for representing the text data and the efficiency of each of the representations was evaluated. This study also introduces a CUDA-based parallel implementation of SOMs that accelerates complaint processing and yields faster results for taking brisk action. The results indicate that TF–IDF representation is better suited for this task as compared to the TF representation. An inspection of the visual results (the resultant maps) depicts that CUDASOM is able to efficiently categorize the complaints related to different products/services into separate groups. As compared to the serial version, the parallel version of the algorithm is significantly faster, demonstrating its applicability for faster analysis of high-dimensional data. In future, we will implement a parallel and distributed SOM in Apache Spark environment and compare its performance in speedup achieved with the preset CUDA-based implementation. Further, we will also employ it for automatic aspect extraction in text documents, especially customer complaints.

Acknowledgments

We express our sincere gratitude to Mr. Pulipaka Sai Ravi Teja and Mr. Harshal Jaiswal for assisting with the annotation task.

References

[1] Cho Y, Im I, Hiltz R, and Fjermestad J. An Analysis of Online Customer Complaints: Implications for Web Complaint Management. In: Proceedings of the Annual Hawaii International Conference on System Sciences [Internet]. IEEE Comput Soc; 2002 [cited 2018 Jun 7]. p. 2308–17. Available from: http://ieeexplore.ieee.org/document/994162/.

[2] Tax SS, Brown SW, and Chandrashekaran M. Customer Evaluations of Service Complaint Experiences: Implications for Relationship Marketing. J Mark [Internet]. 1998 [cited 2018 Jun 7];62(2):60. Available from: www.jstor.org/stable/1252161?origin=crossref.

[3] Hu X, Tang J, Gao H, and Liu H. Unsupervised Sentiment Analysis With Emotional Signals. In: Proceedings of the 22nd International Conference on World Wide Web – WWW '13 [Internet]. New York, NY, USA: ACM Press; 2013 [cited 2019 Apr 7]. p. 607–18. Available from: http://dl.acm.org/citation.cfm?doid=2488388.2488442.

[4] Rothfels J and Tibshirani J. Unsupervised Sentiment Classification of English Movie Reviews Using Automatic Selection of Positive and Negative Sentiment Items [Internet]. 2010. Available from: https://nlp.stanford.edu/courses/cs224n/2010/reports/rothfels-jtibs.pdf.

[5] Zhang J and Fang H. Using Self-Organizing Maps to Visualize, Filter and Cluster Multidimensional Bio-Omics Data. In: Applications of Self-Organizing Maps [Internet]. InTech; 2012 [cited 2018 Jun 7]. Available from: www.intechopen.com/books/applications-of-self-organizing-maps/using-self-organizing-maps-to-visualize-filter-and-cluster-multidimensional-bio-omics-data.

[6] Klose CD. Self-Organizing Maps for Geoscientific Data Analysis: Geological Interpretation of Multidimensional Geophysical Data. Comput Geosci [Internet]. 2006 [cited 2018 Jun 7];10(3):265–77. Available from: http://link.springer.com/10.1007/s10596-006-9022-x.

[7] Deboeck G and Kohonen T. Visual Explorations in Finance: With Self-Organizing Maps. Springer Finance. 1998; xlv, 258.

[8] Claster WB, Dinh H, and Cooper M. Naive Bayes and Unsupervised Artificial Neural Nets for Cancun Tourism Social Media Data Analysis. In: Proceedings – 2010 2nd World Congress on Nature and Biologically Inspired Computing, NaBIC 2010. 2010. p. 158–63.

[9] Claster WB, Hung DQ, and Shanmuganathan S. Unsupervised Artificial Neural Nets for Modeling Movie Sentiment. In: 2010 2nd International Conference on Computational Intelligence, Communication Systems and Networks [Internet]. IEEE; 2010 [cited 2018 Jun 7]. p. 349–54. Available from: http://ieeexplore.ieee.org/document/5616452/.

[10] Claster WB, Caughron M, and Sallis PJ. Harvesting Consumer Opinion and Wine Knowledge Off the Social Media Grape Vine Utilizing Artificial Neural Networks. In: 2010 Fourth UKSim European Symposium on Computer

Modeling and Simulation [Internet]. IEEE; 2010 [cited 2018 Jun 7]. p. 206–11. Available from: http://ieeexplore.ieee.org/document/5703684/.

[11]   Di Capua M, Di Nardo E, and Petrosino A. Unsupervised Cyber Bullying Detection in Social Networks. In: 2016 23rd International Conference on Pattern Recognition (ICPR) [Internet]. IEEE; 2016 [cited 2018 Jun 7]. p. 432–7. Available from: http://ieeexplore.ieee.org/document/7899672/.

[12]   Akay A, Dragomir A, and Erlandsson B-E. Network-Based Modeling and Intelligent Data Mining of Social Media for Improving Care. IEEE J Biomed Health Inform [Internet]. 2015 [cited 2018 Jun 7];19(1):210–8. Available from: http://ieeexplore.ieee.org/document/6851846/.

[13]   Sharma A and Dey S. Using Self-Organizing Maps for Sentiment Analysis. 2013 Sep 16 [cited 2018 Jun 7]. Available from: http://arxiv.org/abs/1309.3946.

[14]   Janetzko H, Jäckle D, and Schreck T. Comparative Visual Analysis of Large Customer Feedback Based on Self-Organizing Sentiment Maps. In: Proceedings of the Third International Conference on Advances in Information Mining and Management IMMM. 2013. p. 147–54.

[15]   Saitoh F. Visualization of Online Customer Reviews and Evaluations Based on Self-Organizing Map. In: 2014 IEEE International Conference on Systems, Man, and Cybernetics (SMC) [Internet]. IEEE; 2014 [cited 2018 Jun 7]. p. 176–81. Available from: http://ieeexplore.ieee.org/document/6973903/.

[16]   Weigang L. A Study of Parallel Self-Organizing Map. 1998 Aug 17 [cited 2018 Jun 7]. Available from: http://arxiv.org/abs/quant-ph/9808025.

[17]   Luo Z, Liu H, Yang Z, and Wu X. Self-Organizing Maps Computing on Graphic Process Unit. In: ESANN. 2005. p. 557–62.

[18]   Sul S-J and Tovchigrechko A. Parallelizing BLAST and SOM Algorithms With MapReduce-MPI Library. In: 2011 IEEE International Symposium on Parallel and Distributed Processing Workshops and PhD Forum [Internet]. IEEE; 2011 [cited 2018 Jun 7]. p. 481–9. Available from: http://ieeexplore. ieee.org/document/6008868/.

[19]   Takatsuka M and Bui M. Parallel Batch Training of the Self-Organizing Map Using OpenCL. In: Lecture Notes in Computer Science (including subseries Lecture Notes in Artificial Intelligence and Lecture Notes in Bioinformatics) [Internet]. Springer, Berlin, Heidelberg; 2010 [cited 2018 Jun 7]. p. 470–6. Available from: http://link.springer.com/10.1007/978-3-642-17534-3_58.

[20]   Hämäläinen TD. Parallel Implementations of Self-Organizing Maps. In: Self-Organizing Neural Networks [Internet]. Physica, Heidelberg; 2002 [cited 2018 Jun 7]. p. 245–78. Available from: http://link.springer.com/10.1007/978-3-7908-1810-9_11.

[21]   Xiao Y, Feng R-B, Han Z-F, and Leung C-S. GPU Accelerated Self-Organizing Map for High Dimensional Data. Neural Process Lett [Internet]. 2015;41 (3):341–55. Available from: http://dx.doi.org/10.1007/s11063-014-9383-4.

[22]   Richardson T and Winer E. Extending Parallelization of the Self-Organizing Map by Combining Data and Network Partitioned Methods. Adv Eng Softw [Internet]. 2015 [cited 2018 Jun 7];88:1–7. Available from: www.sciencedirect. com/science/article/pii/S0965997815000769.

[23]   Moraes FC, Botelho SC, Filho ND, and Gaya JFO. Parallel High Dimensional Self Organizing Maps Using CUDA. In: 2012 Brazilian Robot Symp Lat Am Robot Symp. 2012.

[24]   Cuomo S, De Michele P, Di Nardo E, and Marcellino L. Parallel Implementation of a Machine Learning Algorithm on GPU. Int J Parallel Program [Internet]. 2017 [cited 2018 Jun 7];1–20. Available from: http://link.springer.com/10.1007/s10766-017-0554-6.

[25]   Kohonen T. Essentials of the Self-Organizing Map. Neural Netw [Internet]. 2013 [cited 2018 Jun 7];37:52–65. Available from: www.sciencedirect.com/science/article/pii/S0893608012002596.

[26]   Kohonen T. Self-Organized Formation of Topologically Correct Feature Maps. Biol Cybern. 1982;43(1):59–69.

[27]   Vesanto J. Neural Network Tool for Data Mining: SOM Toolbox. In: Proceedings of Symposium on Tool Environments and Development Methods for Intelligent Systems (TOOLMET 2000) [Internet]. 2000 [cited 2018 Jun 7]. p. 184–96. Available from: http://citeseerx.ist.psu.edu/viewdoc/summary?doi=10.1.1.33.1305.

[28]   Dheeru D and Karra Taniskidou E. UCI Machine Learning Repository [Internet]. 2017. Available from: http://archive.ics.uci.edu/ml.

[29]   Banerjee A, Dhillon IS, Ghosh J, and Sra S. Clustering on the Unit Hypersphere Using Von Mises-Fisher Distributions. J Mach Learn Res [Internet]. 2005;6:1345–82. Available from: http://dl.acm.org/citation.cfm?id=1046920.1088718.

[30]   Vesanto J. SOM-Based Data Visualization Methods. Intell Data Anal [Internet]. 1999 [cited 2018 Jun 7];3(2):111–26. Available from: www.sciencedirect.com/science/article/pii/S1088467X9900013X.

[31]   Ravi K, Ravi V, and Prasad PSRK. Fuzzy Formal Concept Analysis Based Opinion Mining for CRM in Financial Services. Appl Soft Comput [Internet]. 2017 [cited 2018 Jun 7];60:786–807. Available from: www.sciencedirect.com/science/article/pii/S1568494617302910.

[32]   Klöckner A, Pinto N, Lee Y, Catanzaro B, Ivanov P, and Fasih A. PyCUDA and PyOpenCL: A Scripting-Based Approach to GPU Run-Time Code Generation. Parallel Comput [Internet]. 2012 [cited 2018 Jun 7];38(3):157–74. Available from: www.sciencedirect.com/science/article/pii/S0167819111001281.

[33]   Joglekar S. Self-Organizing Maps With Google's TensorFlow. 2015.

[34]   Gorman C. TensorFlow Self-Organizing Map [Internet]. 2018. Available from: https://github.com/cgorman/tensorflow-som/blob/master/LICENSE.

Chapter 13

Wavelet neural network for big data analytics in banking via GPU

Satish Doppalapudi[1,2] and Vadlamani Ravi[1]

Big data is hard to process using conventional technologies and hence calls for massively parallel processing. Machine learning techniques have been widely adopted in several massive and complex data-intensive fields for handling large data. Artificial neural networks (ANNs) are the most common machine learning techniques used for classification, function approximation, dimensionality reduction, classification, etc. Wavelet neural network (WNN) is one of them. The architecture of WNN is having a lot of matrix computations, which can be parallelized by GPU. Theano is used as a programming model for accelerating general-purpose workloads. In our work, we implemented the WNN using Theano. The efficacy of WNN is tested on various bank datasets. In this process, the performance of a conventional CPU implementation of WNN was tested with that of GPU, and the latter was found to be much faster on all datasets.

13.1 Introduction

Nowadays data has become the key for every enterprise. A meaningful chunk of data is generated with the beginning of this digital technology. A massive volume of data is being generated for storing the important information of an organization. Because of the current trends in various technologies, a tremendous amount of data is generated. Massive parallel processing is invariably required to process and analyze big data. Extracting the insights from big data is both challenging and exciting. Application of big data is useful in banking, marketing, finance, and many more fields.

The five Vs—"volume," "velocity," "variety," "veracity" and "value"—are used to signify various dimensions of big data. Not all domains, where big data is prevalent, contain all the five dimensions. Big data is analyzed by scaling up the extant applied statistical and machine learning algorithms. It turns out that many architectures of ANN are well suited for the scaling up because of the presence of

[1]Center of Excellence in Analytics, Institute for Development and Research in Banking Technology, Hyderabad, India
[2]School of Computer and Information Sciences, University of Hyderabad, Hyderabad, India

numerous matrix–vector and matrix–matrix multiplications in the algorithms that train them.

Graphics processing units (GPUs) are specific processors with committed memory that traditionally accomplish the operations through floating-point required for delivering graphics. The latest versions of GPU come with many-core processors that are especially designed to carry out parallel computations.

WNN is a generalized form of radial basis function network (RBFN). Wavelets are used as activation function for a hidden layer in wavelet networks. Universal approximation property is maintained by multidimensional wavelets. The unique values are maintained for nodes of wavelet network that are wavelet coefficients.

WNN is one of the most popular techniques in ANN. Parallelization is done in two ways: horizontally and vertically. WNN can be parallelized vertically by using GPU.

13.2   Literature review

Elgendy and Elragal [1] presented a survey paper on big data analytics. In this paper, they discussed tools and various analytics methods that can be applied to big data, and options that are used by big data analytics operations in different fields for making decisions. Investment or retail banking industries are successfully gaining the benefit from big data analytics in the area of managing the risks; detection and prevention of the fraud. They discussed challenges when dealing with big data. Big data needs appropriate storage, association, administration, cleaning, processing, analyzing, etc. They have discussed in the article that big data increases above challenges due to large volumes, velocities and varieties of data. They discussed future research could target on contributing a plan or structure for big data management that can enclose the previously stated challenges.

Singh and Reddy [2] presented extant literature on big data analytics platforms. In this chapter, they contributed a detailed analysis of various platforms feasible for implementing big data analytics. They have discussed multiple hardware platforms and software frameworks convenient for big data analytics. They explained pros and cons of each of those stages based on different metrics such as fault tolerance, scalability, data I/O rate, data size and iterative task support. They have discussed the advantages and drawbacks of vertical and horizontal scaling and platforms supported for these scalings. The most popular vertical scaling platform is GPU. They discussed choosing an appropriate platform for an application that depends on data size, speed or throughput optimization and the development of a model.

Srivastava and Gopalkrishnan [3] presented a paper on the impact of big data analytics on finance sector. Their intention in this article is to show profitability using big data analytics in the banking sector; they concerned the following aspects: customers buying pattern, management of channels, a grouping of customers and profiling, cross-selling of products, analysis of sentiments and feedback, managing the security and fraud. They suggested future directions for a betterment of the quality of analytics by banks employing different data mining techniques.

Nickolls and Dally [4] presented a paper on GPU computing era. In this article, they described a quick development of GPU architectures from a regular graphics processor to a large parallel multiprocessor that consists of many cores. They also discussed how interestingly choosing GPU with CPU is used in accelerating parallel applications. They explained that GPU that optimizes throughput provides parallel performance efficiently than CPU that is optimizing latency.

Owens *et al.* [5] described the background, hardware and programming model for GPU computing. They have also presented the success of four GPU computations over optimized CPU applications. GPU has become an essential part of contemporary mainstream computing systems. GPU executes the programs parallelly more efficiently, and recently CPU+GPU architectures are becoming extensive.

Theano is a library in python that allows one to optimize, characterize and evaluate mathematical expressions efficiently, which consists of multidimensional arrays [6]. It consists of the following features: uses GPU transparently, having Numpy integration tightly, generation of C code dynamically, efficient symbolic differentiation, optimizing speed and stability, thorough unit testing and self-verification.

Al-Rfou *et al.* [7] presented Theano to the community of machine learning. Theano is employing GPU and CPU mathematical compilers, and it has improved performance. They discussed that it is one of the libraries in python that optimizes, evaluates and defines the mathematical expressions, including multidimensional arrays efficiently. Theano is having an advanced feature like computing gradient automatically, optimization and improvements in numerical ability.

Kamaruddin and Ravi [8] presented a paper on big data analytics used for finding credit card fraud. They explained credit card fraud is one of the severe challenge faced by the banking industries. They implemented particle swarm optimization (PSO) with auto-associative neural network as a hybrid approach for one-class classification in the Spark framework. They parallelized auto-associative neural network. They achieved average classification rate as 89 percent. They suggested the parallelization of PSO as their future work.

Kothapalli *et al.* [9] presented a paper on CPU vs. GPU. They named a term hybrid computing that consists of CPU+GPU. In this article, they suggested that CPU+GPU computing offers lots of advantages at more realistic scale systems with a significant gain in performance and also resource efficiency at huge scale user association. They also showed that the hybrid solution gained good advantage over GPU or CPU alone. They experimented with 13 different workloads. They have demonstrated that hybrid solution on an average is 90 percent efficient in using resources. Their study widened the way for evaluating the hybrid computing in terms of power efficiency, performance models and benchmark suites.

Zhang and Benveniste [10] proposed a paper on wavelet networks. They proposed a wavelet network that is an alternate to feedforward neural networks for nonlinear function approximation using wavelet transform theory. They proposed a backpropagation algorithm for training wavelet network.

Alexandridis and Zapranis [11] presented a paper on a practical guide to WNNs. In this article, they explained applying WNN's statistical model identification framework in various applications. Their proposed algorithm presented very strong and stable results that indicate that it can be implemented in various applications. Their algorithm consists of four steps. The accuracy for full (out) is 97.51 percent, for full (in) is 97.65 percent and reduced (out) is 97.36 percent, reduced (in) is 97.51 percent on breast cancer dataset. They avoided online training or the synthesis of WNN for ensuring the robustness and stability of their proposed algorithm.

Chauhan *et al.* [12] in their study proposed a differential evolution algorithm for training WNN. They tested their algorithm on different datasets and different benchmark datasets for finding bankruptcy prediction. They compared performance of their algorithm with the trained wavelet neural network (TAWNN). Their proposed algorithm scored more than TAWNN in terms of accuracy and sensitivity. They achieved an average of 95 percent for Turkish and 89.99 percent for Spanish and 93.33 percent for US bank datasets.

Becerra *et al.* [13] employed an article on financial distress classification using neural and wavelet networks. They analyzed the use of multilayer perceptron and wavelet networks for predicting financial problems. They introduced a new procedure for developing some wavelet network classifiers. They proposed an algorithm for selecting dilation and translation parameters that render a wavelet network classifier with better characteristics. They achieved an average accuracy as 97.3 percent with WNN. Finally, they concluded by stating that WNNs have more advantages than multilayer perceptron.

Chen *et al.* [14] presented a paper on time-series prediction using a WNN. In this paper, they proposed a local linear WNN (LLWNN). The connections of weights between hidden and output layers are replaced by the local linear model. They used diversity learning and gradient descent method for training LLWNN. This study shows that their proposed model outperformed all models.

Casas [15] presented a paper on the parallelization of neural network training algorithms. They discussed the backpropagation algorithm parallelizing that is used to train their model. They parallelized an algorithm by running it on four processors that have reduced nearly 61 percent of training time than the actual algorithm without parallelization.

Park and Ro [16] presented a paper on the acceleration of ANN. GPUs use Compute Unified Device Architecture (CUDA) as a programming language for accelerating the workloads. They discussed that GPU acceleration is needed for ANN for solving more complex and real-time problems. They accelerated the forwarding computations using CUDA. Their final result is 2.32 times faster when compared to CPU.

Wavelet networks have been used in "short-term load forecasting" [17–21], "time-series prediction" [14,22,23], "signal classification and compression" [24–26], "signal denoising" [27], "static, dynamic and nonlinear modeling" [28] and "nonlinear static function approximation" [29–31]. It is also used in determining the samples of metals like copper and iron [32].

13.3 Techniques employed

Wavelet word is because of Grossmann and Morlet [33]. Localizing the function on scaling and spacing was done by wavelets. They are having more advantages than conventional Fourier methods that are used in analyzing physical situations of signals that consist of discontinuities and sharp spikes. WNN is a model blended with neural network and wavelet theories.

WNN dwells with a feedforward neural network, one hidden layer and activation functions from family of orthonormal wavelet. WNN works as a function estimator.

Two different approaches are there in modeling WNNs:

- First, neural network and wavelet mechanism are implemented separately. By utilizing the wavelet basis with the neurons in the hidden layer, decomposition of the input signal is achieved. The input to the output nodes is wavelet coefficients. Updating of weights can be done by using learning algorithm.
- The second approach is mixed up with the two theories. Translation and dilation of the wavelets together with output weights are changed by using some learning algorithm.

In the first approach, wavelet basis is formed with a dilation and translation of mother wavelet. The former approach is known as WaveNet. The latter approach is known as wavelet.

13.4 Proposed methodology

The architecture of WNN is similar to that of both multilayer perceptron and RBFN in which it is supervised and similar to the former, where it has only three layers same as the latter. However, it is different from both of them in which it incorporates wavelet activation functions. In any case, it also involves a lot of matrix-to-vector and vector-to-matrix multiplications, which indicates that it can be parallelized either horizontally or vertically.

WNN, when utilized on typical datasets that are not big data, produces fast and efficient results with an added advantage of easy implementation.

The parallelized version of WNN is implemented on GPU using Theano framework. There are four logical steps involved in implementing the model in Theano. They are (1) symbolic variable declaration, (2) building a symbolic graph using those variables, (3) compilation of Theano functions, (4) performing the numerical computations using the previous functions.

The training algorithm for WNN using GPU with Theano is as follows:

1. Here we need to select the number of hidden nodes first. Variables for data and parameters that will be used in the model are declared. Implementation of tensor variable is mandatory. Weights $W1$ and $W2$ are used for initializing the weights between input layer and hidden layer and between hidden and output layers

using the shared functions. Translation and dilation parameters are also declared using the shared Theano function up to some random values between (0, 1).

2. The output of the model can be calculated using the parameters $W1$, $W2$, translation and dilation and the data x using a Gaussian wavelet function. The GPU is used to calculate the dot products between x and weight vectors W. The total computation is done by using the tensors in Theano. The computations at each layer are parallelized using Theano.

3. Gradient descent algorithm is used to train WNN. The computation graph of gradient descent is calculated using Theano on GPU. The parallelization of gradient descent is performed by using optimal functions. Optimized gradient descent function has been employed here.

```
dw2 = T.grad (loss, w2)
dtranslation = T.grad (loss, translation)
dw1 = T.grad (loss, w1)
ddilation = T.grad (loss, dilation)
gradient_step = theano.function(
    [x, y],
    updates = ((w2, w2 – epsilon * dw2),
      (w1, w1 – epsilon * dw1),
      (translation, translation – epsilon * dtranslation),
      (dilation, dilation – epsilon * ddilation)))
where epsilon = momentum rate
```

Optimized Categorical cross-entropy is used for calculating the error function here.

```
loss = T.nnet.categorical_crossentropy(a2, y).mean()
```

4. Should return to step (2), the process should go on until it satisfies the loss criteria, with this process, the training process of WNN employing GPU is completed.

13.5   Experimental setup

13.5.1   Datasets description

The CCFraud [34] dataset consists of nearly 1 crore samples. In this work, we have considered real transactions and fraudulent transactions as positive and negative samples, respectively. It consists of 9,403,986 samples as the negative class and 596,014 as the positive class. It contains a total of nine features. The variables in dataset are custID, gender, state, cardholder, balance, numTrans, numIntlTrans, creditLine, fraudRisk. The "fraudRisk" is considered a class variable. It has two class levels, "1" indicates a fraudulent transaction and "0" a genuine transaction. We considered seven features to train the model and removed "custID" as it has all unique values.

The real-time bidding [35] dataset has 1,000,000 samples in it. It consists of 88 attributes in it. It is used in predicting the bidding of a market slot for an advertiser. The class attribute is "convert" here. It has two values, "1" if the person clicked on the the ad and "0" if he did not click. It is an imbalanced dataset. It is having a total of 1,908 positive instances out of 1,000,000 instances.

The polish [36] dataset from the fifth year has 5,910 samples in it. This dataset is about the prediction of bankruptcy in polish banks. It consists of total 65 attributes in it. In this there are 410 bankrupted companies and 5,500 companies that did not bankrupt. There are no missing values in the dataset. In this, class label indicates bankruptcy status after 1 year.

The default of credit card clients [37] dataset is a multivariate dataset that is having a total of 30,000 instances. There are 24 attributes in this dataset. A class variable is used to predict the accuracy of default payments. The class variable is default payments here. It is having two values defaulter and non-defaulter. The value "1" represents defaulter, whereas "0" represents non-defaulter.

The credit card fraud detection [38] dataset consists of 284,807 samples in it. It has 31 attributes in it. This dataset has a class variable that is "1" in terms of fraud and "0" if it is not. The dataset has a total of 492 frauds, so it is an imbalanced dataset. It consists of only numeric variables as input. Those variables are the result of PCA performed on actual data.

13.5.2 Experimental procedure

Parallelizing the neural network by GPU is done by the Theano framework, which is a python library. Theano makes transparent use of GPU if the GPU processor is available. It converts automatically to C++/CUDA programs and accomplishes the complicated mathematical expressions efficiently. All experiments in our study are carried out on systems with 32 GB RAM and eight cores. The GPU device used for all of our experiment is GeForce GT 730. The details about GPU device are depicted in Table 13.1.

13.6 Results and discussion

Accuracy is used to evaluate the performance of the WNN model. The equation for accuracy is as follows:

$$Accuracy = \frac{TP + TN}{TP + FP + TN + FN}$$

where TP is true positive, TN is true negative, FP is false positive, FN is false negative.

Table 13.1   Specifications of GPU

GeForce GT 730 specifications	
Version	GT 730 DDR3, 64-bit
CUDA cores	384
Base clock (MHz)	902
Memory clock	1.8 Gbps
Standard memory configuration	2,048 MB
Memory interface	DDR3
Memory interface width	64-bit
Memory bandwidth (GB/s)	14.4

Table 13.2   Average accuracy obtained on 10-fold cross-validation

Dataset name	Size of the dataset	No of input nodes	No of node in hidden layers	10-FCV
CCFraud	291.7 MB[a]	8	5	93.47[b]
	551.8 MB[c]			82.4[d]
Polish Bank	6 MB	64	30	77.15
Default Credit Card	6.5 MB	23	11	78.25
Credit Card Fraud Detection	94.2 MB	30	16	81.78
Real-Time Bidding	1.1 GB	88	46	90.68

[a]Size of original data.
[b]Result obtained without SMOTE.
[c]Size of data after applying SMOTE.
[d]Result obtained with SMOTE.

Table 13.3   Execution time by the models

Dataset name	Execution time by CPU in seconds	Execution time by CPU+GPU in seconds
CCFraud	9,909.95	9,109.94
	2,266.08	1,170.27
Polish Bank	23.76	15.32
Default Credit Card	136.68	76.52
Credit Card Fraud Detection	500	428
Real-Time Bidding	5,805.078	5,137.18

Tables 13.2 and 13.3 represent the average accuracy and the execution time by the model applied on various datasets, respectively.

CCFraud dataset consists of 10 million records and 8 attributes, including the class label. We have applied stratified random sampling and decreased its size to

1 lakh instances with 8 attributes. Additionally, the dataset is highly unbalanced, so we applied SMOTE (synthetic minority oversampling technique) and shaped a dataset with dimensions $117,879 \times 8$.

The original dataset with 10 million records and 8 attributes is considered as input. We are penalizing the error by increasing the epochs to 100. The WNN model classified the data with 82.4 percent average accuracy on 10-fold cross-validation. The proposed model completed the execution in an aggregate of 117.27 s. The newly formed dataset with 117,879 records and eight attributes is considered as input to the WNN. The model could be able to achieve 93.47 percent average accuracy and completed its execution process in 9,109.94 s with 100 epochs.

Polish Bank dataset consists of 5,910 instances and 64 attributes. The dataset consists of very less positive class in it to detect the fraud. The dataset was highly unbalanced, so we applied SMOTE to balance the dataset. The newly formed dataset consists of 7,140 instances with 64 attributes.

The newly formed dataset is fed into the WNN model for classification. The model could be able to achieve **77.15 percent** average accuracy on 10-fold cross-validation. The proposed model performed in a total of 15.32 s.

Default Credit Card dataset consists of 30,000 instances and 24 attributes, including class label. Initially the total number of attributes without class label is set as input to the WNN, i.e., $30,000 \times 23$. With the epochs set to 200, we could be able to reduce the error. The learning rate was set to 0.9.

The average accuracy obtained on 10-fold cross-validation through the model is **78.25 percent**. The model completed its execution in an aggregate of **76.52** s.

Credit Card Fraud Detection dataset consists of 284,807 instances and 31 attributes along with class label in it. In this dataset 28 attributes are as principal components. In this, there are very less positive class instances, i.e., 492 frauds. As the data is highly unbalanced, we applied SMOTE to balance the dataset.

The newly formed data consists of 347,291 instances and 31 attributes in it. The total numbers of instances and attributes excluding class label are provided as input to the WNN. For reducing the error, we have to set the epoch to 100. By using 16 nodes in the hidden layer the model fetched **81.78 percent** average accuracy on 10-fold cross-validation. The model completed its execution in **428** s with the help of GPU.

Real-Time Bidding dataset consists of 1,000,000 instances and 88 attributes, including the class label in it. There is very less positive class instances, i.e., 1,908 instances in the dataset. So for balancing this highly unbalanced dataset, SMOTE technique is used. A dataset consisting of 1,381,600 instances and 88 attributes is shaped newly after applying SMOTE. Now this new dataset is supplied as input to the model exempting the class label. An error is penalized by setting the epoch to 100.

With the whole setup, the model could be able to classify the test data with **90.68 percent** average accuracy on 10-fold cross-validation. The proposed model executed with an aggregate of **5,137.18** s.

There are various tuning parameters like learning rate and momentum rate. The number of epochs is also considered, but it varies from one dataset to another.

Table 13.4   Parameters used to build to model

Dataset name	Learning rate	Momentum rate	Epochs
CCFraud	0.7	0.01	100
Polish Bank	0.2	0.01	200
Default Credit Card	0.9	0.01	200
Credit Card Fraud Detection	0.7	0.01	100
Real-Time Bidding	0.5	0.01	100

The best combination of these values ensures us to reduce the error. Table 13.4 depicts the different parameters used when building the model.

13.7   Conclusion and future work

The proposed model WNN using Theano on GPU has proved to be successful in acquiring state-of-the-art results. Various financial datasets have been applied to the model, and the average accuracy level is always nearly 80 percent and above. The model became successful by the right selection of various parameters. The execution time by the GPU-based model is less compared to the CPU-based. We tested the model on all datasets mentioned earlier. The results table is mentioned in Section 13.6.

Finally, we foresee our future research direction in a way to use Sigma-Pi-Sigma neural network in combination with WNN for classification problem, and to decrease the data transfer rate when using both CPU and GPU so that the execution time by GPU can be reduced.

References

[1]   Elgendy N and Elragal A. 'Big Data Analytics: A Literature Review Paper'. In: Perner P, editor. *ICDM 2014: Advances in Data Mining Applications and Theoretical Aspects*. Springer, Cham; 2014. p. 214–227. (Lecture Notes in Computer Science; vol. 8557).

[2]   Singh D and Reddy CK. 'A survey on platforms for big data analytics'. *Journal of Big Data*. 2014;2(1):8.

[3]   Srivastava U and Gopalkrishnan S. 'Impact of big data analytics on banking sector: Learning for Indian banks'. *Procedia Computer Science*. 2015;50:643–652.

[4]   Nickolls J and Dally WJ. 'The GPU computing era'. *IEEE Micro*. 2010;30 (2):56–69.

[5]   Owens JD, Houston M, Luebke D, Green S, Stone JE, and Phillips JC. 'GPU Computing'. In: *Proceedings of the IEEE*. IEEE; 2008. p. 879–899.

[6]   Welcome—Theano 1.0.0 Documentation [Internet]. [Accessed 16 Sep 2019]. Available from: www.deeplearning.net/software/theano/.

[7]   Al-Rfou R, Alain G, Almahairi A, *et al.* 'Theano: A python framework for fast computation of mathematical expressions'. arXiv:1605.02688.

[8]   Kamaruddin S and Ravi V. 'Credit Card Fraud Detection using Big Data Analytics: Use of PSOAANN Based One-Class Classification'. In: Proceedings of the International Conference on Informatics and Analytics – ICIA-16. Pondicherry, India: ACM Press; 2016. p. 1–8.

[9]   Kothapalli K, Banerjee DS, Narayanan PJ, *et al.* 'CPU and/or GPU: Revisiting the GPU vs. CPU Myth'. arXiv:1303-2171. 2013.

[10]   Zhang Q and Benveniste A. 'Wavelet networks'. *IEEE Transactions on Neural Networks.* 1992;3(6):889–898.

[11]   Alexandridis AK and Zapranis AD. 'Wavelet neural networks: A practical guide'. *Neural Networks.* 2013;42:1–27.

[12]   Chauhan N, Ravi V and Karthik Chandra D. 'Differential evolution trained wavelet neural networks: Application to bankruptcy prediction in banks'. *Expert Systems with Applications.* 2009;36(4):7659–7665.

[13]   Becerra VM, Galvão RKH and Abou-Seada M. 'Neural and wavelet network models for financial distress classification'. *Data Mining and Knowledge Discovery.* 2005;11(1):35–55.

[14]   Chen Y, Yang B and Dong J. 'Time-series prediction using a local linear wavelet neural network'. *Neurocomputing.* 2006;69(4–6):449–465.

[15]   Casas CA. 'Parallelization of Artificial Neural Network Training Algorithms: A Financial Forecasting Application'. In: *2012 IEEE Conference on Computational Intelligence for Financial Engineering & Economics (CIFEr).* New York, NY, USA: IEEE; 2012. p. 1–6.

[16]   Park JH and Ro WW. 'Accelerating Forwarding Computation of Artificial Neural Network Using CUDA'. In: *2016 International Conference on Electronics, Information, and Communications (ICEIC).* Da Nang, Vietnam: IEEE; 2016. p. 1–4.

[17]   Bashir Z and El-Hawary ME. 'Short Term Load Forecasting by Using Wavelet Neural Networks'. In: *2000 Canadian Conference on Electrical and Computer Engineering Conference Proceedings Navigating to a New Era (Cat No00TH8492).* Halifax, NS, Canada: IEEE; 2000. p. 163–166.

[18]   Benaouda D, Murtagh F, Starck J-L, and Renaud O. 'Wavelet-based non-linear multiscale decomposition model for electricity load forecasting'. *Neurocomputing.* 2006;70(1–3):139–154.

[19]   Gao R and Tsoukalas LH. 'Neural-wavelet methodology for load forecasting'. *Journal of Intelligent and Robotic Systems.* 2001;31(1/3):149–157.

[20]   Ulagammai M, Venkatesh P, Kannan PS, and Padhy NP. 'Application of bacterial foraging technique trained artificial and wavelet neural networks in load forecasting'. *Neurocomputing.* 2007;70(16–18):2659–2667.

[21]   Yao X. 'Evolving artificial neural networks'. *Proceedings of the IEEE.* 1999;87(9):1423–1447.

[22]   Cao L, Hong Y, Fang H, and He G. 'Predicting chaotic time series with wavelet networks'. *Physica D: Nonlinear Phenomena.* 1995;85(1–2):225–238.

[23]   Cristea P, Tuduce R, and Cristea A. 'Time Series Prediction With Wavelet Neural Networks'. In: *Proceedings of the 5th Seminar on Neural Network Applications in Electrical Engineering NEUREL 2000 (IEEE Cat No00EX287)*. Belgrade, Yugoslavia: IEEE; 2000. p. 5–10.

[24]   Kadambe S and Srinivasan P. 'Adaptive wavelets for signal classification and compression'. *AEU – International Journal of Electronics and Communications*. 2006;60(1):45–55.

[25]   Pittner S, Kamarthi S V., and Gao Q. 'Wavelet networks for sensor signal classification in flank wear assessment'. *Journal of Intelligent Manufacturing*. 1998;9(4):315–322.

[26]   Subasi A, Alkan A, Koklukaya E, and Kiymik MK. 'Wavelet neural network classification of EEG signals by using AR model with MLE preprocessing'. *Neural Networks*. 2005;18(7):985–997.

[27]   Zhang Z. 'Learning algorithm of wavelet network based on sampling theory'. *Neurocomputing*. 2007;71(1–3):244–269.

[28]   Billings SA and Wei H-L. 'A new class of wavelet networks for nonlinear system identification'. *IEEE Transactions on Neural Networks*. 2005;16 (4):862–874.

[29]   Jiao L, Pan J, and Fang Y. 'Multiwavelet neural network and its approximation properties'. *IEEE Transactions on Neural Networks*. 2001;12 (5):1060–1066.

[30]   Szu HH, Telfer BA, and Kadambe SL. 'Neural network adaptive wavelets for signal representation and classification'. *Optical Engineering*. 1992;31 (9):1907–1916.

[31]   Wong K-W and Leung AC-S. 'On-line successive synthesis of wavelet networks'. *Neural Processing Letters*. 1998;7(2):91–100.

[32]   Khayamian T, Ensafi AA, Tabaraki R, and Esteki M. 'Principal component-wavelet neural networks as a new multivariate calibration method'. *Analytical Letters*. 2005;38(9):1477–1489.

[33]   Grossmann A and Morlet J. 'Decomposition of hardy functions into square integrable wavelets of constant shape'. *SIAM Journal on Mathematical Analysis*. 1984;15(4):723–736.

[34]   ccFraud Dataset [Internet]. [Accessed 31 Jul 2018]. Available from: https://packages.revolutionanalytics.com/datasets/.

[35]   Real Time Bidding Dataset [Internet]. [Accessed 16 Sep 2019]. Available from: www.kaggle.com/zurfer/rtb.

[36]   Polish Companies Bankruptcy Data Dataset [Internet]. [Accessed 16 Sep 2019]. Available from: https://archive.ics.uci.edu/ml/datasets/Polish+companies+bankruptcy+data.

[37]   Default of Credit Card Clients Dataset [Internet]. [Accessed 16 Sep 2019]. Available from: https://archive.ics.uci.edu/ml/datasets/default+of+credit+card+clients.

[38]   Credit Card Fraud Detection Dataset [Internet]. [Accessed 16 Sep 2019]. Available from: www.kaggle.com/dalpozz/in-depth-skewed-data-classif-93-recall-acc-now/data.

Chapter 14

Stock market movement prediction using evolving spiking neural networks

*Rasmi Ranjan Khansama[1], Vadlamani Ravi[2],
Akshay Raj Gollahalli[3], Neelava Sengupta[3],
Nikola K. Kasabov[3] and Imanol Bilbao-Quintana[4]*

Stock price movement direction prediction is regarded as one of the most difficult and challenging tasks in the real world. An accurate prediction can yield profit to the investors and protect them from financial risk. In this study, we propose three variants of the evolving spiking neural networks (eSNNs) for the stock trend prediction: eSNN model using technical stock indicators (SIs) as input variables – SI-eSNN; a parallel implementation of the SI-eSNN model on a GPU machine – Compute Unified Device Architecture (CUDA)-SI-eSNN; and finally, a model for incremental learning using a sliding window (SW) of data – SW-eSNN. We also propose logistic distribution in place of Gaussian distribution in characterizing the receptive fields. The models are applied on nine large-scale benchmark stock indices of different countries. We considered classification accuracy and area under ROC curve (AUC) to measure the performance of the models in terms of predicting UP or DOWN movements on their daily prices. Our experimental results show that the eSNN model and its parallel implementation achieve a high accuracy of 80%–90% of predicting stock movements from 1 day to 1 month ahead forecasts, which is a significant improvement when compared with the use of traditional AI methods. Also, the performance of eSNN model with logistic receptive fields is compared with that of a deep learning architecture: long short-term memory (LSTM) network. The comparative analysis shows that the proposed model outperformed LSTM in the case of four stock indices out of nine in terms of accuracy. The CUDA-SI-eSNN model performs three to five times faster than the sequential eSNN model. The window-based eSNN model, SW-eSNN, achieved around 75% accuracy on average

[1]Department of Computer Science and Engineering, C. V. Raman Global University, Bhubaneswar, India
[2]Center of Excellence in Analytics, Institute for Development and Research in Banking Technology, Hyderabad, India
[3]KEDRI, Auckland University of Technology, Auckland, New Zealand
[4]Electrical Engineering Department, Engineering School of Bilbao, University of the Basque Country, Bilbao, Spain

across all indexes. As eSNN can be considered as one specific implementation of a comprehensive SNN architecture called NeuCube, future development of improved models is also discussed. The results are promising for a future development of automated trading systems.

14.1   Introduction

Prediction of the stock price index and its trend are considered challenging tasks due to their complexity, non-linearity, dynamic and chaotic nature [1]. In addition, the stock market behaviour is also influenced by sociopolitical movements, investor psychology and so on [2].

Many traditional AI techniques such as artificial neural networks (ANNs) [3,4], support vector machines (SVMs) [5,6], random forest (RF), Kernel Factory (KF) and AdaBoost (AB) [7,8] have been applied to predict the stock price direction or trend [7].

Although many researchers and practitioners have explored several prediction techniques, it is for the first time that we employ eSNNs to develop computational models for stock market trend prediction. We have applied the eSNN model on several stock indices of different countries to test its performance. The eSNNs have already been proven in other domains, such as image recognition [9], taste recognition [10], stroke prediction [11], audio–visual recognition [12] and cyber-fraud detection [13]. In this study, we have proposed three computational variants of eSNN: the first one is an eSNN using stock direction indicators as input variables – SI-eSNN; the second one, CUDA-SI-eSNN, is a parallel implementation of eSNN learning in a GPU machine; the third one is an incremental learning in an eSNN using an SW of data – SW-eSNN.

To measure the performance of these models, we have applied both SI-eSNN and CUDA-SI-eSNN on nine historical stock index datasets of different countries. The performance of these models is based on AUC score and training time. Experimental results showed that the proposed eSNN models achieved a high accuracy of stock movement prediction, while the GPU-based CUDA-SI-eSNN model was three to five times faster than the SI-eSNN model. As eSNN is a specific implementation of a larger and comprehensive SNN architecture and framework, called NeuCube [14,15], the chapter also discusses new directions for future research and development.

The remainder of this chapter is organized as follows. In Section 14.2, we have provided a brief overview of the earlier prediction techniques used for stock price direction prediction. The motivation behind this study is discussed in Section 14.3. In Section 14.4, we have presented the SI-eSNN model and in Section 14.5, the GPU-based CUDA-SI-eSNN model. Section 14.6 describes the benchmark stock indices data and the experimental results with the use of the two models from Sections 14.4 and 14.5. In Section 14.7, we presented the incremental SW-eSNN model and the experimental results with it. We also propose as a future development an incrementally cumulative eSNN (INC-eSNN) model which will utilize more functionality of the NeuCube architecture [16] to further improve the accuracy of stock movement prediction. Section 14.8 contains concluding remarks for future work.

14.2   Literature review

In the last few years, there have been a large number of studies performed on predicting the stock market trend. Both researchers and practitioners have used numerous approaches to predict the stock market trend. Due to the chaotic nature and the complexity of the stock market indices, researchers are still struggling to design techniques that can accurately model the behaviour of their trends. In this section, we present a review of earlier works applied to stock market trend prediction.

There are three primary mechanisms used by researchers and practitioners for the stock price trend prediction: (1) technical analysis, (2) time series forecasting and (3) machine learning and data mining.

Technical analysis is performed using various plots and charts, which is visually interpreted by the analysts to make the decision. Time series forecasting uses past returns to forecast future stock price. These techniques include auto-regressive (AR) methods, moving average (MA) models, autoregressive–moving average (ARMA) models and threshold autoregressive models.

In the last few years, several prediction techniques have been explored to predict stock price movement. As stock market is complex, non-linear, non-parametric and chaotic in nature, many non-linear prediction techniques have been proposed. First, many researchers used ANNs, such as recurrent neural networks (RNNs) [17,18], probabilistic neural networks (PNNs) [19] and evolutionary opti-mized neural networks (NNs) [4] to predict stock price direction by considering several index indicators. Kim [5] investigated SVM for predicting stock price direction on Korea composite stock price index (KOSPI). This study included ten technical indicators as input variables which are calculated from historical price index values such as high, low, open and close. This study showed that SVM could be used as a possible technique for stock price direction prediction. ANN and SVM are two techniques used earlier by many researchers for the forecasting of stock price movement [6]. However, they produced unsatisfactory results.

Ou and Wang [20] applied ten prediction techniques to predict stock price direction of Hang Seng Index of Hong Kong stock market. The prediction techni-ques include Bayesian classification with a Gaussian process, linear discriminant analysis (LDA), quadratic discriminant analysis (QDA), naïve Bayes based on kernel estimation, K-nearest neighbour (KNN) classification, tree-based classifi-cation, ANN, logit model, SVM and least squares SVM (LS-SVM). Their analysis showed that SVM and LS-SVM outperformed other models.

Patel *et al.* [3] used both technical indicators and trend deterministic data representation of technical indicators as input to the model. The study used four prediction techniques such as ANN, SVM, RF and naïve Bayes for predicting the stock price movement. Experiments are performed on two stocks, Reliance Industries and Infosys Ltd, and two stock price indices CNX Nifty and S&P Bombay Stock Exchange (BSE) Sensex. This study showed that the models using trend deterministic data representation of technical indicators outperformed the models with simple technical indicators.

Ballings *et al.* [7] employed different ensemble methods such as AB [21], RF [22] and KF [23] to predict stock price direction of European Stock Index and compared them with the single classifier models such as NNs, logistic regression (LR), SVM and KNN. Experimental results showed that RF was the best performer. Zhang *et al.* [8] presented a new ensemble method integrated with the AB algorithm, probabilistic SVM (PSVM) and genetic algorithm (GA) for stock price trend classification. This study used National Association of Securities Dealers Automated Quotations (NASDAQ) and Shenzhen Stock Exchange (SZSE) to measure the performance of the model. Experimental results showed that this new ensemble method outperformed single classifiers such as PSVM and backpropagation NN.

Deep learning networks are also suitable for time series forecasting. One such architecture is LSTM network, which was introduced by [24]. It differs from traditional NNs in architecture where the data in the same layer is passed to the previous layer in a recurrent manner.

In Table 14.1, we presented an overview of different prediction techniques and stock market indices used in the literature to predict the stock price direction by taking technical indicators as input variables. We provided the list of abbreviations used in this study and their meanings in tables provided in the supplementary information.

14.3 Motivation

From Table 14.1, it is clear that many traditional machine learning techniques have been explored to predict stock price direction and also most of the algorithms have been applied to a single stock index to measure the performance of the model. The third generation of NNs – the SNN – offers a new perspective to explore for the solution of the problem. SNN use spike information representation and spike-time learning rules to capture temporal associations between a large number of temporal variables in streaming data and to predict future events. Different SNN neural models have been developed so far, for a review – see Gerstner and Kistler [38].

One of the successful SNN models is the eSNN [9–13,39], where the number of spiking neurons evolves incrementally in time to capture temporal prototypes from data. The first eSNN model was proposed by Kasabov [39] and further implemented and applied by Wysoski *et al.* [12]. eSNNs are based on the principles of the evolving connectionist systems [39]. An eSNN model consists of an encoding part, which converts a real-valued vector into spikes generated over time, a neuron model and a learning mechanism that calculates the connection weights between the input and the output neurons. eSNNs are now part of a comprehensive SNN architecture for temporal and spatio-temporal data modelling tool, namely, NeuCube [40].

Table 14.1 *Prediction techniques and stock market indices for stock price*
direction prediction used in literature

	Techniques	Stock market indices	GPU-based
[17]	RNN	TSI	No
[18]	RBS+RNN	S&P 500	No
[19]	TDN, RN, PNN	AAPL, IBM, MOT, MSFT	No
[4]	GA+ANN	KOSPI	No
[5]	SVM	KOSPI	No
[25]	FS+ANN	KOSPI	No
[6]	SVM, LDA, QDA, EBNN	Nikkei 225	No
[26]	RF, SVM	NIFTY, CNX, S&P 500	No
[27]	Wrapper, LR, SVM, C 4.5 DT, BP, *K*NN, voting	KOSPI, TSE	No
[20]	LDA, QDA, *K*NN, NB, SVM, LS-SVM, ANN, TBC, BC, Logit	HSI	No
[28]	IBCO+BPNN	S&P 500	No
[29]	MLP, GRNN	KSE	No
[30]	DT+RS	BSE	No
[31]	SVM, ANN	ISE	No
[32]	EPCNNs	S&P 500	No
[33]	SVM	TW50	No
[34]	ANN	PETR4	No
[35]	PCA+SVM	KOSPI, HSI	No
[36]	ANN	BSE, IBM, RIL, OSI	No
[3]	ANN, SVM, NB, RF	NIFTY, BSE-Sensex, Infosys, Reliance	No
[37]	BNNMAS	DAX	No
[7]	LR, ANN, *K*NN, SVM, AB, RF, KF	European Stock Index	No
[8]	AB+PSVM+GA	SZSE, NASDAQ	No
This study	eSNN, CUDA-eSNN	BSE, NIFTY-50, NASDAQ, Nikkei 225, DAX, NYSE-Amex, S&P 500, SSE	Yes

eSNN and NeuCube in general have still not been used in the area of time
series prediction, particularly for stock price trend forecasting. Here, we propose
three variants of eSNN and apply them on benchmark stock indexes to predict their
trends a month ahead.

14.4 The proposed SI-eSNN model for stock trend prediction based on stock indicators

14.4.1 Overall architecture

The architecture of the SI-eSNN model is presented in Figure 14.1. The first layer
is the set of inputs to the model, each of them representing a technical SI. The
research so far has demonstrated that using technical indicators can lead to better

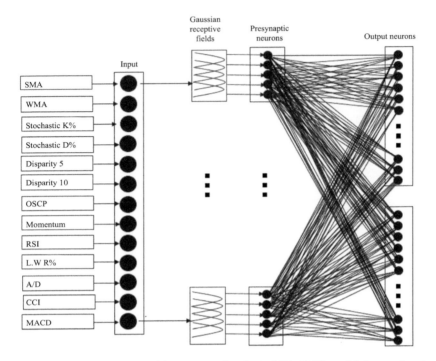

Figure 14.1   Architecture of the proposed technical SI-eSNN model for stock price direction prediction

results than using real stock values as time series and also that there is a lot of research done on selecting the most appropriate technical indicators [3,5,31]. In the model presented in Figure 14.1, the input technical indicators have been selected from [3,5,31] and explained in Table 14.2, but these indicators can be different for different stock prediction applications.

Layer 2 is the encoding layer, where the real value of each input variable (technical indicator) is encoded as trains of spikes generated by several encoding spiking neurons (or also, presynaptic neurons), each of them having a receptive field. The receptive fields of neighbouring neurons are overlapping as Gaussian or logistic functions, and all of them are covering the whole range of the values of this variable. The number of these encoding neurons (receptive fields) can vary, as it is a user-defined parameter. It is optimized in order to obtain better performance from the model.

Layer 3 is the output evolving layer, which evolves output spiking neurons that represent clusters (prototypes) of input vectors that belong to the same class, in this case – class UP and class DOWN. Each output neuron is connected to all the input neurons, and the connection weights are subject to learning from data.

The architecture of the SI-eSNN model for stock price direction prediction allows for incremental learning. It is adaptive to new data when it becomes

Table 14.2   Selected technical indicators and their formulas

Name of the technical indicators (SI)	Formulas[a]
Simple 10-day moving average	$(C_t + C_{t-1} + \cdots + C_{t-9})/10$
Weighted 10-day moving average	$((n) \times C_t + (n-1) \times C_{t-1} + \cdots + C_{t-9})/(n + (n-1) + \cdots + 1)$
Stochastic $K\%$	$((C_t - LL_{t-(n-1)})/(HH_{t-(n-1)} - LL_{t-(n-1)})) \times 100$
Stochastic $D\%$	$\left(\sum_{t=0}^{n-1} K_{t-i}/10\right)\%$
Disparity 5	$(C_t/MA_5) \times 100$
Disparity 10	$(C_t/MA_{10}) \times 100$
OSCP	$(MA_5 - MA_{10})/MA_{10}$
Momentum	$C_t - C_{t-9}$
RSI (relative strength index)	$100 - \dfrac{100}{1 + \dfrac{\sum_{i=0}^{n-1} UP_{t-i}/n}{\sum_{i=0}^{n-1} DW_{t-i}/n}}$
Larry William R%	$((H_n - C_t)/(H_n - L_n)) \times 100$
A/D (accumulation/ distribution)	$(H_t - C_{t-1})/(H_t - L_t)$
CCI (commodity channel index)	$(M_t - SM_t)/(0.015 \times D_t)$
MACD (moving average convergence divergence)	$MACD(n)_{t-1} + (2/(n+1)) \times (DIFF_t - MACD(n)_{t-1})$

[a] C_t is closing price, L_t is low price and H_t is high price at time t, $DIFF_t = EMA(12)_t - EMA(26)_t$, EMA is moving average, $EMA(k)_t = EMA(k)_{t-1} + \alpha \times (C_t - EMA(k)_{t-1})$, α is smoothing factor which is equal to $2/(k+1)$, k is the time period of k-day exponential moving average, LL_t and HH_t imply lowest low and highest high in the last t days, respectively. $M_t = (H_t + L_t + C_t)/3$, $SM_t = \left(\sum_{i=1}^{n} M_{t-i+1}\right)/n$, $D_t = \left(\sum_{i=1}^{n} |M_{t-i+1} - SM_t|\right)/n$, UP_t means upwards price change, while DW_t is the downwards price change at time t.

available. Hence, it can learn new samples without retraining the model on old data. The details of the functioning of the SI-eSNN model are presented next.

14.4.2   Neural encoding

To learn real-valued data, each instance or sample (input vector) is encoded in the form of spikes over time using a neural encoding technique such as rank-order population coding [41,42]. In our study, we have used rank-order population encoding as per [43]. Population encoding maps the input value into a series of spikes over time using an array of Gaussian or logistic receptive fields that describe presynaptic neurons. The centre (C_j) and width (W_j) of each of the Gaussian or logistic receptive field of presynaptic neurons j are defined as

$$C_j = I_{\min}^n + \frac{2j-3}{2} \times \frac{I_{\max}^n - I_{\min}^n}{N-2} \tag{14.1}$$

and

$$W_j = \frac{1}{\beta} \times \frac{I^n_{max} - I^n_{min}}{N - 2} \tag{14.2}$$

where N is the number of receptive fields; n is the range of input variable $n = [I^n_{min}, I^n_{max}]$; the parameter β defines the width of each receptive field. Output of each of the presynaptic neuron j using Gaussian receptive field is defined as

$$output_j = exp\left(-\frac{(x - C_j)^2}{2 \cdot W_j^2}\right) \tag{14.3}$$

Output of each of the presynaptic neuron j using logistic receptive field is defined as

$$output_j = \frac{exp\left(\frac{-(x - C_j)}{W_j}\right)}{\left(1 + exp\left(\frac{-(x - C_j)}{W_j}\right)\right)^2} \tag{14.4}$$

The firing time of each of the presynaptic neurons is defined as

$$\tau_j = T\left(1 - output_j\right) \tag{14.5}$$

where T is the simulation or spike-time interval.

14.4.3   Neural model

For the context of SI-eSNN, Thorpe's neuron model [41] has been used since it is simple and effective. Thorpe's model is based on the timing of each spike, where earlier spike defines stronger weight as compared to later spike. Each neuron in this model can spike at most once. A neuron in this model fires when its postsynaptic potential (PSP) reaches the threshold value. The PSP of neuron i is defined as

$$PSP_i = \begin{cases} 0, & \text{if } fired \\ \sum w_{ji} * mod^{order(j)}, & \text{otherwise} \end{cases} \tag{14.6}$$

where w_{ji} represents the weight of the synaptic connection between presynaptic neuron j and the output neuron i; mod represents modulation factor with a range in between 0 and 1; $order(j)$ defines the rank of presynaptic neurons spike. The first rank will be assigned as 0 and subsequently, rank will be increased by 1 based on the firing time of each presynaptic neuron.

14.4.4   Learning in the output neurons

The eSNN algorithm was first introduced in [9,39]. The learning technique used by the eSNN model is one-pass learning, that is, the model requires one-time presentation of a sample in a feedforward manner. It will create an output neuron for each input sample. The weight vector and a threshold value for each of the output neuron generated towards the training pattern are learned and stored in the repository. However, if this weight vector is similar to the same of the already trained neuron in the repository with some similarity threshold, then it will merge with the most similar one. Merging here means updating the weights as well as the threshold value of the merged neurons. The weight vector and threshold value of the merged neurons update their values by taking the average value of new output neuron weight vector and merged neuron weight vector and the average value of new output neuron threshold and merged neuron threshold, respectively.

Algorithm 1 eSNN training algorithm

1: Initialize neuron repository, $R = \{\}$
2: Set eSNN parameter $mod = [0, 1], C = [0, 1], sim = [0, 1]$
3: **for** $\forall$ input pattern i that belongs to the same class **do**
4: Encode input pattern into firing time of multiple presynaptic neurons j
5: Create a new output neuron i for this class and calculate the connection weights as $w_{ji} = mod^{order(j)}$
6: Calculate $PSP_{max(i)} = \sum_j w_{ji} \times mod^{order(j)}$
7: Get PSP threshold value $\gamma_i = PSP_{max(i)} \times C$
8: **if** The new neuron weight vector $\leq sim$ of trained output neuron weight vector in R **then**
9: Update the weight vector and threshold of the most similar neuron in the same output class group
10: $w = \frac{w_{new} + w*N}{N+1}$
11: $\gamma = \frac{\gamma_{new} + \gamma*N}{N+1}$
12: where N is the number of previous merges of the most similar neuron
13: **else**
14: Add the weight vector and threshold of the new neuron to the neuron repository R
15: **end if**
16: **end for**
17: Repeat above for all input patterns of other output classes

---

14.4.5 *Algorithm for eSNN training*

The eSNN algorithm creates a repository of output neurons for the training patterns. For each training pattern that belongs to the same class, a new output neuron is created and connected to all the presynaptic neurons in the previous layer. The weight for each of the connection from presynaptic neuron j to output neuron i is denoted as w_{ji}. The value of w_{ji} is calculated on the basis of the spike order through a synapse j, which is given in line 5 of Algorithm 1 as $w_{ji} = mod^{order(j)}$, $\forall j$ where j is the presynaptic neuron of output neuron i.

The threshold γ_i of newly created output neuron would be defined as the fraction $C \in \mathbb{R}, 0 < C < 1$ of the maximum PSP $PSP_{max(i)} : \gamma_i = PSP_{max(i)} \times C$.

The weight vector of the newly created output neuron is then compared with the already trained output neurons in the repository. If the newly created output neuron weight vector is less than *sim* of trained neuron weight vectors, then the threshold and weight vector of newly created output neuron are merged with that of the most similar neuron according to

$$w = \frac{w_{new} + w * N}{N + 1} \quad \text{and} \quad \gamma = \frac{\gamma_{new} + \gamma * N}{N + 1},$$

where N is the number of previous merges of the most similar neurons. After the merge operation, the newly created output neuron weight vector is discarded, and the new pattern is presented to model. If none of the trained neurons in the repository is similar, the new output neuron is added to the repository.

14.4.6   Testing (recall of the model on new data)

The testing process involves propagating the spikes that encode the test vector (sample) to all the trained output neurons. The class label for the test sample is defined on the basis of the output class label of the output neuron which fires first.

14.5   The proposed CUDA-eSNN model: a parallel eSNN model for GPU machines

The training and recall procedures for the SI-eSNN model from Section 14.4 consist of two operations. In the first stage, encoding of the input patterns, calculations of the weights and the thresholds are performed, which involve steps 4–7 of the eSNN algorithm. In the second stage, merging of the output neurons is performed, which involves steps 8–14 of the eSNN algorithm. Since the encoding and learning of weights of one input pattern is independent of others except for the merging operation, it is possible to perform both encoding and weight learning operations parallelly in a GPU device using multiple threads. Therefore, we developed a parallel version of the eSNN model that would be suitable for large datasets. The procedure for the GPU-based eSNN algorithm is described in Algorithm 2.

Algorithm 2 CUDA-SI-eSNN algorithm

1: Initialize input patterns array in the device memory with the size being equal to $N \times M$, where N is the number of input patterns and M is the number of input variables.

2: Declare weight matrix in the device memory with size is equal to $N \times P$, where P is the number of presynaptic neurons which is also equal to the number of input variable multiplied by the number of Gaussian receptive fields.

3: Transfer the input patterns data into the GPU memory.

4: Encode input patterns into the firing time of multiple presynaptic neurons j. In this step, each of the threads in the GPU device will calculate the firing time of each of the presynaptic neurons independently. The number of threads is equal to $N \times P$.

5: Calculate the connection weights as $w_{ji} = mod^{order(j)}$. In this step, each tread in the GPU device will calculate the weights independently.

6: Transfer the resulted weight matrix into CPU memory.

7: Calculation of maximum postsynaptic potential $PSP_{\max(i)}$, threshold value γ_i and the merging operation are similar to the equivalent operations of eSNN, which are performed on CPU sequentially.

14.6 Dataset description and experiments with the SI-eSNN and the CUDA-eSNN models

This section describes the datasets, summary statistics of the selected technical indicators and experimental results of applying the two eSNN models on nine benchmark datasets. The datasets used in this study are obtained from Quandl [44,45] and [16]. These datasets cover stock market indices of different countries: BSE, Nikkei 225, NIFTY-50, S&P 500, Dow Jones, NYSE-Amex, DAX, NASDAQ and Shanghai Stock Exchange.

In this study, we selected 13 technical indicators as input variables based on earlier research [3,5,31]. The direction of daily stock price index is categorized as 'UP' or 'DOWN'. If the stock price index at time t is higher than that at time $t + 1$, then the trend is 'DOWN'. If the stock price index at time t is lower than that at time $t + 1$, then the trend is 'UP'. The number of instances of each of the stock index data is given in Table 14.3. The details about selected indicators are given in Table 14.1, and the summary statistics of selected technical indicators for each stock index are provided in the supplementary information.

In the experiments here, the first 70% of the temporal stock data represented by the 13 indicators on a daily basis are used as input variables for training the SI-eSNN and the CUDA-SI-eSNN models, and the future 30% of the time series stock data are used to test the model accuracy.

Experiments in our study were carried on systems with 32 GB RAM and eight cores. The GPU device used for all of our experiment is GeForce GT 730. The details about GPU device is given in Table 14.4.

Classification accuracy and AUC score are used to evaluate the performance of both eSNN and CUDA-SI-eSNN models. Sensitivity and specificity are used to compute the AUC score. The formulas for specificity, sensitivity, accuracy and AUC score are as follows:

$$Specificity = \frac{TN}{TN + FP} \tag{14.7}$$

Table 14.3   The number of instances of UP and DOWN categories in stock market indices

Datasets (no. of instances)	Years covered	Training (70%)			Testing (30%)		
		UP	Down	Total	UP	DOWN	Total
BSE	Jan 2005–Dec 2015	1,020	892	1,912	437	382	819
Nikkei 225	Jan 1987–Jul 2016	2,609	2,483	5,092	1,115	1,067	2,182
NASDAQ	Jan 2005–Dec 2015	1,058	865	1,923	446	378	824
NIFTY-50	Jan 2008–Dec 2015	709	644	1,353	300	279	579
S&P 500	Jan 1962–Jul 2016	5,118	4,473	9,591	2,146	1,964	4,110
Shanghai Stock Exchange	Jan 1998–Jul 2016	1,679	1,470	3,149	685	665	1,350
DJUS	Apr 2005–Jul 2016	997	827	1,824	438	344	782
DAX Index	Jan 1991–Jul 2016	2,413	2,114	4,527	1,044	897	1,941
NYSE-Amex	Jan 1996–Jul 2016	1,957	1,668	3,625	850	704	1,554

Table 14.4   GPU specifications

GeForce GT 730 specifications	
Version	GT 730 DDR3, 64-bit
CUDA cores	384
Base clock (MHz)	902
Memory clock	1.8 Gbps
Standard Memory Config	2,048 MB
Memory interface	DDR3
Memory interface width	64-bit
Memory bandwidth (GB/s)	14.4

$$Sensitivity = \frac{TP}{TP + FN} \qquad (14.8)$$

$$Accuracy = \frac{TP + TN}{TP + FP + TN + FN} \qquad (14.9)$$

$$AUC\ score = \frac{Sensitivity + Specificity}{2} \qquad (14.10)$$

where *TP* is true-positive, *TN* is true-negative, *FP* is false-positive, *FN* is false-negative, where UP is considered as positive class and DOWN as negative class. AUC is the arithmetic mean of the sensitivity and specificity; the cut-off value is chosen as 0.5 while determining the class label in the test phase.

Tables 14.5 and 14.6 present the accuracy and AUC of CUDA-SI-eSNN model for a different number of Gaussian receptive fields on various stock indices.

In Table 14.7, we included the performance of both SI-eSNN and CUDA-SI-eSNN models for the best value of some Gaussian receptive fields. The accuracy of both these models is very high across all stock indexes (between 80% and 90%) and only slightly different between the two models. Table 14.7 also reports the training time needed by both the SI-eSNN and the CUDA-SI-eSNN on the same data. While the latter is two to five times faster, the SI-eSNN training was very fast as well. For example, it took only 40 s to train the SI-eSNN on 5,000 samples for the S&P 500, while it took 20 s on the CUDA-SI-eSNN.

The results of CUDA-SI-eSNN with logistic distribution are presented in Tables 14.8 and 14.9. Logistic distribution was employed in place of Gaussian in [46], where we obtained better results with the former. The experimental results showed that CUDA-SI-eSNN with logistic distribution outperforms the CUDA-SI-eSNN model with Gaussian distribution on all stock indices except on Nikkei 225 stock index. The accuracy of CUDA-SI-eSNN with logistic distribution varies between 82.99% and 90.47%. The results of the CUDA-SI-eSNN with the best value of a number of logistic receptive fields are presented in Table 14.10. The training time of the CUDA-SI-eSNN with logistic receptive fields is different from the training time of the CUDA-SI-eSNN with Gaussian receptive fields for the same number of receptive field due to running of other background processes. The CUDA-SI-eSNN model with logistic receptive fields outperformed the CUDA-SI-eSNN model with Gaussian receptive fields in all stock indices since logistic distribution has higher kurtosis than the Gaussian distribution.

To test whether CUDA-SI-eSNN with logistic distribution significantly outperforms another model, we performed McNemar test. The result of the McNemar test is given in Table 14.11. The McNemar test showed that CUDA-SI-eSNN with logistic distribution significantly outperforms the other model on DJUS, NYSE-Amex and SSE stock indices at 5% statistical significance level.

In addition, we compared the performance of the proposed method with that of a deep learning architecture. Thus, CUDA-SI-eSNN with logistic receptive fields is compared with the standard LSTM network in terms of accuracy on each stock index data and the results are presented in Table 14.12. It is evident that we obtained mixed results, where CUDA-SI-eSNN with logistic receptive fields outperformed LSTM on four stock indices. We used the following hyper-parameter settings for the LSTM: no of LSTM cells (unit): 128; no of layers: 2; activation function for the output layer: sigmoid; and batch size: 60.

14.7 Sliding window (SW)-eSNN for incremental learning and stock movement prediction

While learning in the SI-eSNN and CUDA-SI-eSNN models takes place vector by vector, each vector was learned separately from the others even though the vectors of consecutive days would have some temporal associations. Here we present an SW-eSNN model where a section (a window) of the time series of technical indicator data is used for training a model and a future window – to test it.

Table 14.5 Accuracy and AUC of CUDA-eSNN model with Gaussian distribution for different stock indices

Datasets	BSE			Nikkei 225			NASDAQ			NIFTY-50			S&P 500		
No. of Gaussian receptive fields	Acc. (%)	T.T. (s)	AUC	Acc. (%)	T.T. (s)	AUC	Acc. (%)	T.T. (s)	AUC	Acc. (%)	T.T. (s)	AUC	Acc. (%)	T.T. (s)	AUC
3	82.17	0.84	0.82	81.57	3.3	0.81	84.46	0.89	0.84	76.85	0.61	0.76	82.96	8.51	0.82
4	85.71	1.06	0.86	82.53	4.67	0.82	85.43	1.1	0.85	79.96	0.7	0.79	83.74	9.77	0.83
5	83.88	1.25	0.83	80.33	5.96	0.8	84.22	1.23	0.84	80.13	0.69	0.8	81.16	11.59	0.81
6	85.59	1.36	0.85	84.41	7.15	0.84	84.22	1.24	0.83	77.37	0.79	0.77	82.72	13.78	0.82
7	87.05	1.39	0.87	80.88	8.06	0.8	85.92	1.53	0.86	82.55	0.81	0.82	82.53	18.95	0.82
8	85.47	1.55	0.85	86.15	8.91	0.85	81.79	1.55	0.81	82.03	0.84	0.81	84.03	22.05	0.84
9	88.76	1.65	0.88	82.12	9.68	0.82	84.7	1.67	0.84	81.69	0.93	0.81	82.16	29.05	0.82
10	86.08	1.75	0.86	87.12	10.6	0.87	85.92	1.84	0.85	83.93	0.99	0.83	84.13	35.7	0.84
11	88.64	1.78	0.88	83.73	11.58	0.83	84.7	1.91	0.84	80.31	1.05	0.8	84.5	39.36	0.84
12	87.91	1.88	0.88	86.11	12.41	0.86	83.49	2.04	0.83	82.38	1.08	0.82	81.26	46.94	0.81
13	88.4	2	0.88	83.68	13.15	0.83	84.22	2.19	0.84	84.45	1.18	0.84	84.74	51.51	0.84
14	87.91	2.25	0.88	86.57	14.04	0.86	83.73	2.19	0.83	81	1.22	0.8	84.13	51.88	0.84

Acc., accuracy; T.T., training time.

Table 14.6 Accuracy and AUC of CUDA-eSNN model with Gaussian distribution for different stock indices (continued)

No. of Gaussian receptive fields	Shanghai Stock Exchange			Dow Jones			NYSE-Amex			DAX Index		
	Acc. (%)	T.T. (s)	AUC	Acc. (%)	T.T. (s)	AUC	Acc. (%)	T.T. (s)	AUC	Acc. (%)	T.T. (s)	AUC
3	77.48	1.68	0.77	75.31	0.83	0.74	78.37	2.01	0.77	79.23	2.67	0.79
4	78.14	2.08	0.78	76.59	0.93	0.76	84.04	2.5	0.83	77.64	4	0.77
5	80.74	3.13	0.8	75.31	0.96	0.74	82.75	3.67	0.81	81.55	5.12	0.81
6	80.37	3.3	0.8	78.38	1.05	0.78	80.56	3.96	0.8	82.07	5.79	0.81
7	79.92	3.7	0.79	79.79	1.23	0.79	82.62	4.4	0.82	78.41	6.43	0.78
8	79.18	3.73	0.79	79.28	1.46	0.79	77.79	4.7	0.77	82.22	7.22	0.81
9	79.48	3.76	0.79	78.51	1.49	0.78	82.78	5.1	0.83	82.53	7.76	0.82
10	80.37	4.8	0.8	77.74	1.59	0.77	83.65	5.51	0.82	82.07	8.48	0.81
11	82.66	5.2	0.82	77.62	1.69	0.77	81.78	6.05	0.81	83.41	9.11	0.83
12	79.77	5.33	0.79	79.28	1.77	0.79	86.29	6.45	0.85	84.9	9.66	0.84
13	79.7	5.9	0.79	81.2	1.84	0.8	83.78	6.87	0.83	82.22	10.68	0.81
14	80.44	5.44	0.8	80.17	2.03	0.79	86.42	7.42	0.86	84.75	11.23	0.84

Acc., accuracy; T.T., training time.

Table 14.7   Comparisons of SI-eSNN and CUDA eSNN for the best value of number of Gaussian receptive fields

Dataset	Size of training data	No. of Gaussian receptive fields (best)	eSNN			CUDA-eSNN		
			Accuracy (%)	Training time (s)	AUC	Accuracy (%)	Training time (s)	AUC
BSE	1,912	9	88.15	5.91	0.88	88.76	1.65	0.88
Nikkei 225	5,092	10	87.12	23.67	0.87	87.12	10.6	0.87
NASDAQ	1,923	7	86.04	5.22	0.86	85.92	1.53	0.86
NIFTY-50	1,353	13	83.76	5.98	0.84	84.45	1.18	0.83
S&P 500	9,591	13	84.71	82.56	0.84	84.74	51.51	0.84
Shanghai Stock Exchange	3,149	11	83.18	12.87	0.82	82.66	5.2	0.83
Dow Jones	1,824	13	81.2	8.53	0.8	81.2	1.84	0.8
NYSE-Amex	3,625	14	86.16	20.09	0.86	86.42	7.42	0.86
DAX Index	4,527	12	84.16	24.05	0.84	84.9	9.66	0.84

Table 14.8 Accuracy and AUC of CUDA-SI-eSNN model using logistic distribution for different stock indices

Datasets	BSE			Nikkei 225			NASDAQ			NIFTY-50			S&P 500		
No. of logistic receptive fields	Acc. (%)	T.T. (s)	AUC	Acc. (%)	T.T. (s)	AUC	Acc. (%)	T.T. (s)	AUC	Acc. (%)	T.T. (s)	AUC	Acc. (%)	T.T. (s)	AUC
3	78.14	0.85	0.78	84.87	3.05	0.84	70.87	0.87	0.71	72.02	0.57	0.72	70.85	8.24	0.7
4	77.53	1.01	0.75	86.98	3.32	0.86	83.98	1.12	0.83	78.23	0.64	0.78	79.68	9.16	0.79
5	79.36	1.12	0.78	81.57	3.7	0.81	83.85	1.11	0.83	82.21	0.68	0.82	84.47	11.01	0.84
6	84.37	1.32	0.84	86.29	4.29	0.86	85.19	1.27	0.84	80.65	0.72	0.8	80.58	12.23	0.8
7	86.81	1.38	0.86	81.57	5.07	0.81	87.37	1.81	0.87	83.24	0.76	0.83	83.09	15.37	0.82
8	85.34	1.55	0.85	86.34	6.45	0.86	86.89	1.52	0.86	81.69	0.79	0.81	85.86	19.97	0.85
9	90.47	1.63	0.9	84.55	7.67	0.84	86.77	1.65	0.86	82.03	0.89	0.82	83.81	24.53	0.83
10	86.81	1.74	0.86	86.66	9.73	0.86	85.8	1.74	0.85	83.93	0.96	0.83	84.28	30.96	0.84
11	89.01	1.78	0.89	85.24	10.59	0.85	87.5	1.85	0.87	81.69	1.02	0.81	85.71	35.78	0.85
12	88.03	1.89	0.88	86.38	11.58	0.86	87.01	1.99	0.86	84.8	1.09	0.84	83.5	41.02	0.83
13	89.13	2.03	0.89	86.52	12.87	0.86	86.16	2.05	0.86	85.14	1.15	0.85	84.54	45.49	0.84
14	87.05	2.08	0.87	86.61	13.87	0.86	86.28	2.19	0.86	84.8	1.18	0.84	85.76	49.69	0.85

Table 14.9 Accuracy and AUC of CUDA-SI-eSNN model using logistic distribution for different stock indices (continued)

No. of logistic receptive fields	Shanghai Stock Exchange			Dow Jones			NYSE-Amex			DAX Index		
	Acc. (%)	T.T. (s)	AUC	Acc. (%)	T.T. (s)	AUC	Acc. (%)	T.T. (s)	AUC	Acc. (%)	T.T. (s)	AUC
3	78.74	1.6	0.78	73.91	0.79	0.73	69.75	2.07	0.69	75.32	2.65	0.74
4	78.88	1.95	0.78	74.8	0.81	0.74	81.59	2.43	0.8	77.94	3.63	0.77
5	77.85	2.54	0.77	78.9	0.86	0.78	81.14	3.14	0.8	85	4.78	0.84
6	81.11	3.03	0.81	78	0.92	0.78	81.85	3.63	0.81	81.04	5.59	0.8
7	80	3.23	0.79	79.66	1.05	0.79	86.16	4.15	0.85	80.47	6.24	0.8
8	79.7	3.49	0.79	81.45	1.27	0.81	82.11	4.59	0.81	82.27	6.82	0.81
9	80.29	3.78	0.8	79.79	1.34	0.79	84.42	4.91	0.84	83.51	7.57	0.83
10	81.92	4.15	0.81	79.79	1.46	0.79	84.23	5.34	0.83	82.63	8.11	0.82
11	83.03	4.53	0.83	82.09	1.63	0.81	84.1	5.79	0.83	84.49	8.83	0.84
12	81.55	4.73	0.81	80.56	1.74	0.8	86.62	6.23	0.85	85.67	9.57	0.85
13	81.03	5.1	0.81	82.99	1.81	0.83	83.91	6.87	0.83	84.23	10.25	0.83
14	82.48	5.41	0.81	81.84	1.97	0.81	85.97	7.14	0.85	84.75	11.07	0.84

Table 14.10 Comparisons of SI-eSNN and CUDA-SI-eSNN for the best value of number of logistic receptive fields

Dataset	Size of training data	No. of logistic receptive fields (best)	eSNN			CUDA-SI-eSNN		
			Accuracy (%)	Training time (s)	AUC	Accuracy (%)	Training time (s)	AUC
BSE	1,912	9	90.04	5.78	0.89	90.47	1.63	0.9
Nikkei 225	5,092	10	86.66	22.17	0.86	86.66	9.73	0.86
NASDAQ	1,923	11	88.14	6.14	0.87	87.5	1.85	0.87
NIFTY-50	1,353	13	84.74	5.65	0.84	85.14	1.15	0.85
S&P 500	9,591	8	85.23	40.83	0.85	85.86	19.97	0.85
Shanghai Stock Exchange	3,149	11	83.85	11.83	0.83	83.03	4.53	0.83
Dow Jones	1,824	13	82.87	5.43	0.83	82.99	1.81	0.83
NYSE-Amex	3,625	12	85.94	19.23	0.85	86.62	6.23	0.85
DAX Index	4,527	12	85.16	23.02	0.85	85.67	9.57	0.85

Table 14.11   p *Values of McNemar test for the pairwise
              comparison of performance of CUDA-SI-eSNN
              with logistic distribution and CUDA-SI-eSNN with
              Gaussian distribution*

Stock indices	p Values
BSE	0.648
Nikkei 225	0.8049
NASDAQ	0.794
NIFTY-50	0.4707
S&P 500	0.2693
SSE	0.0442
DJUS	0.0078
NYSE-Amex	0.0001
DAX Index	0.1257

Table 14.12   *Comparisons of CUDA-SI-eSNN with logistic receptive fields
              and LSTM*

Dataset	Size of training data	CUDA-SI-eSNN No. of logistic receptive fields (best)	Accuracy (%)	LSTM Avg. Acc. of 30 run (LSTM)	Variance (LSTM)
BSE	1,912	9	90.47	88.48	0.041
Nikkei 225	5,092	10	86.66	90.37	0.025
NASDAQ	1,923	11	87.50	86.57	0.82
NIFTY-50	1,353	13	85.14	83.14	0.416
S&P 500	9,591	8	85.86	90.36	0.064
Shanghai Stock Exchange	3,149	11	83.03	87.85	0.129
Dow Jones	1,824	13	82.99	78.01	1.940
NYSE-Amex	3,625	12	86.62	90.57	0.100
DAX Index [1.25pt]	4,527	12	85.67	90.58	0.057

Then the window is slid in time, in order to cover the entire time series, where in each experiment, the composition of the training and test datasets differs.

Some experimental results on using the SW-eSNN model for stock price direction prediction on the nine benchmark stock indices are presented in Figure 14.2. A model is first trained with 60-day data and then tested for 20 days ahead prediction. Subsequently, the predicted result is incorporated in the model and the window is slid by 20 days for next 20 days ahead prediction. The X-axis and Y-axis of the graphs represent window number and AUC score, respectively. From the plots, we can see that the average AUC score of the models over all the benchmark datasets varied between 64% and 70%, and for some months it reached 100%. The manifested fluctuation in prediction accuracy across the different windows is expected with this model because the selected window time may be too short, and stock indices depend on many other exogenous variables such as political, ecological, economic and psychological that are not part of the data.

The average AUC score of SW-eSNN incremental approach for both logistic distribution and Gaussian distribution on all stock indices is presented in Table 14.13. This result shows that SW-eSNN incremental approach with logistic distribution outperformed SW-eSNN incremental approach with Gaussian distribution on all stock indices except on NASDAQ stock index.

The incremental approach of SW-eSNN is beneficial over non-incremental approach as it can adapt to the new data and is best suitable for real-time prediction. The performance can be further improved if the two models of SI-eSNN and SW-eSNN are combined into a new model, here called INC-eSNN that can be implemented in an eSNN as part of a NeuCube architecture [40], shown in Figure 14.3.

In NeuCube, the encoded input data as spike trains are used first to train a 3D reservoir (cube) which provides the input spikes to the output classifier (e.g. eSNN). If the learning rate in the SNNr is set to 0, this model is reduced to an eSNN model as the presynaptic neurons of an eSNN model (see Figure 14.1) from the SNN cube.

Algorithm 3 defines the SW-eSNN model which can be used for a continuous, incremental cumulative predictive learning of stock data, theoretically – in a 'lifelong learning mode'.

Algorithm 3 SW-eSNN learning algorithm

1: Train an eSNN model on the whole existing historical data of a stock till time t (as per Algorithm 1).

2: Recall the model to predict the next month $(t+1)$ stock movement.

3: When the next month results are known, train the model incrementally on this data.

4: Aggregate the output neurons if necessary using the aggregation operator and the *sim* parameter.

5: Evaluate the classification error and the AUC so far.

6: Optimize parameters to improve future time accuracy.

14.8   Gaussian receptive fields influence

If we choose the Gaussian receptive fields as encoding method, the design parameters that take part into the neural encoding are only two: N, the number of receptive fields for each feature, and β, a constant that is inversely proportional to

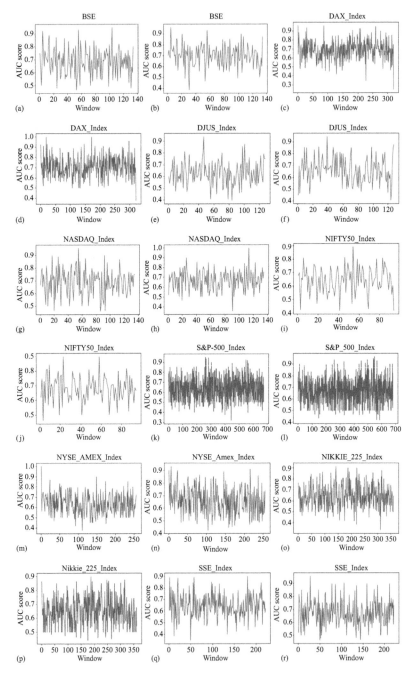

Figure 14.2   Performance of sliding window eSNN (SW-eSNN). GD and LD refer to Gaussian and logistic distributions. (a) BSE(GD) (b) BSE(LD) (c) DAX (GD), (d) DAX(LD) (e) DJUS(GD) (f) DJUS(LD), (g) NASDAQ(GD) (h) NASDAQ(LD) (i) NIFTY-50(GD), (j) NIFTY-50(LD) (k) S&P 500 (GD) (l) S&P 500(LD), (m) NYSE(GD) (n) NYSE(LD) (o) Nikkei 225 (GD), (p) Nikkei 225(LD) (q) SSE(GD) (r) SSE(LD)

Table 14.13   *Average AUC score of SW-eSNN incremental approach using both*
                 logistic and Gaussian distributions

Dataset	eSNN with logistic distribution			eSNN with Gaussian distribution		
	Min. AUC	Max. AUC	Average AUC	Min. AUC	Max. AUC	Average AUC
BSE	0.38	0.96	0.69	0.46	0.95	0.68
Nikkei 225	0.44	0.90	0.64	0.33	0.91	0.64
NASDAQ	0.35	1.00	0.67	0.45	0.95	0.69
NIFTY-50	0.46	0.90	0.68	0.41	0.89	0.64
S&P 500	0.41	0.96	0.67	0.31	0.95	0.63
Shanghai Stock Exchange	0.46	0.95	0.67	0.34	0.89	0.64
Dow Jones	0.40	0.94	0.65	0.39	0.93	0.62
NYSE-Amex	0.42	0.93	0.65	0.37	1.0	0.63
DAX Index	0.37	1.00	0.70	0.25	0.96	0.68

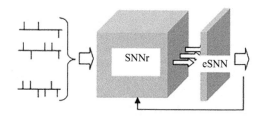

Figure 14.3   A block diagram of NeuCube (from [40])

the width of each field. The influence of these parameters over the performance of
the whole eSNN could be more than $\pm 10\%$.

As [10,39,47,48] explain, when smaller feature values are encoded, the first
neuron to spike tends towards the lower end of the receptive set, and when higher
values are encoded the first neuron to spike tends towards the higher end of the
receptive set. Thus, the receptive fields could be interpreted as a block of neurons
that detect if the feature value is into one of N equally wide range of values. For
example, if N is 3, the range of values from I_{min} to I_{max} could be highly identified
with a field meaning 'low', 'medium' or 'high', or a combination of them.

Some recommended values for the parameters are as follows: there are no
constraints on N but according to [47], the constant β should be in the range of
values $1 \leq \beta \leq 2$. Reference [48] recommends a value of 1.5.

As an example, in Figure 14.4 we can see our results for different N and β
values over BSE dataset. The best AUC score value of 90.50% is achieved with
$N = 17, \beta = 1.05$ and we get very good performances even for $\beta < 1$ that are out
of the literature's recommended range.

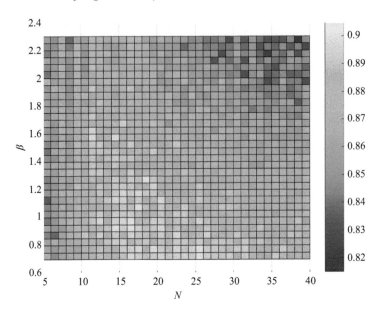

Figure 14.4   AUC score with Gaussian receptive fields over BSE dataset

14.9   Conclusion and future directions

In this study, for stock movement prediction task, we proposed three variants of the eSNNs: a technical indicator model, SI-eSNN; a parallel model on a GPU machine, CUDA-SI-eSNN; and a SW model for incremental learning, SW-eSNN. In all these models, we also proposed logistic distribution in place of Gaussian distribution in characterizing the receptive fields. These three models are applied for stock price direction prediction of nine stock indices: BSE, NASDAQ, Nikkei 225, NIFTY-50, S&P 500, Dow Jones, NYSE-Amex, Shanghai Stock Exchange and DAX Index. For the first two models, the training and testing ratio was 70:30, that is 70% of the data were used for training a model and 30% of the data for testing. Thirteen technical indicators were used as input variables (as shown in Table 14.2), and the daily vectors for the various stock indexes were between 2,000 and 14,000 days. For the incremental SW-eSNN model, the model was trained with 1-year stock market data to predict the following 1-month stock indices, with an SW time of 1 month. The calculated average accuracies were between 65% and 80%. For improved incremental learning, a new algorithm and model is proposed for future exploration, called INC-eSNN, as part of a comprehensive SNN architecture NeuCube [40].

Also, we have done a preliminary analysis using one stock, BSE, while changing the β and N values, an overall accuracy of 90% was achieved. Though this number seems to be relatively good compared to the achieved ones, more research is needed to see why such a huge difference in results was achieved.

The challenging question is related with the values that should be taken to tune the Gaussian receptive fields. Some new ranges could improve the performance of the system.

Further, a comparison of the proposed model with a deep learning network, LSTM, resulted in mixed and inconclusive results.

In the future, we would like to scale up this model in NVIDIA Tesla K-40 (PARAM SHAVAK Super Computer) to detect the trend of big data time series stock indices in real time. One can also explore the development of Spark-based evolving spiking network model to scale out in cluster environment to predict the trend of big data stock indices. Also, one can detect and model the chaos present in the stock index data; if present, use the lagged variables resulting from the state-space representation along with the technical indicators and invoke the classifiers proposed in this study along with Gaussian and logistic receptive fields and technical indicators. A recent study reported the modelling of chaos in financial time series followed by forecasting with NNs [49] that resulted in a very good prediction.

As this is the first study on using eSNN for successful stock movement prediction, we expect that this will open the field for future research towards building autonomous trading systems.

References

[1] Abu-Mostafa YS and Atiya AF. Introduction to financial forecasting. Applied Intelligence. 1996;6(3):205–213.

[2] Tan TZ, Quek C, and Ng GS. Brain-inspired genetic complementary learning for stock market prediction. In: Evolutionary Computation, 2005. The 2005 IEEE Congress on. vol. 3. IEEE; 2005. p. 2653–2660.

[3] Patel J, Shah S, Thakkar P, *et al.* Predicting stock and stock price index movement using trend deterministic data preparation and machine learning techniques. Expert Systems with Applications. 2015;42(1):259–268.

[4] Kim K and Han I. Genetic algorithms approach to feature discretization in artificial neural networks for the prediction of stock price index. Expert Systems with Applications. 2000;19(2):125–132.

[5] Kim K. Financial time series forecasting using support vector machines. Neurocomputing. 2003;55(1):307–319.

[6] Huang W, Nakamori Y, and Wang SY. Forecasting stock market movement direction with support vector machine. Computers & Operations Research. 2005;32(10):2513–2522.

[7] Ballings M, Van den Poel D, Hespeels N, *et al.* Evaluating multiple classifiers for stock price direction prediction. Expert Systems with Applications. 2015;42(20):7046–7056.

[8] Zhang X, Li A, and Pan R. Stock trend prediction based on a new status box method and AdaBoost probabilistic support vector machine. Applied Soft Computing. 2016;49:385–398.

[9] Wysoski SG, Benuskova L, and Kasabov N. Adaptive learning procedure for a network of spiking neurons and visual pattern recognition. In: International Conference on Advanced Concepts for Intelligent Vision Systems. Springer; 2006. p. 1133–1142.

[10] Soltic S and Kasabov N. Knowledge extraction from evolving spiking neural networks with rank order population coding. International Journal of Neural Systems. 2010;20(06):437–445.

[11] Kasabov NK. Evolving connectionist systems for adaptive learning and knowledge discovery: Trends and directions. Knowledge-Based Systems. 2015;80:24–33.

[12] Wysoski S, Benuskova L, and Kasabov N. Adaptive spiking neural networks for audiovisual pattern recognition. In: Neural Information Processing. Springer-Verlag Berlin Heidelberg: Springer; 2008. p. 406–415.

[13] Arya AS, Ravi V, Tejasviram V, *et al.* Cyber fraud detection using evolving spiking neural network. In: Industrial and Information Systems (ICIIS), 2016 11th International Conference on. IEEE; 2016. p. 263–268.

[14] Sengupta N, Ramos JIE, Tu E, *et al.* In: Sgurev V, Piuri V, and Jotsov V, editors. From von Neumann Architecture and Atanasoff's ABC to Neuro-Morphic Computation and Kasabov's NeuCube: Principles and Implementations. Cham: Springer International Publishing; 2018. p. 1–28.

[15] Gholami Doborjeh M, Gholami Doborjeh Z, Gollahalli AR, *et al.* In: Sgurev V, Jotsov V, and Kacprzyk J, editors. From von Neumann Architecture and Atanasoff's ABC to Neuromorphic Computation and Kasabov's NeuCube. Part II: Applications. Cham: Springer International Publishing; 2018. p. 17–36.

[16] NSE – National Stock Exchange of India Ltd. www.nseindia.com/products/ content/equities\\/indices/historical_index_data.htm.

[17] Chiou Y, Liu S, and Tsaih R. Applying reasoning neural networks to the analysis and forecast of Taiwan's stock index variation. Taipei Economics Inquiry, Taipei. 1996;34(2):171–200.

[18] Tsaih R, Hsu Y, and Lai CC. Forecasting S&P 500 stock index futures with a hybrid AI system. Decision Support Systems. 1998;23(2):161–174.

[19] Saad EW, Prokhorov DV, and Wunsch DC. Comparative study of stock trend prediction using time delay, recurrent and probabilistic neural networks. IEEE Transactions on Neural Networks. 1998;9(6):1456–1470.

[20] Ou P and Wang H. Prediction of stock market index movement by ten data mining techniques. Modern Applied Science. 2009;3(12):28.

[21] Freund Y and Schapire RE. A decision-theoretic generalization of on-line learning and an application to boosting. In: European Conference on Computational Learning Theory. Springer; 1995. p. 23–37.

[22] Breiman L. Random forests. Machine Learning. 2001;45(1):5–32.

[23] Ballings M and Van den Poel D. Kernel Factory: An ensemble of kernel machines. Expert Systems with Applications. 2013;40(8):2904–2913.

[24] Hochreiter S and Schmidhuber J. Long short-term memory. Neural Computing. 1997;9(8):1735–1780. Available from: http://dx.doi.org/10.1162/ neco.1997.9.8.1735.

[25] Kim K and Lee WB. Stock market prediction using artificial neural networks with optimal feature transformation. Neural Computing & Applications. 2004;13(3):255–260.

[26] Kumar M and Thenmozhi M. Forecasting stock index movement: A comparison of support vector machines and random forest. 2006.

[27] Huang CJ, Yang DX, and Chuang YT. Application of wrapper approach and composite classifier to the stock trend prediction. Expert Systems with Applications. 2008;34(4):2870–2878.

[28] Zhang Y and Wu L. Stock market prediction of S&P 500 via combination of improved BCO approach and BP neural network. Expert Systems with Applications. 2009;36(5):8849–8854.

[29] Mostafa MM. Forecasting stock exchange movements using neural networks: Empirical evidence from Kuwait. Expert Systems with Applications. 2010;37(9):6302–6309.

[30] Nair BB, Mohandas V, and Sakthivel N. A decision tree—rough set hybrid system for stock market trend prediction. International Journal of Computer Applications. 2010;6(9):1–6.

[31] Kara Y, Boyacioglu MA, and Baykan ÖK. Predicting direction of stock price index movement using artificial neural networks and support vector machines: The sample of the Istanbul Stock Exchange. Expert systems with Applications. 2011;38(5):5311–5319.

[32] Chang PC, Wang DD, and Zhou CL. A novel model by evolving partially connected neural network for stock price trend forecasting. Expert Systems with Applications. 2012;39(1):611–620. Available from: https://doi.org/10.1016/j.eswa.2011.07.051.

[33] Lin Y, Guo H, and Hu J. An SVM-based approach for stock market trend prediction. In: Neural Networks (IJCNN), The 2013 International Joint Conference on. IEEE; 2013. p. 1–7.

[34] de Oliveira FA, Nobre CN, and Zárate LE. Applying artificial neural networks to prediction of stock price and improvement of the directional prediction index – Case study of PETR4, Petrobras, Brazil. Expert Systems with Applications. 2013;40(18):7596–7606.

[35] Wang Y. Stock price direction prediction by directly using prices data: An empirical study on the KOSPI and HSI. International Journal of Business Intelligence and Data Mining. 2014;9(2):145–160.

[36] Bisoi R and Dash PK. A hybrid evolutionary dynamic neural network for stock market trend analysis and prediction using unscented Kalman filter. Applied Soft Computing. 2014;19:41–56.

[37] Hafezi R, Shahrabi J, and Hadavandi E. A bat-neural network multi-agent system (BNNMAS) for stock price prediction: Case study of DAX stock price. Applied Soft Computing. 2015;29:196–210.

[38] Gerstner W and Kistler WM. Spiking neuron models: Single neurons, populations, plasticity. Cambridge, UK: Cambridge University Press; 2002.

[39] Kasabov N. Evolving connectionist systems: the knowledge engineering approach. Springer Science & Business Media; 2007.

[40] Kasabov N, Scott N, Tu E, *et al.* Design methodology and selected applications of evolving spatio-temporal data machines in the NeuCube neuromorphic framework. Neural Networks. 2016;78:1–14. Available from: https://doi.org/10.1016/j.neunet.2015.09.011.

[41] Thorpe SJ and Gautrais J. Rapid visual processing using spike asynchrony. In: Advances in Neural Information Processing Systems. 1997. p. 901–907.

[42] Bohte SM, Kok JN, and La Poutre H. Error-backpropagation in temporally encoded networks of spiking neurons. Neurocomputing. 2002;48(1):17–37.

[43] Schliebs S, Defoin-Platel M, Worner S, and Kasabov N. Integrated feature and parameter optimization for an evolving spiking neural network: Exploring heterogeneous probabilistic models. Neural Networks. 2009;22(5–6):623–632. Available from: https://doi.org/10.1016/j.neunet.2009.06.038.

[44] Quandl Financial, Economic and Alternative Data. www.quandl.com/.

[45] Historical – Indices. www.bseindia.com/indices \\/IndexArchiveData.aspx.

[46] Farquad M, Ravi V, and Raju SB. Analytical CRM in banking and finance using SVM: A modified active learning-based rule extraction approach. International Journal of Electronic Customer Relationship Management. 2012;6(1):48–73.

[47] Schliebs S and Kasabov N. Computational modeling with Spiking Neural Networks. In: Kasabov N, editor. Springer Handbook of Bio-/neuroinformatics. Berlin, Heidelberg: Springer; 2014. p. 625–646.

[48] Bohte SM, Poutre HL, and Kok JN. Unsupervised clustering with spiking neurons by sparse temporal coding and multilayer RBF networks. IEEE Transactions on Neural Networks. 2002;13(2):426–435.

[49] Ravi V, Pradeepkumar D, and Deb K. Financial time series prediction using hybrids of chaos theory, multi-layer perceptron and multi-objective evolutionary algorithms. Swarm and Evolutionary Computation. 2017;36:136–149.

Chapter 15

Parallel hierarchical clustering of big text corpora

Karthick Seshadri[1]

Clustering is a technique that facilitates unsupervised learning of patterns or groups among entities in any application domain. This technique has critical and notable applications in information retrieval, image processing, web mining, computational biology, network security, recommender systems and social network analytics to quote a few. Typically, clustering algorithms are iterative in nature and are designed to operate on huge application datasets. This results in prohibitively excessive demand on computational and storage resources that cannot be met using a single workstation processor. Keeping in mind the advances in parallel processing systems like multicore systems, distributed cluster computers, graphic processing units and programming platforms like Open Multi-Processing (OpenMP), Hadoop, Compute Unified Device Architecture (CUDA) and Message Passing Interface (MPI), it is imperative to design algorithms for tackling the compute and storage demands by applications involving huge datasets. In the recent past, much seminal advancement has been made in the field of parallel clustering algorithms. In this chapter, we highlight seminal research attempts and attempt to weave a timeline illustrating the developments in this happening field with an inference of the pros and cons of each of the proposed algorithms and some open research problems. This is likely to be useful for newbie researchers who would want to pursue their research in designing and analyzing parallel algorithms for clustering.

We begin by emphasizing the significance of designing parallel algorithms for the hierarchical clustering of large-scale text collections. Some of the key challenges involved and the related seminal research attempts are presented in this chapter with a subsequent enlisting of the open research problems.

15.1 Introduction

Due to the rate of information proliferation on the web, it is becoming very difficult for the users to search for the needed information and for the content curators to

[1]Department of Computer Science and Engineering, National Institute of Technology Andhra Pradesh, Tadepalligudem, India

organize information into categories and to identify the category to which a new document belongs. Document directories contain categories of similar documents and help in managing the information explosion on the web. There are several content directories available like Wikipedia (Source: www.wikipedia.org), DMOZ (Source: www.dmoz.org) and Yahoo! (Source: in.yahoo.com) that are developed and maintained through manual and semiautomated mechanisms. This mode of organizing the document directories is prone to error and demands domain knowledge and expertise from the human editors maintaining these directories. Further, with the rapid growth of these content directories, it has become prohibitively time-consuming for the editors to organize and incrementally maintain these directories, keeping in pace with the information explosion. Hence, it is highly desirable to develop automated mechanisms to organize these directories and to transition the supervised algorithms to make them unsupervised or semisupervised. Designing unsupervised clustering algorithms is a challenge due to the semi-structured nature of the textual documents. We recognize a partial structure in terms of the paragraphs, sentences and words; however, unlike tabular databases, no assumptions can be made regarding the order of occurrence of these textual blocks as the order typically varies across various documents. Clustering algorithms can be employed to group similar documents in a web-directory. In other words, given a corpus of unlabeled documents, clustering can label the documents and segment the corpus into cohesive groups, without any training samples. The groups are expected to be formed in such a way that any pair of documents in the corpus belongs to the same group if the documents are similar to each other with respect to a similarity measure and any dissimilar pair of documents belongs to different groups [1].

Typical text-clustering algorithms work on a vector representation of documents that needs to be stored in the main memory to infer document groupings. Even with about a million documents in the corpus and a few thousand unique terms across these documents, it arguably stretches the memory limits available on a single workstation processor [2]. The amount of information in the web is growing everyday with the evolution of new technologies and web portals like Wikipedia, Instagram, Yahoo!, Facebook, Twitter and Google. Such web-scale datasets pose a nontrivial problem to clustering algorithms, in the form of the time and space complexity needs of the algorithm. An important aspect of these unsupervised-learning algorithms that is detrimental to their performance is that, a majority of them are iterative in nature and might run for thousands of iterations before convergence. Though we relax the memory constraint and assume that enough memory is available on a single workstation, the existing sequential text-clustering algorithms might run for a prohibitively long time on a single-processor before emitting any useful grouping [2].

With the advent of novel parallel processing platforms like MPI, OpenMP, CUDA and Hadoop, there is a natural requirement to exploit the available processing power of the underlying parallel computer (multicore, graphics processing units (GPU) and cluster of compute nodes). Hence, there need to port state-of-the-art sequential text-clustering algorithms to their parallel variants to make these algorithms run on web-scale corpuses and to speed them up. Even for document sets that are not web-scale, their processing can be sped up considerably by using parallel variants of the algorithms and the cluster hierarchy constructed can be used for online applications. The arguments cited previously establish a compelling case for designing and analyzing text-clustering algorithms for large-scale corpuses. The case is further supported by the arrival of new parallel computing facilities at the architecture level. Hence, there is a necessity for refactoring sequential algorithms to their parallel counterparts and/or devising new algorithms that can exploit the features of the underlying parallel platform to enhance performance.

Depending upon the nature of the clusters generated by a clustering algorithm, it can be designated as either *flat* or *hierarchical*. A flat-clustering algorithm is one that produces just a set of unordered clusters or groups given a corpus of unlabeled documents as the input. A hierarchical clustering algorithm, on the other hand, produces a hierarchy of clusters, in which we find sets of clusters arranged level-by-level in the hierarchy from the root till the leaf level. The clusters that are part of the same level are to some extent considered to be of the same topical abstraction. Clusters that belong to the adjacent levels are related by a *parent–child* relationship. For example, if the root level contains two clusters on "Music" and "Sports," the next level may contain subtopics of these root topics like "Classical," "Pop" for "Music" and "Cricket," "Baseball" for "Sports." "Classical" and "Pop" are the child clusters of the "Music" cluster, while "Cricket" and "Baseball" are the children of "Sports." In the next level, these child clusters may be subdivided further. It is desirable to infer a hierarchy of clusters while organizing a corpus into a content directory, which can be achieved by an application of a hierarchical clustering algorithm on the corpus. However, hierarchical clustering algorithms are computationally more demanding than the flat-clustering algorithms and hence it is important to parallelize hierarchical document-clustering algorithms to make them scalable when applied on large-scale text collections.

We review the seminal research attempts that help in the design of computationally usable and scalable hierarchical clustering algorithms to automatically organize large-scale text collections like Wikipedia. The major objectives to be achieved toward designing such algorithms are the following:

1. Designing scalable parallel hierarchical document-clustering algorithms for hierarchically organizing large-scale text collections.
2. Analyzing the performance of the proposed parallel hierarchical document-clustering algorithms in terms of the cluster quality, time complexity, space complexity and communication complexity.

The abovementioned major objectives can be achieved by realizing the following sub-objectives:

1. To adapt and parallelize intelligent sequential algorithms for the hierarchical clustering of text documents.
2. To generalize and subsequently parallelize flat-clustering algorithms and enable them to infer a hierarchy of document clusters instead of a flat set of clusters.

3. To explore the possibility of designing and parallelizing hybrid document-clustering algorithms employing complementary and mutually beneficial computational techniques.
4. To propose parallel algorithms based on topic models, for generating probabilistic clusters, for dealing with large collections of lengthy documents.
5. To develop theoretical complexity estimates for characterizing the runtime, space and communication requirements of the proposed algorithms.
6. To design experiments to empirically evaluate and compare the proposed parallel algorithms with respect to the quality of their output hierarchy and running time.

As the focus is more on parallelization and designing algorithms for hierarchical clustering of text documents, this chapter hosts two sections, one each for outlining the related research attempts in (i) designing parallel clustering algorithms and (ii) application of such algorithms to the document-clustering problem. In the recent past, much seminal advancements have been made in the field of parallel clustering algorithms. In the next section, we highlight few representative research attempts and weave a timeline illustrating the developments in this happening field with an inference of the merits and demerits of each of the proposed algorithms and some open research challenges. A variety of clustering algorithms exist and each one has its unique set of pros and cons. Many parallel clustering algorithms have been proposed in the recent past that either are entirely new parallel algorithms or are adapted versions of existing sequential algorithms.

Throughout the subsequent discussions in this chapter, we call the number of clusters/patterns as k, the number of processors as p, the number of features as f, the number of threads as t and the number of data points as n. Figure 15.1 [3] highlights the taxonomy of clustering algorithms, with a clear positioning of this field under

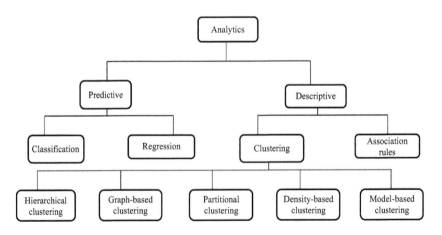

Figure 15.1   Clustering taxonomy

the broad domain of analytics. In the following sections, we have grouped the research attempts in the domain of parallel clustering algorithms depending upon the following factors:

1. nature of the clusters generated (hierarchical or flat, overlapping or nonoverlapping);
2. clustering methodology (agglomerative, divisive, density-based, model-based, probabilistic, graph-based, spectral based, etc.);
3. the platform that is used for parallelization (shared memory or distributed memory, single instruction–stream multiple data–stream (SIMD) or multiple instruction–stream multiple data–stream (MIMD), etc.).

15.2 Parallel hierarchical clustering algorithms

Hierarchical clustering algorithms are known to be computationally intensive and generate a hierarchy of clusters from a given set of data points. There have been numerous research attempts in parallelizing hierarchical clustering algorithms and some of the prominent attempts are highlighted in this section. Li proposed a parallel hierarchical clustering algorithm suitable for an SIMD computer and a method for subsequently computing the cluster validity [4]. In order to reduce the per-processor storage and compute demands, the author proposes a generic way of parallel storage of the similarity/distance matrix and the matrix that keeps track of the clusters inferred. A parallel memory system and an alignment network facilitate this parallel storage and access. The parallel algorithm runs in $O(p^2)$, whereas the sequential algorithm has an order of cubic time (assuming that the number of patterns to be inferred (k) is the same as the number of processors (p)). The parallel storage and access logic proposed in this work is generic enough and can be applied while designing other pattern recognition algorithms. The author has derived separate conditional time-complexity expressions for characterizing the behavior of this algorithm when the number of patterns $k < p$ and $k > p$.

The parallel algorithm proposed by Dahlhaus has two sub-algorithms and is based on computing a minimum spanning tree (MST) of a graph in parallel across multiple processors that amounts to executing a single-linkage clustering algorithm and subsequently identifying the overlapping clusters using parallel prefix-computation in $O(\log n)$ time [5]. Garg *et al.* proposed a parallel version of the balanced iterative reducing and clustering using hierarchies algorithm that exploits a distributed shared-nothing memory Network of Workstations (NoWs) using message-passing [6]. Data is split into equal chunks and every processor operates on the chunk assigned to it and builds a cluster-feature tree, which is a concise representation of the clusters present in the data chunk. A local clustering is performed per processor, which is followed by a global-clustering phase to compute the global mean. The local clustering followed by the global-mean computation repeats until convergence.

15.2.1   Agglomerative clustering

Agglomerative algorithms typically operate on disjoint partitions of data points and generate a set of local clusters that are then merged to form a global cluster set. A parallel hierarchical clustering algorithm suitable for shared memory parallel computers like multicore processors was proposed in [7]. The algorithm divides the dataset into a number of chunks and a dendrogram is constructed for each chunk by using a single-linkage agglomerative construction. Pairs of dendrogram are then assigned to OpenMP threads and are concurrently merged to produce a final dendrogram. Experimental results suggest that the algorithm realizes a speedup of 18–20 on a processor with 36 cores. A distributed version of Hendrix's algorithm called *PINK* was proposed by [8]. Timón *et al.* proposed a parallelization technique for the sequential fuzzy minimals clustering algorithm. Once the clusters are obtained using the parallel algorithm, the authors [9] construct a dendrogram by applying a hierarchical clustering technique. Empirical results suggest that the parallel algorithm achieves a significant speedup at the same time yielding better quality clusters as compared to its sequential variant.

15.2.2   Graph-based clustering

Graph-based clustering (GBC) algorithms are very popular and adopt different clustering strategies based on the class to which a graph belongs. In typical GBC algorithms, vertices represent the data items to be clustered and edges represent the association between data items with the corresponding edge-weights indicating the strength of the association. Graph clustering, especially parallel-graph clustering normally boils down to addressing the following subproblems: (i) identification of subgraphs with a minimum diameter and hence intra-cluster distances; (ii) identification of influential nodes in the graph around which to cluster the rest of the nodes. These influential nodes could be defined differently depending upon the application at hand. One such definition could be the nodes with a relatively higher number of edges incident on them as compared to the other nodes and (iii) in some cases, to identify tight clusters, some researchers use the notion of a clique or its weighted variant that naturally suggests the presence of a cluster [10].

Tsui *et al.* proposed a parallel algorithm with an objective to address the scalability problem when clustering large datasets. The dataset is partitioned into multiple chunks and an MST is computed for each chunk in parallel by the processing elements. The MSTs are then merged using the GBC method that also determines the optimal number of clusters to form. Once the initial sets of merged clusters are formed, the algorithm refactors the clustering arrangement by introducing better intercluster edges, obtains a better MST and hence a better set of clusters [11].

A parallel multilevel multi-threaded algorithm was proposed by LaSalle and Karypis in which the authors construct a series of coarser/smaller graphs from the given graph. The smallest graph in the series of the graphs is clustered using any modularity maximization–based iterative clustering technique and the clusters of the smallest graph are then projected to the next graphs in the series and finally

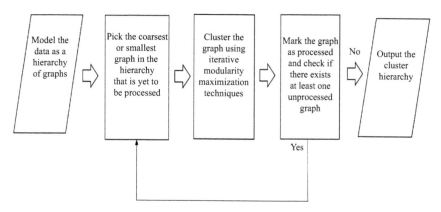

Figure 15.2   Multilevel clustering algorithms

clusters of the original graph are obtained. The authors have released a clustering tool called Nerstrand that is shown to cluster a graph with multimillion vertices and billions of edges in just under two minutes [12]. The methodology adopted by typical multilevel clustering algorithms is depicted in Figure 15.2.

15.2.3   *Partitional clustering algorithms*

Partitioning algorithms operate by considering all the data points as belonging to a single cluster and recursively splitting the cluster to obtain sub-clusters. *K*-Means is a popular algorithm that belongs to this category. Judd *et al.* proposed a data-parallel version of the *K*-means clustering algorithm that comprises two passes: (i) in the first pass the master node splits the dataset into equal subsets and assigns each subset to a slave node. Every slave node executes the *K*-means clustering algorithm on the subset assigned to it and reports the cluster results to the master node. (ii) In the second pass, called a "forcing-pass," pair-wise cluster merging takes place to refine the set of clusters obtained in the first pass. Empirical evaluations done on a standard texture image dataset using a NoWs yielded a reduction of 96% of computations that would otherwise happen in a standard *K*-means algorithm without the following three-fold optimization [13].

A "guaranteed-assignment-sphere" is defined around the centroid of each cluster. The points falling within this sphere are presumed to belong to its host cluster and are not considered for cluster reassignments. If the contents of a cluster do not change across successive passes, then the cluster is assumed to have converged and the points belonging to the cluster are subsequently not considered for any further cluster reassignments. Every data subset has a partial sum stored along with it that characterizes the quality of clusters inferred. If there is any change in cluster membership, only the incremental changes are accounted for, by adding or subtracting an appropriate distance value from the partial sum. This reduces redundant computations.

A parallel version of the *K*-means algorithm was proposed by Kantabutra and Couch to tackle the scalability limitation with the *K*-means algorithm when applied to data points in vector spaces spanned by a large number of dimensions. A designated master processor in a NoWs, splits the dataset into k chunks and assigns each chunk to a single-slave processor. The slave processors then compute the centroids of the respective data chunks and broadcast the chunk centroids to all the processors in the NoWs. Each slave processor then computes the new closest chunk to which each of the chunk members are to be reassigned to, by computing the distance between the chunk point and the chunk centroids. The master announces the start of the next iteration with k new chunks with reassigned chunk points. These parallel iterations continue for a prespecified number of times say i. The time complexity of this approach is reported to be $O(2ik(n/p))$ and showcases an improvement of $O(k/2)$ over the then contemporary parallel versions of the K-means algorithm [14].

The K-means algorithm was parallelized in the work done in [15]. It is done by allocating n/p data points per processor and assigning the task of computing distances for these n/p points to the host processor. This parallelizes the compute-heavy distance calculations. The algorithm was implemented using the MPI framework to achieve a single program multiple data stream parallel operational mode. Empirical evaluation of the algorithm shows a good speedup over the sequential K-means. Forman and Zhang presented a scalable distributed-clustering framework for parallelizing centroid-based clustering algorithms like K-means, K-harmonic-means and expectation–maximization-based fuzzy-clustering algorithms [16]. The key contribution of Forman's framework is the transfer of only a small-sized set of statistics between processors that are used for computing the value of a performance function, which is optimized with respect to the k centroids and the set of data points. The algorithm is theoretically shown to produce the same set of clusters as that of the sequential clustering algorithm and achieves a good speedup when compared to the sequential variants.

A parallelized version of the infamous spatial clustering algorithm "Clustering Large Applications based upon Randomized Search" (CLARANS) was proposed in [17]. The algorithm was implemented using the parallel virtual machine (PVM) framework. It was empirically found to achieve a considerable speedup over the sequential CLARANS variant.

15.2.4   Parallel clustering on SIMD/MIMD machines

Many research attempts in parallelizing clustering algorithms, assume an underlying parallel model of computation. These algorithms are amenable to be implemented on top of specific models like SIMD, MIMD, shared-memory, and distributed-memory parallel processing. Feng *et al.* proposed a parallel algorithm that is amenable to be implemented on top of a cluster of commodity workstations. The key highlight of the algorithm is its ability to leverage the distributed compute power available across commodity machines. Feng's algorithm achieves a better speedup and scalability without compromising the quality of the clusters generated [18]. Pizzuti and Talia proposed a parallel version of a Bayesian-based clustering algorithm called "AutoClass" to be run on MIMD machines. A key highlight of the algorithm is that it performs load balancing of tasks so that all the processors in the multi-computer perform an approximately same amount of work. The authors [19] assert the performance of the proposed algorithm by benchmarking it against the sequential AutoClass algorithm.

A clustering algorithm suitable to be run on a hypercube multi-computer was proposed in [20]. The algorithm extensively makes use of an objective function that minimizes the sum-of-squared distances between the centroids of clusters and the members of a cluster. Initially a random set of k cluster centroids are selected and the cluster membership and the cluster centroids are iteratively updated. This updating is guided by a greedy objective function that attempts to minimize the intra-cluster distance measured using the sum-of-squared distances mentioned previously. Depending upon whether the hypercube network consists of fn processors or fnk, the running time of this algorithm is $O(k + \log(nf))$ or $O(\log(fnk))$, respectively.

Typically, while designing algorithms for SIMD/MIMD machines designers need to check for the cost optimality of the parallel algorithms. Cost optimality is attained when the time complexity of the parallel algorithm when scaled by p is lesser than the time complexity of the best known sequential algorithm that solves the same problem.

15.2.5 Density-based clustering algorithms

A parallel version of the density-based spatial clustering of applications with noise (PDBSCAN) was proposed in [21]. DBSCAN algorithm infers clusters on the basis of the density of the data points in a vector space and can detect arbitrarily shaped clusters very naturally. PDBSCAN uses a distributed spatial index called the dR^* tree to enable faster distributed access to data points. It involves three steps: (i) master processor splits the dataset into subsets and each subset is assigned to a slave processor; (ii) slave processors apply the DBSCAN algorithm on the local subset and infer clusters and (iii) the local clusters are then combined to infer a global set of clusters. An empirical evaluation of the PDBSCAN algorithm shows a near-linear speedup over DBSCAN and scales well with the number of processors and the input size.

Patwary *et al.* proposed a parallelization to the DBSCAN algorithm by exploiting a graph-theoretic strategy using the disjoint set data structure. The algorithm's main goal was to even out the workload across the parallel processing elements and to overcome the typical load imbalance seen in the master–slave parallelization strategies. To achieve this effect, the authors employ a bottom-up strategy for forming clusters using trees. Empirical evaluation reveals a significant speedup over the sequential DBSCAN algorithm on both shared memory and distributed memory multi-computers [22].

15.2.6 Transform-based clustering

Yildirim and Zdogan proposed a parallel clustering algorithm to parallelize an existing sequential-clustering algorithm on the basis of wavelet transforms. The authors [23] designed the algorithm such that the memory footprint per processor and the amount of communication between processors are kept to a minimal extent to enhance the efficiency of the proposed algorithm. The algorithm was implemented on a distributed memory multi-computer that uses MPI for communication and is shown to achieve a significant speedup over its sequential counterpart.

15.2.7   Grid-based clustering

A parallel algorithm to cluster massive datasets containing varying multiple-density regions was proposed in the work done by [24]. The data points are projected onto a grid, and a spatial-partition tree is built. The algorithm exploits data parallelism and forms local clusters using a metric based on the cohesion of the data points falling within a grid. The local clusters are subsequently merged to form global clusters. Empirical evaluation of the parallel algorithm on real and synthetic datasets suggests that the algorithm achieves a near-linear speedup and scales well.

15.2.8   Evolutionary clustering

Clustering algorithms based on evolutionary strategies like genetic algorithm, swarm optimization and ant-colony optimization are arguably easy to parallelize. Babu and Murty proposed parallel evolutionary algorithms, adopting a parallelization strategy on the basis of "master–slave" techniques, where a single-master processor coordinates and controls parallel iterations across multiple–slave processors. The technique adopted by these evolutionary algorithms is to optimize the clustering objective function on the basis of evolutionary techniques through selection, crossover and mutation of individuals representing a set of clusters. The master processor executes the selection operation among parent individuals and feeds the slave processors with the subset of selected parent individuals. The slave processors execute the mutation and crossover operations, compute the objective function on the new population, and feed the new individuals to the master processor. The master processor initiates parallel iterations until the quality of the clusters found, converges to either global optimum or a local optima [25].

Cui *et al.* proposed a parallel clustering algorithm suitable to be run using CUDA on GPUs. The algorithm is nature inspired and is based on multispecies flocking to group similar data points into a cluster. Empirical evaluation of the algorithm revealed that the algorithm achieved a considerable speedup when run on GPUs over uniprocessor systems [26].

15.2.9   Spectral clustering

A parallelization strategy for the power iteration clustering (PIC) algorithm was proposed in the work done by [27]. The objective of this parallelization was to scale the PIC algorithm to large datasets, especially when the similarity matrix could not be fit into the main memory available on a single workstation. The algorithm exploits data parallelism by splitting the similarity matrix across processors and by computing the vector subspace in which the data points are to be projected and subsequently clustered. A key highlight of the algorithm's design is that it is amenable to be implemented on top of a cluster of commodity machines and achieves a significant speedup over the sequential PIC algorithm.

15.2.10   Latent model-based clustering

An earlier work by Seshadri and Iyer [28] proposed a parallelization strategy for a latent semantic indexing–based clustering algorithm. The algorithm has been implemented on both a cluster of workstations interconnected by a local area network (LAN) and a multicore machine. A set of documents is split equally among processing elements and each processor applies singular value decomposition (SVD) on the document–term affinity matrix to reveal the dominant eigen vectors and values. A subspace spanned by the dominant eigen vectors is then constructed and the documents are projected onto this subspace and clustered using an MST-based clustering technique. These local clusters are then merged in parallel by applying the SVD clustering technique on the centroids of the local clusters. If any two centroids fall under the same cluster, then the clusters corresponding to the two centroids are merged.

15.3   Parallel document clustering algorithms

Document clustering may be defined as the problem of segmenting a document corpus into multiple groups such that any pair of documents within a group is more similar to each other than the document pairs that belong to different groups. Hierarchical document clustering is the problem of inferring a hierarchy of groups from a document corpus in such a way that the groups in the root level of the hierarchy represent generic topics, and as we descend down the hierarchy, we find groups that correspond to specific topics. In the hierarchy, if a set of child groups is attached to a parent group then the child groups correspond to the subtopics underneath the parent topic. Hierarchical document clustering is understandably more useful than a naïve flat-clustering of the documents. It helps in organizing the documents in a directory structure and can be effectively used in indexing, searching and maintaining the corpus. It can also be used in novel IR applications like classification, clustering and presenting query results from search engines to enhance IR efficiency and topic-focused crawling of the web.

At the outset there are two types of hierarchical clustering techniques in the literature: (i) agglomerative techniques and (ii) partitional techniques. Both are popular in the document-clustering domain. Though we find many parallel versions of flat-clustering algorithms, arguably, little research effort has gone into parallelizing hierarchical document-clustering algorithms. Majority of the parallel document-clustering algorithms divide the document set into multiple splits and let each processor operate on a split to produce a set of local clusters. The local clusters produced are then combined to form a global cluster set. Irrespective of the underlying parallel programming platform, this parallelization template seems to be prevalent across the proposed algorithms. If the programming is done on the basis of MPI, then the worker nodes perform local clustering and the local clusters are merged by the designated coordinator or the master. Similarly, if the MapReduce (MR) model of programming is employed then the mapper tasks perform local clustering on the splits, and the reducer task combines the local clusters to generate a global set of clusters.

Datta *et al.* proposed an approximate distributed document-clustering algorithm that aims to minimize the synchronization and communication overhead across the nodes in a distributed network [29]. Hammouda and Kamel proposed a distributed document-clustering algorithm based on K-means that exploits the hierarchical structure of the underlying cluster network to compute local clusters using a parallel variant of the K-means algorithm. The local clusters are percolated up the hierarchy to compute the global clusters [30].

Papapetrou *et al.* proposed a distributed text-clustering algorithm that uses a probabilistic approach to assign documents to clusters. The algorithm also uses a distributed hash table to limit the number of clusters against which a document is compared for carrying out this assignment. Empirical evaluation on a dataset containing a million documents was performed to study the scaling characteristics of the algorithm [31]. Li *et al.* proposed a parallel text-document clustering algorithm that uses a similarity metric based on the cosine distance and a link distance. The link distance measures the similarity between the neighbors of two documents and is useful in characterizing the intra-cluster similarity. This algorithm is a parallelized version of the sequential K-means algorithm based on neighbors. The algorithm was empirically evaluated using a cluster of Linux machines interconnected by a LAN and is found to scale well with the number of documents and processors [32].

Aboutabl and Elsayed proposed a parallel hierarchical document-clustering algorithm, in which the documents to be clustered are split equally across the processors and every processor computes a local set of clusters that are then merged with the clusters produced in the neighboring processor. This cluster merging continues until all the clusters that are within a minimum threshold distance of each other are merged. This marks the end of a merging phase, and a new merging phase is initiated to infer the next level in the dendrogram. Empirical evaluations carried out on a smaller document corpus showed a promising speedup [33]. Cathey *et al.* proposed a parallel algorithm on the basis of average-linkage agglomerative hierarchical clustering algorithm. The algorithm is shown to perform in time $O(n^2/p)$ and is also useful as a helper procedure in the parallel Buckshot clustering algorithm [34].

Deb *et al.* evaluated the performance of the distributed RACHET algorithm for clustering a large document corpus. RACHET algorithm constructs local text hierarchies that are then summarized and transmitted to coordinator processors to minimize communication overheads. The coordinators then merge the local hierarchies to generate a global hierarchy [35].

Cao and Zhou parallelized the Jarvis–Patrick algorithm on top of the MR programming framework and studied the scaling characteristics of the proposed parallelization. Cao and Zhou also discuss the open challenges associated with parallelizing a text-clustering algorithm. Dhillon *et al.* proposed a data parallel version of the K-means algorithm to cluster a large collection of documents using the MPI model. Empirical evaluations of the algorithm asserted a near-linear speedup on a 16-node cluster computer [36].

Forman and Zhang proposed a distributed clustering framework using which any centroid-based agglomerative-distributed clustering algorithm can be run across geographically distributed set of compute nodes. The key innovation of the framework is its proposal to transmit only a set of mandatory statistics about a cluster to the coordinator node for merging the local clusters to obtain a set of global clusters [16].

Li and Chung proposed a parallelized version of the bisecting K-means algorithm with an added prediction step to even out the loads across processors to realize an enhanced speedup. Empirical evaluations assert that the algorithm achieves a near-linear speedup and also produces clusters with better purity than the naïve K-means algorithm [37].

Liu *et al.* proposed a master–slave-based parallel algorithm that uses WordNet to compute the similarity between two documents on the basis of semantic information rather than just relying on the word-concordance. Empirical evaluations of the algorithm reveal that it produces clusters with better precision than the clustering algorithms that operate only on the basis of the term frequencies [38].

Mogill and Haglin proposed a parallel document-clustering algorithm that aims at minimizing the number of distance computations done by grouping a set of anchor documents around a pivot document using a data structure called *anchor hierarchy* that also obeys the triangular inequality while computing distances [39].

Zhang *et al.* proposed a parallelization strategy for the CLARANS algorithm on top of a network of computers orchestrated using the PVM tool [17]. Jensen *et al.* proposed a parallelized version of the Buckshot algorithm. The algorithm picks a random sample of a set of $\sqrt{kn}$ documents and applies an agglomerative hierarchical clustering algorithm to identify the cluster centroids. Every document is then assigned to one of the clusters on the basis of its proximity to the centroids [40].

15.4 Parallel hierarchical algorithms for big text clustering

Designing parallel hierarchical clustering algorithms is a notoriously difficult task due to the inherent complexity of hierarchy construction from a big text corpus. Some design issues, especially in the context of big data corpuses, include the following:

1. Repeated scans through the corpus will be prohibitively expensive.
2. The clusters in the hierarchy at the same level should have similar topical granularity.
3. For clustering using representatives (CURE), inferring true representatives of clusters may help speedup cluster inference; however the quantification of the degree to which a document represents the cluster is considered difficult due to the size of the corpus.
4. While designing data-parallel algorithms, deciding which set of documents should be colocated in a processor to optimize data locality is hard to decide,

considering the combinatorially explosive number of ways to split the input across processors.

5. Considering the assorted nature of the topics in big document corpuses, fixing a single model or model parameters will not yield good quality clusters. This forces the usage of multiple models and/or parameters to infer clusters at different abstraction levels and varying contexts.

6. When the underlying contents of documents change or when new documents are added to the input corpus, incremental strategies must be evolved to decide when the model parameters can be updated as opposed to discarding the current model and initiating the learning of a new model to accommodate the change in the input corpus.

The next sub-section discusses some seminal algorithms to perform hierarchical clustering of big text corpuses in a distributed/parallel way. These algorithms attempt to address some of the design issues mentioned previously.

15.4.1   Parallel hierarchical cut clustering

Seshadri and Shalinie proposed a parallel algorithm on the basis of graph cuts to infer a hierarchy of clusters from a big text corpus [41]. The main sledgehammer of Seshadri's algorithm is Flake's clustering algorithm for graphs. Given a connected undirected graph $G = (V, E, w)$, (V: vertex set, E edge set, w: weight function such that $\forall e \in E, w\,(e) \rightarrow R^+$). Flake's algorithm attaches a sink node t to all the vertices in G, such that $\forall (u, v) \in E, w(u, v) = a$, if either u or v is t. The value of alpha lies in the interval [0,1]. Flake's algorithm constructs a cut tree of G, which encodes the all-pair min-cuts in G. Such cut trees are concise encodings of all-pair min-cuts in a given graph. The structure of the cut tree with respect to the sink vertex depends on the alpha value. If alpha value is 0, then the vertex t will be a leaf vertex in the tree. Similarly, if alpha value is 1, then the vertex t will be a hub vertex in a star graph. Pruning t from the cut tree will generate degree(t)-connected components in G. Each connected component is output as a cluster. If alpha value is 0, then the Flake's algorithm generates a single cluster comprising all vertices in V; on the other hand, if alpha value is 1, Flake's algorithm generates $|V|$ singleton clusters that contain a single vertex in V. Therefore, optimal setting of alpha guides the Flake algorithm in generating a legit set of clusters.

Seshadri's algorithm that is entitled parallel hierarchical cut clustering (PHCUT) accepts as input a big text corpus containing a set of documents and executes the following steps to infer a hierarchy of clusters:

1. The document corpus is divided into p equal-sized subsets of documents if there are p processors.

2. Every processor $P_i(1 \leq i \leq p)$ gets a subset and constructs a complete graph G_i in which the documents are vertices and edge weights are cosine distances between the document pairs linked by the edges.

3. Before calculating edge weights, documents are preprocessed and converted to term frequency vectors. As these vectors tend to have a high dimensionality,

they are subjected to SVD and their dimensionality is reduced by considering only the variation in the dominant eigen dimensions. Reduction in the dimensionality helps in speeding up the cosine distance computations.

4. Flake's algorithm is executed on the complete graph G_i. A suitable alpha value is found by performing a *t*-ary search in the range [0,1] that optimizes the ratio of cohesion within clusters to coupling across clusters. Here the value of *t* corresponds to the number of cores in each processor.

5. Every processor P_i generates a set of clusters C_i. r representatives are elected from each cluster in C_i such that the number of representatives from every concentric region around the centroid of the cluster is uniformly distributed across the regions in the cluster.

6. Once the representatives are elected, the local clusters from processors are merged to infer a global set of clusters. This merging happens by following the *TreeSums* parallel algorithm, which is outlined as follows:

    (i)   There are $\lceil \log_2 p \rceil$ parallel iterations labeled $i = 0, 1, \ldots, \lceil \log_2 p \rceil - 1$.
    (ii) In every iteration i, every processor with a rank j in the range $\left[2^i + 1, 2^{i+1}\right]$ receives the local clusters from the processor with the rank $m = j - 2^i$.
    (iii) Flake's algorithm is invoked on the representatives elected from the clusters in the sets C_j and C_m to form a set of clusters C_o.
    (iv) Two clusters, one each from C_j and C_m are merged if a majority of the representatives from the clusters fall under the same cluster in C_o.
    (v)   At the end of the $\lceil \log_2 p \rceil$ parallel merge iterations, processor P_1 has the global set of clusters that corresponds to the leaf-level clusters.

7. The original graph $G = (V, E, w)$ is contracted to obtain a graph $G' = (V', E', w')$. V' contains a vertex corresponding to every leaf-level cluster; E' contains an edge e between each pair of vertices (u,v) in V' with a weight value equal to the normalized total weight of the intercluster edges between u and v. Flake's algorithm is run on the contracted graph G' to obtain the next higher level of clusters in the hierarchy. The alpha value used will be lesser than the alpha value used for inferring the leaf-level clusters as we expect a coarser clustering.

8. Repeated applications of graph contraction and Flake's algorithm on the contracted graph are performed until a single cluster is obtained as depicted in Figure 15.3, when alpha is reduced to zero.

9. In steps 7 and 8 of the algorithm the cores across all the p processors are utilized in performing a parallel search to determine the optimal alpha value to be used for the sink vertex.

The time complexity of the PHCUT algorithm is $O\left((n/p)^3 \log(n/p)\right)$. PHCUT algorithm showed a superior performance to that of Flake's algorithm and CURE algorithm in terms of the metrics such as precision, recall, F-measure and rand index. The reference corpus that was used to assess PHCUT algorithm is a set of a million documents collected from the Wiki and DMOZ repositories. PCHUT exhibited a pronounced speedup as compared to the Flake's algorithm on a 16-node

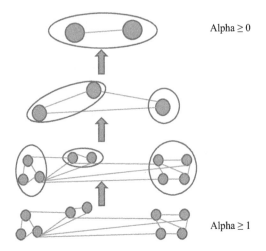

Alpha ≥ 0

Alpha ≥ 1

Figure 15.3   Inferring non-leaf clusters

cluster computing setup orchestrated using the MPI framework. However, PHCUT is known to exhibit the following demerits:

1. Scalability is limited due to the cubic term in the asymptotic complexity of PHCUT.
2. An incorrect merge will cause a cascade of incorrect merges in subsequent levels in the cluster hierarchy.
3. Child clusters are strictly contained inside a single-parent cluster and PHCUT does not infer many-to-one relationships between parent and child clusters.
4. PHCUT does not deal with outliers gracefully and outputs a highly unbalanced hierarchy when the input corpus has outliers.
5. Strict synchronization is required across parallel processors thereby limiting the degree of concurrency.

15.4.2   *Parallel hierarchical latent semantic analysis*

Parallel hierarchical latent semantic analysis (PHLSA) algorithm was proposed by Seshadri *et al.* [42] to overcome some of the demerits of the PHCUT algorithm. PHLSA is a distributed version of the hierarchical latent semantic analysis (HLSA) algorithm. The main cogwheel of the HLSA algorithm is the incremental Arnoldi–Lanczos algorithm to efficiently compute the dominant eigen values and left/right eigen vectors of a matrix one by one. The HLSA algorithm accepts an input text corpus and outputs a hierarchy of clusters and comprises the following steps:

1. A document X term matrix M is framed with n rows and q columns; where n is the number of documents in the input and q is the number of distinct words present in the vocabulary. An entry $M[i,j]$ in the matrix corresponds to the strength of association between the document i and the word j. There are

several term-weighting schemes available in the literature such as term frequency (*tf*) and term frequency–inverse document frequency (*tf–idf*), which can be employed to fill *M*.

2. The initial value for the counter of eigen dimensions *a* is set to 2.
3. Arnoldi–Lanczos algorithm is applied to *M* to incrementally infer the top *a* dominant eigen values and left/right eigen vectors.
4. Each document vector containing *q*-dimensions is projected onto a vector subspace spanned by the *a* prominent eigen vectors to obtain a matrix *M'* with *n* rows and *a* columns.
5. A computationally cheap locality sensitive hash (LSH) function is applied to each document vector to bucket similar document vectors into groups. A complete graph $G = (V, E, w)$ is constructed such that each document vector is a vertex in *V* with a weight function *w(u,v)* defined as follows:

$$w(u, v) = \begin{cases} cosineDist\,(u, v), & \text{if } LSH(u) = LSH(v) \ , \\ cosineDist\,(\mu(LSH(u)), \mu(LSH(v))), & \text{if } LSH(u) \neq LSH(v) \end{cases}$$

If two documents *u* and *v* belong to the same bucket then the distance between them is estimated to be the cosine distance between the corresponding document vectors in the matrix *M'*; otherwise, the cosine distance between the documents is approximated to be the cosine distance between the centroid vectors of the buckets to which *u* and *v* belong. This helps in speeding up the pairwise distance computations, especially in the context of big text corpuses.

6. An MST_a for *G* is constructed from which the $a - 1$ longest edges are pruned to infer *a* connected components. The quality of the connected components (CC_a) or clusters inferred is measured as the sum of the differences between the length of the edges pruned and the sum of the mean and standard deviation of the edge-lengths in the MST. This will rate higher, the MSTs in which the edges pruned are quite longer than the average edge length.
7. The counter *a* is incremented and the steps (3)–(6) are repeated, until the value of *a* reaches a preset maximum limit (or) the rank of the matrix *M*, whichever is lower.
8. The quality of the MSTs is plotted as a function of the eigen dimension counter *a* and without loss of generality, let $a_1 < a_2 < a_3 < \ldots < a_e$ be the *a*-values at which a local maxima is observed in the quality plot.
9. For each $j \in [1, e]$, CC_j is the cluster set emitted by the HLSA algorithm at level *j* in the hierarchy with $j = 1$ being treated as the root level in the hierarchy and $j = e$ as the leaf level in the hierarchy.
10. For all $j \in [2, e]$, links between the child clusters CC_j and the parent clusters CC_{j-1} are obtained by forming a complete weighted bipartite graph between the two and by pruning links with weight values greater than one standard deviation from the mean edge length in the bipartite graph. The weight of an edge in the graph is taken to be the cosine distance between the centroids of the clusters linked by that edge.

Even with the application of incremental Arnoldi iterations and LSH, HLSA is computationally expensive and hence PHLSA was proposed as a data parallel algorithm to speed up HLSA. PHLSA involves the following steps:

1.   The n documents in the corpus are sharded into p sets of size n/p documents each. Each of these subsets is assigned to a processor.
2.   Each processor $P_i \in \{P_1, P_2, \ldots, P_p\}$ runs the HLSA algorithm on the dataset assigned to it and computes a cluster hierarchy H_i.
3.   Pairs of processors synchronize with each other in a lock-step manner for $\log_2 p$ iterations as depicted in Figure 15.4 to merge the local cluster hierarchies to output a global hierarchy, assuming four processing elements.
4.   The merge algorithm accepts two cluster hierarchies H_1, H_2 as inputs and returns a merged hierarchy. The algorithm comprises the following steps:
     (i)   Let CC_e and CC_f be the root-level clusters in H_1 and H_2, respectively.
     (ii)   If $e < f$, H_1 is treated as the parent hierarchy H_p into which the child $H_c = H_2$ is merged. Otherwise, H_2 is treated as the parent hierarchy. The number of eigen dimensions associated with a level in the hierarchy is an indication of the topical abstraction of the clusters at that level. If the number of dimensions is less, then the clusters will be of higher topical abstraction and vice versa.
     (iii) The root set of clusters in the hierarchy H_c is merged with clusters at a level g in H_p such that g is the largest integer less than or equal to the number of eigen dimensions at the level 1 in H_c. This ensures that clusters of similar topical consistency are merged with each other to yield a cohesive hierarchy.
     (iv)   A bipartite graph is formed between the clusters at level 1 in H_c and clusters at level g in H_p. An MST-based graph clustering is performed on

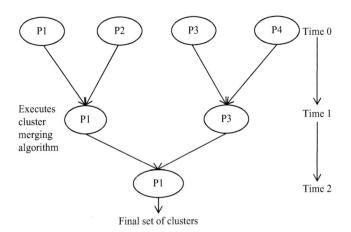

Figure 15.4   Dataflow while merging in PHLSA

the bipartite graph to merge clusters from H_c and H_p. In case a cluster c in H_c does not fall under the same group with any cluster in H_p, the cluster c is attached as a sibling cluster to the cluster closest to c in terms of the cosine distance between cluster centroids.

(v)   After merging a cluster C_1 at level 1 in H_c with a cluster C_2 at level g in H_p, the merge algorithm is recursively called on the sub-hierarchies rooted at C_1 and C_2 to merge the children clusters of C_1 and C_2. The recursion carries on until all the clusters in H_c are merged into semantically equivalent clusters in H_p.

5.   The processor P_1 outputs the cluster hierarchy underlying the big document corpus.

Step 3 of the PHLSA algorithm comprises the following parallel sub-steps:

1.   Each processor with a rank β in $\{1, 3, 5, \ldots\}$ receives the hierarchy $H_{\beta+1}$ from the processor with the rank $\beta + 1$. Processor P_β merges its hierarchy H_β with the hierarchy $H_{\beta+1}$.

2.   Each processor with a rank β in $\{1, 5, 9, \ldots\}$ receives the hierarchy $H_{\beta+2}$ from the processor with the rank $\beta + 2$. Processor P_β merges its hierarchy H_β with the hierarchy $H_{\beta+2}$.

3.   Generalizing this, in the ith parallel iteration ($i \in \{1, 2, \ldots, \lceil \log_2 p \rceil\}$), each processor with a rank β in the set $\bigcup_{j=0}^{\infty} \{1 + j \times 2^i\}$ receives the hierarchy $H_{\beta+2^{i-1}}$ from the processor with the rank $\beta + 2^{i-1}$ and merges the hierarchies H_β and $H_{\beta+2^{i-1}}$.

PHLSA was tested with large text corpuses collected from Wiki and DMOZ. Empirical evaluations reveal that PHLSA performs better than HLSA and PHCUT in terms of running-time and cluster quality measured through F-measure and Rand index. The time complexity of PHLSA is $O((n^2/p^2)q\log(n/p))$, where q is the number of levels inferred. Following are the demerits of PHLSA:

1.   Superquadratic time complexity with respect to the number of documents assigned per processor.
2.   The cluster hierarchy output by PHLSA varies drastically depending upon the way documents are assigned to the processors.
3.   Keeping the matrix M in memory typically requires a heavy memory footprint.
4.   Lack of a theoretically sound technique to identify the parent and the child hierarchies while merging two hierarchies.
5.   PHLSA misses the global perspective as it operates and infers the first-level clusters on the basis of the local context.

15.4.3   *Parallel hierarchical modularity-based spectral clustering*

Parallel hierarchical modularity-based spectral clustering abbreviated as PHMS [43] was proposed by Seshadri *et al.* to overcome the demerits of the PHLSA algorithm. PHMS uses a distributed algorithm, leveraging modularity maximization for finding coarse clusters at the top levels in the hierarchy and a parallel algorithm based on spectral clustering for inferring non-root-level clusters in the hierarchy. Inferring clusters by optimizing the modularity metric exhibits the resolution limit problem, that is, only coarser clusters of a higher topical abstraction can be inferred by modularity maximization. However, variants of spectral clustering technique are good at finding fine-grained clusters in the corpus that are highly focused on a specific topic. Therefore, Seshadri *et al.* have proposed combining the modularity maximization and spectral clustering techniques to infer the cluster hierarchy from big text corpuses. Following are the benefits of combining these techniques especially for crunching big text corpuses:

1. Spectral clustering cannot be directly employed to deal with big text corpuses as the memory required to store the document-feature matrix will be prohibitively large.
2. Modularity maximization first chunks the corpus into manageable-sized sub-corpuses and each of the sub-corpuses can be processed easily using spectral clustering.

PHMS comprises the following three phases:

1. *Coarse clustering*: Clusters in top levels of higher topical abstraction are inferred in this phase using a distributed modularity maximization–based algorithm.
2. *Cluster refinement*: The composition of the clusters inferred in the first phase is refined.
3. *Divisive hierarchy inference*: The rest of the cluster hierarchy in the non-root levels are inferred in this phase by employing a variant of spectral clustering called PIC.

In the first phase, the document corpus is divided into equal-sized subsets and every processor is assigned with a subset. Processors convert document vectors into signatures using an LSH function. A distributed graph is constructed across processors in which each processor holds a subset of vertices/documents and the adjacency list corresponding to these vertices. The weight of the edge between two documents is approximated as the hamming distance between the two document signatures. Subsequent to the distributed graph construction, a localized distributed graph sparsification is performed in which for every vertex u, its adjacency list is sorted in the nondecreasing order of the edge weights and only the top $degree(u)^{\eta}$ edges are retained and the rest of the edges are pruned. Here η is the sparsification factor whose value is in the open interval $(0,1)$. The sparsification step tends to prune out the intercluster edges and retains the intra-cluster edges, thereby making the structure of the underlying clusters explicit for the subsequent steps.

A distributed version of the modularity maximization algorithm is executed in which initially every vertex belongs to its own cluster and there are n clusters. The algorithm reassigns a vertex to the cluster of an adjacent vertex in such a way that this reassignment results in the maximum gain in modularity. Modularity can be loosely defined as the quantification of the deviation in the link-structure of a graph from that of a random graph with the same number of vertices but with randomly induced edges. Hence, modularity is directly proportional to a cohesive clustering arrangement in the link-structure of a graph. The process of reassignment is executed by picking a vertex at random and reassigning it to one of the adjacent clusters until there are no more reassignments possible that increases the modularity metric. Every processor carries out this vertex selection and reassignment on the subset of the vertices assigned to it. The reader may note that this reassignment often may involve reassigning a vertex to the cluster of an adjacent vertex residing in another processor; in such a case, distributed cluster-label propagation is carried out to synchronize the state of the processors with respect to the cluster labels of the vertices held by the processors. Once the process converges, the clusters are output, and a graph contraction is carried out to repeat this process to infer the next higher levels of clusters. The steps involved in the first phase are depicted as a flow-graph in Figure 15.5.

In the cluster refinement phase, the PHMS algorithm merges clusters and corrects any incorrect splits that happened in the first phase due to the approximation of the distances between documents. The centroid of the clusters at a particular level is collated and a modularity–maximization is done on the super-graph constructed with centroid vectors representing nodes and the cosine distances between centroidal vectors representing the edge weights. Any two clusters output by the first phase will be merged if they fall under the same group in the cluster refinement operation performed on the super-graph.

At the end of the first two phases, PHMS outputs a partially constructed cluster hierarchy with only the top few levels of coarser clusters inferred. The steps

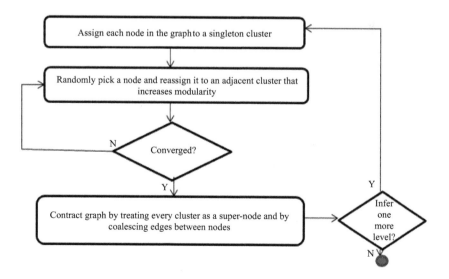

Figure 15.5   Modularity maximization

performed in the last phase of the PHMS algorithm infers the clusters in the bottom-levels and are stated as follows:

1. Compute the k-dominant eigen vectors and values of the Laplacian matrix constructed from the $n \times n$ matrix of pairwise cosine distances between the documents in a coarse cluster.
2. Form a single vector as the corresponding eigen-value weighted linear combination of the top k-dominant eigen vectors.
3. Project the documents onto the single vector inferred in step (2) earlier.
4. Perform K-means clustering in the one-dimensional space and infer k fine-grained clusters.
5. Repeat steps (1) to (4) for every coarse/fine-grained cluster that needs to be split into further subclusters.

$O(n^2/p^2 \log_2 n)$ is the asymptotic time complexity of the PHMS algorithm, which is better than the PHLSA algorithm by a logarithmic factor. PHMS algorithm produces better quality clusters than that generated by modularity maximization techniques like Louvain algorithm or Spectral clustering techniques. Quality of the hierarchy is measured in terms of F-measure and rand index. PHMS exhibits the following demerits:

1. PHMS does not produce good quality clusters when the corpus comprises lengthy documents.
2. PHMS does not produce soft clusters wherein each document can belong to multiple clusters with varying degrees of membership.

15.4.4   Parallel hierarchical latent Dirichlet allocation

Parallel hierarchical latent Dirichlet allocation is abbreviated as PHLDA [44] and has been designed to infer a cluster hierarchy from a big text corpus containing lengthy documents. PHLDA leverages a topic-modeling algorithm proposed by Blei *et al.* called hierarchical latent Dirichlet allocation (HLDA). HLDA is a hierarchical extension to a flat-topic-modeling algorithm called latent Dirichlet allocation (LDA) proposed by Blei *et al.* Given a set of documents LDA fits a topic model in which each topic is interpreted as a probability distribution over the words in the vocabulary and each document is interpreted as a distribution over the topics. HLDA is a computationally intensive algorithm and consumes several iterations before the latent parameters of the model converge. There are parallel/distributed versions of the LDA and HLDA algorithms like AD-LDA proposed by Newman *et al.* and PHLDA proposed by Seshadri *et al.* Unlike the AD-LDA algorithm, the PHLDA algorithm spawns loosely coupled parallel processes that do not require tight synchronization when the processes execute in parallel. Therefore, the PHLDA algorithm is amenable to be implemented on top of a distributed computing environment efficiently. PHLDA algorithm comprises two phases.

1. *Phase 1*: Inference of local hierarchies.
2. *Phase 2*: Merging local hierarchies to form a global hierarchy.

In the first phase of PHLDA, the document corpus is split into equal-sized subsets and assigned to the p processors. Each processor executes the HLDA algorithm in parallel with the other processors to infer a local topic hierarchy. Every node in the hierarchy generated is a distribution over topics. A $p \times p$ matrix of quadratic chi-square distances is computed between the topic distributions in the root node of the local hierarchies. Using this distance matrix as input, the local hierarchies are clustered into groups of topically similar hierarchies. The groups of similar hierarchies are enqueued into a message-queue as the output from the first phase of PHLDA. Each processor in the set of processors, picks a group of local hierarchies from the message-queue in the second phase of PHLDA, merges the local hierarchies in the group (two hierarchies at a time) to form a single topically consistent hierarchy and enqueues it in the output queue. The merge algorithm accepts two hierarchies H_1 and H_2 as input and comprises the following steps:

1. The topic distribution in the root node of H_1 is subtracted from that in H_2 and let the difference be called as the vector γ.
2. The vector γ is fed as the input to a support vector machine (SVM)-based classifier to predict whether H_1 is at a higher level of abstraction than H_2 or vice versa. The hierarchy, that is, at a higher level of topical abstraction is designated as the parent hierarchy H_p into which the other hierarchy designated as the child of H_p will be merged into.
3. The merging process involves construction of a bipartite graph and subsequently clustering the graph to identify the groups of nodes to be merged. This is similar to the hierarchy-merging process in PHLSA with a minor difference in terms of the distance metric used. In PHLDA, the distance metric used is the quadratic chi-square metric, as we need to compute distance between two topic-probability distributions, whereas in PHLSA cosine distance metric was employed.

The process of grouping similar hierarchies in the output queue and invoking the merge algorithm to combine hierarchies in a group continues until the number of hierarchies found in the output queue is more than one. The single hierarchy formed by PHLDA in the output queue is emitted as the global cluster hierarchy. The performance of the PHLDA algorithm was assessed using one million Wikipedia documents. Empirical assessments on corpuses with lengthy documents reveal that PHLDA forms better quality hierarchies than that formed by PHCUT, PHLSA and PHMS. PHLDA is also faster than AD-LDA and the PHCUT algorithm. PHLDA's runtime is in $O(nk\tau/p)$, where τ is the vocabulary size. The following are its demerits:

1. PHLDA produces a hierarchy of inferior quality when the input corpus contains short documents.
2. PHLDA's performance is very sensitive with respect to the quality of the training set used for training the SVM, which is used in determining the parent/ child hierarchy while merging.
3. PHLSA and PHMS outperform PHLDA in terms of running time.

15.4.5   *PHCUT vs. PHLSA vs. PHMS vs. PHLDA*

The speedups realized by the distributed and parallel algorithms PHCUT, PHLSA, PHMS and PHLDA are measured by running these algorithms on a 16-node distributed computing setup orchestrated through MPI. The input was a corpus containing a million documents crawled from Wikipedia. Speedup is measured as the ratio between the running time of the sequential algorithm to that of the parallel/distributed algorithm. Sequential versions of the algorithms Flake, HLSA and HLDA were used for measuring the speedup achieved by PHCUT, PHLSA and PHLDA. However, for PHMS, a hybrid sequential algorithm was employed in which Louvain algorithm was leveraged for generating the top-level clusters in the hierarchy and sequential PIC was used to infer the bottom levels in the hierarchy. The expected ideal speedup value is 64, as each of the distributed compute node is a quad-core processor. The speedups realized by the parallel algorithms are tabulated in Table 15.1. For more details on the experimental setup and statistical tests conducted, the reader is referred to the thesis by Seshadri [45].

As could be observed from Table 15.1, PHMS achieves the maximum speedup followed by PHLSA, PHLDA and PHCUT. This could be attributed to a combination of factors as follows:

1. Distributed modularity maximization.
2. Graph sparsification.
3. Faster parallel PIC on *one*-dimensional document vectors.

The quality of the hierarchy generated by these algorithms can be assessed by comparing the hierarchy with the reference hierarchy from Wikipedia and DMOZ. For assessing the quality of the hierarchy generated, three test sets were orchestrated corresponding to corpuses containing lengthy documents, short documents and a mix of lengthy and short documents. The rand index was computed on the hierarchies as tabulated in Table 15.2. The three test sets contained 25 test cases each, and each test case contained a number of documents in the range of 10,000–20,000. As could be observed from Table 15.2, PHMS performs well on the test set, containing short documents and PHLDA performs better compared to the other three algorithms on

Table 15.1 Speedup achieved—PHCUT vs. PHLSA vs. PHMS vs. PHLDA

Parallel algorithm	Reference sequential algorithm	Speedup
PHCUT	Flake	13.67
PHLSA	HLSA	26.88
PHMS	Louvain + PIC	41.08
PHLDA	HLDA	25.75

Table 15.2 Rand index—PHCUT vs. PHLSA vs. PHMS vs. PHLDA

Test set	PHCUT	PHLSA	PHMS	PHLDA
Short	0.39 ± 0.03	0.54 ± 0.08	0.72 ± 0.08	0.27 ± 0.08
Long	0.57 ± 0.06	0.59 ± 0.07	0.72 ± 0.04	0.78 ± 0.04
Mixed	0.56 ± 0.07	0.60 ± 0.05	0.72 ± 0.05	0.77 ± 0.04

corpuses, containing lengthy documents. The rand index reported in the table is in the $\mu \pm \sigma$ format, where μ is the mean rand-index computed across the 25 test-corpuses in a test set and σ is the standard deviation in the rand-index values.

15.4.6   Research challenges addressed

The following research challenges or objectives have been addressed to a satisfactory extent by the algorithms PHCUT, PHLSA, PHMS and PHLDA.

1. To determine the number of levels in the hierarchy and the number of clusters per level automatically without supervision.
2. To generalize intelligent flat-clustering algorithms to their hierarchical variants.
3. To infer hierarchies in which there are many-to-one relationships between parent clusters and child clusters, respectively.
4. To design a suitable merging logic that can merge hierarchies generated by parallel processing elements into a single consistent hierarchy by taking into consideration the topical granularities of the clusters being merged.
5. To devise efficient and effective cluster-quality metrics to infer the number of clusters in a hierarchy and to validate the hierarchies generated by the parallel hierarchical clustering algorithms.
6. There are still many intelligent sequential clustering algorithms that need to be ported to the hierarchical variants to leverage the compute-power available in parallel computers.
7. To summarize the contents of the hierarchy generated and effectively leverage the summary for information retrieval tasks.
8. To design and analyze faster parallel hierarchical clustering algorithms that can be scalable and still generate hierarchies comparable to that of their sequential variants.
9. To develop platform-agnostic parallel hierarchical clustering algorithms that can be ported to different parallel programming platforms with a minimal human effort.
10. To develop parallel versions of hierarchical clustering algorithms across various genres like agglomerative, divisive, model-based, probabilistic and spectral-based, and to integrate these parallel versions into an unified framework that can facilitate selection and application of one of the suitable algorithms to the problem at hand.

15.5   Open research challenges

Following are some of the open research challenges that could be taken up by researchers who wish to work in this domain:

1. Designing cost models to approximate the resource requirement of the algorithm in terms of running time, memory and communication costs. These models ought to be created in such a way that their parameters can be tuned to different algorithms and distributed/parallel computing platforms.

2. The MPI parallel programming framework was used for evaluating the performance of PHCUT, PHLSA, PHMS and PHLDA. However, there are other programming frameworks like CUDA and MR that can be tested for the suitability of running these parallel/distributed algorithms. In fact, these algorithms can be refactored to utilize specific idioms in the target parallel programming platforms and the improvement in the performance can be quantified.

3. The parallel algorithms can be refactored to accommodate the incremental addition or removal of documents to or from the corpus. The challenge here lies in adjusting the clusters without rerunning the algorithm on the entire corpus.

4. The parallel algorithms can be redesigned to track the topical evolution happening in the corpus over a period of time. This is challenging and requires designing sequence models to characterize the temporal evolution of topics over time.

5. The applicability of these parallel algorithms in non-text-related datasets can be explored.

15.6   Concluding remarks

This chapter discusses the problem of inferring a hierarchy of clusters from a big text corpus. The problem involves several challenges due to the scale of the input and the inherent theoretical minimum nonlinear computational complexity of typical hierarchical clustering algorithms. The chapter hosts a discussion on several kinds of parallel hierarchical clustering algorithms like density-based, grid-based, graph-based, spectral-based, latent-model-based among others. The chapter also outlined the key challenges faced while designing parallel or distributed algorithms for inferring a hierarchy of clusters/topics in a big text corpus. Detailed design issues involved in and the algorithmic nitty-gritty of four seminal parallel or distributed algorithms were discussed as follows:

1. *Parallel hierarchical cut clustering (PHCUT)*: This algorithm was based on graph-cuts and is a parallel version of the infamous Flake's algorithm. The algorithm uses the Gomory–Hu cut tree to encode the pairwise min-cuts in the graph modeling the document corpus. The algorithm outputs a hierarchy that almost mimics the hand-curated categories in the reference corpuses like Wikipedia and DMOZ. The algorithm exhibits a pronounced speedup as compared to the sequential Flake algorithm.

2. *Parallel hierarchical latent semantic analysis (PHLSA)*: This parallel algorithm takes the document-feature matrix as input and infers a sequence of vector subspaces in which the clusters in different levels of the hierarchy are inferred. Data parallelism was exploited using which local hierarchies are independently inferred from subsets of the corpus and the local hierarchies are merged in parallel to generate a global hierarchy.

3. *Parallel hierarchical modularity-based spectral clustering (PHMS)*: This distributed algorithm is a hybrid between a distributed modularity-based maximization algorithm and a parallel spectral clustering algorithm. Modularity

maximization is leveraged to infer coarse clusters whereas spectral clustering is employed to infer fine-grained clusters. The algorithm exhibits a good clustering performance in terms of cluster quality and runtime, over algorithms like Louvain and PIC.

4. *Parallel hierarchical latent Dirichlet allocation (PHLDA):* This is a distributed version of the stochastic topic-modeling algorithm called HLDA. The algorithm infers probabilistic clusters or topics. Every document is modeled as a probability distribution over topics and a topic is defined as a probability distribution over the words in the vocabulary. PHLDA exhibits a good speedup over the sequential HLDA algorithm and produces good quality clusters when subjected to a corpus containing lengthy documents.

We concluded the discussion of these algorithms with a performance comparison of the algorithms, which was followed by an enumeration of the research challenges addressed by the four algorithms and the open research challenges that are yet to be addressed by researchers in this domain.

References

[1] Jain AK, Murty MN, and Flynn PJ: 'Data Clustering: A Review', ACM Computing Surveys, 1999, 31(3), pp. 264–323.

[2] Newman D, Asuncion AU, and Smyth P: 'Distributed Algorithms for Topic Models', Journal of Machine Learning Research, 2009, 10(1), pp. 1801–1828.

[3] Han J and Kamber M: 'Data mining: Concepts and techniques', Morgan Kaufmann, Massachusetts, USA, 2000.

[4] Li X: 'Parallel Algorithms for Hierarchical Clustering and Cluster Validity', IEEE Transactions on Pattern Analysis and Machine Intelligence, 1990, 12 (11), pp. 1088–1092.

[5] Dahlhaus E: 'Parallel Algorithms for Hierarchical Clustering and Applications to Split Decomposition and Parity Graph Recognition', Journal of Algorithms, 2000, 36(2), pp. 205–240.

[6] Garg A, Mangla A, Gupta N, *et al.*: 'PBIRCH: A scalable parallel clustering algorithm for incremental data', In: IDEAS, 2006, pp. 315–316.

[7] Hendrix W, Patwary MMA, Agrawal A, *et al.*: 'Parallel hierarchical clustering on shared memory platforms', In: HiPC. IEEE Computer Society, 2012, pp. 1–9.

[8] Hendrix W, Palsetia D, Patwary MMA, *et al.*: 'A scalable algorithm for single-linkage hierarchical clustering on distributed-memory architectures', In: Proceedings of IEEE Symposium on Large-Scale Data Analysis and Visualization. Los Alamitos, CA, USA, 2013, pp. 7–13.

[9] Timón I, Soto J, Pérez-Sánchez H, and Cecilia JM: 'Parallel Implementation of Fuzzy Minimals Clustering Algorithm', Expert Systems and Applications, 2016, 48(1), pp. 35–41.

[10] Pavan M and Pelillo M: 'Dominant Sets and Pairwise Clustering', IEEE Transactions on Pattern Analysis and Machine Intelligence, 2007, 29(1), pp. 167–172.

[11]   Tsui SR, Wang WJ, and Chen SS: 'Parallel clustering based on partitions of local minimal-spanning-trees', In: PAAP Conference. IEEE, 2012, pp. 111–118.

[12]   LaSalle D and Karypis G: 'Multi-Threaded Modularity-Based Graph Clustering Using the Multilevel Paradigm', Parallel and Distributed Computing, 2015, 76(1), pp. 66–80.

[13]   Judd D, McKinley PK, and Jain AK: 'Large-Scale Parallel Data Clustering', IEEE Transactions on Pattern Analysis and Machine Intelligence, 1998, 20(8), pp. 871–876.

[14]   Kantabutra S and Couch AL: 'Parallel K-Means Clustering Algorithm on NoWs', NECTEC Technical Journal, 1999, 1(6), pp. 243–247.

[15]   Dhillon I and Modha D: 'A data clustering algorithm on distributed memory multiprocessors', In: 5th ACM SIGKDD, Large-Scale Parallel KDD Systems Workshop, 1999, pp. 245–260.

[16]   Forman G and Zhang B: 'Distributed Data Clustering Can Be Efficient and Exact', SIGKDD Explorations, 2000, 2(2), pp. 34–38.

[17]   Zhang Y, Sun J, and Zhang Y: 'Parallel implementation of CLARANS using PVM', In: Proceedings of the 2004 International Conference on Machine Learning and Cybernetics, 2004, pp. 1646–1649.

[18]   Feng Z, Zhou B, and Shen J: 'A Parallel Hierarchical Clustering Algorithm for PCs Cluster System', Neurocomputing, 2007, 70(4–6), pp. 809–818.

[19]   Pizzuti C and Talia D: 'P-AutoClass: Scalable Parallel Clustering for Mining Large Data Sets', IEEE Transactions on Knowledge and Data Engineering, 2003, 15(3), pp. 629–641.

[20]   Ranka S and Sahni S: 'Clustering on a Hypercube Multicomputer', IEEE Transactions on Parallel and Distributed Systems, 1991, 2(2), pp. 129–137.

[21]   Xu X, Jger J, and Kriegel HP: 'A Fast-Parallel Clustering Algorithm for Large Spatial Databases', Data Mining and Knowledge Discovery, 1999, 3(3), pp. 263–290.

[22]   Patwary MA, Palsetia D, and Agrawal A: 'A new scalable parallel DB-SCAN algorithm using the disjoint-set data structure', In: Proceedings of the International Conference on High Performance Computing, Networking, Storage and Analysis. SC 2012, Los Alamitos, CA, USA, IEEE Computer Society Press, 2012, pp. 62:1–62:11.

[23]   Yildirim AA and Zdogan C: 'Parallel WaveCluster: A Linear Scaling Parallel Clustering Algorithm Implementation With Application to Very Large Datasets', Parallel and Distributed Computing, 2011, 71(7), pp. 955–962.

[24]   Xiaoyun C, Yi C, Xiaoli Q, et al.: 'PGMCLU: A novel parallel grid-based clustering algorithm for multi-density datasets', In: Proc. of the 1st IEEE Symposium on Web Society, 2009, pp. 166–171.

[25]   Babu GP and Murty MN: 'Clustering With Evolution Strategies', Pattern Recognition, 1994, 27(2), pp. 321–329.

[26]   Cui X, Charles JS, and Potok TE: 'The GPU enhanced parallel computing for large scale data clustering', In: CyberC IEEE Computer Society, 2011, pp. 220–225.

[27] Yan W, Brahmakshatriya U, and Xue Y: 'p-PIC: Parallel Power Iteration Clustering for Big Data', Parallel and Distributed Computing, 2013, 73(3), pp. 352–359.

[28] Seshadri K and Iyer KV: 'Parallelization of a Dynamic SVD Clustering Algorithm and Its Application in Information Retrieval', Software: Practice & Experience, 2010, 40(10), pp. 883–896.

[29] Datta S, Giannella C, and Kargupta H: 'Approximate Distributed K-Means Clustering over a Peer-to-Peer Network', IEEE Transactions on Knowledge and Data Engineering, 2009, 21(10), pp. 1372–1388.

[30] Hammouda KM and Kamel MS: 'Hierarchically Distributed Peer-to-Peer Document Clustering and Cluster Summarization', IEEE Transactions on Knowledge and Data Engineering, 2009, 21(5), pp. 681–698.

[31] Papapetrou O, Siberski W, and Fuhr N: 'Decentralized Probabilistic Text Clustering', IEEE Transactions on Knowledge and Data Engineering, 2012, 24(10), pp. 1848–1861.

[32] Li Y, Luo C, and Chung SM: 'A Parallel Text Document Clustering Algorithm Based on Neighbors', Cluster Computing Journal, 2015, 18(2), pp. 933–948.

[33] Aboutabl AE and Elsayed MN: 'A Novel Parallel Algorithm for Clustering Documents Based on the Hierarchical Agglomerative Approach', Computer Science and Information Technology, 2011, 3(2), pp. 152–163.

[34] Cathey R, Jensen EC, Beitzel SM, *et al.*: 'Exploiting Parallelism to Sup-Port Scalable Hierarchical Clustering', Information Science and Technology, 2007, 58(8), pp. 1207–1221.

[35] Deb D, Fuad MM, and Angryk RA: 'Distributed hierarchical document clustering', In: Proc. of the 2nd International Conference on Advances in Computer Science and Technology, ACST'06, 2006, pp. 328–333.

[36] Cao Z and Zhou Y: 'Parallel text clustering based on MapReduce', In: Second International Conference on Cloud and Green Computing, 2012, pp. 226–229.

[37] Li Y and Chung SM: 'Parallel Bisecting k-Means With Prediction Clustering Algorithm', Supercomputing Journal, 2007, 39(1), pp. 19–37.

[38] Liu G, Wang Y, Zhao T, *et al.*: 'Research on the parallel text clustering algorithm based on the semantic tree', In: 6th International Conference on Computer Sciences and Convergence IT (ICCIT), 2011, pp. 400–403.

[39] Mogill J and Haglin DJ: 'Toward parallel document clustering', In: IPDPS Workshops. IEEE, 2011, pp. 1700–1709.

[40] Jensen EC, Beitzel SM, Pilotto AJ, *et al.*: 'Parallelizing the buckshot algorithm for efficient document clustering', In: Conference on Information and Knowledge Management. ACM, 2002, pp. 684–686.

[41] Seshadri K and Shalinie SM: 'Parallelization of a Graph-Cut Based Algorithm for Hierarchical Clustering of Web Documents', Concurrency and Computation: Practice & Experience, 2015, 27(17), pp. 5156–5176.

[42] Seshadri K, Iyer KV, and Shalinie SM: 'Design and Evaluation of a Parallel Document Clustering Algorithm Based on Hierarchical Latent Semantic

Analysis', Concurrency and Computation: Practice & Experience, 2019, 31(13), pp. 1–20.

[43] Seshadri K, Mercy SS, and Manohar S: 'A Distributed Parallel Algorithm for Inferring Hierarchical Groups From Large-Scale Text Corpuses', Concurrency and Computation: Practice & Experience, 2018, 30(11), pp. 1–18.

[44] Seshadri K, Mercy SS, and Kollengode C: 'Design and Evaluation of a Parallel Algorithm for Inferring Topic Hierarchies', Information Processing and Management, 2015, 51(5), pp. 662–676.

[45] Seshadri K: 'Design and Performance Evaluation of Parallel Algorithms for Hierarchical Clustering of Large Text Collections', Ph.D. thesis, Anna University, 2017.

Chapter 16

Contract-driven financial reporting: building automated analytics pipelines with algorithmic contracts, Big Data and Distributed Ledger technology

Wolfgang Breymann[1], Nils Bundi[2] and Kurt Stockinger[1]

Future regulatory reporting should be automated to make it more efficient. Moreover, automation enables the supervising authorities to effectively oversee and identify risks of individual financial institutions and the entire financial market. During the last years, we have developed new technologies that are important to reach this goal. These technologies include (i) a suitable standardized representation of financial contracts, (ii) a standardized way of carrying out financial analytics, (iii) Big Data technology required to process hundreds of millions of financial contracts and (iv) Distributed Ledger and Smart Contract technology to create a secure layer for automated reporting. In this work, we provide an overview of these technological elements that are required to reach an earlier established vision of future financial risk reporting.

16.1 Introduction

A more stable and efficient financial system is essential for a thriving economy, and effective, state-of-the-art regulation, and supervision are indispensable ingredients to support this goal. Indeed, during the 2008 financial crisis, the world financial system was on the edge of a financial meltdown, and the extent of regulatory shortcomings became apparent. A total financial collapse was averted only by massive public sector intervention. As to the underlying reasons, the Basel Committee on Banking Supervision pointed towards the inadequacy of banks' information technology (IT) and data architectures to support the broad management of financial risks [1]. This is because regulatory reports typically relied on the collection of data in a standard that did not support forward-looking analysis, used inflexible aggregation criteria, used summary statistics that resulted in the loss of

[1]School of Engineering, Zurich University of Applied Sciences, Winterthur, Switzerland
[2]School of Business, Stevens Institute of Technology, Hoboken, NJ, USA

critical information, lacked the ability to see the interdependencies in financial markets and were only available months after the reporting period. The aggregate measures produced by traditional methods are rigid, infrequent and not available when needed. The current limitations are illustrated by the *inability to measure, even imprecisely, the risks inherent in the development of subprime lending, securitization and risk transfer in the run-up to the 2007 crisis* [2]. The severe consequences for both single financial institutions and the whole (global) financial system have been a painful experience for the entire world. To avert similar events in the future, which bear the risk of long-term damage to the economy and collapse of social well-being, it is essential to speedily address the failings revealed by that crisis [3].

Unfortunately, the new regulatory rules introduced over the 12 years since the crisis have only partially addressed these issues. For example, the reporting of over-the-counter derivatives trades to Trade Repositories was mandated, and millions of transactions were reported as required. However, the heterogeneity of the data formats used prevented the analysis of the data, which turned this reporting into a high-cost requirement with little regulatory benefit. The new stress tests imposed on large banks are an important advance compared to what was done before the crisis. However, they are also very high-cost exercises whose benefits are limited in a number of important dimensions. Performing the analytics and reporting the results of the stress tests takes the banks month to complete. Each bank uses its own models and accounting rules to do the analytics, which means that regulators cannot make comparisons between the results reported by different banks. And, the stress tests do not provide insight into the interdependencies between systemically important banks. At the same time, the banks' costs of the new regulations have skyrocket and are estimated at least 15%–20% of operational costs.

Here, we present elements of a new approach towards financial reporting with the goal to efficiently and effectively oversee and identify the financial risk of financial institutions and financial markets. More specifically, we will discuss the following: (i) the collection of granular data in a standard that enables current and forward-looking analysis; (ii) an approach towards financial analytics that supports flexible, near-time data aggregation according to situation-dependent criteria; (iii) forward-looking financial and risk analysis; (iv) stress tests that provide near-time results that can also include inter-bank comparisons and identify critical interdependencies; (v) Big Data technology for timely and flexible risk assessment at the financial institution (micro-prudential) and financial market (macro-prudential, i.e., systemic) level; (vi) an automated pull-based approach towards financial reporting using Blockchain/Distributed Ledger technology (DLT) and smart contracts.

Clearly, a suitable standard for the collection of granular data is required as basis for all subsequent analytical tasks. There are various competing standardization initiatives, e.g., Fibo [4] of the EDM council or—more recently—ISDA's CDM initiative [5]. Unfortunately, these standards fall short of meeting an essential requirement, namely the support of forward-looking financial analysis. To our knowledge, the ACTUS standard [6] is the only standardized digital representation of financial contracts that meets this requirement. It does so by standardizing the financial contracts, which are the basic building blocks of the financial system. The special feature of this standard is that it does not only focus on data standardization but, in addition, provides standardized algorithms that generate the future cash flows encoded in the financial contract. These cash flows, in turn, provide the basis for all kinds of financial analytics. In addition, cash flows of all types of contracts can be compared with one another. In this way, ACTUS provides standardization at the deepest technological level, similar to standards as TCP/IP that ensures the working of the Internet.

Notice that this data is highly structured. The case for structured data has been made by Brammertz and Mendelowitz [7]. We agree with this view. Our belief relies on the fact that the financial system has a so-called bow tie (or hour glass) structure [8] that is found in many complex systems where high variability of input and output must be reconciliated with efficiency and robustness. Such systems typically consist of a small core with restricted variability that ensures efficiency and robustness while input and output fan out. For the financial system, this core consists of the financial contracts and ACTUS provides a standardization of this core that—going beyond mere classification—makes its operation more robust and efficient. Accordingly, we chose the ACTUS standard as the starting point of our approach.

Generating the context-dependent cash flows of all the contracts on the books of a financial institution is a simulation approach based on granular data. An ACTUS-based simulation is thus similar to a simulation in meteorology or other fields of science. It is the most promising approach for studying complex systems. Indeed, weather forecasts all over the world have become astonishingly reliable during the last decade. This is thanks to a worldwide measurement infrastructure (which requires a suitable standardization of data and models) and the ICT advances during the last decades.

Transferred to the financial sector, this means simulating the future cash flows of all financial contracts on the books of a financial institution and, by extension, ideally of the whole financial system for chosen assumptions about the financial–economic environment. All analytical metrics can then be computed from these cash flows. The crucial property that makes this possible is the fact that—with the exception of risk measures—all analytical metrics can be obtained from the cash flows of the financial contracts by linear mathematical operations, i.e., by (possibly weighted) aggregation. Such operations can be executed very fast by standard software. Therefore, flexible aggregation according to situation-dependent criteria will be available once the cash flows of all financial contracts can be evaluated quickly enough. Even though simulating (parts of) the financial system on a granular (contract by contract) level is a formidable computational task, we do not believe it to be beyond the challenge of weather forecasting or other large volume data-processing tasks. However, while the meteorological infrastructure evolved over decades in a collaborative effort, no such infrastructure exists for the financial system.

For the analytics we need, in addition, a modified formulation of financial analytics, which is presented in Section 16.3. Given the possibility to simulate the cash flows generated by the contract of financial institutions and ideally the whole financial system, the flexible aggregation of financial analytics according to situation-dependent criteria can then be provided.

We tested that such an approach does indeed work with real financial data. For this exercise, we used data from the Centralized Securities Database of the European Central Bank (ECB). We mapped this data to the ACTUS data standard, and we carried out an ACTUS-based analysis for a portfolio of government bonds [9]. Later, we investigated various parallel programming technologies based on Hadoop and Apache Spark to enable large-scale financial system simulation and analysis [8]. Such a system ultimately *enables near-time stress tests and Monte Carlo simulation of the whole financial system on a daily basis, similar to the daily weather forecast.*

As to financial reporting, we designed a reporting concept that uses a replication of legacy financial contracts by Smart Contracts Blockchain/DLT based environment and the ACTUS standard as basis for an automated, granular pull-based reporting approach [10]. Such an approach is already used in [11] and is also mentioned in two recent discussion papers on possible future reporting approaches [12,13].

The outline of this chapter is as follows. We start with an overview of the ACTUS standard in Section 16.2. In Section 16.3, it follows the cash-flow-based formulation of financial analytics. Section 16.4 shows how to use ACTUS in practice by presenting the results of an ACTUS-based analytics carried out on a portfolio of European government bonds. Section 16.5 is devoted to results of how ACTUS scales on cloud-based Big Data technology. The design of a possible pull-based automated financial reporting system by means of Blockchain/DLTs and smart contracts is the subject of Section 16.6, and finally, Section 16.7 concludes.

16.2   The ACTUS methodology

The ACTUS concept of standardization of contract modelling [6] goes back to [14]. The analytical process is organized in form of a data supply chain as depicted in Figure 16.1 (see also [9]). The main parts are **input elements**, **raw results**, and **analytical output**. They are described in turn.

Input elements: The input elements consist of financial contracts and the relevant financial–economic environment in form of risk factors. This separation reflects the separation of the known (the financial contracts) and the unknown (the risk factors) [15]. More precisely, **financial contracts** consist of contract data and algorithms. The contract algorithms encode the legal contract rules that describe the intended cash flows exchange between the contract's counterparties (who is paying how much when to whom under which circumstances) while the contract data provides the parameters that are required for the full contract specification. The contract information completely reflects the intentions of the counterparties and therefore is the only fully known and determined reality in the financial world. **Risk factors** determine the state of the financial and economic environment, whose future states have strong random elements and can only be described by the means of probability theory, e.g., stochastic processes. Risk factors are further divided into factors for market risk, counterparty risk and all the remaining risk factors which are lumped together in a third catch-all category called 'Behaviour'. This distinction is important because the modelling of

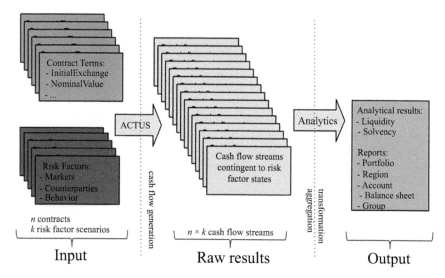

Figure 16.1 *Analytical methodology. Adapted from [9] by permission from Springer Nature*

market risk and credit risk is governed by the principles of financial mathematics such as the absence of arbitrage while there are no such guiding principles for the third category. The most important market risk factors are interest rates, foreign exchange rates, stock and commodity indices. Counter party risk factors typically consists of credit ratings and/or default probabilities.

Typically, both contract data and risk factor information is needed for generating the cash flows encoded in a contract. The reason is that the contract rules often refer to market information such as interest rates in the case of a variable rate bond. Notice that, despite the stochastic nature of the risk factors, the future development of the state of a contract is completely determined for a given (i.e., known or assumed) risk factor scenario.

Raw results: The raw results are cash flow streams together with some auxiliary information obtained as output of the contract algorithms. Assuming n contracts and k risk factor scenarios, there will be $n \times k$ cash flow streams consisting of a handful to hundred(s) events each. Since there are millions of contracts on a bank's balance sheet and a Monte Carlo (MC) simulation does contain up to 10,000 or even more risk scenarios, the size of the data can easily be of the order of terabytes for large institutions. This requires the use of Big Data technologies, see Section 16.5.

Analytical output: Different types of financial analysis such as liquidity and solvency calculations are carried out on top of the raw results. This encompasses the analysis of liquidity, value and income as well as sensitivity analysis and different kinds of risk measures. Important is the possibility to flexibly aggregate according to different criteria. This requires an adaptation of the mathematical formulation of the analytics. This is the subject of the following section.

16.3   The mathematics of ACTUS

The objective of this section is to formulate a cash-flow-based approach towards financial analytics in a rigorous way, such that it will provide the mathematical foundation of an ACTUS-based approach towards financial analytics. This approach must be formulated in terms of operators on cash flows. Most of these operators are linear, which is one of the reasons why ACTUS is such a powerful concept. Carrying out this approach is a scientific program. Here, only a few important elements can be sketched.

16.3.1   *Contract terms, contract algorithms and cash flow streams*

As already mentioned earlier, a financial contract essentially defines who pays how much, when, to whom, and under which conditions. Thereby, every payment is a cash flow from a party A to a party B, and a financial contract can be specified by providing a list with all the cash flows that are expected to occur during its lifetime. An example is provided in Table 16.1. However, this may be somewhat cumbersome, in particular, if there are many equal cash flows on a regular schedule as, for example, in the case of the 30-year bond. This is why rules are defined that implicitly encode the payments. The following example of a real government bond issued by the Hellenic Republic [16] illustrates this 'encoding' in natural language that matches the cash flow schedule listed in Table 16.1:

THE HELLENIC REPUBLIC
€ 3,000,000,000 4.75 per cent. Notes due 2019
Issue Price: 99.133%

The € 3,000,000,000 4.75 per cent. Notes due 2019 (the "Notes") of the Hellenic Republic (the "Republic") will bear interest at the rate of 4.75 per cent per annum. Interest on the Notes will be payable annually in arrear on 17 April of each year (each an "Interest Payment Date"). The first payment of interest will be paid on 17 April 2015.
The Notes will mature on 17 April 2019.

The text is composed of sentences with embedded quantitative elements that describe the whole list of payments (i.e., the cash flow stream as shown in Table 16.1) intended by the contract under all circumstances considered.

The quantitative elements in this description are called *contract terms*. The mandatory and optional contract terms and their form are described by the ACTUS Data Dictionary [6]. Some of the contract terms are displayed in Table 16.2. The previous text contains the rules that generate the set of payments, i.e., the contract's cash flow stream $X = \{x(t_i)\}_{i=1}^{n}$ when they are applied to the contract terms $\mathscr{C}$. In general, additional input external to the contract is needed, namely the relevant financial-economic environment $\mathscr{E}$ in the form of the risk factors mentioned in the previous section. An example is the reference interest rate, e.g., the LIBOR 6-month rate, that is required, e.g., for fixing the new interest rates in the case of variable rate contracts.

Table 16.1 The contractual payment events of the € 3,000,000,000 4.75 per cent Notes of the Hellenic Republic

Time	Type	Currency	Amount
2014-04-17	Initial exchange	€	2,973,990,000
2015-04-17	Interest payment	€	−142,500,000
2016-04-18	Interest payment	€	−142,500,000
2017-04-17	Interest payment	€	−142,500,000
2018-04-17	Interest payment	€	−142,500,000
2019-04-17	Interest payment	€	−142,500,000
2019-04-17	Maturity	€	−3,000,000,000

Table 16.2 Extract of the ACTUS Data Dictionary grouped by contract terms

ACTUS group name	ACTUS contract term
	ContractType
	StatusDate
Contract identification	ContractRole
	LegalEntityIDRecordCreator
	ContractID
Counterparty	LegalEntityIDCounterparty
	CycleAnchorDateOfInterestPayment
	CycleOfInterestPayment
Interest	NominalInterestRate
	NominalInterestRate2
	DayCountConvention
	AccruedInterest
	Currency
	AmortizationDate
	ContractDealDate
	InitialExchangeDate
	PremiumDiscountAtIED
	MaturityDate
	NotionalPrincipal
Notional principal	CycleAnchorDateOfPrincipalRedemption
	CycleOfPrincipalRedemption
	NextPrincipalRedemptionPayment
	PurchaseDate
	PriceAtPurchaseDate
	TerminationDate
	PriceAtTerminationDate
	XDayNotice
	MarketValueObserved
	CycleAnchorDateOfRateReset
Rate Reset	CycleOfRateReset
	RateSpread
	MarketObjectCodeRateReset

The cash flow generating rules can be mathematically defined as a mapping from the contract terms $\mathscr{C}$ and the risk factor environment $\mathscr{E}$ to the contract's cash flow stream:

$$\mathscr{A} : (\mathscr{C}, \mathscr{E}) \mapsto X. \tag{16.1}$$

This mapping is digitally represented by an algorithm, the so-called ACTUS Contract Algorithm that takes the contract terms and the risk factors as input and provides the payments as output. The output can be generated either as one payment $x(t_i)$ at a time, as is required for transaction systems, or at once as the entire cash flow stream X, as is needed for financial analytics.

As in the remainder of this chapter we are interested in analytics, we will now turn to a closer description of the cash flow streams and the evaluation of the analytical metrics liquidity, value and income, which are used in Sections 16.4 and 16.5.

16.3.2   Description of cash flow streams

A cash flow stream can always be decomposed into a series of individual cash flows $x_\alpha^\beta(t)$ which describes a payment received by party α (lower index) from party β (upper index) at time t. If we change the sign, the payment flows the other way, namely party β receives a payment from party α:[*]

$$x_\beta^\alpha(t) = -x_\alpha^\beta(t). \tag{16.2}$$

Notice that an individual payment always involves exactly two parties even in cases where more than two parties are involved in the contract that generates this payment. A cash flow stream X is a series of payments among these parties:

$$X = \left\{ x_{\alpha_i}^{\beta_i}(t_i) \right\}_{i=1}^n.$$

Standard financial contracts have two parties A and B that exchange cash flows[†] so that

$$\alpha_i, \beta_i \in \{A, B\}.$$

It is obvious that symmetry rule (16.2) for individual cash flows directly carries over to a respective symmetry rule for a two-party cash flow stream X_A^B:

$$X_A^B = -X_B^A. \tag{16.3}$$

---

[*]Such a rule is called a symmetry rule in mathematics.
[†]Nothing excludes that more than two cash flow exchanging parties are involved in a given financial contract. However, the total cash flow stream of a multi-party contract can always be decomposed into pairwise cash flow streams. Therefore, we restrict the discussion to two-party contracts.

16.3.2.1 The actors view and the contract's standard cash flow stream

To ensure easy, unambiguous aggregation, well-defined sign rules are required for the cash flow streams. Indeed, the cash flow stream generated by a contract depends on the role that this contract plays for the party under consideration. The most common roles are those of the investor (asset position) or the issuer (liability position).[‡] We define the

standard cash flow stream $\hat{X}_A^B$

generated by an ACTUS contract by the following conventions:

1. Incoming cash flows are counted positive:

$$x_A^B(t)\begin{cases} > 0 & \text{if } A \text{ receives } x_A^B(t) \text{ from B,} \\ < 0 & \text{if } B \text{ receives } x_A^B(t) \text{ from } A. \end{cases} \tag{16.4}$$

2. $\hat{X}_A^B$ is generated from the point of view of the *investor* (asset position). Notice that here A, who is considered the record creator, has the role of the investor.

Asset and liability positions can then be described by a binary variable ρ with the following definition:

$$\rho = \begin{cases} +1 & \text{actor is investor,} \\ -1 & \text{actor is issuer.} \end{cases} \tag{16.5}$$

With this assumption, the actual cash flow stream is given as

$$\rho_\alpha \hat{X}_A^B, \quad \alpha \in \{A, B\}$$

with $\rho_A = +1$ and $\rho_B = -1$. We thus have

If A is the investor : $X_A^B = \rho_A \hat{X}_A^B = +\hat{X}_A^B,$ \hfill (16.6)

If A is the issuer : $X_B^A = \rho_B \hat{X}_A^B = -\hat{X}_A^B.$ \hfill (16.7)

16.3.3 Standard analytics as linear operators

All financial analytics can be computed from the contracts' cash flow stream. Moreover, this can be done in a quite straightforward and conceptually simple way because nearly all financial analytics can be described through linear operations on the contract's cash flows stream. We will show this for the basic analytics *value*, *income* and *liquidity*. These quantities are needed for the evaluation of the financial statements of an institution, namely balance sheets, P&L statement (profit and loss) and cash flow statement, respectively, but it requires an additional aggregation over

---

[‡]Short selling is treated as being equivalent to the issuer role.

the contracts on the book.[§] Again thanks to the linearity property, the analytical results obtained for a single contract can be aggregated up to an institution's total book by simply adding up the results. Notice that for this rule to work from a practical point of view, it is important to ensure that the cash flows always appear with the correct sign in the system. This will be ensured by systematically using the standard form $\hat{X}_A^B$ for a contract's cash flow stream and by assigning the variable ρ according to the contract's role on the book of the analysing party.

The major intrinsically non-linear financial analytics are risk measures because of their sub-linearity property that expresses the possibility of diversification.[¶]

Let us now consider the different quantities in turn. We start with liquidity because it is the simplest one.

16.3.3.1   Liquidity

Liquidity is the cash flow stream aggregated over a given time interval (or time bucket). Let us consider the series of points in time:

$$(\tau_0 < \tau_1, < \cdots < \tau_k).$$

We define now a time bucket system (TBS) $\mathscr{B}$ as a partition of the time interval $(t_0, t_k]$ into time buckets b_j:

$$\mathscr{B} = \{b_1, \cdots, b_k\} \tag{16.8}$$

with

$$b_j = (\tau_{j-1}, \tau_j] \text{ for all } j = 1, \ldots, k. \tag{16.9}$$

Notice that the parenthesis at the left indicates that τ_{j-1} is excluded from the interval and the square bracket at the right indicates, the τ_j is included, following the usual convention in mathematics.

Then, the marginal liquidity $L = (l_1, \ldots, l_k)$ is a vector of dimension k with

$$l_j = \sum_{t_i \in b_j} x_A^B(t_i). \tag{16.10}$$

In a more compact way, we can write for the liquidity vector:

$$L = \mathscr{L}_{\mathscr{B}} X_A^B, \tag{16.11}$$

where $\mathscr{L}_{\mathscr{B}}$ is the liquidity operator associated with TBS $\mathscr{B}$. Thus, the liquidity vector is the result of applying the liquidity operator associated with a given time bucket system to a given cash flow stream. It is straightforward and easy to show that $\mathscr{L}_{\mathscr{B}}$ is a linear operator. Indeed, if we consider the weighted sum $aX_A^B + bY_A^B$

[§]In this context the term *book* is an accounting term and is a synonym for general ledger.
[¶]Diversification means that the risk of a portfolio of assets is *less than the sum* (=sub-additive) of the risks of the individual assets.

of two cash flow streams X_A^B and Y_A^B, then for arbitrary real-valued weighting constants a and b we find the following:

$$a\mathscr{L}_{\mathscr{B}}X_A^B + b\mathscr{L}_{\mathscr{B}}Y_A^B = \mathscr{L}_{\mathscr{B}}(aX_A^B + bY_A^B).$$

16.3.3.2 Value

Here, we only consider the net present value (NPV). The NPV at time t, $V_t(x(t_i))$, of a cash flow $x_A^B(t_i)$ from party B to party A occurring at time t_i is obtained by discounting this cash flow from t_i to the evaluation time t. For this evaluation we need the interest rate $s(\tau_i)$ with term $\tau_i = t_i - t$, and we get[||]

$$V_t(x(t_i)) = x_A^B(t_i)\exp(-s(\tau_i)\tau_i).$$

The NPV of a cash flow stream X_A^B is then the sum of the NPVs of all its individual cash flows:

$$V_t(X_A^B) = \sum_{i=1}^{n} x_A^B(t_i)\exp(-s(\tau_i)\tau_i). \tag{16.12}$$

This is a weighted sum of the cash flows of X, which mathematically can be expressed as a linear operator $\mathscr{D}_{\mathscr{Y}}$ attached with yield curve $\mathscr{S}$:

$$V_t(X) = \mathscr{D}_{\mathscr{Y}}X_A^B. \tag{16.13}$$

Now, we can go a step further and consider an MC simulation where we want to compute the expected value of $V_t(X_A^B)$ obtained from a whole sample of yield curves $\mathscr{S}_k$ which has been generated by some stochastic model. This can then be written as the mathematical expectation E_t with respect to analysis time t,[**]

$$V_t(X_A^B) = E_t[\mathscr{D}_{\mathscr{Y}}X_A^B]. \tag{16.14}$$

We can express this equation in operator language:

$$V_t(X_A^B) = \mathscr{V}_t X_A^B. \tag{16.15}$$

with

$$\mathscr{V}_t(\cdot) := E_t[\mathscr{D}_{\mathscr{Y}}\cdot].$$

[|]For mathematical simplicity, we here use continuous discounting even though in practice discrete discounting with the correct compounding period must be used. This does not affect the gist of our argument.

[**]Notice that (16.14) is not yet fully specified. We should indicate the measure that is used to evaluate the expectation. Usually, the risk neutral measure is used. In this case, the discounting operator $\mathscr{D}$ uses the risk-neutral interest rates, possibly with a spread. We can also use the real-world measure. In that case, $\mathscr{D}$ indicates a suitable deflator.

The linearity of the value operator follows immediately from the linearity of both, the discounting operator and the expectation.

16.3.3.3 Income

Income is the derivative of value with respect to time:

$$I_t = \frac{dV_t}{d\tau}\bigg|_{\tau=t}. \tag{16.16}$$

Again, we can identify the income operator $\mathcal{I}_t$ with the derivative in this formula so that we can write the following:

$$I_t = \mathcal{I}_t X_A^B. \tag{16.17}$$

16.3.3.4 Aggregation over contracts

Cash flow streams can be aggregated over contracts. This aggregation is also a linear operator. Let us consider the aggregation of the cash flow stream of two contracts for party A, namely one with party B_1,

$$X_A^{B_1} = \{x_A^{B_1}(t_i) \text{ for all } i\}_{i=1}^n,$$

and one with party B_2,

$$Y_A^{B_2} = \{x_A^{B_2}(t_i) \text{ for all } i\}_{i=1}^n.$$

The aggregated cash flow stream is obtained as a union of both:

$$X_A^B = \{x_A^\beta(t_i)\beta \in \{B_1, B_2\}\}_{i=1}^n.$$

Here we consider only contracts which are assets for party A. A similar union is obtained for all liability contracts, and the off-balance sheet contracts can be treated in a similar way. We can then apply the analytical operators for liquidity, value and income on the union of the cash flow streams and reorder the resulting equations. But because of the linearity property we can equally well first compute liquidity, value and income for the individual contracts and aggregate the contract-level results by simply summing them up.

To summarize, the main analytical metrics can be expressed in terms of linear operators so that (i) their evaluation only involves (possibly weighted) sums and (ii) these contract-level results can be aggregated at arbitrary level by simply summing them up.

16.4 ACTUS in action: proof of concept with a bond portfolio

In this section, we summarize an ACTUS proof of concept with bond data that has been reported in [9] as an example for ACTUS-based financial analytics. The data

Table 16.3   Overview over the portfolio composition

Sample overview: # Contract s: 3809

Sector (according to European System of Accounts 2010 issued by the European Union)

	Central Government	State Government	Local Government	Social security funds
# Ctrs.	1290	1944	491	84

Country (according to ISO 3166-1 system)

	AT	BE	CY	DE	ES	FI	FR	GR	IE	IT	MT	NL	PT	SI	SK
# Ctrs.	149	413	46	1712	346	31	478	102	29	219	81	108	42	33	20

Key attributes (according to the ACTUS data dictionary)

Contract Deal Date		Maturity Date		Cycle Of Interest Payment				
Earliest	Latest	Earliest	Latest	1M-	1Q-	1Y-	6M-	NULL[3]
1986-06-20	2015-03-31	2015-04-01[1]	2090-11-08[2]	4	391	2237	474	703

Notional Principal [EUR]			Nominal Interest Rate [%]		
Min	Median	Max	Min	Mean	Max
0.0[4]	76,690,000	38,530,000,000	0.0[3]	1.55	23.19

[1]Matured bonds, [2]Data quality issue, [3]Zero coupon bonds, [4]Data quality issue

has been obtained from the Centralized Securities Database of the ECB, which contains all securities issued in the Euro area and all securities worldwide held by institutional investors in the Euro area. For technical reasons, we had to limit the analysis to bullet bonds (i.e., bonds with full amortization at maturity).[††] The analysis was performed on 1 May 2015. We used all bullet bonds with maturity date later than the analysis date. This amounted to a total of 3,809 bonds. The breakdown of the portfolio according to different criteria is shown in Table 16.3.

[††]For other securities, the information contained in the upper layer of the CSDB was not sufficient for ACTUS, and during the time that W.B. spent at ECB, it was not possible to access the deeper layer of the database.

ACTUS contract events

Date	Value	Type	Current	Nominal	Rate	Accrued
2015-05-01	0.00	AD0	EUR	3,000	0.0475	5.54
2016-04-17	142.50	IP	EUR	3,000	0.0475	0.00
2017-04-17	142.50	IP	EUR	3,000	0.0475	0.00
2018-04-17	142.50	IP	EUR	3,000	0.0475	0.00
2019-04-17	142.50	IP	EUR	3,000	0.0475	0.00
2019-04-17	3,000.00	MD	EUR	0	0.00	0.00

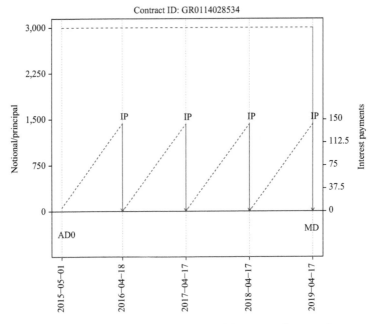

*Figure 16.2   Cash flows in Mio EUR generated by a Greek central government
bond displayed in tabular form (top) and as graphics (bottom)*

Since the portfolio consists only of bullet bonds and, at this stage, we do not
take into account credit risk, the contract events with the cash flow streams are fully
defined by the contract terms and no risk factor information is required to compute
them. Figure 16.2 displays an example of these raw results for one contract: a
Greek central government bond (ISIN GR0114028534) with a nominal of 3 billion
EUR that matures on 17 Apr 2019 (cf. Section 16.3.1 for details about this bond).
For each contract in the sample, the series of contract events starts with the analysis
date (event type AD0) which marks the reference date at which the analysis is
conducted. It follows a series of interest payments (event types IP) and at the end,
the repayment of the principal at maturity (event type MD).[‡‡] It is this data that is

---

[‡‡]Notice that events prior to the analysis event are not printed as they are in the past (w.r.t. the analysis
date) and hence are not relevant for forward-looking analysis.

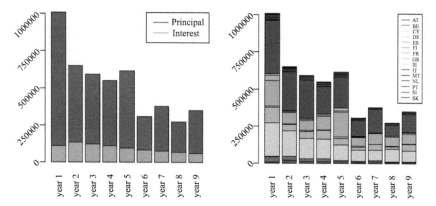

Figure 16.3 *Liquidity analysis of the bond portfolio for the years 2015 (year 1) until 2023 (year 9) in million EUR. Reprinted from [9] by permission from Springer Nature*

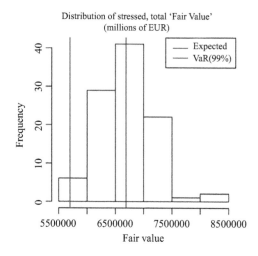

Figure 16.4 *Value distribution of the bond portfolio obtained by a Monte Carlo simulation. Reprinted from [9] by permission from Springer Nature*

the raw results that serve as input for all further analysis. By suitable aggregation, arbitrary analytical metrics can be computed. Here, we show results for liquidity in Figure 16.3 (cf. (16.11)) and for the market value in Figure 16.4 (cf. (16.14)). Figure 16.5, finally, displays liquidity results under credit risk.

For liquidity analysis, the cash flows must be aggregated according to a time bucket system as defined in Section 16.3.3.1. Here, we chose yearly aggregation for nine legal years, starting in 2015. The results are displayed in Figure 16.3. In

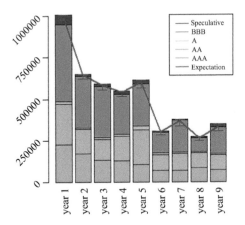

Figure 16.5   Liquidity analysis, including default risk. x and y axes are the same as in Figure 16.2. Reprinted from [9] by permission from Springer Nature

Table 16.4   EUR yield curve as of 1 May 2015 (rates are displayed in percentage)

Tenors	3M	1Y	2Y	5Y	7Y	10Y	20Y
Rates	−0.282	−0.259	−0.207	0.0309	0.200	0.417	0.807

addition to the aggregation over time buckets, aggregation has also been carried out according to additional criteria. The left panel shows aggregation according to the type of payment, which can be extracted from the event types. Here, we only have interest payments (green bars in the figure) and the repayment of the principal (red bars). The total amount of interest payments decreased over time, as one would expect because more and more bonds mature. Notice that in 2015, only 8 months are left (May–December), which explains that the amount of interest payment is smaller than for the full year 2. The length of the red bars only decreases on average, which indicates that there tend to be more bonds with short maturity than with long maturities.

In the right panel, the additional aggregation criterion is the issuing country. The figure shows the relative amount of outstanding payments (interest and principal) for the different countries of the Euro area. The total yearly amount is equal to the amount in the left panel, as it should be.

Let us now turn to value. The nominal value is just the aggregated principal of all the bonds, i.e., the sum of the red bars in the graph on the left in Figure 16.3. For the market value, on the other hand, we must discount the cash flows generated by the contracts with the market interest rates. Since at this stage we neglect default risk we only need to consider the risk-free yield curve for discounting. The NPV of a financial contract at to the analysis date t_0=1 May 2015 is obtained according to (16.13). The values of the risk-free EUR yield curve as of 1 May 2015 are shown in Table 16.4 for a typical set of tenors $\tau = t - t_0$. Rates for arbitrary tenors are obtained by inter-polating these rates.

In order to compute risk measures of an object under consideration, be this a single contract, a portfolio or an entire institution, we need to evaluate a distribution of the value of this object. In order to obtain such a distribution, we need to recalculate the value for a sample of risk scenarios. In the present case, this would mean a sample of yield curve scenarios.

Since the nominal value does not depend on the yield curve, we will trivially obtain the same value, whatever the interest rate scenario. Equation (16.13), on the other hand, does depend on the yield curve so that we expect non-trivial results. This is demonstrated by carrying out an MC simulation with a sample of 100 randomly generated modifications of the observed yield curve. This means that we computed the NPV of the whole portfolio for any yield curve modification in the sample, which results in the sample of NPVs displayed in Figure 16.4. It shows a distribution with the sample average indicated by the blue line and the 95% value-of-risk (i.e., the 5% quantile) indicated by the red line.[§§]

At last, we incorporated a simple default model. Specifically, we assume that default occurs with a probability implied by the country ratings and if a default occurs at time t, all cash flows from this time on are stalled. The modified liquidity result obtained with these assumptions is indicated by the red line in Figure 16.5. This is a probabilistic result. Noticeable is that in 2015 there is hardly any difference while in 2023 the red line is at the lower border of the speculative tranche. This means that according to this model the speculative bonds are likely to default within 9 years.

In order to get an idea of the error bars, we performed a simple simulation with a Markov model in which the transition probabilities are given by the migration matrix for credit ratings. For details, the reader is referred to [9].

16.5 Scalable financial analytics

Now we proceed to the description of the use of Big Data technology in order to analyse millions of financial contracts in reasonable time. The analysis is performed in two steps: (i) the implementation of the non-linear mapping (16.1) from the contract terms and risk factors to the cash flows and (ii) the evaluation of the analytical metrics defined by linear operators as those for liquidity, value and income in Section 16.3.3. In particular, we describe how ACTUS can be used with Apache Spark in order to parallelize and scale up the financial calculations. We summarize the results of an experiment carried out on the Amazon cloud with up to 512 CPU cores to analyse up to 96 million contracts, which originally has been reported in [8].

Apache Spark [17] employs a data-parallelism architecture where typically a large data set is spilt into smaller parts. These parts are then distributed onto various

---

[§§]Notice that the form of the distribution does not have real meaning because the yield curve sample was not generated by an interest rate model calibrated to historical data as for real risk measurement exercises it should be.

machines of a computer cluster—for instance, either with the Hadoop Distributed File System[¶¶] or with the Amazon S3-file system.[|||] Each compute node of the Spark cluster performs the same calculations in parallel, however, on a different part of the whole data set.

Spark provides two different mechanisms for parallel processing that are relevant for our problem, namely user-defined functions (UDFs) and Spark-SQL. A UDF can be any program code that is written, for instance, in Java or R. Spark executes this program code in parallel where again each Spark node performs calculations on a subset of the whole data. The advantage of UDFs is that existing programs can easily be parallelized without major code-rewriting. Spark-SQL, on the other hand, enables a parallel execution of SQL statements. The advantage of that approach is that when a problem can be formulated as an SQL query, Spark can further optimize the query execution based on the statistics acquired by a query optimizer [18]—similar to the query optimizer of parallel database systems. We expect this to hold for the linear part of the analytics.

We designed a Big Data architecture that can take advantage of both UDFs and Spark-SQL. The major objective is to evaluate which kind of approach is more suitable for the problem of Big Data financial analytics.

Figure 16.6 shows three different Big Data architecture designs, namely (a) the so-called *UDF-only on-the-fly* architecture; (b) *Mixed on-the-fly* architecture and (c) *Materialized* architecture.

Panel (a): *UDF-only on-the-fly* architecture. The results obtained from the non-linear analytics are not materialized but the linear analytics is carried out 'in memory'. All financial calculations are performed using Spark-UDFs and only the end results are materialized, i.e., they are stored on the underlying file system. Note that we distinguish between *non-linear analytics*, i.e., the calculations of cash flows based on ACTUS and *linear analytics*, i.e., financial calculations such as *nominal value, liquidity* and *fair value*.

Panel (b): *Mixed on-the-fly* architecture. Here we proceed as in the previous case with the difference, however, that the linear analytics is performed in Spark-SQL rather than as Spark-UDF. For that approach, we had to rewrite all linear analytics codes in SQL.

Panel (c): *Materialized* architecture. In this case, the non-linear analytics is again performed as Spark-UDFs as in the previous case. However, the intermediate cash flow results are materialized, i.e., they are stored in the file system. The intuition of this approach is to apply a mechanism commonly used in database and data warehousing systems where the results of long-running calculations are materialized such that subsequent queries can directly access these results without recalculation. Moreover, note that in approach (c) the linear analytics can either be performed using Spark-UDFs or Spark-SQL. The idea is to study how our financial analytics can benefit from materializing intermediate results and thus improve the performance of subsequent linear calculations.

[¶¶]https://hadoop.apache.org
[|||]https://aws.amazon.com/s3/

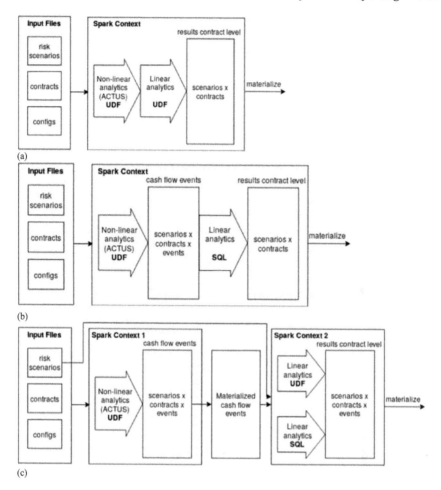

Figure 16.6   Big Data architecture designs. (a) On-the-fly architecture with UDF linear analytics. (b) On-the-fly architecture with SQL linear analytics. (c) Materialized architecture with both UDF and SQL linear analytics. Reprinted from [9] by permission from Springer Nature

We evaluated each design on three different financial calculations: *nominal value*, *liquidity* (cf. (16.14)) and *fair value* (cf. (16.11)). The goal of these experiments was to investigate how well our approach scales for performing financial analytics on millions of financial contracts running on Big Data architecture. Moreover, we wanted to know whether Spark-UDFs or Spark-SQL is the better architectural design choice for large-scale financial analytics.

All experiments were executed on Amazon Web Services running Spark 2.3 using the Java interface of Spark and ACTUS. Our compute cluster consisted of 32 machines of type m3.2 large. Each compute node had 30 GB RAM, 16 vCPUs and 2.5 GHz clock speed. Hence, the total memory size of our cluster was 960 GB with 512 vCPU cores.

For our experiments we used up to 96 million financial contracts with a total size of 30 GB. The size of the materialized cash flows was 450 GB.

Figure 16.7 shows the performance of financial analytics leveraging the *on-the-fly* architecture where linear analytics are performed with Spark-UDF and Spark-SQL. Notice that the figure shown in log–log-scale has two different descriptions of the *x*-axis. The bottom part shows the number of vCPU cores while the top part shows the number of financial contracts in millions. The basic idea is to analyse our results based on a strong scaling assumption, which means that as we increase the number of processor cores, we also increase the size of the data set. Hence, optimal (ideal) scaling would result in a horizontal line, i.e., the execution time remains constant when we simultaneously double the number of processors as well as the amount of data.

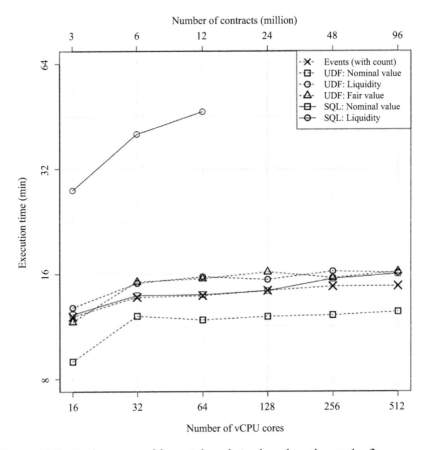

Figure 16.7   *Performance of financial analytics based on the on-the-fly architecture. Linear analytics is based on Spark-UDF and Spark-SQL. Reprinted from [9] by permission from Springer Nature*

In general, we can observe that executing financial analytics using Spark-UDFs performs better than Spark-SQL. Note, for instance, that the liquidity calculations based on Spark-SQL only show three data points, i.e., for 16, 32 and 64 vCPU cores. The reason is that Spark-SQL has main memory issues and hence does not scale beyond 64 vCPUs cores. We can also observe that most calculations show almost optimal linear scaling starting from 32 vCPUs cores. For 16 vCPU cores the communication overhead of the system has a negative performance impact. Again, the interested reader is referred to [8] for more details.

Figure 16.8 shows the performance of financial analytics based on the *materialized* architecture. The interesting feature is a trend opposite of what we observed before. In particular, in this case Spark-SQL performed better than Spark-UDF. The reason is that the Spark-SQL query optimizer can take advantage of the materialized results and thus speed up the performance of queries that repeatedly use the same pre-calculated results. Also note that for the analytics based on Spark-UDFs there are only two data points, namely for 16 and 32 vCPU cores. Again, the reason for not scaling up to a higher number of cores is due to Spark's main memory issues.

In summary, our experiments demonstrate that we can scale Big Data financial calculations up to 512 vCPUs cores showing almost (ideal) linear scaling. In the case that intermediate (cash flow) results are not materialized, Spark-UDF performs better than Spark-SQL. On the other hand, if intermediate results are materialized and data is reused in subsequent queries, Spark-SQL performs better than Spark-UDF since the SQL query optimizer can efficiently leverage materialized intermediate results.

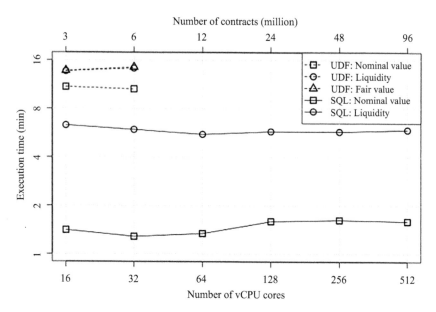

Figure 16.8   Performance of financial analytics based on the materialized architecture. Linear analytics is based on Spark-UDF and Spark-SQL. Reprinted from [9] by permission from Springer Nature

Assuming that a mid-sized bank has on the order of 10 million contracts, the results demonstrate that we perform financial analytics over all contracts of 10 major banks in only about 16 min.

16.6   Towards future automated reporting

Speed and timeliness, flexibility and global scale of risk monitoring are major features of an effective regulatory policy tool. In practice, however, reporting systems are complex and heterogeneous over multiple hierarchical levels leading to data fragmentation, quality and consistency problems and, thus, induce significant organizational inefficiencies, including high reconciliation and compliance cost for the industry [1,10,19]. Difficulties in collecting necessary position-level data, comparing data coming from different sources, or aggregating similar data, etc. are frequently reported [20–22].

As a result, current monitoring processes, i.e., reporting and analysis, experience considerable difficulties to deliver the required performance. Essentially, existing data architecture and organization as well as IT infrastructure are 'unfit-for-purpose' and impede the goals of effective policymaking [1].

Two opposing reporting paradigms are *data pull* and *data push*. In the push paradigm, supervised entities 'upload' their prepared data in the format required by the supervising agency. For the reasons discussed earlier, the push reporting process is often time-intensive for the reporting institutions and results in inconsistent aggregate data sets. Following the pull reporting paradigm, on the other hand, a supervisory agency directly fetches data from the IT systems of the supervised entities. This process is controlled and initiated by the agency in a fully automated way [11]. Thereby, agencies are able to pull the specific data they require at the time when needed. As a result, the pull approach gives the supervising agencies more flexibility in terms of what data they pull from which entity and at what time. At the same time, pull data also reduces the reporting burden on the side of the supervised entities.

As an example, the National Bank of Rwanda has implemented a pull data reporting system through which it fetches relevant information directly from the IT systems of more than 600 supervised financial institutions, including commercial banks, insurance companies, microfinance institutions, pension funds, forex bureaus, telecom operators and money transfer operators. Through this reporting system, data is fetched in a fully automated fashion with frequencies ranging from every 15 min to every 24 h depending on the type of the entity concerned [11]. Similarly, in two recent papers, the pull approach is explicitly mentioned as a possible way for future reporting [12,13].

A first essential building block for such automated reporting facilities is a common financial product data dictionary according to which position-level data is represented and made available consistently across reporting entities for pull data by supervising agencies. In the previous sections, we have presented ACTUS as an alternative data dictionary with these capabilities. Furthermore, we have shown that the ACTUS algorithms provide essential intermediate analytical results that provide the basis for all kinds of reports. Moreover, we have demonstrated that these algorithms scale near-linearly in the number of positions reported. This makes the ACTUS analytical model a formidable basis for effective financial system monitoring.

A second crucial building block is the IT infrastructure supporting automated reporting facilities. While this can be solved with standard IT systems, as in the example of the National Bank of Rwanda, novel technologies such as DLT offer entirely new possibilities for automated reporting.

In [10] the authors propose a new ACTUS and DLT-based RegTech reporting infrastructure as 'a new layer of algorithmic regulation functionality that spans over existing financial technology systems, processes and data formats'. In that model, the operational position-level data continues to live in banks' proprietary databases but is replicated as a 'digital doppelgänger' in a so-called deep dynamic transaction document (DTD). This deep DTD reflects the actual data in near-real time and is accessible to third-parties such as supervisory agencies who can use them, e.g., for pull reporting purposes.

Figure 16.9 outlines the RegTech reporting infrastructure and the deep DTD as well as the ACTUS data and algorithmic model at its heart. Smart contracts in a DLT environment are used to build a novel layer of *algorithmic regulation functionality* on top of the deep DTD that automates certain reporting processes. This results in a further reduction of operational inefficiencies around regulatory

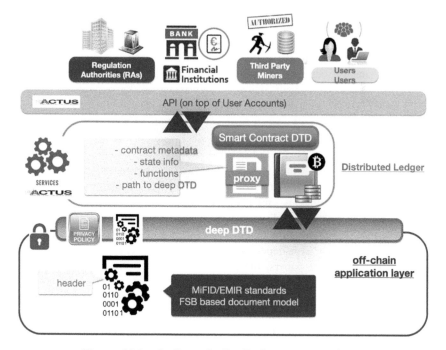

Figure 16.9   Outline of a RegTech reporting solution

reporting for both the supervised entities and the supervisory agencies. At the same time, agencies do not only get access to near-real-time positions data but also to reports derived therefrom. A first simplified implementation of the deep DTD and algorithmic regulation functionality is presented and discussed in [23] and supports the viability of such an approach.

While a viable model, the DTD approach introduces a critical interface between the bank systems maintaining the original records and the DTD carrying the digital doppelgänger. Obviously, the model demands that the doppelgänger records are always synchronized with the source, leading to well-known data problems and related operational inefficiencies. The reason for this design is that it does not require the banks to change their internal systems but only to provide a mapping onto the DTD. It is intended as an interim solution that supports an automated pull approach while leaving the legacy financial contracts in place. Eventually, the DTD should acquire legal value so that the legacy contracts are replaced with smart contracts representing digital positions.

In fact, the ACTUS Protocol, an initiative building on the ACTUS standard and providing financial product templates that can be issued and their entire lifecycle managed on DLT aims at achieving exactly this [24]. Figure 16.10, borrowed from the cited report, presents the architecture of digital financial assets according to the ACTUS Protocol. The very goal is to leverage DLT as a joint ledger for recording and managing the full life cycle of all sorts of financial products. Thereby, these products are defined using the ACTUS data model and encoded in smart contracts and, as a result, represent standardized and fully digital financial assets. Once the contract is issued the parties involved, or a mandated third party, can iterate through the life cycle of the asset and compute the remaining balance, make repayments, and update the asset state accordingly directly on the DLT and without maintaining the original in a proprietary database. Similarly, also leveraging the ACTUS standard Cardano-based

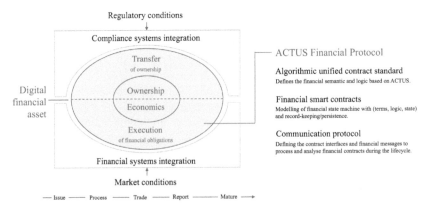

Figure 16.10   Architecture of DLT-based digital financial assets according to the ACTUS Protocol

Marlowe*** and Substrate-based Katallassos [25] work towards the same goal. The interesting aspect here is that while being implemented on entirely different DLT frameworks, still no data mapping and normalization has to be done in order to achieve the automated pull reporting paradigm because they are following the same data model, namely the ACTUS Data and Algorithmic Standard.

16.7 Conclusion

Already 12 years have passed since the last financial crisis. According to the economic historian Charles Kindleberger [26, p. 264], there have been on average a financial crisis every 10 years. No evidence suggests that this dynamics will change if we will not be able to better harness the financial system. For this purpose, however, more effective supervision must be in place. This is all the more urgent in view of the ongoing digitization of the financial sector.

Fortunately, we are in the possession of the necessary technology. This chapter has presented a concept of financial reporting and the technological elements required to implement it. What is still missing is the integration of all these elements into a working system in order to show that this concept can indeed be implemented. There is no time to lose.

Acknowledgements

Many fruitful discussions with Willi Brammertz, Jefferson Braswell, Francis J. Gross, Petros Kavassalis and Allan I. Mendelowitz are gratefully acknowledged. We also acknowledge financial support from the Swiss National Science Foundation (project no. IZCNZ0-174853) and the Innosuisse Innovation Agency (project no. 25349.1 PFES-ES).

References

[1] Bank for International Settlement—Basel Committee on Banking Supervision. Principles for effective risk aggregation and risk reporting; 2013.

[2] UBS AG. Shareholder report on write-downs; 2008. Visited April 2014. Available from: http://maths-fi.com/ubs-shareholder-report.pdf.

[3] Committee on Economic and Monetary Affairs, European Parliament, Rapporteur: El Khadraoui, Saïd. Report on Shaow Banking (2012/2115 (INI)). Report no. A7-0354/2012. Strassbourg, 2012. Visited May 2021. Available from: www.europarl.europa.eu/doceo/document/A-7-2012-0354_EN.pdf.

***See GitHub for more information: https://github.com/input-output-hk/marlowe/blob/master/docs/tutorial-v1.3/actus-marlowe.md.

Handbook of big data analytics, volume 2

[4] Bennett M. The financial industry business ontology: Best practice for big data. Journal of Banking Regulation. 2013;14(3–4):255–268.

[5] ISDA. What is the ISDA CDM. ISDA; 2019.

[6] ACTUS Financial Research Foundation. Algorithmic contract type unified standards; 2018. Available from: https://actusfrf.org.

[7] Brammertz W and Mendelowitz AI. Limits and Opportunities of Big Data for Macro-Prudential Modeling of Financial Systemic Risk. In: DSMM'14: Proceedings of the International Workshop on Data Science for Macro-Modeling. Association for Computing Machinery, New York, NY, United States; 2014. p. 1–6.

[8] Stockinger K, Bundi N, Heitz J, *et al.* Scalable architecture for Big Data financial analytics: user-defined functions vs. SQL. Journal of Big Data. 2019;6(1):46.

[9] Breymann W, Bundi N, Heitz J, *et al.* In: Braschler M, Stadelmann T, and Stockinger K, editors. Large-Scale Data-Driven Financial Risk Assessment. Cham: Springer International Publishing; 2019. p. 387–408. Available from: https://doi.org/10.1007/978-3-030-11821-1_21.

[10] Kavassalis P, Stieber H, Breymann W, *et al.* An innovative RegTech approach to financial risk monitoring and supervisory reporting. The Journal of Risk Finance. 2018;19(1):39–55.

[11] Broeders D and Prenio J. Innovative technology in financial supervision (suptech) – The experience of early users. Bank for International Settlement – Basel Committee on Banking Supervision; 2013.

[12] Bank of England. Transforming data collection from the UK financial sector. Bank of England; 2020.

[13] Drvar M, Turner J, Piechocki M, Stiegeler E, and Münch D. The future of data collection and data management: Agile RegOps for digitalizing the regulatory value chain. BearingPoint Software Solutions GmbH, Frankfurt; 2020.

[14] Brammertz W, Akkizidis I, Breymann W, *et al.* Unified Financial Analysis. Wiley, Chichester; 2009.

[15] Brammertz W, Mark R, and Mendelowitz AI. Certainty, Risk and Uncertainty in Finance; 2020. Submitted to the Journal of Risk Finance.

[16] The Hellenic Republic. € 3,000,000,000 4.75 per cent. Notes due 2019, Offering Circular; 2014.

[17] Zaharia M, Xin RS, Wendell P, *et al.* Apache Spark: A unified engine for big data processing. Communications of the ACM. 2016;59(11):56–65.

[18] Armbrust M, Das T, Davidson A, *et al.* Scaling spark in the real world: Performance and usability. Proceedings of the VLDB Endowment. 2015;8 (12):1840–1843.

[19] Jenkinson N and Leonova IS. The importance of data quality for effective financial stability policies – Legal entity identifier: A first step towards necessary financial data reforms. Financial Stability Review. 2013;17:101–110. Available from: https://ideas.repec.org/a/bfr/fisrev/20111710.html.

[20] Financial Stability Board (FSB). Implementation and effects of the G20 financial regulatory reforms; 2015. Available from: www.fsb.org/wp-content/uploads/Report-on-implementation-and-effects-of-reforms-final.pdf.

[21] Chen K, Fleming M, Jackson J, *et al.* An analysis of CDS transactions: Implications for public reporting. Federal Reserve Bank of New York Report; 2011. Available from: www.newyorkfed.org/medialibrary/media/research/staff_reports/sr517.pdf.

[22] Gordon M. Reconciliations: The forefront of regulatory compliance procedures. Journal of Securities Operations & Custody. 2017;8(4). Available from: www.lseg.com/markets-products-and-services/post-trade-services/unavista/articles/reconciliations-forefront-regulatory-compliance-procedures.

[23] Sel M, Diedrich H, Demeester S, *et al.* How Smart Contracts Can Implement 'Report Once'. In: Paper submitted to the Data for Policy Conference 2017. Mimeo, London; 6–7 September 2017.

[24] Svoboda M. The ACTUS Financial Protocol – Creating the web for digital financial assets and unlocking the full potential of finance and blockchain; 2019. Available from: https://medium.com/at-par/the-actus-financial-protocol-839a3d8f52dc.

[25] França B, Radermacher S, and Trinkler R. Katallassos: A standard framework for finance; 2019.

[26] Kindleberger CP. A Financial History of Western Europe. Taylor & Francis, London; 2005.

Overall conclusions

Vadlamani Ravi and Aswani Kumar Cherukuri

This volume covers applications and parallel architectures of machine learning. Cyber security, e-commerce and finance are considered representative domains, where big data algorithms were proposed. Parallel and distributed version of a few neural network architecture and clustering algorithms are proposed. The list of application domains covered in this volume is by no means exhaustive. Huge potential for developing novel, parallel and distributed machine learning algorithms still exists in fields such as healthcare, bioinformatics, medicine, cyber fraud detection, cyber security, financial services fraud detection, supply chain management, physics, chemistry, agriculture. One of the future directions would include parallelizing hybrids of second, third and fourth generation of neural networks to solve complex problems. For instance, multi-layer perceptron, spiking neural network and long short-term memory network could be hybridized and parallelized.

Index